Economic expansion in the Byzantine empire

In this book Dr Harvey shows that, if we adopt a broader definition of feudalism, the economic developments of the Byzantine empire and the medieval west were far more comparable than Byzantine historians have been prepared to admit.

Previous interpretations have linked economic trends too closely to the political fortunes of the state, and have consequently regarded the twelfth century as a period of economic stagnation. Yet there is considerable evidence that the empire's population expanded steadily during the period covered by this book, and that agricultural production was intensified. The volume of coinage in circulation increased in the eleventh and twelfth centuries and towns also revived. Furthermore, the economically positive aspects in the development of feudal relations of production – the inter-relationship between towns, trade and the rural economy – serve only to reinforce the point that the disintegration of the Byzantine empire in the late twelfth century should no longer be associated with economic decline.

Dr Harvey's conclusions will affect all future inter-pretations of the general course of Byzantine history. In particular the appreciation that there is no incompatibility between the development of the landed wealth of a feudalising aristocracy and the growth of commerce and urbanisation will call for a reassessment of the whole nature and social structure of the Byzantine economy.

Economic expansion in the
Byzantine empire
900–1200

ALAN HARVEY

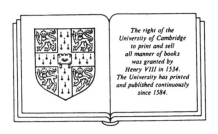

CAMBRIDGE UNIVERSITY PRESS

Cambridge
New York   Port Chester
Melbourne   Sydney

CAMBRIDGE UNIVERSITY PRESS
Cambridge, New York, Melbourne, Madrid, Cape Town, Singapore, São Paulo

Cambridge University Press
The Edinburgh Building, Cambridge CB2 8RU, UK

Published in the United States of America by Cambridge University Press, New York

www.cambridge.org
Information on this title: www.cambridge.org/9780521371513

© Cambridge University Press 1989

This publication is in copyright. Subject to statutory exception
and to the provisions of relevant collective licensing agreements,
no reproduction of any part may take place without the written
permission of Cambridge University Press.

First published 1989
First paperback edition 2002

A catalogue record for this publication is available from the British Library

Library of Congress Cataloguing in Publication data
Harvey, Alan, 1953–
Economic expansion in the Byzantine Empire, 900–1200 / Alan Harvey.
p.   cm.
Bibliography.
Includes index.
ISBN 0 521 37151 1
1. Byzantine empire – Economic conditions.   I. Title.
HC294.H37   1989
330.9495′02–dc20   89-9791   CIP

ISBN 978-0-521-37151-3 hardback
ISBN 978-0-521-52190-1 paperback

Transferred to digital printing 2008

Contents

Acknowledgements		page vii
Abbreviations		viii
Glossary		xiii
Maps		xvii
	Introduction	1
1	The early medieval period	14
2	Demographic growth and social relations	35
3	Taxation and monetary circulation	80
4	Agricultural production	120
5	The pattern of demand	163
6	Interaction between town and country	198
	Conclusion	244
	Bibliography	269
	Index	293

v

Acknowledgements

This work is an expanded version of my doctoral thesis, and the receipt of a postdoctoral fellowship granted by the Economic and Social Research Council made its completion for publication possible. I owe a great debt of thanks to Professor Anthony Bryer, Dr John Haldon, Professor Rodney Hilton, Dr Rosemary Morris and, especially, Mr Michael Hendy for reading this work and suggesting many improvements. I should also like to thank Professor Margaret Alexiou for her help in interpreting the Ptochoprodromic literature and Professor Leslie Clarkson and Dr Margaret Crawford for their helpful advice on the subject of diet. Naturally, all responsibility for mistakes and weaknesses in argument is entirely mine. I should also like to thank my parents for their encouragement throughout the duration of this work.

Abbreviations

Anna Comnène, *Alexiade*
Anna Comnène, *Alexiade*, ed. B. Leib. (3 vols., Paris, 1967)

Ashburner, 'The Farmer's Law'
W. Ashburner, 'The Farmer's Law', *Journal of Hellenic Studies*, 30 (1910), pp. 85–108; 32 (1912), pp. 68–95

Attaleiates
Michaelis Attaliotae Historia, ed. I. Bekker (Bonn, 1853)

Benjamin of Tudela
A. Asher (ed. and trans.), *The Itinerary of Rabbi Benjamin of Tudela* (New York, 1840)

Bryennius
Nicephori Bryennii Historiarum Libri Quattuor, ed. P. Gautier (Corpus Fontium Historiae Byzantinae IX) (Brussels, 1975)

Cecaumenos, *Strategicon*
B. Wassiliewsky, V. Jernstedt, *Cecaumeni Strategicon* (St Petersburg, 1896, reprinted Amsterdam, 1965)

Chilandar
L. Petit, *Actes de Chilandar*, I, *Actes grecs* (Actes de l'Athos V), *Vizantijskij Vremennik*, 17 (1910), supplement 1

Constantine Porphyrogenitus, *De Cerimoniis*
Constantini Porphyrogeniti Imperatoris De Cerimoniis Aulae Byzantinae Libri Duo, ed. J. J. Reiske (2 vols., Bonn, 1829)

DAI
Constantine Porphyrogenitus, *De Administrando Imperio*, 2nd edn ed. G. Moravcsik and R. J. H. Jenkins (Washington, 1967)

Darrouzès, *Épistoliers*
J. Darrouzès, *Épistoliers byzantins au Xe siècle* (Paris, 1960)

Dionysiou
N. Oikonomides, *Actes de Dionysiou* (Archives de l'Athos IV) (Paris, 1968)

Docheiariou
N. Oikonomides, *Actes de Docheiariou* (Archives de l'Athos XIII) (Paris, 1984)

Abbreviations

Dölger, *Beiträge*	F. Dölger, *Beiträge zur Geschichte der byzantinischen Finanzverwaltung besonders des 10. und 11. Jahrhunderts* (Leipzig, Berlin, 1927)
Dölger, *Schatzkammern*	F. Dölger, *Aus den Schatzkammern des heiligen Berges* (Munich, 1948)
Engrapha Patmou, I	E. L. Branouse, *Byzantina Engrapha tes Mones Patmou*, I, *Autokratorika* (Athens, 1980)
Engrapha Patmou, II	M. Nystazopoulou-Pelekidou, *Byzantina Engrapha tes Mones Patmou*, II, *Demosion Leitourgon* (Athens, 1980)
To Eparchikon Biblion	*To Eparchikon Biblion. The Book of the Prefect. Le Livre du préfet*, with an introduction by I. Dujčev (London, 1970)
Esphigménou	J. Lefort, *Actes d'Esphigménou* (Archives de l'Athos VI) (Paris, 1973)
Gautier, 'Grégoire Pakourianos'	P. Gautier, 'Le typikon du sébaste Grégoire Pakourianos', *Revue des Études Byzantines*, 42 (1984), pp. 5–145
Gautier, 'La diataxis de Michel Attaliate'	P. Gautier, 'La diataxis de Michel Attaliate', *Revue des Études Byzantines*, 39 (1981), pp. 5–143
Gautier, 'Pantocrator'	P. Gautier, 'Le typikon du Christ Sauveur Pantocrator', *Revue des Études Byzantines*, 32 (1974), pp. 1–145
Geoponica	H. Beckh, *Geoponica sive Cassiani Bassi de Re Rustica Eclogiae* (Leipzig, 1897)
Goudas, 'Vatopedi'	M. Goudas, 'Byzantiaka engrapha tes en Atho hieras mones tou Batopediou', *Epeteris Hetaireias Byzantinon Spoudon*, 3 (1926), pp. 113–34
Hesseling and Pernot, *Poèmes prodromiques*	D.-C. Hesseling and H. Pernot, *Poèmes prodromiques en grec vulgaire* (Amsterdam, 1910)
JGR	J. Zepos and P. Zepos, *Jus Graeco-Romanum* (8 vols., Athens, 1931–62)
Karayannopulos 'Fragmente'	J. Karayannopulos, 'Framente aus dem Vademecum eines byzantinischen Finanzbeamten', in *Polychronion. Festschrift F. Dölger* (Heidelberg, 1966), pp. 318–34
Laurent, *La Vie merveilleuse*	V. Laurent, *La Vie merveilleuse de saint Pierre d'Atroa* (Subsidia Hagiographica 29) (Brussels, 1956)

Lavra, I	P. Lemerle, A. Guillou, N. Svoronos and D. Papachryssanthou, *Actes de Lavra*, I, *Des origines à 1204* (Archives de l'Athos V) (Paris, 1970)
Lavra, II	P. Lemerle, A. Guillou, N. Svoronos and D. Papachryssanthou, *Actes de Lavra*, II, *De 1204 à 1328* (Archives de l'Athos VIII) (Paris, 1977)
Lavra, IV	P. Lemerle, A. Guillou, N. Svoronos and D. Papachryssanthou, *Actes de Lavra*, IV, *Études historiques. Actes serbes. Compléments et index* (Archives de l'Athos XI) (Paris, 1982)
Lemerle, *Les Plus Anciens Recueils*	P. Lemerle, *Les Plus Anciens Recueils des miracles de saint Démétrius et la pénétration des Slaves dans les Balkans*, I, *Le texte*, II, *Commentaire* (2 vols., Paris, 1979, 1981)
Michael Choniates	S. Lampros (ed.), *Michael Akominatou tou Choniatou ta Sozomena* (2 vols., Athens 1879–80)
Migne, *Patrologia Graeca*	J.-P. Migne, *Patrologiae Cursus Completus, Series Graeca* (Paris, 1857–)
MM	F. Miklosich and J. Müller, *Acta et Diplomata Graeca Medii Aevi* (6 vols., Vienna, 1860–90)
Nicetas Choniates	*Nicetae Choniatae Historia*, ed. J. A. van Dieten (Corpus Fontium Historiae Byzantinae XI) (Berlin, 1975)
Nicolas, I, Patriarch	R. J. H. Jenkins and L. G. Westerink, *Nicolas I, Patriarch of Constantinople. Letters* (Dumbarton Oaks, 1973)
'Nikon Metanoeite'	S. Lampros, 'Ho bios Nikonos tou Metanoeite', *Neos Hellenomnemon*, 3 (1906), pp. 129–228
Pantéléèmôn	P. Lemerle, G. Dagron and S. Ćirković, *Actes de Saint-Pantéléèmôn* (Archives de l'Athos XII) (Paris, 1982)
Petit, 'Kosmosotira'	L. Petit 'Typikon du monastère de la Kosmosotira près d'Aenos (1152)', *Izvestija Russkogo Arheologičeskogo Instituta v Konstantinopole*, 13 (1908), pp. 17–77
Petit, 'Notre Dame de Pitié'	L. Petit, 'Le monastère de Notre Dame de Pitié en Macédoine', *Izvestija Russkogo Arheologičeskogo Instituta v Konstantinopole*, 6 (1900), pp. 1–153

Abbreviations

Prôtaton	D. Papachryssanthou, *Actes du Prôtaton* (Archives de l'Athos VII) (Paris, 1975)
Psellos, *Chronographie*	Michel Psellos, *Chronographie ou histoire d'un siècle de Byzance (976–1077)*, ed. E. Renauld (2 vols., Paris, 1926–8)
Psellos, *Scripta Minora*	*Michaelis Pselli Scripta Minora*, ed. G. Kurtz and F. Drexl (2 vols., Milan, 1936–41)
Sathas, *MB*	K. N. Sathas, *Mesaionike Bibliotheke* (7 vols., Athens–Paris, Venice–Paris, 1872–94)
Scylitzes	*Ioannis Scylitzae Synopsis Historiarum*, ed. J. Thurn (Corpus Fontium Historiae Byzantinae V) (Berlin, 1973)
Stadtmüller, *Michael Choniates*	G. Stadtmüller, *Michael Choniates, Metropolit von Athen* (Orientalia Christiana Analecta 33) (Rome, 1934)
Svoronos, 'Recherches sur le cadastre byzantin'	N. Svoronos, 'Recherches sur le cadastre byzantin et la fiscalité aux XIᵉ et XIIᵉ siècles: le cadastre de Thèbes', *Bulletin de Correspondance Hellénique*, 83 (1959), pp. 1–145
Tafel and Thomas, *Urkunden*	G. L. F. Tafel and G. M. Thomas, *Urkunden zur älteren Handels- und Staatsgeschichte der Republik Venedig* (3 vols., Vienna, 1856–7)
Theophanes	*Theophanis Chronographia*, ed. C. de Boor (2 vols., Leipzig, 1883–5)
Theophanes Continuatus	*Theophanes Continuatus, Ioannes Cameniata, Symeon Magister, Georgius Monachus*, ed. I. Bekker (Bonn, 1838)
Timarione	R. Romano, *Pseudo-Luciano, Timarione* (Naples, 1974)
Vasilievskij, 'Meletios'	V. G. Vasilievskij, 'Nikolaou ek Methones kai Theodorou tou Prodromou syngrapheon tes ib' hekatontaheteridos bioi Meletiou tou neou', *Pravloslavnyi Palestinskij Sbornik*, 17 (1886), pp. 1–69
'Vie d'Athanase'	L. Petit, 'Vie de Saint Athanase l'Athonite', *Analecta Bollandiana*, 25 (1906), pp. 5–89
Vie de Cyrille Philéote	E. Sargologos, *La Vie de saint Cyrille le Philéote, moine byzantin (†1110)* (Subsidia Hagiographica 39) (Brussels, 1964)
'Vie de Philarète'	M. H. Fourmy and M. Leroy, 'La vie de S. Philarète', *Byzantion*, 9 (1934), pp. 85–170
Vie de Théodore de Sykéôn	A. J. Festugière, *Vie de Théodore de Sykéôn* (Subsidia Hagiographica 48) (Brussels, 1970)

'Vie du patrice Nicétas'	D. Papachryssanthou, 'Un confesseur du second iconoclasme: la vie du patrice Nicétas (†836)', *Travaux et Mémoires*, 3 (1968), pp. 309–51
'Vita S. Lucae Stylitae'	H. Delahaye, 'Vita S. Lucae Stylitae', *Les Saints stylites* (Subsidia Hagiographica 14) (Brussels, 1923), pp. 195–237
Xénophon	L. Petit, *Actes de Xénophon* (Actes de l'Athos I), *Vizantijskij Vremennik*, 10 (1903), supplement 1
Xéropotamou	J. Bompaire, *Actes de Xéropotamou* (Archives de l'Athos III) (Paris, 1964)
Zographou	W. Regel, E. Kurtz and B. Korablev, *Actes de Zographou* (Actes de l'Athos IV), *Vizantijskij Vremennik*, 13 (1907), supplement 1
Zonaras	*Ioannis Zonarae Epitome Historiarum*, ed. M. Pinder and T. Büttner-Wobst (3 vols., Bonn, 1841–97)

Glossary

This glossary does not attempt to give comprehensive definitions of every possible meaning of each term, only to elucidate the meaning of the terms as they appear in this work.

AERIKON   a judicial fine later commuted into a cash payment
AKTEMON   a dependent peasant without oxen
ALLELENGYON   the collective responsibility of a fiscal unit for the taxes imposed on that unit
ANGAREIA   compulsory labour service
APOROS   an impoverished peasant, possibly referring specifically to peasants with property valued at less than fifty *nomismata*
ARCHONTES   holders of honorific titles or offices in the administration, in practice the landowning elite who dominated in towns
ATELES   not owing any tax-payment, therefore landless
AULE   courtyard surrounded by buildings which could be leased to tenants
BOIDATOS   a dependent peasant with one ox
CHARISTIKARIOS   lay landowner given responsibility for the control of the temporal affairs of a monastery
CHORION   a village, but in technical documents also a fiscal unit
COLONUS   peasant tied to the land, which he cultivated, by the late Roman state
DEKATEIA   a tax-payment of a tenth (see also *morte, pakton*)
DEMOSIARIOI   *paroikoi* who were established on lands belonging to the state
DEMOSION   the basic land-tax
DIKERATON   supplementary tax raised at the rate of one-twelfth of the basic land-tax
DIOIKETES   official responsible for the collection of the land-tax

xiii

xiv *Glossary*

DROMOS administrative department responsible for foreign affairs and the maintenance of the road network among other duties

DYNATOS a person designated as powerful owing to the position which he occupied in the state's military or administrative hierarchies or in the church

ELATIKON supplementary tax additional to the *demosion* and exacted at a flat rate

ELEUTHEROS literally meaning free, but referring in the archives to peasants who were free from all fiscal responsibilities to the state or any private landowner and were therefore landless

ENNOMION a tax on the pasture of animals

EPEREIA a general term for requisitioning

EPIBOLE the rate of *epibole* was the equation between the area of a fiscal unit and the basic land-tax imposed on it (excluding the supplementary taxes). All land in the fiscal unit was included in the calculation, including land which had received relief from taxation in the form of a *sympatheia*. The application of this procedure to Lavra's estates in the late eleventh and early twelfth centuries differed from the standard procedure, because the monastery was treated as a special case

EPISKEPSIS a complex of properties belonging to the state

ERGASTERION either a workshop or a place of retail trade or an establishment combining both functions

EXKOUSSEIA a transfer of revenues and other peasant obligations from the state to a private landowner. Usually, the documents stipulated the number of peasants covered by the *exkousseia* and the range of obligations which the state was willing not to exact from them. The landowner would then benefit from these obligations

FOLLIS low-value copper coin, 288 to the *nomisma*

GENIKON SEKRETON the state's fiscal department

HEXAFOLLON flat-rate surcharge imposed with the land-tax

HYPERPYRON top-value gold coin in the reformed coinage of Alexios Komnenos

KANISKION a quantity of food and drink supplied to fiscal officials by the rural population

KAPNIKON a tax on households

KLASMA land which had been granted tax-relief for thirty years and was then withdrawn from the fiscal unit and became the property of the state

Glossary

KLERIKOS a person who exercised some lowly function in the church and was settled on metropolitan and episcopal land under conditions comparable to those regulating the settlement of *paroikoi*

KOMMERKION a tax of a tenth on commercial transactions

LIBELLIKON DEMOSION tax-payment imposed on klasmatic land and levied at one-twelfth the rate of the ordinary *demosion*

LIBELLOS document confirming the sale of klasmatic land by the state to a private individual

LOGISIMON an attribution of fiscal revenues by the state to a private landowner. It took various forms, including payment by the administration or directly by peasants to the beneficiary without the intervention of the state

METOCHION a subordinate monastery under the control of another, more powerful monastery

MILLIARESION silver coin worth one-twelfth of a *nomisma*

MISTHIOS a hired labourer

MODIOS a unit of surface measurement equivalent to about a tenth or a twelfth of a hectare or a measurement of the capacity of boats or of quantities of produce

MORTE a payment of a tenth of the produce, equivalent in the late Byzantine period to a feudal rent, indicating that the cultivator had the status of *paroikos*

NOMISMA gold coin

NOMISMA THEOTOKION *nomisma* featuring a representation of the Theotokos, in some cases clearly the electrum *nomisma*, in others possibly the *hyperpyron*

NOMISMA TRACHY a term used to refer to debased *nomismata* of the eleventh century and to some denominations of the reformed coinage of the twelfth century

NOMISMA TRIKEPHALON *nomisma* with three heads or figures represented on it. Through most of the twelfth century it referred to the electrum coin, but a reference to coins of Isaac II clearly refers to the top-value *hyperpyron*

PAKTON a payment of rent (sometimes identified with the *dekateia* and *morte*) by the *paroikos* to a landowner in theory at the standard rate of one *nomisma* for ten *modioi*

PAROIKOS a peasant established on land belonging to either a private landowner or the state. He paid the *pakton*, not simply the standard land-tax, to the landowner

xvi *Glossary*

PENES   an independent peasant farmer without substantial resources

PERIORISMOS   the delimitation of the boundary of a property

PRAKTIKON   a document drawn up by the state's fiscal officials listing the obligations of peasants to their landowner

PROASTEION   a property on which the landowner was not resident and which was cultivated by peasant farmers

PRONOIA   an attribution of fiscal revenues to a soldier in return for military duties. These grants were not hereditary in the twelfth century

PTOCHOS   an impoverished person

SOLEMNION   an annual payment of a fixed sum from the state's fiscal revenues to a beneficiary, usually a church or a monastery

STASIS   peasant landholding with household

STICHOS   a line in a tax-register in which the property of an individual landowner and its tax-payment were recorded

STRATEIA   a property whose owner was liable to supply the state with a soldier for the thematic army

STRATIOTES   the owner of a military property, not always identical with the soldier who performed the military obligation incumbent on the land. The term later applied to the holder of a *pronoia*

SYMPATHEIA   relief from taxation on a property which had been abandoned by its cultivator, intended to avoid increasing the burden on the remaining members of the fiscal unit through the system of collective responsibility for the taxes of the entire unit

SYNETHEIA   supplementary tax, imposed at a flat rate in addition to the basic land-tax

TELOS   tax-payment

TETARTERON   light-weight gold coin introduced in the tenth century. The term was later used to refer to the low-value copper coin of the reformed currency in the twelfth century

TYPIKON   a document prescribing the rules by which a monastery was administered and the monks' lives regulated

ZEUGARATOS   a dependent peasant with two oxen

ZEUGARION   either a ploughteam with two oxen or a peasant landholding corresponding roughly to the area which could conveniently be cultivated by a peasant with two oxen

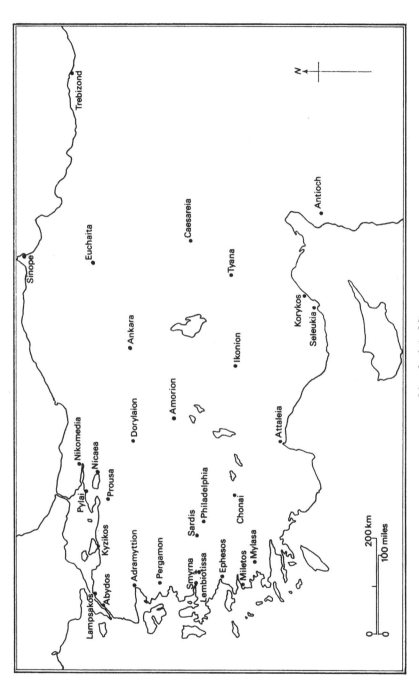

Map 1. Asia Minor

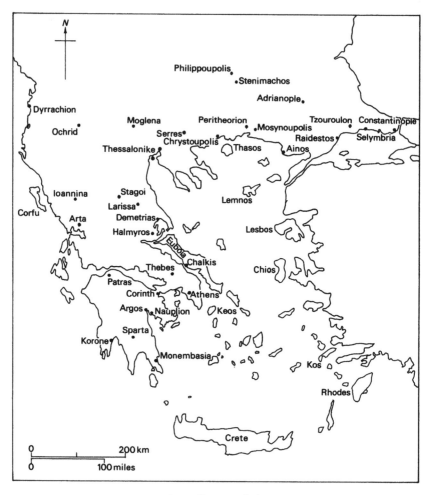

Map 2. The Balkans and the Aegean

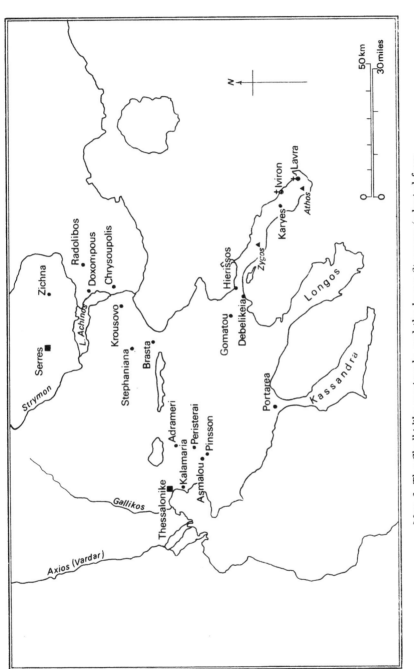

Map 3. The Chalkidike peninsula and the lower Strymon (adapted from *Lavra*, I, p. 57; *Lavra*, IV, pp. 74–5, 100–1, 115; and *Esphigménou*, p. 23)

Introduction

The Byzantine social formation[1] consisted overwhelmingly of peasant producers. The fundamental characteristic of the peasantry is that the family is the most important unit of production and it has effective control (but not necessarily ownership) of the means of production. Peasant families are usually associated in larger groups with certain collective interests which may vary from one society to another. The family forms a socio-economic unit and depends mainly on the labour of its own members. Additional labourers, when necessary, are usually obtained from the same community and belong to the same social class. The familial units produce mainly for their own subsistence. Some artisanal activity may occur in the village, but it is still a household activity and these artisans are derived from the peasantry and usually combine their industrial activity with agriculture. They produce for consumption within the village, not exchange outside the village.[2] Peasant producers formed the economic base of Byzantine society. Their own requirements were not restricted to consumption needs, but included the storage of sufficient seed for next year's crop and the provision of food for livestock. They also had to replace their instruments of production whenever necessary. Peasant production depended on a

---

[1] This term is used to refer to a specific, historical combination of modes of production organised under the dominance of one of them; see P. Anderson, *Passages from Antiquity to Feudalism* (London, 1974), p. 22 n. 6; M. Godelier, *Perspectives in Marxist Anthropology* (Cambridge, 1977), pp. 18, 63–9; and J. F. Haldon, 'Some Considerations on Byzantine Society and Economy in the Seventh Century', *Byzantinische Forschungen*, 10 (1985), pp. 101–2 n. 61. See also B. Hindess and P. Q. Hirst, *Pre-capitalist Modes of Production* (London, 1975), pp. 13–15. F. Favory, 'Validité des concepts marxistes pour une théorie des sociétés de l'Antiquité. Le modèle impérial romain', *Klio*, 63 (1981), pp. 313–30, uses the term in a completely different sense.

[2] R. H. Hilton, *The English Peasantry in the Later Middle Ages* (Oxford, 1975), p. 13; D. Thorner, 'Peasant Economy as a Category in Economic History', in T. Shanin (ed.), *Peasants and Peasant Societies* (Harmondsworth, 1971), pp. 202–18.

2   *Economic expansion in the Byzantine empire*

balance between needs and a distaste for manual labour which restricts the intensity of agricultural production (at least when land is not in short supply). Once enough is being produced to satisfy needs there is little incentive to extend cultivation further, unless pressure is put on the peasant community by some outside authority to alienate part of its produce. The production of a surplus was essential for economic development (although on its own insufficient for this purpose). In Byzantium the surplus was expropriated by political coercion and it supported the imperial bureaucracy, the army, the church and secular landowners.[3]

The state played the major part in expropriating surplus wealth from the direct producers. Its revenues, as in the late Roman period, were largely based on a very comprehensive system of land-taxation, where land was graded according to its quality and use and the tax-payment fixed accordingly. The tax-registers of every fiscal unit were revised regularly. The system was inherited from the later Roman empire and, in spite of subsequent alterations, it reflects a large measure of administrative continuity.[4] A large part of the superstructural apparatus of Byzantium had been carried over from the Roman empire. This was the fundamental difference between Byzantium and the medieval west, where the breakdown of Roman institutions was more extensive. Constantinople remained the major centre of consumption in the empire owing to the demands of the imperial court and the administrative hierarchies of church and state. The state was responsible for all issues of money, which it coined to meet its administrative and military expenses. It reclaimed the gold coinage through taxation. So the state left its own clear imprint on monetary and commercial activity.[5]

In these respects continuity between late Antiquity and the Middle Ages is apparent. Nevertheless, the extent of continuity should not be exaggerated. Some important changes in social organisation did take place. The cities had been centres of local government, exacting revenues for themselves and the state from their territories. This

---

[3] For the concept of the surplus, see E. R. Wolf, *Peasants* (New Jersey, 1966), pp. 4–10; and M. Godelier, *Rationality and Irrationality in Economics* (London, 1972), pp. 270–4. See also B. Kerblay, 'Chayanov and the Theory of Peasantry as a Specific Type of Economy', in Shanin (ed.), *Peasants and Peasant Societies*, pp. 150–60.

[4] For the technical aspects of Byzantine taxation, see Dölger, *Beiträge*; and Svoronos, 'Recherches sur le cadastre byzantin', pp. 1–145.

[5] M. F. Hendy, *Studies in the Byzantine Monetary Economy c. 300–1450* (Cambridge, 1985).

Introduction

3

institutional link between the cities and their rural areas was ruptured, resulting in a decline in the importance of the cities in social and economic terms. Some retained a certain importance owing to the administrative role attributed to them by the state and the church. Others had no real importance except as a fortified centre for the inhabitants of the region and perhaps as a local centre for petty commodity exchange on a very small scale.[6]

Although there was only a partial breakdown of the institutions of Antiquity, the change was enough to permit the slow rise of a new aristocracy. A new system of provincial administration, based on the themes, unified civil and military authority and gave great powers to the generals in command of these administrative units. Gradually, through service to the state, a powerful provincial officer class was able to build up its economic, social and military power to such an extent that it became a centrifugal force undermining the territorial and jurisdictional unity of the empire. No longer based in the classical urban centres of western Asia Minor, its strength lay in the rugged interior of the peninsula.[7] The other source of wealth for the aristocracy was service in the central administration in Constantinople. Traditionally, the course of Byzantine history has been seen in terms of the struggle between these two opposing factions in the aristocracy, civil and military, for control of the state; this conflict reached its climax in the eleventh century, culminating in the triumph of the military faction through the seizure of power by the Komnenoi.[8] This is a great oversimplification and there has been a justified reaction against it recently.[9] Certainly, there is no clear dichotomy between the two groups, but the distinction does have a certain amount of validity. One group derived their power from service in the capital and could bring influence to bear on the emperor more easily, but had less scope for action independent of the state. The provincial magnates had greater *de*

---

[6] Haldon, 'Some Considerations on Byzantine Society and Economy in the Seventh Century', pp. 75–112.

[7] *Ibid.*, pp. 94–5; G. Ostrogorsky, *History of the Byzantine State*, 2nd English edn, trans. J. M. Hussey (Oxford, 1968), p. 96.

[8] Ostrogorsky, *History*, pp. 320–50; S. Vryonis, *The Decline of Medieval Hellenism in Asia Minor and the Process of Islamization from the Eleventh through the Fifteenth Century* (Berkeley, Los Angeles, London, 1971), pp. 70–7.

[9] G. Weiss, *Oströmische Beamte im Spiegel der Schriften des Michael Psellos* (Munich, 1973), pp. 90–7; P. Lemerle, *Cinq études sur le XIe siècle byzantin* (Paris, 1977), p. 258. The term 'aristocracy' is used more for convenience than with any precise technical content; see the introduction to M. Angold (ed.), *The Byzantine Aristocracy IX to XIIIth Centuries* (Oxford, 1984), pp. 1–9.

4   Economic expansion in the Byzantine empire

facto autonomy of action. There was, of course, much blurring and overlapping between the two groups owing to familial and social connections, which made it difficult for the state to take effective measures to restrict the economic and social power of the magnates. The emperor always needed their political and military support, which was based firmly on their economic strength, and the aristocracy needed the benefits which could accrue from imperial favour. So there was a community of interest between the emperor and the aristocracy, but underlying this were the centrifugal tendencies inherent in the economic strength and social authority of the aristocracy.

Landowners received the advantages of imperial benevolence not only through gains made from service in the administration, but from grants of land and fiscal privileges. Even where the state conceded the fiscal revenues of an estate to a landowner, it still exercised an important function in establishing the payments to be made by the peasants to the landowner. The comprehensiveness of the state's fiscal apparatus asserted itself even when the state was abandoning its taxes from a property. Fiscal officials drew up the *praktikon*, the register detailing the peasants' obligations, and handed it over to the landowner. The *praktikon* was revised at regular intervals by the state's officials to take into account any changes in the number and wealth of the peasants or in the fiscal privileges of the landowner.[10] So one uniform fiscal system was in operation and the revenues were divided between the state, the lay aristocracy and the church.[11] It should be stressed that most fiscal privileges were not all-embracing and even privileged landowners usually still owed a tax-payment to the state.

An important consideration is whether there were any fundamental distinctions between the properties of secular and ecclesiastical landowners. The latter had greater stability. They were not subject to division among heirs (a subject about which little is known) and they were less seriously affected by (but not totally immune from) the vicissitudes of political intrigue. Otherwise there was probably little fundamental difference between the two categories of landed property. Surviving documents relating to lay estates show no real differences from monastic estates in the way in which the properties were exploited. An important factor was the uniformity of the state's fiscal

[10] For the technical procedure, see Dölger, *Beiträge*, pp. 100–1; and Svoronos, 'Recherches sur le cadastre byzantin', pp. 60–2.

[11] E. Patlagean, '"Économie paysanne" et "féodalité byzantine"', *Annales ESC*, 30 (1975), pp. 1371–96.

Introduction 5

system, which ensured that the same range of obligations was imposed on the peasants on both secular and ecclesiastical land. The scope of the privileges which landowners received from the state depended on the influence they were able to exert at Constantinople, and the division between secular and ecclesiastical properties was irrelevant in this respect.[12] There is no reason to think that economic and demographic trends on ecclesiastical estates were any different from those on lay estates. This is particularly important owing to the preeminent position of the documents from monastic archives in the surviving source material. It suggests that conclusions drawn from monastic documents reflect economic trends in general.[13]

The range of obligations which the state transferred to privileged landowners was wide and included rents in cash and kind and labour services. Usually, the state retained rights to certain obligations, while transferring others to the landowner. An important consequence of the state's role in this procedure was that the rents and other obligations then owed to the landowner had been devised for the convenience of the state to expedite the proper functioning of the administration. The state was mainly interested in cash revenues paid in gold. It exacted payments in kind to maintain its officials in the performance of their duties in the provinces and to ensure the army's food supply. Labour services were enforced for military reasons (work on fortifications) and to keep the state's network of communications in good repair. Agricultural labour services were never a great concern of the state. Consequently, there was an institutional restraint on the enforcement of extensive labour services performed by dependent peasants on their landowners' properties. Byzantium never witnessed large-scale demesne farming by compulsory labour services.

The position of independent peasant farmers in this social formation has been the subject of controversy.[14] They had full rights of landownership as long as they made their fiscal payments to the state. Their economic position was sometimes insecure, at the mercy of

---

[12] For these privileged properties, see below, p. 71.

[13] See also A. E. Laiou-Thomadakis, *Peasant Society in the Late Byzantine Empire. A Social and Demographic Study* (Princeton, 1977), p. 12. For the close social contacts between monastic leaders and members of the aristocracy, see R. Morris, 'The Political Saint of the Eleventh Century', in S. Hackel (ed.), *The Byzantine Saint* (Studies Supplementary to Sobornost 5) (London, 1981), pp. 43–50.

[14] G. Ostrogorsky, *Quelques problèmes d'histoire de la paysannerie byzantine* (Brussels, 1956); P. Lemerle, *The Agrarian History of Byzantium from the Origins to the Twelfth Century. The Sources and Problems* (Galway, 1979).

6   *Economic expansion in the Byzantine empire*

harvest failures and the excesses of the state's fiscal machinery. The state's requirement that taxes be paid in high-value gold coins must have been a problem for many peasant communities, helping to intensify differences in wealth among the villagers. There was always a tendency for independent peasants to be subordinated to large landowners, but the speed of this process should not be exaggerated. The state's need of the support of powerful individuals and institutions led it to attribute landless peasants to these landowners as *paroikoi* (dependent peasants); consequently, as the population increased, *paroikoi* of either the state or of private landowners made up a larger proportion of the peasantry. When peasants were subsumed under landowners, the state, through its role in the attribution of revenues to landowners, was responsible for the rigorous legal coercion on the peasantry to alienate part of its produce to the landowner. The latter did not have to rely on his own, often considerable power, as he also had the backing of the state. The independent peasantry was gradually squeezed between the state and powerful landowners. Although the state did take legal measures to prevent independent peasants from being bought out or forced out by large landowners, the relative importance of communities of independent producers tended to decline, because they were unable to acquire new land and bring it under cultivation as rapidly as larger landowners.

How to define the social structure of Byzantium has been the source of endless controversy. The traditional dividing-line has been between those historians who apply the term 'feudalism' to Byzantium and those who resolutely deny its validity.[15] Ostrogorsky has attempted to define Byzantine feudalism in terms comparable to those of traditional western historiography. He regards the *pronoia* as a Byzantine equivalent of the fief, and it was only with the widespread adoption of this institution by Alexios I (so he claims) that Byzantine society became fully feudalised.[16] There are several problems with this interpretation. The similarities between the *pronoia* and the fief are very superficial. Many important features associated with the fief, such as vassalage and the oath of fealty, did not occur with the *pronoia*, which was a simple attribution of fiscal revenues and, perhaps, temporary ownership of the

---

[15] The standard work on Byzantine feudalism is G. Ostrogorsky, *Pour l'histoire de la féodalité byzantine* (Brussels, 1954). Lemerle has always taken the opposite view with great vigour; see *Cinq études*, pp. 186–7.

[16] Ostrogorsky, *History*, pp. 371–2; Ostrogorsky, *Pour l'histoire de la féodalité byzantine*, pp. 26ff. For the development of this institution, see below, p. 72.

Introduction 7

land in return for military service. The major objection to Ostrogorsky's interpretation is that the *pronoia* was a much more marginal phenomenon in Byzantium than the fief in western Europe. Leading aristocrats did not hold their land by *pronoia*. The pyramid effect of subinfeudation was absent in Byzantium, although there is evidence for the existence of aristocratic retinues. The *pronoia* grant involved only fiscal revenues, not jurisdictional rights over *paroikoi*. Its impact on Byzantine society was much less than that of the fief in western Europe.

The historians who see feudalism in the traditional, narrow sense which characterises discussion of the subject among most western medievalists, understandably deny the concept any validity in relation to Byzantium. However, the value of such a rigid, narrow concept of feudalism is strictly limited because it leaves out of sight the overwhelming mass of the population in any feudal society, and its use as an analytical category is therefore restricted. It is preferable to adopt a wider definition of the term. Feudalism will be regarded as a mode of production consisting of the forces of production (the material basis of the productive process) and the relations of production (the relations between landowners and peasantry). In feudalism the bulk of the direct producers, who were peasant farmers, were subordinated to a landowning aristocracy. Although the peasant household and the village community were the base of feudalism, they were not specific to it. The essential factor was the exploitative relationship between landowners and dependent peasants by which the surplus labour of the peasantry was transferred to the landowners in the form of rents in cash or kind or through the performance of labour services. The essential feature of this relationship was the political coercion which the landowner could exert on the peasant household to ensure that he received the payments. As the peasantry actually had control of the means of production (except in cases where labour services were exacted by the landowner), the landowners had to exercise some sort of compulsion to expropriate surplus produce.[17]

How far does this definition of feudalism correspond to conditions in Byzantium? Clearly, surplus labour extracted by the state to provide for the imperial court, a centralised bureaucracy and a large army cannot be considered in this light. Some historians have tended to confuse the

---

[17] R. H. Hilton (ed.), *The Transition from Feudalism to Capitalism* (London, 1976), p. 30; R. H. Hilton, 'Agrarian Class Structure and Economic Development in Pre-industrial Europe: A Crisis of Feudalism', *Past and Present*, 80 (1978), pp. 3–19.

8 Economic expansion in the Byzantine empire

appropriation of rent by the state with feudalism,[18] but this reduces feudalism to such a vague concept that it has little analytical value. The definition of feudalism outlined above has more relevance for the estates of members of the aristocracy or the monasteries, about whose lands we are relatively well informed. Where the state conceded extensive fiscal claims to landowners, the latter must have exercised some sort of coercion over the peasantry, but this is not well documented. This conflict between the centralised state and feudalism was a distinctive feature of Byzantine history. The development of feudalism was restricted by the survival of the state apparatus of late Antiquity, but it did eventually become a formidable threat to the integrity of the centralised state.

These issues have provoked much debate and controversy among historians. Ostrogorsky represents the old orthodoxy which has been subjected to telling criticisms in recent years. In his view Byzantium survived the crisis of the seventh and eighth centuries owing to the greater importance of communities of independent peasants in this period and to the formation of a new category of military lands – peasant farms with an obligation to provide a soldier for the state. The peasantry is represented as the backbone of the state.[19] Certainly, peasant farmers were more easily controlled by the state than powerful aristocratic clans, making it easier for the state to exercise its authority. But there was little differentiation in economic activity. These peasants were primarily engaged in subsistence farming and were involved in commerce only on a very limited scale to obtain the cash required for their tax-payments. Consequently, there was little economic vitality in the early Middle Ages.

Ostrogorsky's judgement on the process of feudalisation is negative. By the tenth century the rise of feudal magnates threatened the social balance which Byzantium had achieved in the early Middle Ages. The subordination of previously free peasants to large landowners undermined the authority of the central government and consequently much of Asia Minor was lost to the Seljuk Turks in the eleventh century.[20] He even goes so far as to claim that the independent peasant largely

---

[18] L. E. Havlík, 'The Genesis of Feudalism and the Slav Peoples', in V. Vavrinek (ed.), *Beiträge zur byzantinischen Geschichte im 9.–11. Jahrhundert* (Prague, 1978), pp. 133–4. The contrast between state tax-raising and the extraction of rent by landowners, representing two different economic systems, has been strongly emphasised by C. J. Wickham, 'The Uniqueness of the East', *Journal of Peasant Studies*, 12, parts 2–3 (1985), pp. 166–96.

[19] Ostrogorsky, *History*, pp. 133–4.   [20] *Ibid.*, pp. 272–350.

Introduction 9

disappeared, leaving only *paroikoi* belonging either to the state or to feudal landowners.[21] Not only is this an unwise assertion given the limited nature of the surviving source material, but the distinction between an independent peasant and a *paroikos* of the state is never clearly established. Ostrogorsky represents feudalisation as a process of decadence.[22]

Other historians, who have not followed Ostrogorsky's use of the concept of feudalism, agree with him in retaining the eleventh century as a critical turning-point in Byzantine history. The interpretations of Lemerle and Svoronos have been modified somewhat to place greater emphasis on the later decades of the eleventh century. Originally, both regarded that century as a period of demographic decline and Svoronos presented a very pessimistic picture of a decrease in agricultural production.[23] Subsequently, he conceded that there is some evidence of expansion in the urban economy, but he is reluctant to admit any similar trend in the rural economy. He concludes that during the course of the eleventh century whatever expansion there might have been came to an end and stagnation prevailed.[24] His conclusions complement those of Lemerle, who sees the first part of the eleventh century as a time of expansion. He emphasises the innovative role of ministers such as Nikephoritzes and the greater activity of the senate in politics during the century, but he sees the accession of Alexios Komnenos as marking a definitive end to such expansion and as the reply of an aristocratic conservatism. As he himself admits, such conclusions have to be examined in the light of evidence relating to the rural economy. He raises the possibility of a decline in production caused by the extension of large estates.[25]

Much discussion in the eastern European literature on Byzantine agrarian history has centred around the specific characteristics of Byzantine feudalism and the extent to which it is comparable with feudalism in western Europe.[26] Generally, Soviet scholars place the

[21] Ostrogorsky, *Quelques problèmes*, pp. 22–4.
[22] Ostrogorsky, *Pour l'histoire de la féodalité byzantine*, p. 92.
[23] N. Svoronos, 'Société et organisation intérieure dans l'empire byzantin au XIe siècle: les principaux problèmes', in *Proceedings of the XIIIth International Congress of Byzantine Studies, Oxford 1966* (London, 1967), pp. 384–9. Lemerle, *The Agrarian History*, p. 188 n. 2.
[24] N. Svoronos, 'Remarques sur les structures économiques de l'empire byzantin au XIe siècle', *Travaux et Mémoires*, 6 (1976), pp. 62–3.
[25] Lemerle, *Cinq études*, pp. 251–312, esp. p. 310.
[26] In particular the important contribution of H. Köpstein, 'Zu den Agrarverhältnissen', in F. Winkelmann *et al.*, *Byzanz im 7. Jahrhundert* (Berlin, 1978), pp. 1–72. See also

10   *Economic expansion in the Byzantine empire*

origin of Byzantine feudalism in the seventh century. An exception is Lipsic, who regards the late Roman colonate as a sort of 'proto-feudalism'.[27] The major problem with her approach is that the *coloni* were bound to the soil by the state in order to secure its own fiscal revenues, creating a sharp distinction between the *colonus* and the dependent peasant under feudalism. She also stresses the importance of the Slav invasions, which supposedly provided the manpower to consolidate communities of independent peasants and to bring new land into cultivation.[28] For Sjuzjumov and others Byzantine feudalism originated in the free peasant communities, but was definitely established only in the tenth and eleventh centuries.[29] Sjuzjumov stresses the importance of the growth of commercial and artisanal activities, linking this question with the extension of feudal social relations. He connects economic developments too closely with the political fortunes of the state, and the presentation of the eleventh century as one of economic decline as well as political crisis is open to question.[30] An exception is Kazhdan, who was the first historian to regard the early medieval period as one of profound urban decline in Byzantium, with a subsequent revival in the eleventh and twelfth centuries. He represents the seventh century as the critical period for the evolution of medieval society. The disappearance of the ancient

---

V. Hrochova, 'La place de Byzance dans la typologie du féodalisme européen', in Vavrinek (ed.), *Beiträge*, pp. 31–45. K.-P. Matschke, 'Sozialschichten und Geisteshaltungen', *XVI Internationaler Byzantinistenkongress. Akten. Jahrbuch der Österreichischen Byzantinistik*, 31/1 (1981), pp. 189–212. Most of the Soviet literature is inaccessible to me, but some has been translated. See *Le Féodalisme à Byzance. Problèmes du mode de production de l'empire byzantin, Recherches Internationales à la Lumière du Marxisme*, 79 (1974). See also Z. V. Udal'cova and K. V. Chvostova, 'Les structures sociales et économiques dans la Basse-Byzance', *XVI Internationaler Byzantinistenkongress. Akten, Jahrbuch der Österreichischen Byzantinistik*, 31/1 (1981), pp. 131–47; and G. G. Litavrin, 'Zur Lage der byzantinischen Bauernschaft im 10.–11. Jh. Strittige Fragen', in Vavrinek (ed.), *Beiträge*, pp. 47–70. For summaries of Soviet work, see A. P. Kazhdan, 'La byzantinologie soviétique en 1974-75', *Byzantion*, 49 (1979), pp. 506–53 and preceding volumes; I. Sorlin, 'Les recherches soviétiques sur l'histoire byzantin de 1945 à 1962', *Travaux et Mémoires*, 2 (1967), pp. 489–564; and I. Sorlin, 'Publications soviétiques sur le XIᵉ siècle', *Travaux et Mémoires*, 6 (1976), pp. 367–98.

[27] E. Lipchits, 'La fin du régime esclavagiste et le début du féodalisme à Byzance', *Le Féodalisme à Byzance*, p. 27.

[28] E. Lipchits, 'La ville et le village à Byzance du VIᵉ siècle jusqu'à la première moitié du IXᵉ siècle', *Le Féodalisme à Byzance*, p. 52.

[29] Sorlin, 'Les recherches soviétiques sur l'histoire byzantin de 1945 à 1962', p. 497. Z. Oudaltsova, 'À propos de la genèse du féodalisme à Byzance', *Le Féodalisme à Byzance*, pp. 37–9.

[30] M. I. Siouzioumov, 'Le village et la ville à Byzance aux IXᵉ–Xᵉ siècles', *Le Féodalisme à Byzance*, pp. 65–74.

Introduction 11

urban life-style had already begun, but it was accelerated by the contraction of towns and the increased importance of a barter economy from the middle of the seventh century. The Byzantine social structure also became more simplified. Dependent peasants became fewer and, owing to urban decline and the reduced importance of the provincial aristocracy, there was no significant intermediate level between the bureaucratic elite of the capital and the bulk of the population, mainly independent peasants. He also produces some evidence to contradict the view that the Komnenian period was a time of steady decline and includes literary evidence that agriculture might have been more prosperous in the twelfth century. Evidence of craft production suggests that by the twelfth century Constantinople no longer held a monopoly in the production of goods, especially silk. There appears to have been an economic shift away from Constantinople to the provinces, even though the capital still retained control of the manufacture of many luxury goods. This did not produce a new urban economy or ideology. Cautious attitudes to markets persisted and, in contrast to the west, provincial towns failed to develop their own identity, but were dominated by local magnates and administrators. Kazhdan also emphasises the concentration of power by the Komnenoi and a small group of related families through their monopolisation of military commands, and he considers their restructuring of the aristocracy as a new development closer to the feudal model of the west.[31]

The interpretation of some Soviet scholars show too much confidence in the existence of feudalism as early as the seventh century. Although it was certainly a time of fundamental transformation, emphasis on the importance of communities of independent peasants is incompatible with a definition of feudalism which is based on the subordination of peasant producers to private landowners. Some historians have used

---

[31] See the publications in English of A. P. Kazhdan and G. Constable, *People and Power in Byzantium. An Introduction to Modern Byzantine Studies* (Dumbarton Oaks, 1982); A. P. Kazhdan, in collaboration with S. Franklin, *Studies on Byzantine Literature of the Eleventh and Twelfth Centuries* (Cambridge, 1984), pp. 23–86; A. P. Kazhdan and A. W. Epstein, *Change in Byzantine Culture in the Eleventh and Twelfth Centuries* (Berkeley, 1985), pp. 1–73; A. P. Kazhdan and A. Cutler, 'Continuity and Discontinuity in Byzantine History', *Byzantion*, 52 (1982), pp. 429–78. See also his critical assessment of the work of Litavrin and Lemerle, 'Remarques sur le XIᵉ siècle byzantin à propos d'un livre récent de Paul Lemerle', *Byzantion*, 49 (1979), pp. 491–503. In his later work he uses a definition of feudalism which is closer to the traditional usage of western historiography and is in contrast to his earlier work, which is summarised by Sorlin, 'Les recherches soviétiques sur l'histoire byzantin de 1945 à 1962', pp. 489–565 *passim*; and Sorlin, 'Publications soviétiques sur la XIᵉ siècle', pp. 367–80.

12 *Economic expansion in the Byzantine empire*

the concept 'centralised feudal rent' to account for the role of the state in expropriating surplus labour.[32] Although the superficial form in which the surplus was appropriated did not differ whether the state or a feudal landowner was the beneficiary, it made a fundamental difference to the social structure. The state's role in fixing the level of payments made by the peasantry to landowners and in restricting the privileges of the latter was one aspect of the conflict between the centralised state, which survived from Antiquity, and the developing feudal social relations.

These problems need to be examined with a rigorous interrogation of the source material, but it will be useful first to consider in general terms how much scope this social formation gave for economic expansion. It must have had a largely restrictive influence. The major productive unit was the peasant household with a limited capability for making improvements to the land. Peasant communities probably achieved a certain amount through drainage and irrigation, but the most important method of producing more was simply to increase the area under cultivation. These considerations apply also to large properties, because they were divided up mainly among peasant cultivators. However, it is possible that the expansion of feudal estates did have some beneficial effects on Byzantine agriculture. Technological innovations were absent, but an equally important consideration is whether the potential of the land was more effectively exploited within the limits of the technology available to the Byzantines. The capacity of large landowners to bring extensive tracts of new land under cultivation quickly has already been mentioned. They also had the resources to effect large-scale irrigation works and to spend large sums on viticulture and arboriculture, which did not bring returns for several years. These improvements added to the revenues from agriculture, but the most important way of increasing feudal revenues was simply to acquire more peasant cultivators.

The development of towns and trade was closely linked to the

---

[32] Sorlin, 'Les recherches soviétiques sur l'histoire byzantin de 1945 à 1962', p. 502; Sorlin, 'Publications soviétiques sur le XIᵉ siècle', pp. 376–7; Oudaltsova, 'À propos de la genèse du féodalisme à Byzance', pp. 42–3. This concept has also been used by Soviet historians working on the absolutist state of early modern Europe, which followed upon the crisis of medieval feudalism and is represented as a renewal of feudal domination; see P. Anderson, *Lineages of the Absolutist State* (London, 1974), pp. 15–42, esp. p. 35. Whatever value the concept has in analysing this historical situation, it is of very dubious utility when applied to the Byzantine state, whose apparatus for surplus expropriation was a direct continuation from the later Roman empire.

Introduction   13

condition of the rural economy. The degree of occupational special-isation in towns depended first on the production of a large enough surplus by the rural population to support the urban population. The market for urban goods was closely linked to trends in the rural economy. The consumers of high-value luxury goods were the officials of the state and church and wealthy landowners. If revenues from the land were increasing, more could be spent on urban products. Therefore, an increase in agricultural production would have led to an increased ability to provision towns, greater activity in urban markets and an upsurge in commodity production. The discussion of the internal dynamic of the Byzantine social formation – its capacity for economic expansion – has to take into account the extent of, and the limitations to, urban growth. The fortunes of the towns offer a very clear reflection of developments in the economy as a whole.

Chapter 1

The early medieval period

The tension between the bureaucratic state and the provincial magnates did not come to the fore until the tenth and eleventh centuries. In the early Middle Ages (the seventh to the ninth century) the power of these magnates was developing. This period was a transitional one which saw the decline of the old senatorial aristocracy, based in the major cities of Antiquity, and the gradual rise of the military aristocracy. The origins of Byzantine feudalism can be traced to these centuries when the magnates exploited the authority which they derived from their role in the provincial administration to consolidate their economic power. During this transitional period the Byzantine social structure was marked by the relatively greater importance of independent peasant producers who owned their own land and paid the tax on it directly to the state.

The main evidence for the changes which occurred in the seventh century is contained in the Farmer's Law. Although communities of independent peasant farmers were known in the late Roman period,[1]

---

[1] The Farmer's Law has been the subject of considerable controversy, and widely divergent views about its origins and nature have been advanced. For the edition of the text, see Ashburner, 'The Farmer's Law', pp. 97–108. According to G. Ostrogorsky, 'Über die vermeintliche Reformtätigkeit der Isaurer', *Byzantinische Zeitschrift*, 30 (1930), pp. 394–400, it was an official law-code issued by Justinian II. This is very improbable. There is no indication in the text that it was an official law-code decreed at a specific time by any emperor. It is better regarded as a practical handbook put together for the convenience of judges who had to handle the most common everyday cases and would have found the Justinianic code too bulky. Although the attribution of the code to Justinian II is unfounded, the compilation probably dates from the late seventh or early eighth century. It is a unique source for the early medieval village community, but its uniqueness presents a problem as there is little other source material from the same period to complement it. See F. Dölger, 'Ist der Nomos Georgikos ein Gesetz Justinians II?', in *Paraspora. 30 Aufsätze zur Geschichte, Kultur und Sprache des byzantinischen Reiches* (Ettal, 1961), pp. 241–62; and N. Svoronos, 'Notes sur l'origine et la date du code rural', *Travaux et Mémoires*, 8 (1981), pp. 487–500. See also H. Hunger, *Die hochsprachliche profane Literatur der Byzantiner* (2 vols., Munich, 1978), II, pp. 440–1; and D. Simon, 'Provinzialrecht

14

The early medieval period

they did not have the same importance in the social structure of late Antiquity as they did in the early medieval centuries. By the end of the seventh century the Roman colonate had disappeared as a result of the political, social and military upheavals of the time.[2] When the *paroikos* appears in the later Byzantine sources there are important differences from the *colonus adscripticius*. The latter was bound to the soil by law and his *pekoulion* was legally the property of the landowner.[3] Neither of these conditions applied to the status of the Byzantine *paroikos*.[4] Another important consideration was that the state's reason for tying *coloni* to the soil was to secure its fiscal revenues,[5] but no such consideration affected the status of the Byzantine *paroikos*. The break in continuity was sharp. Although there is some evidence for the survival of large estates, the early Middle Ages was most important as a transitional period preceding the development of feudal social relations.

This has been denied by some historians, who claim that it attaches too much significance to the absence of any reference to the *colonus* in the Farmer's Law.[6] This argument ignores a fundamental change in legal terminology reflected in the Farmer's Law. The word used in the code to denote a peasant cultivator, *georgos*, had been used in the late Roman legislation to denote a *colonus adscripticius*. The conditions on which the peasant farmers of the Farmer's Law held their land were far less restricting than those to which the *colonus* was subject. The code is not altogether precise about the exact legal status of the peasant producer. Where it refers to a peasant cultivating his own land, two

und Volksrecht', in D. Simon (ed.), *Fontes Minores*, I (Frankfurt am Main, 1976), pp. 102–16. For the village community of the late Roman period, see E. Patlagean, *Pauvreté économique et pauvreté sociale à Byzance, 4ᵉ–7ᵉ siècles* (Paris, 1977), pp. 238–40; and M. Loos, 'Quelques remarques sur les communautés rurales et la grande propriété terrienne à Byzance (VIIᵉ–XIᵉ siècles)', *ByzantinoSlavica*, 39 (1978), pp. 3–18.

[2] For the general political background, see Ostrogorsky, *History*, pp. 92–146.

[3] Lemerle, *The Agrarian History*, pp. 21–4 believes that in practical terms the difference between the *coloni libri* (*misthotai*) and *coloni adscripticii* was not very great. See also Köpstein, 'Zu den Agrarverhältnissen', pp. 7–8; and A. H. M. Jones, *The Later Roman Empire 284–602. A Social, Economic and Administrative Survey* (2 vols, Oxford, 1964), II, pp. 796–803.

[4] *Paroikos* was used to translate *colonus* in the late Roman period, but the difference in the word's usage in the sixth century and the Byzantine period was considerable; see Ostrogorksy, *Quelques problèmes*, p. 67. For alternative opinions, see G. Weiss, 'Die Entscheidung des Kosmas Magistros über das Parökenrecht', *Byzantion*, 48 (1978), pp. 477–500; and C. Mango, *Byzantium. The Empire of New Rome* (London, 1980), p. 47.

[5] A. H. M. Jones, 'The Roman Colonate', *Past and Present*, 13 (1958), pp. 1–13; Jones, *The Later Roman Empire*, II, p. 796; Lemerle, *The Agrarian History*, p. 25.

[6] Mango, *Byzantium. The Empire of New Rome*, p. 47.

16 Economic expansion in the Byzantine empire

interpretations are possible. The peasant might have enjoyed complete rights of ownership or simply the right of possession. The same interpretations can be made where the term *kyrios* is used. The most important conclusion which can be derived from the code is that these direct producers had the right to dispose freely of their land. Peasants had complete freedom to exchange lands or to alienate them in other ways. By the end of the seventh century the legal conditions on which peasants held their land had been greatly relaxed.[7]

The Farmer's Law contains clear indications of differences in wealth and status within the village community. Such economic stratification among the peasantry was unquestionably a fundamental cause of the later extension of large properties, but at this stage the trend had not been fully developed. At the bottom of the social structure slaves continued to be used in agriculture. Surprisingly, all the references to them in the code concern animal raising, work which was the most difficult to supervise. It seems that they were not used in large numbers in arable cultivation. Probably, slavery was a marginal factor in agricultural production in most regions.[8] There are also mentions of wage labourers. The community might employ a herdsman, shepherd, or a guard for their fruit trees.[9] It cannot be assumed that these were landless labourers. They were probably among the smaller peasant landowners in the village.

Economic differentiation is apparent in the clauses relating to leaseholding. Two types of lease were regulated by the code, the *hemiseia* and the *morte*. The former involved a division of the harvest in half shares between the lessee and the lessor. The code is not specific about the terms on which the lease was granted, but it allows for some variations in the conditions according to individual agreements. The lessee probably met the expenses of cultivation and the lessor the fiscal burden. The code envisaged these agreements being made when the owner of the land was too impoverished to cultivate the land effectively.

---

[7] Ashburner, 'The Farmer's Law', chs. 3–5, 11–15, pp. 98–9; Köpstein, 'Zu den Agrarverhältnissen', pp. 41–2. See also the chapters by Angelov, Maslev and Köpstein in H. Köpstein and F. Winkelmann (eds.), *Studien zum 7. Jahrhundert in Byzanz. Probleme der Herausbildung des Feudalismus* (Berlin, 1976).

[8] Ashburner, 'The Farmer's Law', chs. 45–7, 71–2; Lemerle, *The Agrarian History*, pp. 37–8. The standard work on Byzantine slavery is A. Hadjinicolaou-Marava, *Recherches sur la vie des esclaves dans le monde byzantin* (Athens, 1950).

[9] Ashburner, 'The Farmer's Law', chs. 23–9, 33–4. The *misthotoi* of the Farmer's Law were wage labourers and should not be confused with the *misthotai*, the *coloni libri* of the sixth century legislation; see Köpstein, 'Zu den Agrarverhältnissen', pp. 45–7.

The early medieval period 17

Other factors might easily have been involved. The owner might have left the village or he might have had too much land to cultivate personally and found the share-cropping arrangement more convenient than hiring labour. So this type of lease was probably used by peasants with relatively small properties and also by those with quite extensive lands.[10] The *morte* is equally problematic. The payment was a tenth of the crop, but this was only a customary payment without any legal basis. It has been suggested that the lessor (*chorodotes*) was a large landowner;[11] this was not necessarily the case. The lack of evidence about the terms of such contracts makes it difficult to attribute any precise status to the *chorodotes*. The expression could easily have been used both for an absentee landowner or a member of the village community.[12] The *morte* seems to have been a customary payment. By the later period it had become a feudal rent, a private payment exacted by the landowner. Where the state levied the payment, it signified that it was exercising the full rights of landownership, not simply those of tax-collector.[13] Whether the *morte* of the Farmer's Law had acquired this significance must remain an unresolved question.

The state's interest in the fiscal unit played an important part in accentuating differences in peasant wealth. Its main concern, naturally, was the collection of its revenues, and any absentee peasant who continued to pay his taxes had full rights of ownership over the land. This is likely to have happened only if his family was large enough to cultivate the land in his absence or if additional hired labour was readily available. If he did not make his payments, he forfeited his rights. The taxes on the abandoned property were claimed from the remaining villagers through the collective responsibility of the members of the fiscal unit for its tax-burden. Consequently, more land was accumulated

---

[10] Ashburner, 'The Farmer's Law', chs. 11–15; Lemerle, *The Agrarian History*, pp. 38–9; Köpstein, 'Zu den Agrarverhältnissen', pp. 48–9; P. A. Yannopoulos, *La Société profane dans l'empire byzantin des VIIe, VIIIe et IXe siècles* (Louvain, 1975), p. 196. Some light is thrown on this type of contract by two model agreements of the late Byzantine period. In both cases the lessee was responsible for the costs of cultivation and the maintenance of the land. The yield from a vineyard was divided into half shares, but the lessor received only a third of the harvest from an arable field, presumably because a large part of the crop was needed for the following year's seed. See Sathas, *MB*, VI, pp. 620–2.

[11] Ashburner, 'The Farmer's Law', chs. 9–10, and his commentary, *Journal of Hellenic Studies*, 32 (1912), p. 83.

[12] Lemerle, *The Agrarian History*, p. 38, emphasises that these clauses do not necessarily refer to large landowners.

[13] Laiou-Thomadakis, *Peasant Society*, pp. 216–21.

18   *Economic expansion in the Byzantine empire*

by the wealthier villagers, who had the means to cultivate the land and pay the taxes.[14]

The intensification of economic stratification in the village community was probably checked in the early medieval period by the availability of land. There are clear indications of demographic contraction at this time. Results from archaeological surveys show a sharp reduction in the number of inhabited sites in Boiotia and in the Ayiofarango valley in Crete and it is likely that other surveys will reveal a broadly similar trend.[15] The transfers of population by different emperors also suggest that some areas were sparsely inhabited.[16] The evidence of contraction in urban sites cannot be used automatically as an indicator of rural depopulation, but it is unlikely that the countryside escaped the effects of political instability and regular invasions. The fertile but more vulnerable lowlands were often abandoned, as peasants sought security in better-protected but rougher terrain which did not have the resources to support a dense population.[17]

Land was readily available and the Farmer's Law laid down the procedure for its allocation. Uncultivated land was divided up among members of the village community. This might have been land which had been abandoned recently by a previous cultivator or simply land which had long been unproductive. Until this land was divided up among the villagers, it remained the property of the community. If a mill was built on common land the community was entitled to expropriate it after meeting the expenses of its construction. Once a

---

[14] Ashburner, 'The Farmer's Law', chs. 18, 19; Lemerle, *The Agrarian History*, pp. 40–1; Köpstein, 'Zu den Agrarverhältnissen', p. 47 n.4. Another way in which rich peasants accumulated land was to receive property as security for loans; see Ashburner, 'The Farmer's Law', ch. 67; and A. E. Laiou, 'A Note on the Farmer's Law, Chapter 67', *Byzantion*, 41 (1971), pp. 197–204.

[15] J. L. Bintliff and A. M. Snodgrass, 'The Cambridge/Bradford Boeotian Expedition: The First Four Years', *Journal of Field Archaeology*, 12 (1985), pp. 149, 158–60; D. Blackman and K. Branagan, 'An Archaeological Survey of the Lower Catchment of the Ayiofarango Valley', *Papers of the British School at Athens*, 72 (1977), pp. 77–8.

[16] P. Charanis, 'The Transfer of Population as a Policy in the Byzantine Empire', *Comparative Studies in Society and History*, 3 (1961), pp. 140–54; P. Charanis, 'Observations on the Demography of the Byzantine Empire', in *Proceedings of the XIIIth International Congress of Byzantine Studies, Oxford 1966* (London, 1967), pp. 445–63.

[17] I. Dujčev (ed.) *Cronaca di Monemvasia* (Palermo, 1976), p. 16; J. F. Haldon and H. Kennedy, 'The Arab–Byzantine Frontier in the Eighth and Ninth Centuries: Military Organisation and Society in the Borderlands', *Zbornik Radova Vizantološkog Instituta*, 19 (1980), pp. 99–101. For the abandonment of the island of Skiathos, see Lemerle, *Les Plus Anciens Recueils*, I, p. 231, ch. 296. For the evidence from urban sites, see below, pp. 24–30.

The early medieval period 19

division of land had taken place, the community had no claims to any water-mill because the land was in private ownership. In contrast a farmer who planted a tree on an undivided piece of land retained possession of it, even if the land later came into the possession of another farmer. Intercultivation of arable land and olive trees was probably quite common and on a small scale would not have been too detrimental to the owner of the land.[18]

A strong incentive to bring new land under cultivation was given to a peasant who entered woodland belonging to another farmer with the owner's consent. The cultivator was entitled to the produce of the land for three years before it reverted to its original owner. Although three years is a short time, the arrangement was very advantageous to the cultivator. When woodland is cleared by fire, the abundance of ash fertilises the soil and for the first few years yields are high. The cultivator is also spared the labour involved in hoeing because, after burning, the soil is loose and free of weeds. The first cultivator was likely to get the best out of the soil and, when the owner regained possession, he had to work hard to maintain good yields.[19]

As the land was readily available, the size of the peasant family was probably the determining factor of the extent of the peasant farm. The theory of a peasant economy which Chayanov constructed is relevant here. It postulates a balance between the consumption requirements of the peasant household and the drudgery of manual labour. As the composition of the family changes, so does the area which it cultivates.[20] The theory works best for thinly populated areas, where there is plenty of available land. As pressure on the land increases and wage labour is easier to find, economic stratification among the peasantry is intensified. Even in the early Middle Ages the tendency towards stratification in the village community was present, but the most extreme consequences of this process were mitigated by the greater availability of land. In later centuries differences in wealth in village communities became much more pronounced.[21]

---

[18] Ashburner, 'The Farmer's Law', chs. 8, 32, 81, 82; Lemerle, The Agrarian History, pp. 41–5; Köpstein, 'Zu den Agrarverhältnissen', pp. 50–1; Loos, 'Quelques remarques', pp. 5–6 n.19. For intercultivation in the Roman period, see K. D. White, Roman Farming (London, 1970), p. 124.

[19] Ashburner, 'The Farmer's Law', ch. 17; E. Boserup, The Conditions of Agricultural Growth (Chicago, 1965), p. 24.

[20] Kerblay, 'Chayanov and the Theory of Peasantry as a Specific Type of Economy'.

[21] A very idealised impression of the village community has been advanced by Yannopoulos, La Société profane, pp. 177, 183. He claims that it was a pacific, tightly

20   *Economic expansion in the Byzantine empire*

An important development which strengthened the economic position of the peasantry was the establishment of the military lands (*stratiotika ktemata*). The owners of a *strateia* (military land) had a responsibility to provide a properly equipped soldier for the thematic army. The origins of this system are shrouded in obscurity, but it certainly arose out of the budgetary difficulties of the state during the seventh century after the loss of Egypt, Syria and Palestine and the consequent decline in the state's revenues. It then faced the problem of maintaining its military forces with much reduced resources. Therefore the responsibility for the supply of arms and equipment was transferred from the state to the individual soldier. Some compensation for this change was, of course, necessary and it took the form of land. As the retreating armies withdrew into Asia Minor, it is likely that plots of land were attributed to the soldiers to facilitate this change or, alternatively, the soldiers were billeted on peasant families who received additional land to cope with the obligation. The state could have used abandoned land for this purpose or it might have dismembered some of its own properties. The details of the development of this system of military lands are obscure, but the overall effect must have been to make more land available to an independent peasantry.[22]

Economic contraction was also reflected in the greater scarcity of money in circulation. The number of mints producing copper coinage declined sharply in the seventh century. In the late Roman period Thessalonike, Kyzikos and Nikomedia had operational mints, but by about 630 they had all been closed and production was centralised at Constantinople. It seems that there was no provincial mint again until the ninth century, when one was probably established at Thessalonike after the reform of the copper *follis* in the joint reign of Michael II and Theophilos.[23] The reduction in coin output is reflected in the very small quantities of coins dating from the second half of the seventh and the

---

knit community based on a spirit of mutual aid. This is contradicted by the Farmer's Law. The crimes and misdemeanours with which the code was concerned give a completely different impression. See also, *Vie de Théodore de Sykéôn*, pp. 89–90.

[22] This paragraph is based on Hendy, *Studies in the Byzantine Monetary Economy*, pp. 619ff. The subject has provoked considerable discussion; see J. F. Haldon, *Recruitment and Conscription in the Byzantine Army, c. 550–950. A Study of the Origins of the Stratiotika Ktemata* (Vienna, 1979), pp. 66–81; R.-J. Lilie, 'Die zweihundertjährige Reform: Zu den Anfängen der Themenorganisation im 7. und 8. Jahrhundert. II. Die "Soldatenbauern"', *ByzantinoSlavica*, 45 (1984), pp. 190–201; and W. T. Treadgold, *The Byzantine State Finances in the Eighth and Ninth Centuries* (New York, 1982), p. 13. For later developments of this system, see below, p. 38.

[23] Hendy, *Studies in the Byzantine Monetary Economy*, pp. 417–20, 424–5.

The early medieval period

eighth centuries which have been uncovered on archaeological sites. At Corinth and Athens a sharp decline in monetary circulation is apparent from the reign of Constantine IV and lasted until the mid ninth century at Corinth and the tenth century at Athens. However, there was an anomalous find of sixty-one copper coins from the reign of Philippikos (711–13). They probably reached Athens through military activity, but this was only an isolated interlude in a long period of decline.[24] A broadly similar pattern is found on sites in Asia Minor. At Ephesos and Sardis coins from the reigns of Phokas, Heraklios and Constans II were numerous and the decline starts with the reign of Constantine IV. At Ephesos there is a gap until the reign of Leo VI (apart from two coins of Constantine V). At Sardis, where the quantity of coins is larger and they have been systematically examined, there are only ten coins from the same period. Work on other sites in Asia Minor has revealed a broadly similar pattern.[25] The situation in Constantinople was different because the functioning of the capital's mint ensured the availability of coinage there.[26]

The economic and social basis for a flourishing urban economy was undermined during the early Middle Ages. Recovery from the Slav, Persian and Arab attacks was a painfully protracted process. One reason for this was the break in the institutional link between the cities and their territories, which had been a characteristic of the ancient world, and the inability of the state to pay for the cities' upkeep. However the most important factor was that the conditions of

---

[24] J. M. Harris, 'Coins found at Corinth', *Hesperia*, 10 (1941), p. 153; M. Thompson, *The Athenian Agora*, II, *Coins from the Roman through the Venetian Period* (Princeton, 1954), pp. 4–5, 71–75; Hendy, *Studies in the Byzantine Monetary Economy*, pp. 419–20, 659–62. The evidence from Kenchreiai, Sparta and elsewhere in Greece suggests a similar pattern; see below, p. 86.

[25] C. Foss, *Ephesus after Antiquity. A Late Antique, Byzantine and Turkish City* (Cambridge, 1979), pp. 197–8; G. E. Bates, *Byzantine Coins. Archaeological Explorations at Sardis*, I (Cambridge, Massachusetts, 1971), pp. 1–2, 85–140; Hendy, *Studies in the Byzantine Monetary Economy*, pp. 640–1. P. Grierson, 'Byzantine Coinage as Source Material', in *Proceedings of the XIIIth International Congress of Byzantine Studies, Oxford 1966* (London, 1967), pp. 324–5, suggests that the 'contracting use of coins in towns may have been balanced by its greater use in the countryside' in the early Middle Ages and he cites evidence from Alishar Huyuk, where the coin sequence ended in the early seventh century, probably due to the abandonment of the town. In the same region the excavators were able to purchase thirteen coins of Constans II as well as later anonymous *folleis*; see H. H. Van der Osten, *The Alishar Huyuk. Seasons of 1930–2*, part 3 (Chicago, 1937), pp. 317–18. However, it seems likely that the coins of Constans II were connected with military activity and the gap from that reign until the eleventh century suggests a long period of decline.

[26] Hendy, *Studies in the Byzantine Monetary Economy*, p. 499 n.247.

22   *Economic expansion in the Byzantine empire*

agricultural production were not favourable to the continued existence of an urban economy. Demographic decline was accompanied by a contraction in the area under cultivation. Unstable political and economic conditions made the revenues derived from agriculture more uncertain,[27] causing a reduction in the demand from landowners for urban products. The relatively greater importance of independent peasant farmers from the seventh century also implies a sharp contraction in commercial exchange. Their emphasis on the direct provision of the household did not stimulate commerce. The reduction of the volume of coinage in circulation was part of the same phenomenon. It is a likely hypothesis that non-monetary forms of exchange assumed a greater significance in most communities. The sources give a few hints of economic contraction. Nikephoros accused Constantine V of accumulating so much treasure from taxation that agricultural prices slumped. The account is vitriolic and we need not believe that wheat was actually sold at sixty *modioi* and barley at seventy *modioi* a *nomisma*. Nikephoros was, naturally, unaware that economic contraction and the decline in the amount of money in circulation made revenues from agriculture more unremunerative.[28]

In spite of these adverse economic conditions the fate of Byzantine towns in the early Middle Ages has been the subject of great controversy. Most historians have emphasised economic decline in the seventh century, but some have claimed that an urban economy continued to exist.[29] Ostrogorsky has used the lists of bishops attending church councils in an attempt to prove the case for urban continuity.[30] The lists give a useful indication of the fate of towns at a time when little is known of them, because even towns of relatively little significance would have had bishops. One important qualification has to be made before they can be interpreted. If a town continued to be the seat of a

[27] J. F. Haldon, 'Some Remarks on the Background to the Iconoclast Controversy', *ByzantinoSlavica*, 38 (1977), p. 175 n.50. The importance of the connections between the rural and urban economies will be discussed in greater detail in chapter 6.

[28] *Nicephori Archiepiscopi Constantinopolitani Opuscula Historia*, ed. C. de Boor (Leipzig, 1880), p. 76.

[29] F. Dölger, 'Die frühbyzantinische und byzantinisch beeinflusste Stadt (V.–VIII. Jahrhundert)', in *Atti del 3° Congresso Internazionale di Studi sull'Alto Medioevo, 1956* (Spoleto, 1959), pp. 65–100; G. Ostrogorsky, 'Byzantine Cities in the Early Middle Ages', *Dumbarton Oaks Papers*, 13 (1959), pp. 47–66; P. Tivchev, 'Sur les cités byzantines aux XIe–XIIe siècles', *ByzantinoBulgarica*, 1 (1962), pp. 145–82; E. Frances, 'La ville byzantine et la monnaie aux VIIe–VIIIe siècles', *ByzantinoBulgarica*, 2 (1966), pp. 3–14; Vryonis, *The Decline of Medieval Hellenism*, pp. 6ff; Haldon and Kennedy, 'The Arab–Byzantine Frontier', pp. 87–97; M. Angold, 'The Shaping of the Medieval Byzantine "City"', *Byzantinische Forschungen*, 10 (1985), pp. 1–37.

[30] Ostrogorsky, 'Byzantine Cities', pp. 52–61.

The early medieval period 23

bishopric, it does not necessarily follow that its economic life continued unabated as in the late Roman period. The evidence of urban continuity extracted from Byzantine authors has also to be treated with caution. When a chronicler refers to a town as well populated, the judgement has to be set against the standards of his time, not those of the sixth century. The conciliar lists reveal a dramatic reduction in the number of sees in the Balkans by 680, reflecting the absence of Byzantine authority in much of the peninsula. Most of the sees which did survive were coastal towns in Thrace and Greece. By 787 and 879 a large number of new bishoprics were founded as Byzantine control was reestablished. The lists give a different impression of Asia Minor. Most of the bishoprics of the late Roman period continued to be represented at the councils.[31] This only demonstrates the extent of Byzantine political control. It would be misleading to conclude on this basis that the economic life of these towns continued to flourish. The conciliar lists give evidence only of the continuity of settlement; evidence of economic trends has to be sought elsewhere.

The impetus behind urban vitality could be administrative, military or commercial. The dramatic decline of the seventh and eighth centuries reduced the importance of commerce, and any continuity in economic activity was due to the demands and expenditure of the state. Consequently, Constantinople recovered much more rapidly than provincial towns. During these centuries, which preceded the effective development of feudal social relations, it exercised an almost monopolistic role as an urban centre, reflecting the dominant position of the imperial bureaucracy in the social formation of Byzantium. Unlike provincial towns, which underwent a profound transformation from late Roman *poleis* to fortified medieval towns, Constantinople retained the political and economic functions which it had performed in late Antiquity. It continued its role as a centre of consumption meeting the requirements of the court and imperial and ecclesiastical administrations. Following the loss of Egypt and Syria, it became dependent for its grain supply on its Thracian hinterland, the west coast of Asia Minor, Bithynia and the Pontos.[32] It was not immune from the general

---

[31] *Ibid.*, pp. 54–8. For more recent analyses of these lists, see R.-J. Lilie, '"Thrakien und Thrakesion". Zur byzantinischen Provinzorganisation am Ende des 7. Jahrhunderts', *Jahrbuch der Österreichischen Byzantinistik*, 26 (1977), pp. 7–47, esp. 35–46; and Hendy, *Studies in the Byzantine Monetary Economy*, pp. 69–85, 90–100.

[32] R.-J. Lilie, *Die byzantinische Reaktion auf die Ausbreitung der Araber. Studien zur Strukturwandlung des byzantinischen Staates im 7. und 8. Jahrhundert* (Munich, 1976), pp. 213ff.

24   *Economic expansion in the Byzantine empire*

economic decline, but was able to recover much more rapidly than provincial towns. The worst time for the capital appears to have been the eighth century. By the early part of the century some parts of the city had fallen into disrepair.[33] The aqueduct of Valens, which had been destroyed by the Avars in 626, was not repaired again until 766.[34] Demographic decline can be inferred from the transfer of population from Hellas to the capital after the plague of 747.[35] The existence of agricultural plots inside the walls of the city should not be given an exaggerated importance. Theophanes does mention vineyards and gardens, but this was true of all periods and was not a unique phenomenon confined to the eighth century, although it probably occurred on a larger scale then than later.[36] Constantinople's recovery was quick and the basic character of the city remained unchanged. By 800 signs of expansion in its Thracian hinterland, giving its food supply greater security, were apparent to Arab writers.[37] The main pre-occupation of the state was to ensure that the population did not become too large. Legal provisions concerning the distance between houses were revived, and building on land which had previously been used for agriculture was restricted, a reflection of the state's determination to prevent the growth of an unruly urban mob in the capital.

The continuity in economic activity in Constantinople was in vivid contrast to the great changes which took place in provincial towns. Whereas economic decline was relatively short-lived in the capital and recovery was quick, elsewhere adverse economic conditions led to a more protracted decline and a fundamental urban transformation. The

---

[33] Averil Cameron and J. Herrin (eds.), *Constantinople in the Early Eighth Century. The Parastaseis Syntomai Chronikai* (Leiden, 1984), p. 28.

[34] Theophanes, I, p. 440. Great importance is attached to this by J. L. Teall, 'The Grain Supply of the Byzantine Empire 330–1025', *Dumbarton Oaks Papers*, 13 (1959), pp. 102–3; and Mango, *Byzantium. The Empire of New Rome*, p. 80. However, the city was not totally dependent on this aqueduct and we know nothing of its water resources in relation to the number of its inhabitants. See also W. Müller-Wiener, *Bildlexikon zur Topographie Istanbuls* (Tübingen, 1977), pp. 271–85, whose dating of the repair of the aqueduct to 758 is incorrect.

[35] Theophanes, I, p. 429; C. Mango, *Le Développement urbain de Constantinople (IVe–VIIe siècles)* (Paris, 1985), pp. 51–62.

[36] Theophanes, I, p. 423. For agricultural production in Constantinople at the start of the thirteenth century, see G. Downey, 'Nikolaos Mesarites: Description of the Church of the Holy Apostles at Constantinople', *Transactions of the American Philosophical Society*, 47 (1957), pp. 863, 897–8. This was a not uncommon occurrence throughout medieval and early modern Europe; see below, p. 201.

[37] E. W. Brooks, 'The Campaign of 716–718 from Arabic Sources', *Journal of Hellenic Studies*, 19 (1899), p. 23.

The early medieval period 25

cities of the later Roman empire were, theoretically, self-governing units responsible for the administration of their own territories. The city was the seat of local magistrates and the council. Although the councils' functions and finances were increasingly usurped by provincial governors, who were responsible for much of the building of late Antiquity, the council had to elect officials to collect taxes, impose levies and perform other functions for the government. Consequently, the cities played a much more immediate role in the exaction of taxation from the countryside than in the Byzantine period. The revenues from the cities' territories contributed to the maintenance of civic opulence, and emperors tried frequently to ensure that civic finances were kept free from the control of the provincial governor. The standard of public building in many cities of late Antiquity makes a fairly impressive display of prosperity by comparison with subsequent centuries.[38] The ending of this institutional link between a city and its hinterland, a fundamental characteristic of the ancient city, gave Byzantine towns a very different appearance from their ancient predecessors, and the worsening fortunes of the towns' landowning class deprived the provinces of any urban dynamism in the early medieval centuries. They were generally unable to recover quickly from the effects of invasions, except where the state took a direct interest for military or administrative reasons. Some towns disappeared; others were transferred to new, more secure locations. Some survived better than others because of their strategic importance. Economic interests were subordinated to military considerations.

These generalisations apply to both Asia Minor and the Balkans. For Asia Minor the descriptions of Arab writers give an impression of a society consisting of villages and fortresses but few cities. Although Ibn Khurdadhbiy did describe Nikomedia, Nicaea, Ephesos, Amorion and Ankara as cities, they were in fact fortresses rather than cities like the *poleis* of Antiquity.[39] The case of Ankara illustrates this clearly. It was a very important strategic centre and one of the earliest thematic capitals. Its military and strategic role should have stimulated some economic activity, but the archaeological evidence shows that the town was greatly reduced by comparison with the wealthier city of late

---

[38] Jones, *The Later Roman Empire*, II, pp. 712–13, 724–37; R. L. Scranton, *Corinth*, XVI, *Medieval Architecture in the Central Area of Corinth* (Princeton, 1957), pp. 6–26; C. Foss, *Byzantine and Turkish Sardis* (Harvard, 1976), pp. 20–2, 39–52; Foss, *Ephesus*, pp. 46–95; C. Foss, 'Archaeology and the "Twenty Cities" of Byzantine Asia', *American Journal of Archaeology*, 81 (1977), pp. 469–86.

[39] Haldon and Kennedy, 'The Arab–Byzantine Frontier', pp. 96–7; Angold, 'The Shaping of the Medieval Byzantine "City"', p. 5.

26 Economic expansion in the Byzantine empire

Antiquity.[40] In the frontier areas, which were most vulnerable to Arab raids, towns suffered very badly. Tyana's exposed situation in a plain led to its capture by the Arabs in 709 and its inhabitants moved to Magida, a more secure place. Faustinopolis was probably destroyed early in the Arab raids and its was eclipsed by the neighbouring fortress at Loulon. Neither Malakopea nor Osiena appear to have survived the Arab attacks and other towns like Komana, Arabissos and Taranta never regained their earlier prosperity.[41] Movements of population also occurred elsewhere in the Anatolian peninsula. At Priene the inhabitants moved to a steep *akropolis*, where new fortifications were added in the seventh and eighth centuries. The population of the Phrygian city of Kolossai transferred to a nearby mountain site, where the Byzantine town of Chonai developed.[42] Usually the old site was maintained, but the medieval architecture had a decidedly military character. The early medieval fortifications normally encompassed only a part of the inhabited area of the late antique period, but they also offered a refuge for people living outside the fortifications.[43]

The extent of the decline is clear in the cases of Ephesos and Sardis, both of which have provided significant archaeological evidence. They were important cities in the late Roman period, especially Ephesos, but had limited strategic importance in the face of the military problems of the seventh century. Ephesos developed into two separate fortified centres, a walled town by the harbour and a fortress on the hill of Ayasuluk. Some of the wealthiest Roman quarters were abandoned, which suggests a substantial reduction in population even if some people still lived outside the walls. The harbour gradually silted up, aqueducts fell into disuse and each part of the town had to ensure its own water-supply.[44] Statements in written sources about economic activity at Ephesos must be treated with caution. It is likely that the annual fair held there during the reign of Constantine VI was important by the standards of commercial fairs in the eighth century. However, Theophanes's figure for the revenues of the fair, 100 pounds of gold, is

---

[40] C. Foss, 'Late Antique and Byzantine Ankara', *Dumbarton Oaks Papers*, 31 (1977), pp. 29–87, esp. 72–84. The existence of *kommerkiarioi* based in the town should not be interpreted as a sign that trade occurred on a large scale; see Hendy, *Studies in the Byzantine Monetary Economy*, pp. 626–34.

[41] F. Hild, *Das byzantinische Strassensystem in Kappadokien* (Vienna, 1977), pp. 46, 52, 69, 78–9, 88, 93, 102.

[42] Foss, 'Archaeology and the "Twenty Cities" of Byzantine Asia', pp. 479, 484.

[43] *Ibid.*, pp. 472–84; C. Foss, 'The Persians in Asia Minor and the End of Antiquity', *English Historical Review*, 90 (1975), pp. 721–47.

[44] Foss, *Ephesus*, pp. 103–15.

The early medieval period

difficult to believe. It is so obviously a convenient round figure that its accuracy must be questioned; the archaeological evidence of economic contraction would suggest that it is exaggerated.[45] The evidence of maritime traffic in the life of St Gregory Dekapolites should also not be given too much importance. There is no certainty that the boats actually sailed from the old harbour of Ephesos and not from Phrygela. The account does not allow us to judge the importance of this traffic in comparison with that of the preceding or later periods. It shows only that there was a certain amount of contact with Constantinople. There is no indication of the regularity of transactions, the products which were involved, the scale of the trade, nor of the persons who controlled it. The deterioration of the harbour at Ephesos would have militated against trade on a large scale. A clear indication of economic decline was that the old city was eventually replaced by a fortified inland site.[46] Nevertheless, the town did retain some importance. It was still a substantial place by comparison with towns like Sardis, Magnesia and Pergamon.[47]

The decline of Sardis was more dramatic. It was reduced to a cluster of small settlements around a fortification. Some parts of the late antique city were no longer inhabited. Military reconstruction took place in the middle of the seventh century.[48] In the cases of towns which appear to have been relatively unscathed, Smyrna and Attaleia, this is probably due to lack of evidence. Nicaea retained its old walls, so it is difficult to determine whether any reduction in the settlement occurred there. But instances of urban contraction are easy to find throughout Asia Minor.[49]

The same general pattern applies to the Balkans. In some parts of the interior there was no continuity between many late Roman and

---

[45] Theophanes, I, p. 469. In western Europe the existence of large fairs was an indication of a not very highly developed economy. In late medieval Europe many fairs declined as the towns became more commercially developed and usurped the functions of fairs; see N. J. G. Pounds, *An Economic History of Medieval Europe* (London, 1974), pp. 354–61. If the fair at Ephesos was important, it would have been as a place where expensive merchandise, brought from long distances, was exchanged, but we have no precise details about the fair.

[46] F. Dvornik, *La Vie de saint Grégoire le Décapolite et les slaves macédoniens au IXe siècle* (Paris, 1926), p. 53; Vryonis, *The Decline of Medieval Hellenism*, p. 10; Foss, *Ephesus*, p. 119.

[47] Foss, *Ephesus*, p. 115.   [48] Foss, *Sardis*, pp. 53–61.

[49] Foss, 'Archaeology and the "Twenty Cities" of Byzantine Asia', pp. 469–86; Foss, 'The Persians in Asia Minor and the End of Antiquity', pp. 721–47. These studies present the causes of urban decline in a much too simple fashion, but their presentation of the archaeological evidence is useful.

28   *Economic expansion in the Byzantine empire*

medieval settlements. Numerous towns, including Stobi and Sirmium, had ceased to exist by the seventh century. For other towns, such as Serdika, Adrianople, Mesembria, Naissos and Philippoupolis, there is evidence of some continuity of settlement.[50] In Thessaly Phthiotid Thebes is not mentioned again in the sources after the seventh century along with a few other less important towns.[51]

There is strong evidence of decline in some major urban centres of the Balkans. Thessalonike was subjected to attacks by Avars and Slavs. In these unstable conditions the town's hinterland was probably able to support only a limited population and occupational specialisation must have been restricted. In the early seventh century a large proportion of the town's residents were caught unawares by an Avar attack while they were outside the walls gathering in the harvest.[52] During a later siege, in 662, the leading men of the town were alleged to have exported their stores of wheat rather than conserve them for the siege. Additional supplies were sent by the emperor and when there was still a shortage the townsmen imported grain from Thessaly.[53] It is difficult to determine from a literary text the extent of economic decline. Perhaps many of the inhabitants who took part in the collection of the harvest were not full-time agriculturalists. However, the insecure hold of the town on its hinterland must have caused a reduction in its wealth and there is some archaeological evidence of buildings falling into disuse.[54] At times the town became a focal point for refugees, its resources were greatly strained and imports became necessary.

A sharp contraction in economic activity in Corinth and Athens can be established with greater certainty from the results of excavations. In both towns, buildings which were destroyed around the end of the sixth

---

[50] H. Ditten, 'Zur Bedeutung der Einwandlung der Slaven', in H. Winkelmann *et al.*, *Byzanz im 7. Jahrhundert. Untersuchungen zur Herausbildung des Feudalismus* (Berlin, 1978), pp. 113–19. See also Mango, *Byzantium. Empire of New Rome*, pp. 69–70; G. Gomulka, 'Bemerkungen zur Situation der spätantiken Städte und Siedlungen in NordBulgarien und ihrem Weiterleben am Ende des 6. Jahrhunderts', in Köpstein and Winkelmann, *Studien zum 7. Jahrhundert in Byzanz. Probleme der Herausbildung des Feudalismus*, pp. 35–42.

[51] Avramea, A. P., *He Byzantine Thessalia mechri tou 1204. Symbole eis ten historiken geographian* (Athens, 1974), pp. 145–6.

[52] Lemerle, *Les Plus Anciens Recueils*, I, p. 137 lines 9–16, p. 185 lines 31–6. It is implied in the first passage that soldiers were also involved in the collection of the harvest.

[53] *Ibid.*, p. 214 lines 9–19, p. 221 lines 3–11. See also Teall, 'The Grain Supply of the Byzantine Empire', pp. 121–3.

[54] C. Bakirtzis, 'He agora tes Thessalonikes sta palaiochristianika chronia', in *Praktika tou 10ou Diethnous Synedriou Christianikes Archaiologias*, II (Thessalonike, 1984), pp. 5–19.

The early medieval period 29

century were not reoccupied and the inhabited area on both sites contracted sharply. The supply of coinage became scarce from the middle of the seventh century and there is no evidence of any extensive industrial or commercial life.[55] There is also evidence of extensive abandonment of the excavated area of Sparta.[56] Other sites in southern Greece are not so well known. At Patras the inhabitants moved from the late Roman site, located by the sea, to a fortified hill a little inland.[57] Olympia appears to have been deserted from the seventh century and Monembasia was established mainly because of the defensive potential of the site.[58] At Thebes the most important town in central Greece, the settlement was confined to the Kadmeian hill and again there is evidence of a prolonged abandonment of part of the town.[59]

The contraction of urban markets and the general demographic decline created serious problems for landowners, but the seventh, eighth and ninth centuries also saw some fundamental developments which led to the growth of feudal social relations in later centuries. Although some continuity of large estates in the seventh century can be discerned, the source material is limited. It relates only to church lands and graphically illustrates the problems which confronted large landowners at this time. Those in Constantinople or its vicinity probably suffered less than provincial landowners. Heraklios decreed that *klerikoi* from cities and villages in the provinces were not to be attributed to churches in the capital. This reinforcement of earlier Justinianic legislation reflects the difficulties which landowners had in retaining their labour-force at a time of severe population decline. In 691–2 it was decreed that *klerikoi* who abandoned their churches owing to invasion had to return afterwards. Such legislation was probably unenforceable in practice, but it shows that, although the church

[55] K. M. Setton, 'The Archaeology of Medieval Athens', in *Essays in Medieval Life and Thought, Presented in Honor of Austin Patterson Evans* (New York, 1955), pp. 227–58; T. L. Shear, 'The Athenian Agora: Excavations of 1972', *Hesperia*, 42 (1973), pp. 395–8; Thompson, *The Athenian Agora*, II, pp. 3–4; Scranton, *Corinth*, pp. 27–33; P. Charanis, 'The Significance of Coins as Evidence for the History of Athens and Corinth in the Seventh and Eighth Centuries', *Historia*, 4 (1955), pp. 163–72.

[56] C. Bouras, 'City and Village: Urban Design and Architecture', *XVI Internationaler Byzantinistenkongress. Akten. Jahrbuch der Österreichischen Byzantinistik*, 31/1 (1981), p. 622.

[57] H. Saranti-Mendelovici, 'À propos de la ville de Patras aux 13e–15e siècles', *Revue des Études Byzantines*, 38 (1980), pp. 219–32.

[58] Dujčev, *Cronaca di Monemvasia*, p. 14; A. Bon, *Le Péloponnèse byzantin jusqu'en 1204* (Paris, 1951), pp. 49–55; G. L. Huxley, 'The Second Dark Age of the Peloponnese', *Lakonikes Spoudes*, 3 (1977), pp. 84–110.

[59] Bouras, 'City and Village: Urban Design and Architecture', p. 623.

30   Economic expansion in the Byzantine empire

retained extensive properties, they must have become less remunerative owing to the greater instability of its labour-force.[60]

The extent to which the late Roman senatorial and municipal aristocracy survived this period is unknown, but it is tempting to speculate that, because they were more vulnerable to political vicissitudes, the break in continuity may have been sharper than on ecclesiastical estates. By the early eighth century there are indications of the early stages of the accumulation of landed wealth by military commanders in the provinces. They owed their wealth to the great civil and military authority delegated to them by the state. Provincial officials had greater power than in the sixth century and the instability of the period gave them great opportunities to acquire large tracts of land.[61] In the first reign of Justinian II the future emperor Leo III had moved with his family to Mesembria in Thrace. In Justinian's second reign Leo presented him with a gift of 500 sheep. No further details are given by Theophanes, but it is likely that Leo owned extensive grazing lands.[62]

The Anatolian plateau, in particular, offered great scope for extensive grazing. Not surprisingly this region became the power-base of the military aristocracy. The properties for which we are best informed for the eighth century belonged to Philaretos. We do not know by what means the properties were acquired or whether his family exercised important functions in the administration. The details given in his hagiography probably exaggerate his wealth, but this is unimportant. They can be regarded as an illustration of the wealth which a nobleman in Asia Minor might have owned in the eighth or ninth century. There were forty-eight estates, scattered in three regions, Paphlagonia, Pontos and Galatia, but the main value of his property lay with the herds. Large tracts of pasture would have been required for 600 cattle, 800 grazing

---

[60] Köpstein, 'Zu den Agrarverhältnissen', p. 65. For the meaning of the term *klerikos* at a later period, see N. Svoronos, 'Les privilèges de l'Église à l'époque des Comnènes: un rescrit inédit de Manuel 1er Comnène', *Travaux et Mémoires*, 1 (1965), pp. 361–2 n. 175. For the grant of a saltworks by Justinian II to the church of St Demetrios in Thessalonike with an exemption from taxation, see A. Vasiliev, 'An Edict of the Emperor Justinian II, September 688', *Speculum*, 18 (1943), pp. 1–13; and H. Grégoire, 'Un édit de l'empereur Justinien II, daté de septembre 688', *Byzantion*, 17 (1944–5), pp. 119–24. The inscription has been reedited by J. M. Spieser, 'Inventaires en vue d'un recueil des inscriptions historiques de Byzance, I. Les inscriptions de Thessalonique', *Travaux et Mémoires*, 5 (1973), pp. 156–9.

[61] J. F. Haldon, 'Some Remarks on the Background to the Iconoclast Controversy', pp. 174–5; Haldon and Kennedy, 'The Arab–Byzantine Frontier', pp. 98f.

[62] Theophanes, I, p. 391.

The early medieval period 31

horses and 12,000 sheep. This type of farming is best suited to the resources of the Anatolian plateau and afforded greater security than arable farming at a time when military operations were a threat to agricultural production.[63] Philaretos was not a *nouveau riche* as has sometimes been claimed.[64] Part of his property consisted of a very impressive patrimonial house.[65] If a large part of his wealth was inherited it must have been accumulated by the first half of the eighth century at the latest and possibly considerably earlier. These estates have been cited by Köpstein as an example of the continuation of old forms of large property in the early Middle Ages,[66] but the information in the text does not permit such precision. Admittedly, there is no mention of dependent peasants, but this is inconclusive. Slaves are mentioned, but there is no evidence that they were engaged in agricultural production and were not simply domestic slaves. The life also reveals the difficulties which military instability created for some landowners and how others took advantage of the situation to increase their properties. One reason for the break-up of Philaretos's estates was the Arab raids. Other landowners and peasants in his village, Amnia, exploited his difficulties to seize his land. By the late eighth century there was an elite group of landowners there, referred to in the life as the leading men of the village.[67]

As Byzantium recovered from the military crises of the seventh and eighth centuries, conditions became more favourable for agricultural production. The state and private landowners were able to consolidate their economic base. Some of the state's properties were organised into *kouratoria*. They were extended by Nikephoros I, who attributed to the *kouratoria* those lands which had been confiscated from religious houses. Little is known of monastic lands, but they had probably increased greatly as a result of the generosity of the iconodule empress Irene, and Nikephoros's measure can be seen as a reaction against his

---

[63] 'Vie de Philarète', pp. 113–15; Hendy, *Studies in the Byzantine Monetary Economy*, pp. 208–9. H. Evert-Kappesova, 'Une grande propriété foncière du VIIIᵉ siècle à Byzance', *ByzantinoSlavica*, 24 (1963), pp. 32–40, emphasises the importance of pastoral rather than arable exploitation. For the advantages of pastoral farming at this time, see Haldon and Kennedy, 'The Arab–Byzantine Frontier', pp. 100–1.

[64] By, for instance, J. W. Nesbitt, 'The Life of St Philaretos (702–792) and its Significance for Byzantine Agriculture', *Greek Orthodox Theological Review*, 14 (1969), pp. 150–8; and L. Bréhier, 'Les populations rurales au IXᵉ siècle d'après l'hagiographie byzantine', *Byzantion*, 1 (1924), p. 180.   [65] 'Vie de Philarète', pp. 135–7.

[66] Köpstein, 'Zu den Agrarverhältnissen', pp. 61–4.

[67] 'Vie de Philarète', pp. 115–17, 137 line 1; Köpstein, 'Zu den Agrarverhältnissen', pp. 63–4.

32   *Economic expansion in the Byzantine empire*

predecessor's policy.[68] In the second period of iconoclasm the *patrikios* Niketas was forced to retreat to estates which he owned (or had given to a monastery) near the capital or to the estates of sympathisers.[69]

The evidence of large landownership among the laity is even more fragmentary. A woman of senatorial rank, who lived in Nicaea, owned a village near the monastery of St Peter of Atroa on Olympos.[70] A smaller property was owned by the parents of Basil I. Nevertheless, it was more than a modest peasant holding. They did not cultivate it directly themselves, but during the harvest they personally supervised the labourers.[71] Basil was reputed to have bought properties in Macedonia out of the money which he received from Danielis. The account of Danielis's wealth is frequently cited as evidence for the existence of large properties in the ninth century, but there are considerable problems in interpreting it. Her wealth was concentrated in the Peloponnesos and is supposed to have included eighty estates and thousands of slaves. The Peloponnesos had been organised as a theme for only about fifty years and such an accumulation of properties in a short period is unlikely. The details are difficult to believe unless Danielis was of Slav extraction and the accumulation of these properties preceded the reimposition of Byzantine rule in the region.[72]

The gradual spread of large estates was carried out partly at the expense of peasant producers. A peasant suffering from bad harvests might have contracted debts or built up arrears in his tax-payments; the resources to cultivate his land might have been diminished if bad yields restricted the quantity of seed available for the following year's crop. In such circumstances land might be pledged as security for a loan or the peasant might be bought out by a richer villager or a large landowner. A peasant in debt might have abandoned his land and migrated.[73] This tendency for the property of impoverished peasants to be purchased by large landowners was naturally apparent throughout

[68] Theophanes, I, pp. 486–7; Zonaras, III, p. 306. In the late eighth century the *higoumenos* of the monastery of Heraklion in Bithynia owned patrimonial estates in the European part of the empire; see F. Halkin, 'La vie de saint Nicéphore, fondateur de Médikion en Bithynie', *Analecta Bollandia*, 78 (1960), p. 408. See also Mango, *Byzantium. Empire of New Rome*, p. 48.   [69] 'Vie du patrice Nicétas', pp. 325–9.

[70] Laurent, *La Vie merveilleuse*, pp. 169–71. She is said to have freed her slaves as a pious act (*ibid.*, p. 173), but there is no indication that their work had been agricultural and not domestic.

[71] The text does not specify whether the labourers were hired seasonally or were dependent peasants working on a landowner's field; see Theophanes Continuatus, p. 218.

[72] *Ibid.*, pp. 228, 318–21; Loos, 'Quelques remarques', pp. 10–11; Mango, *Byzantium. Empire of New Rome*, p. 48. The Slav connection is suggested by Hendy, *Studies in the Byzantine Monetary Economy*, pp. 206–7.   [73] 'Vie de Philarète', pp. 117–19.

The early medieval period 33

Byzantine history and had significant results only over a very long period. A few examples prior to the tenth century are given in the sources. St Nikephoros founded the monastery of Medikion in a village which had been purchased from peasant cultivators who had owned it in common. In 897 the monastery of St Andrew purchased land to the east of Thessalonike from a peasant family.[74]

The first indications of the development of feudal social relations are found in the early ninth century. The earliest mention of the *paroikos* is given in Theophanes's account of Nikephoros I's fiscal practices. He imposed the *kapnikon* (hearth tax) on the *paroikoi* of the *orphanotropheion* (orphanage), other pious houses, monasteries and churches.[75] The passage is very terse. It does not tell us whether the *kapnikon* already existed but had not been imposed on ecclesiastical property, possibly owing to the privileges granted by Irene, or whether it was a new imposition devised by Nikephoros. Also, we do not know the terms on which the *paroikos* occupied the land. A very early instance of the grant of peasants by the state to a large landowner occurred in the Peloponnesos at about the same time. Following an unsuccessful rebellion, Nikephoros attributed the defeated Slavs and all their familial property to the metropolitan of Patras. These peasants also had obligations to the state as well as to the metropolitan. They had to maintain *strategoi* (commanders of the themes), other state officials and foreign envoys. Their precise obligations to the metropolitan are not clear. They were later stipulated in a chrysobull of Leo VI (which does not survive) and the metropolitan was forbidden from increasing their payments. He did not have as extensive claims as later chrysobulls allowed landowners over their *paroikoi*. Porphyrogenitos referred to the Slavs as *enapographomenoi*, which was the technical term in the Justinianic legislation for the *coloni adscripticii*. It cannot, however, be assumed that the *coloni* survived into the ninth century. Porphyrogenitos, a pedantic antiquarian, was simply using an archaic expression for its own sake. The affair is best regarded as a precursor of later grants of *paroikoi* to large landowners, which appear regularly in the sources from the tenth century. It shows how the state, by conceding some of the claims over the peasantry to large landowners, was laying the base for the development of feudalism.[76]

---

[74] Halkin, 'La vie de saint Nicéphore', pp. 413–14; *Lavra*, I, no. 1. For the purchase of properties in Bithynia by the *patrikios* Niketas, see 'Vie du patrice Nicétas', pp. 327, 337.

[75] Theophanes, I, pp. 486–7; Zonaras, III, pp. 306–7.

[76] *DAI*, pp. 229–33. For a different interpretation, see Yannopoulos, *La Société profane*, pp. 219–21.

34   *Economic expansion in the Byzantine empire*

The state's fiscal apparatus also created difficulties for independent peasant producers. Basil I tried to alleviate some of these problems by administrative actions which anticipate the concerns of the tenth-century legislation. The form in which the tax-registers were drawn up was altered. Previously, the payment of a fiscal unit was listed summarily, but now the payments for each entry were listed individually so that the small landowners who owed only a small fraction of a *nomisma* were not coerced into paying a larger proportion of the total payment.[77] Village communities faced the problem that the state insisted on payment of the total obligation of a fiscal unit in gold *nomismata*, except for fairly small amounts. This gave the wealthier landowners of the village a lever to pressurise the smaller landowners into handing over rather more in small change than they theoretically owed. Another measure involved abandoned land. According to the Farmer's Law the tax-payment on these lands and the right to exploit them were transferred to other members of the fiscal unit.[78] This procedure no longer happened automatically. Fiscal officials suggested the reallocation of such lands to other landowners to increase the state's revenues from taxation. It is uncertain that the lands remained in the fiscal unit. Probably they had been detached from it and transformed into klasmatic lands owned by the state, but were being exploited in some way (most likely as pasture) by villagers, and Basil was reluctant to deprive them of this resource by selling the land to more wealthy landowners.[79] The affair suggests an awareness of the potential political threat to the state from the growing social and economic power of the provincial nobility, a development which was to be intensified in the following century.

[77] Theophanes Continuatus, p. 261.
[78] Ashburner, 'The Farmer's Law', ch. 18.
[79] Theophanes Continuatus, pp. 346–8; Lemerle, *The Agrarian History*, pp. 71–2; Haldon, *Recruitment and Conscription*, pp. 52–4. By the time of the compilation of the Fiscal Treatise in the tenth century the standard procedure was to grant tax-relief on abandoned land to the fiscal unit for up to thirty years. Then it was detached from the unit and became klasmatic land, which the state disposed of as it wished; see Dölger, *Beiträge*, pp. 118–20. This procedure was gradually phased in. The collective responsibility of the fiscal unit is apparent in the second 'vexation' of Nikephoros I, but his fourth was to remove all the *kouphismoi*; see Theophanes, I, p. 486. For the *kouphismos*, as relief from taxation, see Dölger, *Beiträge*, p. 119 lines 19–30. The transfer of the fiscal burden of abandoned lands onto neighbouring landowners remained a possible course of action for the administration at a much later period; see *Lavra*, I, no. 43 lines 6–12. The two alternatives seem to have coexisted for a long time, but by the reign of Basil I the procedure of granting tax-relief had become more usual.

Chapter 2

Demographic growth and social relations

A major theme of Byzantine history is the gradual reduction in importance of independent peasant producers, as dependent peasants belonging to both the state and private landowners increased in numbers and the tension between the state and its provincial magnates intensified in the tenth and eleventh centuries. This was reflected in attempts by tenth-century emperors to protect the territorial integrity of peasant villages by legislation. The state's main concern in taking this course was, naturally, to safeguard its own fiscal revenues. It is significant that the term *chorion* was used in official documents to denote a fiscal unit as well as its more general meaning of village. The tenth-century legislation was intended to prevent landowners, who did not already have land in any *chorion*, from buying their way into it and gradually coming to dominate the other smaller landowners in the *chorion*. This was one feature of the development of feudal social relations; another was the intensification of differences in wealth within peasant communities. A variety of forms of agricultural exploitation is revealed in the Fiscal Treatise, a tenth-century document which outlines the basic workings of the land-tax.[1] The pattern of land tenure became more complex with the extension of the area which the villagers were cultivating. The establishment of *agridia* (separate fields away from the main settlement but inside the boundaries of the fiscal unit) was a response to increased crowding around the main settlement.

---

[1] Inequalities in wealth among the villagers appear greater in the Fiscal Treatise than in the Farmer's Law, but the two texts cannot be compared simply, as in G. Ostrogorsky, 'La commune rurale byzantine. Loi agraire – Traité fiscal – Cadastre de Thèbes', *Byzantion*, 32 (1962), pp. 139–66, esp. 147–53. The two documents were drawn up for specific and different reasons, which make comparisons difficult. The Farmer's Law was a practical handbook concerned with the regulation of petty misdemeanours in the village and the Fiscal Treatise is an informed description of the working of the taxation system. Only the other evidence from the tenth century makes it possible to draw conclusions about economic and social trends.

36　　Economic expansion in the Byzantine empire

Some villagers, who did not possess as large an extent of the gardens around the settlement as other villagers, might move away from the settlement and bring land into cultivation elsewhere in the fiscal unit. When a peasant died leaving several heirs, he might bequeath his land in the village to some and that outside the village to others. If the latter was a considerable distance from the village, it was more convenient to move away from it.[2] The complexities of land tenure are well illustrated by the five categories of preemption rights, which were intended to give peasants the first option to purchase land sold by other villagers. The first three all applied to landowners where properties were intermingled with those of the seller, the other two to landowners whose properties were simply contiguous.[3]

Such a concentrated settlement and complicated tenurial pattern was probably an irritant to a wealthier peasant who owned slaves and large numbers of cattle, but if sufficient land was available he could move elsewhere in the fiscal unit where it was possible to farm in a more rational way.[4] The Fiscal Treatise also defines the *proasteion* (estate), which differed significantly from other lands in the fiscal unit. Its owner was not a resident of the territory, and the estate was cultivated by slaves, wage labourers or (although the treatise does not say so specifically) by tenant farmers.[5] The range in social status was great: slaves, wage labourers, independent peasant farmers and large landowners. The discussion of the *agridion* is particularly significant. It shows how wealthier peasants with the resources to bring more land under cultivation were increasing their wealth and how economic

---

[2] Dölger, *Beiträge*, p. 115 lines 21–3, pp. 135–6; G. Ostrogorsky, 'Die ländliche Steuergemeinde des byzantinischen Reiches im X. Jahrhundert', *Vierteljahrschrift für Sozial- und Wirtschaftsgeschichte*, 20 (1927), pp. 17–20; Loos, 'Quelques remarques', p. 8; Lemerle, *The Agrarian History*, p. 77.

[3] *JGR*, I, p. 202; Ostrogorsky, 'Die ländliche Steuergemeinde', pp. 32–5; Lemerle, *The Agrarian History*, p. 92 n. 2.　　　[4] Dölger, *Beiträge*, p. 115 lines 33–37.

[5] *Ibid.*, p. 115 lines 39–43, pp. 134–5; Ostrogorsky, 'Die ländliche Steuergemeinde', pp. 20–1; Loos, 'Quelques remarques', p. 8; Lemerle, *The Agrarian History*, p. 77; M. Kaplan, 'Remarques sur la place de l'exploitation paysanne dans l'économie rurale byzantine', *XVI Internationaler Byzantinistenkongress. Akten II, Jahrbuch der Österreichischen Byzantinistik*, 32/2 (1982), pp. 105–14; M. Kaplan, 'Les villageois aux premiers siècles byzantins (VIème–Xème siècles): une société homogène?', *Byzantino-Slavica*, 43 (1982), pp. 202–17. The references to slaves present a problem. Although the Farmer's Law contains evidence of the use of slaves in agricultural production, from the tenth century onwards the evidence is slight and, where it exists, we cannot be certain that it does not refer to domestic slaves. The term *misthios* is also problematic. It usually means wage labourer, but could also mean tenant farmer in this context; see Kaplan, 'Remarques sur la place de l'exploitation paysanne dans l'économie rurale byzantine', p. 113 n. 30.

Demographic growth and social relations 37

stratification was being intensified. The Fiscal Treatise also discusses another category of peasant cultivators, the *chorooikodespotai*, who were generally better-off than most villagers. They were farmers in the *ktesis*, a separate fiscal unit identical to the *chorion* for all practical purposes of tax-collecting. The only difference was that the *ktesis* consisted of scattered settlements instead of a nucleated village,[6] indicating a larger area of land in the ownership of the *chorooikodespotes* and possibly a greater concentration on pastoral farming.

The Fiscal Treatise gives an idealised version of the variations in wealth in a village community. The tenth-century legislation, which was intended to prevent the expansion of the properties of powerful landowners (the *dynatoi*) at the expense of the peasantry, shows that the gulf between rich and poor peasants was becoming greater. The villagers, who were given the right to repurchase land which they had alienated, were designated by different terms – *ptochos, penes* and *aporos*. Some distinctions have to be made between these terms. The first implies outright poverty where begging was necessary for subsistence, while the *penes* (best translated as weak) was obliged to work hard to survive.[7] The legislation envisaged a *penes* alienating property worth 100 *nomismata*. The *aporos* was defined by Constantine Porphyrogenitos as having a fortune no larger than fifty *nomismata*, but this is probably a survival from earlier legislation with little contemporary relevance and this category of peasant cannot be precisely defined.[8]

The legislation reinforced variations in peasant wealth.[9] Although the weaker peasants (*penetes*) were given the right to repurchase the land which they had sold from the time of the famine of 927–8 onwards, most villagers were unlikely to have been able to raise the cash. The state recognised this and repayments were made in kind by allowing the purchaser the usufruct of the land for a number of years.[10]

---

[6] Dölger, *Beiträge*, p. 115 lines 13–20, pp. 134–5; Ostrogorsky, 'Die ländliche Steuergemeinde', pp. 16–17; Lemerle, *The Agrarian History*, pp. 77–8.

[7] J. Leclerq, 'Aux origines bibliques du vocabulaire de la pauvreté', in M. Mollat (ed.), *Études sur l'histoire de la pauvreté* (2 vols., Paris, 1974), I, pp. 35–43.

[8] *JGR*, I, pp. 216, 242. For a discussion of this terminology, see R. Morris, 'The Powerful and the Poor in Tenth-Century Byzantium: Law and Reality', *Past and Present*, 73 (1976), pp. 3–27. See also Kazhdan and Constable, *People and Power*, p. 167.

[9] For general discussion of the tenth-century legislation, see Ostrogorsky, 'Die ländliche Steuergemeinde', pp. 14–16; Ostrogorsky, *History*, pp. 269–315 *passim*; Lemerle, *The Agrarian History*, pp. 85–156; Loos, 'Quelques remarques', pp. 15–18; and Morris, 'The Powerful and the Poor in Tenth-Century Byzantium', pp. 3–27.

[10] *JGR*, I, p. 242. Constantine VII had allowed the *aporoi* to reclaim their land without making any repayment, but this was rescinded later in his reign; see *JGR*, I, pp. 240–1.

38   Economic expansion in the Byzantine empire

If the original owner was unable to reclaim his land, his rights were transferred to other members of the fiscal unit. Compensation had also to be given for improvements made to the land by the powerful, until this stipulation was rescinded by Basil II in 996.[11] Consequently, the wealthiest villagers or a powerful landowner established in the village before the famine were the most likely beneficiaries of the legislation, because they were able to make the repayments. The trend towards the concentration of more wealth in the hands of fewer villagers was alluded to by Romanos I, who piously declared that those raised to a higher level ought to remain in their initial situation and ought not to extend their wealth at the expense of their neighbours.[12] The well-known case of Philokales illustrates the process. Originally one of the villagers, he had risen to the rank of *protobestiarios* and gained possession of the whole of his village, transforming it into his own estate, until Basil II intervened, restoring the land to the poorer peasants and leaving Philokales with only the lands for which he had originally paid taxes.[13]

The legislative provisions about *idiosystata* had a similar effect. The *idiosystaton* was a property which had been detached from the fiscal unit and established as a separate unit with its own boundaries. When an *idiosystaton* came onto the market, the purchaser claiming the right of preemption was obliged to buy the whole property or to withdraw from the deal, and he had four months in which to make the payment. The short time-limit and the need to maintain the integrity of the *idiosystaton* made it difficult for any but the wealthiest villagers or the community as a whole to complete the transaction.[14]

The intensification of differences in peasant wealth is also apparent in the legislation about military lands (*stratiotika ktemata*).[15] The *stratiotes* (the owner of military land) had to maintain property to the value of at least four pounds of gold. Previously, the obligation had been customary, but in the tenth century it became compulsory to register the property in the military *kodikes*. The same value was attached to the *strateia* (military holding) for the fleets of the themes of the Aegean, Samos and the Kibyrraiotes. The *strateia* for the imperial and other fleets

---

[11] *Ibid.*, p. 210.   [12] *Ibid.*, p. 211.   [13] *Ibid.*, p. 265.

[14] *Ibid.*, p. 217. For the *idiosystaton*, referred to as *idiostaton* in the Fiscal Treatise, see Dölger, *Beiträge*, p. 116 lines 19–23.

[15] On the military lands, see Lemerle, *The Agrarian History*, pp. 115–56; H. Ahrweiler, 'Recherches sur l'administration de l'empire byzantin aux IX⁰–XI⁰ siècles', *Bulletin de Correspondance Hellénique*, 84 (1960), pp. 5–24; and Haldon, *Recruitment and Conscription*, pp. 41–65.

Demographic growth and social relations 39

was valued at only two pounds.[16] Later, Nikephoros Phokas raised the limit for armoured cavalry to twelve pounds.[17] A landowner with this much wealth might be better categorised as a petty member of the provincial elite than as a peasant. It was much in excess of the property of most *stratiotai*. One reason for the strain on the system was the division of land among heirs. The *strateia* could be made up of the combined lands of several cultivators. The owner of military lands was entitled to dispose of the land by will in unequal shares to relatives or outsiders. If he died intestate, his property was divided up equally among his heirs.[18] In some cases such divisions probably led to the creation of very small peasant holdings which were scarcely viable and the pressure to alienate them increased. On the other hand, the landowner who possessed the full value of the *strateia* was quite prosperous. The sources do not give many prices of properties for comparison, but one suggestive figure is available. In 897 the monastery of St Andrew purchased some peasant property consisting of arable fields, a disused vineyard, a meadow, press and a courtyard (*aule*) for sixty-one *nomismata* and an enclosed vineyard for another seven *nomismata*.[19] The owner of military land valued at four pounds (288 *nomismata*) was clearly one of the wealthier members of the village community.

The parents of St Luke the Stylite came into this category. They were able to live in comfortable self-sufficiency, finance Luke in the performance of his military duties and supply him with provisions. Probably only a minority of soldiers were able to provide their own food. A large number were less wealthy and relied on the state for provisions.[20]

The existence of a substantial section of impoverished *stratiotai*, among other reasons possibly due to successive divisions among heirs, is confirmed by the *adoreia*, the term applied to relief granted to impoverished owners of military lands. The beneficiaries retained the

---

[16] *JGR*, I, pp. 222–3. Where previously more than four pounds had been registered, the additional land was to remain inalienable. The legislation was the culmination of the transfer of the obligation from the *stratiotes* personally to the land which he held; see Haldon, *Recruitment and Conscription*, pp. 41–2, 48–9.

[17] *JGR*, I, p. 256; Lemerle, *The Agrarian History*, pp. 129–31; Ahrweiler, 'Recherches sur l'administration', pp. 16–19; Haldon, *Recruitment and Conscription*, pp. 43–4.

[18] *JGR*, I, p. 223; Haldon, *Recruitment and Conscription*, pp. 48–50.

[19] *Lavra*, I, no. 1. For the meaning of the term *aule*, see Lemerle, *Cinq études*, p. 109 n. 93.

[20] 'Vita S. Lucae Stylitae', pp. 199–201; Haldon, *Recruitment and Conscription*, p. 45 n. 73.

40   *Economic expansion in the Byzantine empire*

same privileges[21] as other *stratiotai*, but as they were needy (*epideeis*) they were exempted from service.[22]

These divergences in the wealth of *stratiotai* are reflected in the legislation's provisions. Under no circumstances was the alienation of military lands permitted, but when transactions took place between *stratiotai* the terms on which the land was restored to its proper owner varied according to the means of the parties. A prosperous *stratiotes* who purchased the military lands of a poor (*aporos*) *stratiotes* was liable to the same penalty as a powerful landowner (*dynatos*); an *aporos* who bought from a well-off *stratiotes* was entitled to reclaim the price.[23] This trend towards intensified economic stratification among the owners of military lands was complementary to that affecting ordinary villagers.

This was one aspect of the problems with which the legislation was concerned. It dealt mainly with the extension of large properties through the purchase of peasant lands. This process was probably intensified after the famine of 927–8 and the long winter of 934.[24] The real problem confronting the central government was the consolidation of the political, military and economic power of the provincial elite. Their military power was based on their control of the thematic armies and was probably reinforced by the exercise of patronage and the maintenance of private retinues. Some families obtained a firm control of the highest positions in the provincial administration over successive generations.[25] The most powerful magnates were based in the interior of Asia Minor. Most of the plateau is best suited to extensive grazing and the wealth of many magnates was probably solidly based on large-scale ranching. This would automatically have led to conflicts with peasant producers domiciled in the sunken basins and river valleys of the plateau, because these areas, more favourable for sedentary agriculture, were needed for winter pasture. Later, under Turkish rule, the conflict of interest between sedentary farmers and pasturalist nomads was a

---

[21] For details of these privileges, see chapter 3.

[22] *JGR*, I, p. 224; Constantine Porphyrogenitus, *De Cerimoniis*, I, p. 696; Lemerle, *The Agrarian History*, p. 119 n. 2; Ahrweiler, 'Recherches sur l'administration', p. 14; Haldon, *Recruitment and Conscription*, p. 53 n. 92.

[23] *JGR*, I, p. 225.

[24] The famine is represented as an event of major importance by the legislation. Purchases made by the *dynatoi* from the *penetes* after this time could be rescinded. For the long winter, see the accounts of Theophanes Continuator, Symeon Magister and George the Monk in Theophanes Continuatus, pp. 417–18, 743, 908–9. See also Lemerle, *The Agrarian History*, pp. 94–7; and Morris, 'The Powerful and the Poor in Tenth-Century Byzantium', p. 8.

[25] Vryonis, *The Decline of Medieval Hellenism*, pp. 24–5 n. 132.

Demographic growth and social relations

recurring problem.[26] Disputes were no doubt resolved more abruptly in the Byzantine era because the herds were owned not by marginal groups, but by a very powerful elite which controlled the administration and judiciary in these provinces. The major aristocratic families were found in the themes of the Anatolikon, Cappadocia and Paphlagonia, regions which were the most easily exploited by large-scale pasture farming. There the subordination of peasant farmers to the *dynatoi* probably happened very fast. In the more fertile Aegean coastal region of Asia Minor there is no solid evidence for the existence of such powerful families, and large sections of the peasantry retained their independence until much later.[27] The administration was particularly determined to ensure that the powerful did not make substantial encroachments on peasant communities in this region: two of the novels were concerned with abuses by the powerful in the theme of Thrakesion. The state was also concerned to restrict the magnates' gains in the fertile, newly conquered territories in the east, which were turned into extensive state properties.[28]

The legislation was largely a response to the economic and military strength of a powerful group of magnates who constituted a political threat to the central administration. This is most apparent in Basil II's novel of 996, which abolished the forty-year time-limit within which claims against the powerful had to be made and abolished their right to repayment of the price of the purchase and to compensation for improvements. He also confiscated the property of several magnates and imposed on the powerful the taxes of peasants who had failed to make their payments.[29]

Lemerle has seen the legislation in terms of two different status

---

[26] *Ibid.*, pp. 188–90, 258–85, discusses at great length the problems caused by the nomads.

[27] For the most comprehensive discussion of the regional distribution of magnates in Asia Minor, see Hendy, *Studies in the Byzantine Monetary Economy*, pp. 100–7. See also Vryonis, *The Decline of Medieval Hellenism*, p. 25 n. 132; and I. Djuric, 'La famille des Phocas', *Zbornik Radova Vizantološkog Instituta*, 17 (1976), pp. 189–296 (French summary, pp. 293–6). For the properties of Eustathios Maleinos in Cappadocia, see Scylitzes, p. 340. See also L. Petit, 'Vie de St Michel Maléinos', *Revue de l'Orient Chrétien*, 7 (1902), pp. 550, 557. For other families, see J. F. Vannier, *Familles byzantines. Les Argyroi (IXe–XIIe siècles)* (Paris, 1975); and W. Seibt, *Die Skleroi. Eine prosopographisch-sigillographische Studie* (Vienna, 1976).

[28] Hendy, *Studies in the Byzantine Monetary Economy*, pp. 104–6. For the gains which could accrue from successful military operations, see Theophanes Continuatus, p. 427.

[29] *JGR*, I, pp. 262 ff; Scylitzes, p. 347; Lemerle, *The Agrarian History*, pp. 79–80, 104–5; Morris, 'The Powerful and the Poor in Tenth-Century Byzantium', pp. 3–27.

42 Economic expansion in the Byzantine empire

groups rather than economic classes. The problem with this approach is that it analyses the social structure of Byzantium in terms set down by the Byzantines themselves rather than those of the modern historian. Romanos I's definition of the *dynatoi* (powerful) included high civil and military officials, members of the senatorial order, officials of the themes and leading ecclesiastical dignitaries. Lemerle concludes from this definition that Romanos was more worried about civil and ecclesiastical dignitaries than the owners of large estates. The argument is artificial, because the easiest way to categorise the powerful was according to such positions. Lemerle argues that the powerful were not necessarily rich and the weak (*penetes*) not necessarily poor.[30] Certainly, a parvenu who was rising up through the administration would have consolidated his gains by buying land, but most officials, especially in the highest positions in the provincial administration, were already members of magnate families and the legislation was intended to prevent them from bringing direct producers into dependence on them.

Large estates were extended not only by simple purchases but by force or by the dubious use of legal contrivances. The legislation imposed fines on landowners who seized the property on which military service was imposed and reduced the *stratiotes* to the status of a *paroikos*.[31] The problems which aggressive neighbours created are well illustrated by the attacks on the property of St Nikon's church. It was vulnerable to the seizure of its animals by neighbouring Slavs and by Michael Choirosphaktes, a powerful local landowner.[32]

The most blatant examples of seizures of property are provided by the *Peira*, an eleventh-century legal compilation. The son of a *patrikios*, Baasakios was alleged to have entered an island, Gazoura, by force and seized property. It was incumbent on the plaintiffs to establish his guilt with eyewitness evidence. If they were able to prove how much they had lost, the case would be decided accordingly; if not, the judge would have to give a ruling according to their incomes.[33]

The activities of the Skleroi were more notorious. They were a very powerful family whose wealth was based in the Anatolikon theme. As numerous allegations of robbery, whipping and imprisonment were brought against Basil Skleros it was decided that, once proof of

---

[30] Lemerle, *The Agrarian History*, p. 107.
[31] *JGR*, I, pp. 262–72. For allegations against the metropolitan of Patras that his church had appropriated military land, see Darrouzès, *Épistoliers*, pp. 101–2.
[32] 'Nikon Metanoeite', pp. 194, 196, 201, 206–7.
[33] *Peira*, XL, 12, *JGR*, IV, pp. 176–7.

Demographic growth and social relations

victimisation by Skleros was established, the plaintiffs were to be given precedence in deciding how much had been taken.[34] Two accusations of seizure of property were made against Romanos Skleros. In the first case he took possession of the property of some villagers and then came to an agreement with them over its transfer. In the second his agent arbitrarily transferred lands, animals and movable wealth from some villagers to others (presumably Skleros's own *paroikoi*). The court ordered the restoration of all the property, its produce from the time of the seizure and all the offspring of the animals. Twice the value had to be given as compensation for work animals.[35]

The complaints in the legislation of usurpations effected fraudulently by state officials and of judicial partiality cannot be proved owing to the sparse evidence from actual cases. Basil II's legislation made provision for the invalidation of actions by officials which were considered detrimental to the state's interest. It alleged that the tax-assessors had been responsible for numerous frauds. Irregularities had been found in the chrysobulls and these were not allowed legal validity because the administrators who compiled them had not been present in the locality. The surveys in the chrysobulls of the properties affected by these privileges were valid only if they were also included in the records of the *genikon sekreton* or if there was other confirmatory evidence. The chrysobulls which had been issued in the early part of Basil's reign, before the fall of Basil the *parakoimomenos*, were automatically void unless they had received the emperor's personal approval. Perhaps these provisions did reflect a widespread use of fraudulent devices by the powerful, but it is equally likely that Basil was contriving a pretext to take strong action against his political enemies.[36]

The abolition of the forty-year time-limit on the claims for the restoration of property was justified by accusations that the powerful were bribing officials in order to pass through the time-limit unscathed.[37] The law continued to be enforced in the eleventh century. Eustathios Romaios expelled the powerful from land which had been acquired since the famine. He also had to allocate the produce of the

---

[34] *Peira*, LXIX, 5, *JGR*, IV, pp. 256–7; Seibt, *Die Skleroi*, pp. 67–8.
[35] *Peira*, XLII, 18, 19, *JGR*, IV, pp. 177–8; S. Vryonis, 'The Peira as a Source for the History of Byzantine Aristocratic Society in the First Half of the Eleventh Century', in *Near Eastern Numismatics, Iconography, Epigraphy and History. Studies in Honor of George C. Miles* (Beirut, 1974), pp. 279–84. The Romanos Skleros of these chapters cannot automatically be identified with the brother of Constantine IX's mistress, Maria Skleraina; see Seibt, *Die Skleroi*, p. 76.
[36] *JGR*, I, pp. 267, 270–1.   [37] *Ibid.*, p. 263.

44   *Economic expansion in the Byzantine empire*

land during the period of illegal occupation.[38] In fiscal units where the land was owned both by the powerful and by villagers, he laid down the principle that each individual owned the land corresponding to the entry in the tax-register and the villagers (not the powerful) were entitled to all the remaining lands which had been abandoned by other villagers.[39]

One of Basil's most important rulings, that a *dynatos* was not allowed to use unwritten evidence against a weak peasant (*penes*), was given practical application by Romaios. The monks of a monastery *tou neastou* had been in possession of land in a fiscal unit (*chorion*) *tes gordiou* for 128 years. When the land was transferred to the villagers by a metropolitan, the monks appealed and produced written evidence for the purchase of a property outside the fiscal unit. Romaios decided that the villagers would have the land inside the *chorion* and the monastery the land outside. The monk's possession of the land for 128 years did not entitle them to ownership because they only produced witnesses and did not have written evidence to support their claims to the land inside the fiscal unit.[40]

On a superficial examination these decisions warn against easy assumptions that the purpose of the legislation was frustrated by the state's own officials who had intimate links with provincial landowners and an identity of economic interests. It is significant that some villagers had the resources to take cases to such a high court, where they would obtain favourable verdicts. Nevertheless, these decisions survive in the sources as model cases and it cannot be assumed that general judicial practice in the provinces followed the same course. In provincial courts the judges would have been more directly exposed to the pressures of the powerful and probably had close social connections with them. Another factor was the ability of the administration to put verdicts into effect. It is possible that the Skleroi were able to exploit their great influence to nullify unfavourable verdicts in practice. The specific evidence to resolve this question is lacking.[41] Even though the legislation remained officially in force, its impact from the second half of the eleventh century onwards was undermined by the introduction of

---

[38] *Peira*, IX, 2, *JGR*, IV, p. 38.

[39] *Peira*, XV, 10, *JGR*, IV, pp. 52–3.

[40] *Peira*, XXIII, 3, *JGR*, IV, pp. 85–6.

[41] The identity of interests between officials in the administration and landowners has been emphasised by Ostrogorsky, *History*, p. 275. The decision of the judge Samonas (*Lavra*, I, no. 4) has been interpreted as evidence of judicial partiality; see G.

Demographic growth and social relations

interpolations into the texts of the novels reducing the severity of the restrictions on the activities of the powerful.[42] The effectiveness of the legislation has been a contentious issue. Ostrogorsky, pointing to Romanos III's abrogation of Basil II's measure imposing the tax-arrears of the peasantry on the powerful and the end of the sequence of legislation with the novel of 996, concluded that the state no longer had the will to protect the free peasantry, which rapidly disappeared.[43] This is an oversimplification, because independent peasants did not disappear dramatically. Their position in the Byzantine social structure gradually became less significant, as large properties belonging to the state and private landowners expanded. As the state came to depend more in subsequent centuries on the revenues from its own properties, the enforcement of the tenth-century legislation became less important. But it should not be dismissed out of hand as an inevitable failure. It was probably least successful in those provinces where powerful magnate families were most solidly entrenched and could most easily subvert the legislation. It is more likely to have had an effect in other provinces where the magnates' position was weaker, notably the Thrakesion theme and the newly conquered regions in the east, where the state was better placed to impose its authority.[44]

The extension of large properties was accompanied by the formulation of a clearer definition of the legal relations between landowners and their *paroikoi* (dependent peasants). In the tenth century Kosmas Magistros ruled that the landowner was not allowed to expel a *paroikos* from his land if he had been settled there for forty years – the *Peira* laid down a time-limit of thirty years. If the *paroikos* abandoned the land, it reverted back to the landowner, whose only obligation to the peasant concerned the materials from the latter's building. The *paroikos* had no authority to alienate the land in any way.[45]

Ostrogorsky, 'The Peasant's Pre-emption Right: An Abortive Reform of the Macedonian Emperors', *Journal of Roman Studies*, 37 (1947), pp. 120–2. It is impossible to agree with this conclusion. The property in question was bounded on three sides by lands belonging to the *dynatoi* and probably by the sea on the other side. Also the property was an *idiosystaton* and therefore claims had to be made within four months, but this time-limit had elapsed. See Lemerle, *The Agrarian History*, pp. 157–60.

[42] Svoronos, 'Les privilèges de l'Église', pp. 348–52; Lemerle, *The Agrarian History*, pp. 202–3.   [43] Ostrogorsky, *History*, pp. 322–3.

[44] Hendy, *Studies in the Byzantine Monetary Economy*, pp. 100–7.

[45] Weiss, 'Die Entscheidung des Kosmas Magistros', p. 480; *Peira*, XV, 2, 3, *JGR*, IV, p. 49; Lemerle, *The Agrarian History*, pp. 178–81.

46 *Economic expansion in the Byzantine empire*

In practice the situation was quite fluid, but we have to rely on later evidence in this respect. Thirteenth-century archive material shows that servile holdings were transferred without the permission of the landowner. *Paroikoi* sometimes lived outside the estates of the landowner, but this did not cause problems as long as they continued to meet their obligations. The *paroikos* did not have the right to abandon one landowner for another, but he could hold land from more than one landowner.[46]

The state played an important role not only in sanctioning the number of *paroikoi* whom a landowner was entitled to have on his property with fiscal privileges, but in establishing the payment which they owed to him according to the basic principles of the state's fiscal system. There was a fundamental distinction between the peasant who owned his own land and paid taxes to the state and the *paroikos* who was installed on the property of a landowner. In addition to other obligations the *paroikos* had to pay a rent; the *morte* or *dekateia* was technically a payment of a tenth of the produce of the land, but could also take the form of a payment in cash. In cases where the state's *paroikoi* had a small plot of their own land, the state would collect both the *morte* and the land-tax (*telos*) in its capacity as landowner as well as tax-collector.[47]

The extent of the obligations of the *paroikos* to the landowner varied according to the terms of the privileges which the state conceded. The administration exacted a wide range of obligations from the rural population; in addition to the basic land-tax these included payments in kind to maintain officials and soldiers and also the performance of labour services. It continued to claim the impositions which it chose not to concede to the landowner. The bureaucratic fiscal system imposed a large degree of uniformity on the obligations of the peasantry, but there

---

[46] Ostrogorsky, *Quelques problèmes*, pp. 41–74 *passim*; M. Angold, *A Byzantine Government in Exile. Government and Society under the Laskarids of Nicaea (1204–61)* (Oxford, 1975), pp. 133–7.

[47] *Engrapha Patmou*, I, no. 30; II, no. 67; Laiou-Thomadakis, *Peasant Society*, pp. 216–21. See also Angold, *A Byzantine Government in Exile*, pp. 134–5. The *morte* had already evolved into a feudal rent by the end of the eleventh century. *Paroikoi* belonging to another landowner encroached upon the lands of the monastery of Xerochoraphion and had to acknowledge the monastery's right of ownership and pay the *morte* from these fields to the monastery; see N. Wilson and J. Darrouzès, 'Restes du cartulaire de Hiéra-Xérochoraphion', *Revue des Études Byzantines*, 26 (1968), pp. 31–4, no. 9 l. 16. This feudal rent is also referred to in the sources as *pakton*; see *Dionysiou*, p. 104. In the *praktikon* granted to Andronikos Doukas in 1073 the *pakton* was clearly distinguished from the *telos*; see *Engrapha Patmou*, II, no. 50.

Demographic growth and social relations   47

were local variations in conditions. The number of days of labour services to which *paroikoi* were liable varied according to local custom,[48] but they were less onerous than in some other feudal societies. Consequently, in Byzantium dependent tenure was characterised by the payment of an additional surcharge rather than the performance of regular week-work, which was the distinctive feature of English serfdom. As has already been mentioned, the state was responsible for the limited imposition of labour services. It exacted corvees for its own military purposes – the maintenance of fortifications – and for the upkeep of communications. It had little need of agricultural labour services, which accounts for their restricted use in Byzantium.

A much neglected factor in the development of large properties was a growth in the population. It was of great importance because in the absence of technological improvements in Byzantine agriculture the most significant way to increase production was simply to extend the area under cultivation. The problem of establishing population trends has to be tackled if a proper assessment of the economic fortunes of Byzantium is to be made. Yet the subject has provoked conflicting statements from historians. Some have even argued for demographic decline in the eleventh century.[49] Although precise figures are, of course, lacking, the sources do reveal a general pattern of population increase in these centuries. Not only did this development contribute to the expansion of large properties, but it can be safely assumed that the state's revenues from its own properties increased for the same reason. The gains from the greater availability of manpower were divided between the state and feudal landowners, so that *paroikoi* became a relatively larger element of the rural population compared with

---

[48] Laiou-Thomadakis, *Peasant Society*, p. 181.
[49] H. Antoniadis-Bibicou, 'Démographie, salaires et prix à Byzance au XIe siècle', *Annales ESC*, 27 (1972), pp. 215–46, esp. 217–22; Svoronos, 'Société et organisation intérieure', pp. 384–5; but see his modified comments 'Remarques sur les structures économiques', pp. 62–3, where he places the onset of demographic stagnation in the late eleventh century. See also Charanis, 'Observations on the Demography of the Byzantine Empire', pp. 456–61, who postulates demographic growth in the Balkan provinces until the end of the twelfth century, but does not substantiate this view with firm evidence; see the criticisms of D. Jacoby, 'Une classe fiscale à Byzance et en Romanie latine: les inconnus du fisc, eleuthères ou étrangers', *Actes du XIVe congrès international des études byzantines, Bucharest 1971* (2 vols., Bucharest, 1974–5), II, p. 142 n. 17; and Lemerle, *The Agrarian History*, pp. 188 n. 2, 246. For a different assessment, see J. Lefort, 'Une grande fortune foncière aux X–XIIIe siècles: les biens du monastère d'Iviron', in *Structures féodales et féodalisme dans l'Occident méditerranéen (X–XIIIe siècles). Bilan et perspectives de recherches* (Collection de l'École Française de Rome 44) (Rome, 1980), pp. 736–7.

48 *Economic expansion in the Byzantine empire*

independent peasants. The expansion of large estates and the privileges granted by the state allowing peasants to be installed on these properties were symptomatic of a growth in population. Large landowners, who had the resources to bring extensive tracts of land under cultivation quickly, were able to absorb surplus, landless peasants on their estates. Most chrysobulls concerned with the installation of *paroikoi* stipulated that only peasants without any fiscal obligations to the state were to be settled on these estates. They were referred to in the texts as *ateleis*. The definition of the term was that they possessed no land of their own and therefore had no responsibility for the *demosion* or the *strateia*, nor any obligation to the *dromos* or any other fiscal charge.[50] The number of peasants who could be settled on these estates was limited by the administration. This had been seen as the consequence of a limited supply of manpower for which the state and private landowners were competing.[51] But the concern of the state was purely fiscal. It was simply curtailing the number of peasants over whom it was abandoning its fiscal claims. The most important factor is that the peasants were landless. By settling them on their properties large landowners were helping to extend the area under cultivation, a very clear indication of an increase in population.

This hypothesis rests on the assumption that the state was able to restrict landowners to the terms of the chrysobulls and that these landowners were not able to any significant extent to take peasants from other lands instead of landless peasants. Usually the state had the authority and the will to impose its rights in this respect. The *sigillion* recording the names of twenty-four *paroikoi* whom Nea Mone settled on the property of Kalothekia stipulated that if any were later found owing any payments to the state their old obligations would be reimposed regardless of the monastery's privileges.[52] Regular assessments by fiscal officials ensured that a close check was kept on the numbers of dependent peasants installed on these estates. In 974 Symeon, the *ekprosopou* of Thessalonike and Strymon, investigated the holders of *strateiai* and the *prosodiarioi demosiarioi* (dependent peasants of state lands) who had fled onto the estates of *archontes* and the church. He

[50] *JGR*, I, p. 617; *Engrapha Patmou*, I, no. 18.
[51] Ostrogorsky, *Quelques problèmes*, p. 16; Antoniadis-Bibicou, 'Démographie, salaires et prix à Byzance au XIe siècle', p. 220.
[52] MM, V, p. 7. For the localisation of the estate *ton Kalothekion* in the Aegean coastal region of Asia Minor opposite Chios, see H. Ahrweiler, 'L'histoire et la géographie de la région de Smyrne entre les deux occupations turques (1081–1317) particulièrement au XIIIe siècle', *Travaux et Mémoires*, 1 (1965), p. 68.

Demographic growth and social relations 49

made an assessment of the *kastron* of Hierissos, reimposing their taxes on the *demosiarioi* he found and leaving landowners with the *paroikoi* to whom they were entitled by chrysobull and who were not *demosiarioi*.[53]

This procedure was common. In the late twelfth century similar enquiries were made in the theme of Mylasa and Melanoudion. The monastery of St Paul on Latros was found in possession of considerably more *paroikoi* than were accounted for by its chrysobulls. The revenues from the extra *paroikoi* were transferred to the state. Another assessment with the same objectives was made in the same theme in 1189. The titles of military, ecclesiastical and monastic properties were examined. On this occasion the monastery was found to be in possession of only the *paroikoi* and land to which it had legitimate claims.[54]

The regularity with which landowners obtained confirmation of previous chrysobulls is an indication of the readiness of fiscal officials to enforce the state's claims. The status of *paroikoi* was a frequent source of contention between landowners and the administration. They were classified in the *praktika* according to the number of oxen which they possessed. Whenever they acquired additional animals, problems might arise. When an *aktemon*, a peasant without oxen, obtained a ploughteam, the tax-collector often ignored an earlier chrysobull unless it referred specifically to *zeugaratoi* (peasants with two oxen) and not simply *paroikoi*.[55]

It can safely be assumed that the restrictions on the privileges were usually enforced and that the grants of *paroikoi* are, indirectly, evidence of an increase in population. Unfortunately, the documents rarely give details of the surface area on which the peasants were settled and the increase in the area under cultivation usually cannot be calculated. Precise information is available in only a few cases. The clearest indication of an increase in rural manpower comes from the estates of the Athonite monastery of Iviron. In 1047 the monastery's properties amounted to about 10,800 acres and there were 246 *paroikoi* installed on these lands. By the beginning of the twelfth century the number of peasant families had risen to 294, even though confiscations had reduced the extent of the monastery's properties. By the early fourteenth century the monastery had 460 *paroikoi*, but the extent of its lands had

---

[53] *Lavra*, I, no. 6; Lemerle, *The Agrarian History*, pp. 167–8. For the similar activities of Theodore Kladon in 975, see Ostrogorsky, *Quelques problèmes*, pp. 12–14.

[54] MM, IV, pp. 317–19.

[55] For the exploitation of this loophole by successive *praktores* of Samos, see *Engrapha Patmou*, I, no. 19. See also Petit, 'Notre Dame de Pitié', p. 35 lines 4–6; and Lemerle, *The Agrarian History*, pp. 243–4.

50   *Economic expansion in the Byzantine empire*

not increased.[56] One particularly important property was the village of Radolibos, which came into Iviron's possession in 1098. In 1103 there were 122 *paroikoi* settled on this property. By the early fourteenth century this figure had risen to 222.[57] No doubt short-term fluctuations are concealed within this general pattern of expansion, but the documentation is not comprehensive enough to reveal them. But the most important trend is very clear. A steady increase in population from the mid eleventh to the early fourteenth century led to a dense settlement on Iviron's estates.

Elsewhere information about the balance between manpower and land is available in only a limited number of cases, but they do reveal a similar pattern. The monastery of the Theotokos at Strymitza received a property of 500 *modioi* with an exemption for twelve landless peasants (*ateleis paroikoi*) and six ploughteams from Alexios I. Each pair of oxen corresponded to eighty-three *modioi*.[58] By the middle of the twelfth century a considerable expansion in the area under cultivation had taken place. In 1152 all twelve *paroikoi* possessed oxen and the monks obtained an exemption for these *zeugaratoi* and all the land in their possession. Six had been installed on the 500 *modioi* which had originally been given to the monastery. The other six were exploiting land outside the monastery's property and the state conceded this land to it. Some doubts arose about the amount of land to which they were entitled, owing to a confusion in the rates of taxation of different fiscal units in the same region. Therefore the earlier privilege was used as the basis for the new grant and it was decided that the six *zeugaratoi* were entitled to 500 *modioi*.[59] The most important features of the procedure

---

[56] Lefort, 'Une grande fortune foncière', pp. 740–1. For the confiscation of some of Iviron's properties, see below, p. 70.

[57] Lefort, 'Une grande fortune foncière', pp. 736–41; J. Lefort, 'Le cadastre de Radolibos (1103), les géomètres et leurs mathématiques', *Travaux et Mémoires*, 8 (1981), pp. 269–313.

[58] The ploughteams were intended to cultivate this *topos* of 500 *modioi*. Another 162 *modioi*, which included the monastic building, were not taken into account in the equation; see Petit, 'Notre Dame de Pitié', pp. 28–9. The *modios* was approximately one tenth of a hectare; see E. Schilbach, *Byzantinische Metrologie* (Munich, 1970), pp. 66–70.

[59] Petit, 'Notre Dame de Pitié', pp. 34–40. The affair was quite complicated because the 1,176 *modioi* whose *periorismos* is given in the *praktikon* also included some fields cultivated by *paroikoi* of the state and the figures in the text do not add up properly. The lands of the state's *paroikoi* amounted to 166 *modioi*; 1,010 *modioi* should have been left to the monastery, but the *praktikon* gives a total of only 749 *modioi*. The most likely explanation is that the lower figure excluded some of the less productive land in the *periorismos*. The monastery also received an *aporos topos* of 100 *modioi* which had been abandoned for a considerable length of time. The treasury recognised the

Demographic growth and social relations 51

were that it gives a rough estimate of the area which a peasant with a pair of oxen might cultivate (although this was subject to considerable variation) and it shows how the acquisition of landless peasants by a privileged landowner led to the extension of the area under cultivation.

These *paroikoi* at Strymitza held slightly more land than those at Radolibos in 1103, where the average holding was 50 to 60 *modioi*.[60] Few other documents give both the extent of an estate and the number of peasants cultivating it. Only in isolated instances are there figures to compare with the Strymitza documentation. The estate of Galaidai, which was included in the properties donated to Andronikos Doukas in 1073, consisted of 762 *modioi*. Twelve *paroikoi* were installed there, nine *zeugaratoi* and three *aktemones*. Leaving aside the latter, each pair of oxen was equivalent to eighty-four *modioi*. Allowing for the small plots cultivated by the *aktemones*, the extent cultivated was slightly less. Cultivation of about eighty *modioi* by each *zeugaratos* accords well with the evidence for Strymitza.[61]

On some of Lavra's estates the peasantry held more land. In 1104 the monastery surrendered Barzachanion to the state and received Lorotomou and Asmalou, two properties near Thessalonike, in exchange. The total extent of Barzachanion was 6,962 *modioi*. Its arable land and first-class meadow amounted to 3,549 *modioi*. Four of the *paroikoi* owned two ploughteams each and the other eleven had one each.[62] The maximum average for each pair of oxen was 196 *modioi*. It would have been less if the meadow had been extensive. It is not known whether all the land was assigned to the *paroikoi*, but it seems likely because the estate was far removed from Lavra's other properties.

The twelfth-century evidence for Lorotomou and Asmalou can be compared with information from the early fourteenth century, a

monastery's ownership of 849 *modioi* which was cultivated by the twelve *paroikoi zeugaratoi*. This works out to about 70 *modioi* for each ploughteam, not the original figure of 83, but the *periorismos* made no mention of the *topos* of 162 *modioi* which Alexios had given to the monastery and brings the total area which it owned to just over 1,000 *modioi*; see ibid., pp. 43–4. There was still uncultivated land in the area. In addition to the *aporos topos* which was conceded to the monastery, other *stichoi* consisted of *aporos ge* and had been abandoned for a long time; see ibid., p. 39.

[60] Lefort, 'Une grande fortune foncière', pp. 736–7, gives the figure of five hectares for a *zeugaratos* at Radolibos; see J. Lefort, 'Radolibus: population et paysage', *Travaux et Mémoires*, 9 (1985), pp. 195–234.

[61] *Engrapha Patmou*, II, no. 50 lines 167–75, 305–10. There are clear indications that some of the other properties in this *episkepsis* were less intensively cultivated in 1073; see below, p. 138.

[62] *Lavra*, I, no. 56, lines 30–3; Svoronos, 'Remarques sur les structures économiques', p. 56 n. 27.

52   *Economic expansion in the Byzantine empire*

comparison which reveals a significant increase in the number of peasants established there by 1321. In 1104 Lorotomou was assessed at 2,048 *modioi*, all land of the first quality. It contained twenty-one peasant households, nine with a pair of oxen, seven with one ox and five without any. Assuming that the whole estate was cultivated by these *paroikoi*, each pair of oxen corresponded to 164 *modioi*. This figure takes no account of the peasants without oxen (*aktemones*). The officials in charge of the transfer of the properties worked on the principle that one *zeugaratos* corresponded to two *boidatoi* (peasants with one ox) or four *aktemones*. This gives a revised average of 150 *modioi* for each *zeugaratos*.[63] These averages are rather schematic and there might have been variations in the amount of land which a peasant household could cultivate according to the labour-power available to each household. Nevertheless, they give a useful indication of the balance between land and manpower on the estate in 1104. In 1321 there were sixty peasant households on the estate, a threefold increase over the earlier figure, and the surface area of the estate had not increased. Thirty-four of these households possessed two oxen and eight owned one ox.[64] The twelfth and thirteenth centuries had witnessed a steady growth of population on this estate, which was being much more intensively exploited by 1321.

The calculations for the property at Asmalou are slightly more complicated, but the same trend is apparent. It was assessed at $4,982\frac{1}{2}$ *modioi*, of which 980 *modioi* was land of the first quality, 300 *modioi* of second quality and the remaining $3,702\frac{1}{2}$ *modioi* land of third quality. The latter was intended to compensate for the mountainous and pasture land at Barzachanion. The category of third quality was applied to unploughed land, possibly stony, mountainous or marshy, but not necessarily always totally unsuitable for future cultivation. Here it can be left out of consideration. Each of the $10\frac{1}{2}$ peasant ploughteams corresponded to 122 *modioi* of first- and second-class land.[65] Lavra was also allowed to settle another ten *zeugaratoi* at Asmalou and

---

[63] *Lavra*, I, no. 56 lines 49–51. The document gives no evidence that there were also oxen belonging to the landowner on this estate.

[64] *Lavra*, II, no. 109 lines 200–65. The estate is called Lorotomou in the earlier document and Loroton in the later one. For their identification as the same estate, see *Lavra*, I, p. 290; and J. Lefort, *Villages de Macédoine. Notices historiques et topographiques sur la Macédoine orientale au moyen âge*, I, *La Chalcidique occidentale* (Paris, 1982), pp. 93–6.

[65] *Lavra*, I, no. 56 lines 47–9. For the type of land assessed as third class, see Schilbach, *Byzantinische Metrologie*, pp. 239–40.

Demographic growth and social relations   53

Lorotomou,[66] a change which permitted a more intensive exploitation of the land. In the next two centuries settlement on this estate became much denser. Much of the uncultivated third-class land of 1104 was brought under the plough. By 1321 there were sixty-eight peasant households, almost a five-fold increase since 1104 and the number of oxen had increased about four-fold.[67]

The only other comparable information for this period concerns the properties which the monastery of Patmos had on Leros and Leipso. In 1099 it obtained an exemption for twelve *paroikoi* – four to be settled on Leipso and four on each of two estates, Parthenion and Temenia, on Leros. The text does not state specifically that they were *zeugaratoi*, but the monastery's complete exemption from all obligations to the state entitled it to them.[68] The *praktikon* assessing the quality of the land on these estates had been compiled in 1089. The cultivated area had possibly been extended by 1099, but there is no evidence that substantial changes had taken place. All three properties were very extensive, but the main emphasis was on pastoral farming and there was a limited amount of arable land. At Parthenion it amounted to 409 *modioi*, an average of just over 100 *modioi* for each *paroikos*. At Temenia there was only 259 *modioi* of arable and on Leipso 400 *modioi*.[69] Except for the estate at Temenia the figures suggest an average of about 100 *modioi* for each *paroikos*. By the mid twelfth century some expansion had occurred. The emperor Manuel confirmed the original grant of *paroikoi*, their entitlement to oxen, and added another six *zeugaratoi*. The only condition, as in the original grant by Alexios, was that they should be *ateleis*, owing no obligations to the state. That the monks originally requested the grant of extra *zeugaratoi* suggests that there was already an available supply of landless peasants on these islands.[70] There is a gap in the evidence until the middle of the thirteenth century. The monastery had lost control of Temenia and Parthenion in the first half

---

[66] *Lavra*, I, no. 56 lines 82–3.
[67] *Lavra*, II, no. 109 lines 133–99. In this document the property is called Hagia Euphemia. The identification with Asmalou has been made on the basis of the information in the *periorismoi* of various Athonite texts; see *Lavra*, I, p. 290; and Lefort, *Villages de Macédoine*, I, pp. 157–60. In 1117 Docheiariou obtained an estate, Rousaiou, with eight *zeugaratoi*. The property was assessed at 6,111 *modioi*, but no specific figures are given for arable cultivation. In 1341 there were seventeen peasant households on the property, but there is evidence that the property had been abandoned not long before 1338; see *Docheiariou*, nos. 4, 5, 19, 20.
[68] *Engrapha Patmou*, I, no. 18.
[69] *Ibid.*, II, no. 52 lines 64–5, 98–9; and for the details concerning Leipso, *ibid.*, II, p. 61.
[70] *Ibid.*, I, no. 19.

54　　　　Economic expansion in the Byzantine empire

of the century and when they were restored in 1254 there were twenty *paroikoi* on these properties. By 1263 this figure had risen to thirty-one, fifteen at Parthenion, sixteen at Temenia.[71]

The size of peasant holdings varied according to local farming conditions and the density of settlement in each region. The sources suggest that in the late eleventh and early twelfth centuries the average holding of a peasant with a pair of oxen was about 80 to 100 *modioi*.[72] The figure is very approximate and should not be attributed an exaggerated importance because of the variations which have been demonstrated, but it can be used as a rough guide to put into perspective the scale of the extension of the cultivated area on other estates. Usually, the documents record only the number of landless peasants (*ateleis paroikoi*) which the beneficiary of the privilege was allowed to install on his land. Several of these grants were received by the monasteries in the Chalkidike in the tenth century. Prodromos, near Thessalonike, received an exemption for thirty-six *ateleis paroikoi* from Constantine VII, and the monastery *tou Atho* was allowed to install seventy on its estates in the Kassandra peninsula. Kolobou received an exemption for forty *ateleis paroikoi* from Romanos II.[73] That these estates were able to absorb so many landless peasants indicates that a significant expansion in the region's economy was in progress. The limitations of the source material and the lack of information about these estates at other times make precision impossible and only a general indication of economic trends is available, but there is no doubt that population was increasing in the peninsula in the mid tenth century and extensive tracts of new land were being brought into productive use.

The evidence from Lavra's properties in the peninsula suggests that the expansion was sustained over a long period. Its *metochion* (subordinate monastery), St Andrew at Peristerai, had been allowed by Constantine VII to install 100 *paroikoi* on its estates on the usual conditions. In 1079 Lavra received a new exemption for another 100, provided that they were obtained from the descendants of *paroikoi*

---

[71] *Ibid.*, II, nos. 65, 68.

[72] Usually, 150 *modioi* is suggested as the average size; see Svoronos, 'Remarques sur les structures économiques', p. 52 n. 6; and Schilbach, *Byzantinische Metrologie*, pp. 67–70. Schilbach takes into account evidence of much larger peasant holdings dating from the early fifteenth century which inflate his average.

[73] F. Dölger, 'Ein Fall slavischer Einsiedlung im Hinterland von Thessalonike im 10. Jahrhundert', *Sitzungsberichte der bayerischen Akademie der Wissenschaft. Philosophisch–historische Klasse* (1952), pp. 6–7.

Demographic growth and social relations

already established on its estates.[74] Demographic expansion on these estates made it necessary for the monks to obtain this extension of their earlier privilege.

It is possible to follow the installation of peasants on Lavra's estate at Chostiane in the theme of Moglena over a period of about 100 years. When it was given to Leo Kephalas in 1086 there were only twelve *paroikoi*, some with one ox, others with none. In 1115 the property came into Lavra's possession and by 1181 there were sixty-two *paroikoi*, all of them with a pair of oxen. Manuel had given Lavra thirty and Alexios II another twenty. There were probably other *paroikoi* installed on the estate in 1181 in excess of the total allowed by imperial privileges. The chrysobulls of Manuel and Alexios II do not survive and the conditions of the privileges which they conferred are not known. It is possible that they transferred to Lavra state *paroikoi* who had been settled on neighbouring lands, but such concessions were rare. The grants usually referred to peasants with no obligations to the state and the increase in the number of *paroikoi* was most likely the result of demographic increase in the region. It was accompanied by an improvement in the resources of the peasantry. They had all acquired ploughteams and the surface area which they cultivated can be estimated conservatively at 5,000 *modioi*, a very substantial increase in production.[75]

The middle decades of the twelfth century were marked by a fairly generalised trend of demographic increase. The extension of ecclesiastical estates through a combination of illegal usurpation and an increase in the cultivated area owing to population growth is well attested by Manuel's legislation. These estates were expanding beyond the limits laid down in earlier privileges. In 1148 the claims of the metropolitans and bishops and of Hagia Sophia were confirmed, even where their titles to property were incomplete or contrary to imperial legislation.[76] However, fiscal officials continued to reclaim lands which had been held by Hagia Sophia, including *sympatheia* (land granted tax-

---

[74] *Lavra*, no. 38 lines 22–6, and p. 58 n. 12.
[75] *Lavra*, no. 48 line 8, no. 65 lines 17–19, 30, 75. We do not know whether the monastery played an active role in maintaining the numbers of oxen belonging to the *paroikoi* or simply left the matter to the peasants. The former is quite likely, because the animal wealth of the *paroikoi* affected the assessments of their obligations to the monastery.
[76] *JGR*, I, pp. 376–7. For the most comprehensive discussion of this legislation, see Svoronos, 'Les privilèges de l'Église', pp. 325–91. See also P. Charanis, 'The Monastic Properties and the State in the Byzantine Empire', *Dumbarton Oaks Papers*, 4 (1948), pp. 82–92.

56   *Economic expansion in the Byzantine empire*

relief) and klasmatic land. In 1153 the state renounced its claims to all the state land which was in the church's possession at that time.[77] In 1158 all the monasteries in the region of Constantinople were confirmed in the possession of all the property which they held at that time, even if its possession had been illegal.[78] Illegally held land probably included extensive stretches of land recently brought into cultivation, for which the monasteries had no exemptions and were not paying taxes.

The gains which the monasteries of Strymitza and Patmos made at this time have already been mentioned. There is also evidence for a considerable expansion on the estates of the metropolitan of Corfu and the bishop of Stagoi. In one chrysobull the metropolitan received an exemption for eighty *paroikoi* and forty *klerikoi*. Another exemption involved twenty-four houses inside the *kastron* of Corfu and fifty outside the *kastron*. A *sigillion* gave the metropolitan twenty *paroikoi* who were free and had no obligation to the state.[79] The bishop of Stagoi had received earlier privileges from Nikephoros III and Alexios in respect of peasants with nineteen ploughteams. By 1144 the estates contained forty-six *klerikoi* with ploughteams.[80]

The evidence for demographic increase is supported by the revival of towns after the upheavals of the early Middle Ages. As the relations between town and country will be examined in detail later,[81] a few general remarks must suffice here. After a sharp contraction of urban sites in the later sixth and seventh centuries, towns began to recover from the ninth and tenth centuries and expanded significantly in the eleventh and twelfth centuries. There is some variation within this general pattern, because the Turkish influx into Asia Minor caused great disruption in the late eleventh and early twelfth centuries. Archaeological evidence from both Europe and Asia Minor shows an increase in the size of urban settlements from the ninth and tenth centuries onwards. This was accompanied by a notable upsurge in new towns. It was clearly a reflection of demographic growth (although urban development cannot be explained in purely demographic terms). It would be a mistake to explain the urban revival in terms of a shift in population from the country to the towns.[82] As death-rates in pre-

---

[77] *JGR*, I, pp. 379–80.   [78] *Ibid.*, pp. 381–4.

[79] MM, V, pp. 14–16; Svoronos, 'Les privilèges de l'Église', pp. 361–3.

[80] C. Astruc, 'Un document inédit de 1163 sur l'évêché thessalien de Stagi', *Bulletin de Correspondance Hellénique*, 83 (1959), pp. 213–15; MM, V, pp. 270–1; Svoronos, 'Les privilèges de l'Église', pp. 364–5; Lemerle, *The Agrarian History*, pp. 220–1.

[81] See below, chapter 6.

[82] Mango, *Byzantium. The Empire of New Rome*, p. 57.

Demographic growth and social relations 57

industrial societies tend to be higher in towns than in the country, urban development gives a very strong indication of an upward population trend in the rural economy.

The beginning of urban recovery was accompanied by signs of revival in the rural economy. In the tenth century large tracts of klasmatic land (abandoned land which had reverted to the state) were sold by the state. The buyers included powerful monasteries, peasants and the inhabitants of Hierissos, some of whom were quite wealthy. In 941 a major sale of klasmatic land was undertaken by the *epoptes* (tax-assessor) of Thessalonike, Thomas Moirokouboulos. The low price at which the land was sold (fifty *modioi* for each *nomisma*) indicates that large areas had not been intensively cultivated previously; the Arab and Bulgar raids early in the century might have had an adverse effect on the region's economy. The monastery of St Andrew at Peristerai purchased two properties in the peninsula of Kassandra. One consisted of 800 *modioi* and the other 1,000 *modioi*. Of these, 1,200 *modioi* were said to have been under cultivation and the other 600 unexploited. The monastery paid thirty-six *nomismata*. Another 100 *modioi* were sold to a peasant, Nicolas, for two *nomismata*. Both had to contribute their share to the payment of twelve *nomismata* for the *libellikon demosion* on all the klasmatic land sold in the region at that time.[83] At the same time Moirokouboulos sold klasmatic land in the region of Hierissos at the same price and a *libellikon demosion* of almost exactly one *milliaresion* for 100 *modioi* was imposed. As the sale price was the same in both regions, it is likely that the rate of taxation was the same. A *libellikon* of twelve *nomismata* would have corresponded to 14,000 *modioi*, a very large amount of land to sell at once. It seems that this payment involved only the lands which were sold in Kassandra. The total payment on those sold near Hierissos is not known. These lands included 950 *modioi* which were sold to thirteen peasants. In 956 the land was reassessed, the price was doubled and nineteen extra *nomismata* were paid by Xeropotamou, which took possession of the properties.[84] Either the peasants who made the original payment were unable to pay the additional amount or the land was arbitrarily transferred to the monastery. The first explanation is the more likely. It illustrates how the

[83] *Lavra*, I, nos. 2, 3. The *libellikon demosion* was the tax on klasmatic land, assessed at a rate of $\frac{1}{12}$ of the normal land-tax; see Dölger, *Beiträge*, pp. 120, 123. The reference to the land which was already being exploited shows that some recovery had already begun while these klasmatic lands were under state control.

[84] *Xéropotamou*, no. 1. For the procedure involved in the sale of klasmatic land, see the notes to *Lavra*, I, no. 11.

58 Economic expansion in the Byzantine empire

technical procedures imposed by the state could exert pressure on the direct producers and how economic recovery was exploited by landowners to build up large properties, with the result that independent peasants came to form a relatively small proportion of the rural population.

Other purchases were made by the inhabitants of Hierissos and its neighbouring villages. The boundary between their lands and those of the Athonite monasteries needed a clear delimitation, which the official had failed to make at the time of the sale.[85] An attempt was made to resolve the problem in 942–3. The monks made extensive claims on the basis of a chrysobull of Basil I giving them the right to the land from the *enoria* of Hierissos to the interior of Athos. The dispute revolved around the exact meaning of the term *enoria*. The monks interpreted it as referring not to the fiscal unit but to the *kastron* of Hierissos. They claimed all the land as far as the monastery of Kolobou, while the villagers asserted that their klasmatic land extended as far as the Zygos. Moirokouboulos drew up a boundary which was more favourable to the purchasers of the klasmatic land than to the monks. The fields and waste land towards the Zygos came into the possession of the monks, but all the land between the boundary and Kolobou was defined as klasmatic and belonging to the villagers and inhabitants of Hierissos. Although they did not obtain all they claimed, the boundary was fairly close to the Zygos and they also received over 2,000 *modioi*, about which they had been in dispute with Kolobou. In contrast the monks received only a small quantity of arable land of inferior quality.[86] A year later the boundary was redrawn by the *strategos* of the theme accompanied by the metropolitan of Thessalonike. As they were acting on an imperial *prostagma*, it is probable that the monks were trying to get the frontier changed in their favour. The *periorismos* established by Moirokouboulos has not survived, but it seems that no substantial alterations were made to it.[87] The dispute is a clear example of expansion in the rural economy creating a need for boundaries to be more clearly established.

Evidence for the regular sale of klasmatic land in the eleventh century is contained in the cadaster of Thebes, although there is nothing to

---

[85] *Prôtaton*, no. 4.

[86] *Prôtaton*, no. 5 and pp. 56–9. For the dispute between the inhabitants of the *kastron* of Hierissos and Kolobou, see *ibid.*, p. 58 n. 112.

[87] *Prôtaton*, no. 6 and pp. 58–9. The text states that the boundary was established according to the actions of Moirokouboulos.

Demographic growth and social relations

suggest that these sales were comparable in scale to those in the Chalkidike during the previous century, an indication that the region was already fairly densely settled. Within each of the two main fiscal units of the cadaster there are subdivisions introduced by very brief topographical indications, but not the detailed *periorismoi* (descriptions of the boundaries) which were essential for self-contained fiscal units. They must have had some connection with the preceding fiscal unit, but for some reason had been detached from it. They are best regarded as klasmatic land which had been alienated by the state. A precise dating of this procedure cannot be established. Some of the taxes had been imposed by an official, Merkourios, in the second quarter of the eleventh century, but the group survives in a mutilated form and the full extent of the operation is unknown. As the group follows on from an earlier subdivision, it is likely that the latter already had their taxes imposed earlier in the century. Even such rough estimates cannot be made for the klasmatic land in the rest of the cadaster. It leaves only an impression of more land being brought steadily into cultivation during the century.[88] Oikonomides has pointed out that although klasmatic lands are often mentioned in the documents of the eleventh century, there is no indication that they were sold at low prices as in the tenth century.[89] The documentation permits only a tentative conclusion, but if this hypothesis is correct, it suggests that demand for land was increasing in the eleventh century.

Another form of rural colonisation was the settlement of slaves on their own plots of land. The process was most notable when a large landowner had numerous slaves, but sometimes the slave of a peasant family received part of the family's land. When the Tzagastes family sold their property to St Andrew of Peristerai, the *legaton* of their freed slave was excluded from the transaction.[90] The most explicit example of this

---

[88] Svoronos, 'Recherches sur le cadastre byzantin', pp. 44–6, 52–3; A. Harvey, 'Economic Expansion in Central Greece in the Eleventh Century', *Byzantine and Modern Greek Studies*, 8 (1982–3), pp. 21–8. The evidence for the alienation of klasmatic land outside this region in the eleventh century is more scattered. Leo Kephalas received a property of 334 *modioi* from Alexios, and Gregory Pakourianos obtained *libelloi*, the documents accompanying the grant of klasmatic land, for two *choria*; see *Lavra*, I, no. 44; and Gautier, 'Grégoire Pakourianos', p. 127. For the acquisition of the klasmatic property of Dobrobikeia by Iviron early in the eleventh century, see below, p. 61. For the allocation of klasmatic land to an imperial *episkepsis*, see *Docheiariou*, no. 3 line 44.

[89] N. Oikonomides, 'L'évolution de l'organisation administrative de l'empire byzantin au XIe siècle (1025–1118)', *Travaux et Mémoires*, 6 (1976), p. 137.

[90] *Lavra*, no. 1 lines 19–20.

60   *Economic expansion in the Byzantine empire*

procedure is found in the will of Eustathios Boilas. By 1059 he had freed all his slaves. Some had already received properties or gifts of money. In his will two were given *zeugotopia* and two others *boidotopia*. Others were bequeathed cash payments. The will indicates that at some stage all the freed slaves received lands with complete rights of ownership.[91] The same procedure is apparent in the will of Kale Pakouriane, although this text is not so precise. She bequeathed animals to 'her men' and to her freed slaves. One freed slave received a *zeugarion*, two others *boidia*. Two of her men received a *zeugarion* each and three a *boidion*. The document does not state that they received land with the animals, but the close association between the *zeugarion* and the amount of land a pair of oxen could plough makes this a distinct possibility.[92] However, even in these instances where large landowners were involved, this practice had only a very slight importance in relation to the broad economic trends of the period.

The general trend of the extension of the area under cultivation conceals temporary fluctuations, where land fell vacant for a period and was then reclaimed for cultivation. Usually this did not happen on a large enough scale to affect the long-term trend. The only exception was in Asia Minor in the late eleventh century, which will be discussed later.[93] In the European provinces there were no major upheavals but the sources do reveal some small-scale fluctuations. In 1080 Lavra and Xeropotamou settled a dispute over a vineyard which had fallen out of use. Lavra claimed it as part of the property which had been donated to it by Constantine and Maria Lagoudes in 1014. As the land had been neglected, Xeropotamou, which had its own neighbouring property, exploited the situation and usurped the vineyard.[94] Occasionally, properties were ineffectively exploited because the landowner was resident in a town some distance away.[95]

The effect of such fluctuations was usually to concentrate land-ownership in fewer hands, as large landowners with greater resources were responsible for bringing land back into cultivation. In some villages east of the Strymon, where the Amalfitan monastery owned lands, many inhabitants had fled to other villages or estates and in 1081 the monastery's claim to the abandoned lands was guaranteed by

[91] Lemerle, *Cinq études*, pp. 26–7 lines 192–231 and p. 61. See also Ostrogorsky, *Quelques problèmes*, pp. 72–3.

[92] I. Iberites, 'Ek tou archeiou tes en hagio orei hieras mones ton Iberon. Byzantinai diathekai', *Orthodoxia*, 6 (1931), pp. 367–8.

[93] See below, p. 67.   [94] *Lavra*, I, no. 40.

[95] *Docheiariou*, no. 3 line 28, no. 4 line 14.

Demographic growth and social relations

chrysobull.[96] On a much smaller scale Constantine Triphyles, who owned land near Thessalonike, purchased two neighbouring plots in 1097; one was a vineyard of about three *modioi* which had been neglected, the other consisted of two *modioi* which was lying uncultivated with just a few fruit trees.[97]

The demographic problem can be complicated by signs of contraction and expansion in the same region. The archbishop Theophylaktos complained that the peasants on his estates were fleeing from the state's exactions, but this was partly rhetorical exaggeration.[98] Another complaint was that officials were imposing heavier taxes than they ought for the *zeugarion*. The number of *zeugaria* exceeded those for which the archbishop had an exemption, implying that some expansion had occurred in the preceding decades.[99]

The best indication of economic fluctuations were the grants of *sympatheiai*. It has been suggested that their regularity from the middle of the tenth century onwards reflected the growing unproductivity of many lands, corresponding to a demographic decline.[100] The *sympatheia* was a remission of taxes, which could be granted if the land had become unproductive, but it could operate for a maximum of thirty years before the land reverted to the state. It cannot therefore be indicative of a long-term trend, only of short-term fluctuations. It can be attributed to the migration of peasants, a common enough phenomenon, without the need for any misleading conclusions about demographic decline to be drawn. The incidence of *sympatheiai* in the cadaster of Thebes is more than counterbalanced by the new fiscal units, which had been created out of klasmatic land alienated by the state.[101] The effect of this procedure is clearly illustrated by the fate of the fiscal unit of Dobrobikeia. In the late tenth century it was abandoned and tax-relief was granted on its twenty-four peasant holdings. Before 1031 the property had become klasmatic and had been acquired by Iviron. By 1042 seven peasant holdings were under cultivation and a new tax-payment was assessed. In 1104 there were twenty-eight peasant families on this estate. In this instance fluctuations in the rural

---

[96] *Lavra*, I, no. 43 lines 1–12.

[97] *Ibid.*, no. 53 lines 2–18.

[98] Migne, *Patrologia Graeca*, CXXVI, cols. 529, 532; D. Xanalatos, *Beiträge zur Wirtschafts- und Sozialgeschichte Makedoniens im Mittelalter, hauptsächlich auf Grund der Briefe des Erzbischofs Theophylaktos von Achrida* (Munich, 1937), p. 37.

[99] Bryennius, pp. 327–9; Xanalatos, *Beiträge*, pp. 40–1.

[100] Antoniadis-Bibicou, 'Démographie, salaires et prix à Byzance au XIᵉ siècle', pp. 221–2.   [101] See above, p. 59.

62   *Economic expansion in the Byzantine empire*

economy worked to the advantage of a powerful landowner at the expense of the peasant community.[102]

As new land was brought into cultivation, disputes arose over landownership because boundaries had not been clearly defined or in some cases were flagrantly ignored. The *paroikoi* of the *metochion* of St Andrew at Peristerai brought into cultivation land which was claimed by the inhabitants of the *kastron* Adrameri. After the latter had resisted pressure from the monks to renounce their claims, a compromise was arranged and the inhabitants of the *kastron* received a pound of gold in compensation for the land. Although the community was strong enough to resist the encroachments of the monastery, it probably had fewer resources than the monastery to bring large tracts of new land under the plough rapidly. It was better off in the short term receiving the cash payment, but in the long term was weakened by the encroachment on its land.[103]

Lavra and Iviron clashed over property at Kamena near Hierissos. It belonged to Lavra, but had been usurped and brought under cultivation by Iviron. Two neighbouring peasants had alienated their land to Iviron. Then the monastery encroached upon Lavra's land and destroyed the old boundary marks. A new *periorismos* was made in 1071 to safeguard Lavra's lands.[104]

In the mid twelfth century Lavra had to defend its estate, Archontochorion, against infringements by *paroikoi* who belonged to *stratiotai* holding a neighbouring property as a *pronoia*. In 1162 an enquiry by the *doux* of Thessalonike found that *paroikoi* were installed inside the boundaries of the monks' land. A river ran between the two estates; the monks' property was to the west, that of the *stratiotai* to the east. The installation of the *paroikoi* had taken place earlier in the century. Lavra had granted previous holders of the *pronoia* land near the river on the west bank to be cultivated by their *paroikoi*. The monks had imposed two conditions on the lease. The grant was restricted to the life-time of the *stratiotai* with whom the transaction was made and the *paroikoi* were not allowed to build houses on the west bank. The second condition had been broken. When the land was restored to Lavra, the *paroikoi* were obliged to transfer their houses to the other side of the river.[105]

---

[102] J. Lefort, 'En Macédoine orientale au Xe siècle: habitat rural, communes et domaines', in *Actes du IXe congrès de la société des historiens mediévalistes de l'enseignement supérieur public, Dijon 1978* (Paris, 1979), pp. 251–72.   [103] *Lavra*, I, no. 37.

[104] *Ibid.*, no. 35. For another case on Athos, see Dölger, *Schatzkammern*, no. 104.

[105] *Lavra*, I, no. 64.

Demographic increase led to the creation of quite small peasant holdings in some regions. In 1089 a *metochion* (dependent monastery) of Xenophon in Kalamaria had 300 *modioi* of land, in which nine peasant families were established, an average of only thirty-three *modioi* each.[106] In the region of Thebes a rough indication of the size of many familial holdings can be obtained by hypothetical calculations based on the tax-register. The tax-register simply lists the owners of the land and does not give the size of the peasant holdings, but the tax-payments can provide rough approximations. It will be assumed that the rate of *epibole* (the equation between the surface area and the amount of tax) averaged 150 *modioi* for each *nomisma* in tax-payments in the region covered by the tax-register.[107] The major problem with this approach is that some entries involve more than one *stasis* (peasant holding) and others only a part of a *stasis*. Where several landowners had a share in the ownership of a peasant holding, the small tax-payments imposed on each of them could give a misleading impression of the size of the property.[108] However, this is not a serious difficulty because the majority of entries involve more than one peasant holding. Consequently, in most cases the tax-payment exaggerates the size of the peasant holdings.[109] As most entries include a complete *stasis*, the breakdown of tax-payments, excluding the relief granted by *sympatheiai*, accurately reflects economic stratification among the direct producers. In the Theban region there was a handful of large peasant holdings. Only two entries involved payments of two *nomismata*,[110] six had payments over one *nomisma* and a few others payments between a half and one *nomisma*.[111] The number of small holdings was much greater. Thirty-one entries had a payment of less than $\frac{1}{2}$ *nomisma*. In eighteen of these cases, it was less than $\frac{1}{4}$ *nomisma*, although thirteen included at

---

[106] *Xénophon*, no. 1 lines 222–3. For other figures, see the discussion above, p. 50.

[107] For the imposition of this rate on land of second quality, see *Esphigménou*, no. 5. For good-quality land the rate of taxation was higher; see *Lavra* I, no. 44, which involves a rate of *epibole* of about 75 *modioi* to the *nomisma*. Both documents are of the late eleventh century, about the time of the final revision of the tax-register. The extremely low rate of payment on Lavra's estates has no relevance to this question because the monastery was exceptionally privileged; see *Lavra*, I, no. 58. The following argument is derived from Harvey, 'Economic Expansion in Central Greece', pp. 26–7.

[108] Svoronos, 'Recherches sur le cadastre byzantin', p. 14 lines 68–77.

[109] *Ibid.*, pp. 17–18 lines 39–60, involve entries which all contain more than one complete *stasis*. Consequently, the tax-payment gives an exaggerated impression of their size; yet in all six cases the payment was less than $\frac{1}{4}$ *nomisma*.

[110] *Ibid.*, p. 11 lines 1–2, 12–13.

[111] *Ibid.*, pp. 11–19. Using Svoronos's notation, the relevant entries are 1c1, 2c1, 4a1, 5b1, 5f1, 5f11, which all paid at least one *nomisma*, and 2d1, 5e1, 5f12, 6a1, which all paid $\frac{1}{2}$ *nomisma* or more.

64   Economic expansion in the Byzantine empire

least one whole *stasis*. Using the hypothetical rate of *epibole*, a payment of $\frac{1}{4}$ *nomisma* can be equated with 37 *modioi* (about 7 to 8 acres). Several properties were much smaller. That of Nicolas the *ptochos*, with a payment of $\frac{5}{48}$ *nomisma*, could not have been more than 3.5 acres.[112] However, this calculation does not take into account the supplementary taxes, which were not incorporated into the rate of *epibole*, but were added to form the total tax-payment recorded in the tax-register.[113] Therefore the calculations tend to overestimate the size of peasant holdings. Although the variation in their size was considerable, only a few were substantial and there was a significant stratum of small holdings by the late eleventh century. Possibly, many peasants were living near the subsistence level, but our evidence is insufficiently precise for firm conclusions to be drawn.

The initiative behind the extension of the area under cultivation probably came from the peasantry rather than the landowner in most cases. The latter merely reacted to the increase in the number of peasant households by seeking new privileges from the state to protect himself from the claims of fiscal officials. The intermittent grants to landowners of *paroikoi*, who were unknown to the treasury, were often merely a formal reflection of a slow, long-drawn-out process of expansion. This was especially true in those cases where the state restricted the terms of the grants to descendants of *paroikoi* who were already installed on the landowner's property. These instances contrast sharply with the more spectacular, but less typical examples of large-scale colonisation projects which were undertaken in less densely populated regions by large landowners.

The sources inform us only of the projects instigated by Boilas and Pakourianos. Boilas brought an extensive area under cultivation on the eastern border in the 1050s. When he arrived there, the land was heavily wooded and inhospitable. It was reduced by fire and axe and two estates (*proasteia*), seven villages and another property, Bouzina, were created.[114] Boilas's example cannot be used as evidence of a general trend owing to the special circumstances in which he settled in

---

[112] *Ibid.*, p. 18 lines 66–70.

[113] For the various supplementary charges, see *ibid.*, pp. 81–3. See also Dölger, *Beiträge*, pp. 59–60; and below, p. 97.

[114] Lemerle, *Cinq études*, pp. 22–3, 59. The area in which Boilas settled is uncertain. S. Vryonis, 'The Will of a Provincial Magnate, Eustathius Boilas (1059)', *Dumbarton Oaks Papers*, 11 (1957), pp. 275–6, suggests the district of Taiq in the theme of Iberia. Lemerle, *Cinq études*, pp. 44–7, believes the estates were located in the region of Edessa, but see Kazhdan, 'Remarques sur le XIe siècle byzantin', pp. 492–6.

the east as a political exile. It does, however, show the impact which a large landowner with some resources could have on the economy of a locality in just a few years. Boilas's resources were limited in comparison with those of Gregory Pakourianos, who undertook a more impressive colonisation programme in Bulgaria in the late eleventh century. His patrimonial property had been in the east, but it had been lost owing to the Turkish advance in Asia Minor. He moved to the west with the great advantage of imperial favour. He build new *kastra* and monasteries and created new villages. The details of his activities are largely unknown because the *typikon* lists only the bare subject matter of the privileges which he received, but the text does show that two *kastra* were constructed in the village of Stenimachos. Unfortunately, there are no details about the most interesting aspect of Pakourianos's activities, the creation of new villages.[115] Possibly, other landowners who moved from Asia Minor to the European provinces at this time also engaged in similar activities in other regions. It is particularly significant that Pakourianos's work of colonisation took place at exactly the time when, according to some historians, stagnation set in in the rural economy.[116]

There are also instances of the colonisation of previously thinly populated regions by monastic communities. On Athos over two dozen monasteries had been founded by the end of the tenth century.[117] By 1045 Lavra alone contained over 700 monks.[118] Other monastic centres were established on mount Galesios by Lazaros,[119] in Boiotia by

[115] Gautier, 'Grégoire Pakourianos', pp. 35–7, 127 lines 1796–1800.
[116] Svoronos, 'Remarques sur les structures économiques', pp. 62–3. See also the cautious remarks of Lemerle, *Cinq études*, pp. 310–11. It has been suggested by H. Antoniadis-Bibicou, 'Villages désertés en Grèce: un bilan provisoire', in *Villages désertés et histoire économique, XIᵉ–XVIIIᵉ siècles* (Paris, 1965), pp. 343–417 (especially p. 364, where she gives figures for the numbers of deserted villages in Greece in successive centuries), that the eleventh century was notable for the desertion of large numbers of villages, reflecting a downward demographic trend. The methodology of this work is suspect. Nowhere does the author state how she obtained her figures. Until she offers convincing evidence to substantiate her claims, it is best to ignore them. She has repeated her argument more recently in 'Mouvement de la population et villages désertés: quelques remarques de méthode', in *Actes du XVᵉ congrès international d'études byzantines, Athènes – septembre 1976, IV, Histoire. Communications* (Athens, 1980), pp. 19–27, where she makes a simplistic and uncritical link between the development of feudal social relations and the abandonment of villages, an assumption which also is not supported by solid evidence.
[117] *Prôtaton*, pp. 86–93.
[118] *Ibid.*, no. 8 lines 93–4. It is not clear whether this figure included the monks in Lavra's *metochia* outside the peninsula.
[119] R. Janin, *Les Églises et les monastères des grands centres byzantins* (Paris, 1975), pp. 241–5.

66 Economic expansion in the Byzantine empire

Meletios,[120] and on Patmos by Christodoulos. The latter is a good illustration of the process. In the *praktikon* of 1088 the island was described as completely deserted, covered in bushes, inaccessible, and very dry owing to an inadequate water-supply. Of the 627 *modioi* which were considered suitable for arable cultivation, only 160 *modioi* could be brought under the plough immediately. The rest needed clearing with pickaxes and hoes. Before Christodoulos's death, in 1093, twelve peasant holdings had been installed on Patmos.[121] Expansion favoured the larger monasteries at the expense of the smaller. Many new monasteries were established with inadequate resources to maintain their property, which fell into disuse. They were often attributed to wealthy institutions, which had the resources to bring land into productive use. The cases of monasteries which fell on bad times are indicative of short-term fluctuations within the general trend of economic expansion which accentuated the inequalities between wealthy and small monasteries.[122]

Regional variations in the demographic trend are difficult to discern. By the eleventh century settlement was probably denser in coastal regions which had long been under Byzantine control (but even here there was still room for further expansion). Pakourianos's activities suggest that some parts of Bulgaria still had room for extensive colonisation in the late eleventh century. Other significant variations in the density of settlement and the chronology of population increase are probably concealed by the deficiency of the source material, but the general trend in the European provinces in these centuries is one of expansion.[123]

---

[120] Vasilievskij, 'Meletios', pp. 15, 17–18, 48.

[121] *Engrapha Patmou*, II, nos. 51, 54; P. Karlin-Hayter, 'Notes sur les archives de Patmos comme source pour la démographie et l'économie de l'île', *Byzantinische Forschungen*, 5 (1977), pp. 189–215, esp. 190–2, 198–201.

[122] *JGR*, I, pp. 249–52. For specific instances of Lavra's acquisition of impoverished monasteries, see *Lavra*, I, nos. 8, 10, 11, 12, 61, 62; Lemerle, *The Agrarian History*, pp. 108–14; Charanis, 'The Monastic Properties and the State', pp. 55f; and I. M. Konidares, *To dikaion tes monasteriakes periousias apo tou 9ou mechri tou 12ou aiona* (Athens, 1979), pp. 136–7. See also Basil II's comments on monasteries and *eukteria* (oratories) established by peasants and their appropriation by bishops (*JGR*, I, pp. 267–9). An alternative method of dealing with the same problem was to grant ailing monasteries to a *charistikarios* who was able to restore their fortunes; see H. Ahrweiler, 'Charisticariat et les autres formes d'attribution de fondations pieuses aux Xe–XIe siècles', *Zbornik Radova Vizantološkog Instituta*, 10 (1967), pp. 1–27; P. Lemerle, 'Un aspect du rôle des monastères à Byzance: les monastères donnés à des laïcs, les charisticaires', *Comptes-rendus des séances de l'Académie des Inscriptions et Belles-Lettres* (1967), pp. 9–28; and Weiss, *Oströmische Beamte*, pp. 145–52.

[123] Much useful information about settlement patterns may eventually be obtained from archaeological surveys in areas about which little is known at present. Recent work

Demographic growth and social relations

The most important contrast was between Asia Minor and Europe. The estates around Miletos which Andronikos Doukas received in 1073 were not so effectively exploited,[124] but owing to lack of comparable evidence at other times it is not known whether this was a temporary or a more permanent situation. Given the dearth of reliable archive evidence from Asia Minor before the thirteenth century, the main outline depends on the historians of the period. The most important river valleys of western Asia Minor were regularly raided from the late eleventh century. Further inland the areas which were most frequently fought over became depopulated. The insecurity provoked by the situation, particularly the abandonment of land and the flight to safer areas, probably had more serious repercussions than the physical damage inflicted by the Turks. Repopulation of the countryside in some more badly affected areas took place only after the Komnenian emperors built extensive fortifications in rural areas. The restitution of order in western Asia Minor enabled the demographic trend to resume its upward course after the setbacks of the late eleventh and early twelfth centuries and it reached its peak in the thirteenth century.[125]

Demographic expansion was accompanied by the reduction of a larger proportion of the population to the status of *paroikoi*. The state and the landowning aristocracy divided up the spoils from the increase in rural manpower and the extension of the area under cultivation. The state had always been the largest landowner, but in the eleventh century it concentrated more heavily on exploiting land with its own *demosiakoi paroikoi*. Much of the land recovered in the tenth century in the south and east of Anatolia was retained under the state's direct administration.[126] The new *sekreton epi ton oikeiakon* appears in the sources in 1030. Its creation may have been connected to the exploitation of the lands confiscated by Basil II or reclaimed by the

---

in the lower catchment of the Ayiofarango valley in Crete concludes that there is no archaeological evidence for settlement there between the middle of the seventh century and the end of the twelfth century, but qualifies this by suggesting that the present ignorance of coarse pottery used in Crete might conceal some eleventh- and twelfth-century occupation of the valley; see Blackman and Branigan, 'An Archaeological Survey of the Lower Catchment of the Ayiofarango Valley', pp. 77–8.

[124] Lemerle, *The Agrarian History*, pp. 209–11; M. Angold, *The Byzantine Empire 1025–1204. A Political History* (London, 1984), p. 65.

[125] Elsewhere recovery was not so successfully effected. The fertile agricultural hinterland of Attaleia was so unsafe that the town had to import its grain supply. For a comprehensive account of the impact of the Turkish invasions, see Vryonis, *The Decline of Medieval Hellenism*, pp. 143–84, 216–23. For the agricultural prosperity of the western coastal region in the thirteenth century, see Angold, *A Byzantine Government in Exile*, pp. 103–4.

[126] Hendy, *Studies in the Byzantine Monetary Economy*, p. 104.

68   Economic expansion in the Byzantine empire

treasury in accordance with his legislation. Land was also allocated to new *euageis oikoi* (religious houses) under the state's control. After these institutions had met their obligations, the surplus revenues from their lands were at the disposal of the state. In some cases these revenues were alienated, but usually only for a brief period. These institutions were another mechanism by which the state organised the exploitation of its properties.[127]

For a long time a balance was maintained between the divergent interests of the state and feudal landowners. The state maintained this balance by permitting landowners to install only landless peasants as *paroikoi* on their estates. In this way the financial interests of the state were not impaired. It usually retained its claim to the *demosion* (land-tax) even in cases where the landowner received a complete exemption from other charges.[128]

Some significant developments occurred in the 1070s and 1080s. Powerful landowners were able to exploit the debasement of the coinage to make tax-payments which in real terms were less than their theoretical obligations.[129] Confronted by a grave political and military crisis, the state had to make more extensive concessions to the aristocracy, whose support it desperately needed. The chrysobulls issued in these decades were in general much more generous to landowners. Lands which had previously been owned by the state were transferred to private landowners with a greater regularity. The long-term consequence was to strengthen the economic position of the landowning elite at the state's expense.

One of the more spectacular examples was the grant to Andronikos Doukas of a group of properties which had previously belonged to the *episkepsis* of Alopekai. The revenues totalling 307 *nomismata* had previously been collected by the *sekreton ton euagon oikon*. Not long before, Doukas had also received the *episkepsis* of Miletos.[130] Pakouri-

---

[127] Oikonomides, 'L'évolution de l'organisation administrative', pp. 135–41. See also Lemerle, *Cinq études*, pp. 272–85; and Lefort, 'Une grande fortune foncière', pp. 733–4. For an instance of the state retaining control of klasmatic land and attributing it to an imperial *episkepsis*, see *Docheiariou*, no. 3 line 44.

[128] See the list of charges from which Lavra's properties were exempted by Nikephoros III (*Lavra*, I, no. 38 lines 28–52). For Lavra's payment of the *demosion*, see *ibid.*, no. 50. After Nea Mone received extensive privileges in 1044, it owed only the *demosion*; see *JGR*, I, p. 617.

[129] See below, p. 90.

[130] *Engrapha Patmou*, II, no. 50; Svoronos, 'Remarques sur les structures économiques', pp. 54–6 n. 25; Ostrogorsky, *Pour l'histoire de la féodalite byzantine*, pp. 302–10. The

Demographic growth and social relations 69

anos, too, received extensive privileges. An imperial *pittakion* granted a *logisimon* giving him the right to take all the taxes from his properties.[131] Attaleiates received a less extensive privilege which limited his tax-payment to the amount he was already paying when he received his chrysobull from Michael VII.[132]

Extensive privileges were given not only to major aristocratic figures like Doukas and Pakourianos, but also on a smaller scale to lesser magnates like Leo Kephalas. He did not own a substantial patrimony, but acquired his lands by imperial donation owing to his military achievements. Only one of his four estates had a tax-payment incumbent on it.[133] In the other cases the state sacrificed all the revenues. For example, the estate Ano was detached from the *episkepsis* of Macedonia and the fiscal revenues of Chostiane, which had been collected by the provincial administration of Moglena, were removed from the records of the theme by a *logisimon*.[134]

The tax-payments of two properties in Kos which Christodoulos received were completely abolished.[135] Later, when he conceded all his properties on the island to the state in exchange for Patmos, that island was completely exempted from all obligations to the state, including the land-tax.[136] The state also conceded to Christodoulos its claims to the fiscal revenues from the properties of Parthenion and Temenia on Leros and the small island of Leipso.[137]

The most generous fiscal privileges which Alexios I conceded were issued mainly in the first part of his reign when the state's authority was temporarily undermined by political and military crises. They became much less common after Alexios had firmly reestablished imperial

figure for the total revenues is suspect, but the gaps in the text made it difficult to assess the accuracy of the arithmetic in the document. For the *episkepsis*, see Dölger, *Beiträge*, pp. 151–2. See also Lemerle, *The Agrarian History*, pp. 209–11; and Hendy, *Studies in the Byzantine Monetary Economy*, pp. 133–4, who links the *episkepsis* of Miletos and Alopekai with those of Sampson and Ta Malachiou, which were in the possession of the Kontostephanos and Kamitzes families in 1204.

[131] Gautier, 'Grégoire Pakourianos', p. 129 line 1820; Lemerle, *Cinq études*, pp. 181–3.
[132] Gautier, 'La diataxis de Michel Attaliate', pp. 103–5.
[133] *Lavra*, I, no. 44.
[134] *Lavra*, I, nos. 48, 49. The other estate which Kephalas received had only recently come into the state's possession through confiscation; see *ibid.*, no. 45; and Lemerle, *The Agrarian History*, p. 208.
[135] *Engrapha Patmou*, I, no. 4.
[136] *Ibid.*, no. 6.
[137] *Engrapha Patmou*, II, no. 52; Karlin-Hayter, 'Notes sur les archives de Patmos', pp. 203–4.

70   Economic expansion in the Byzantine empire

authority.[138] Alexios's generosity was restricted to a fairly narrow circle. His rule was notable for the way in which he advanced the interests of members of the imperial family and a small group of related families at the expense of other sections of the aristocracy. In particular, he was very harsh in his treatment of the senatorial aristocracy, which was excluded from the most important titles and offices.[139]

The most extensive concessions of fiscal revenues were made early in the reign to close relatives. The state's claim to the land-tax in the peninsula of Kassandra was transferred to the emperor's brother Adrian and the revenues were collected by Adrian's own men, the most far-reaching form of *logisimon*.[140] Another brother, Isaac, also received the same type of *logisimon*. The extent of the area whose revenues were alienated is not known, but it was in the region of Thessalonike.[141] Some of the revenues which were conceded to Isaac came from land which had been in the possession of Iviron until it was confiscated by the state.[142] John Doukas and Nikephoros Melissenos also gained from the confiscation of Iviron's land.[143] These privileges were of a great significance because they were part of the policy of concentrating power increasingly in the hands of members of the imperial family and a few related families. The Komnenoi did this more thoroughly than previous emperors – a new stage in the conflict between the centralised state and the feudal tendencies which were becoming more clearly developed. The empire itself was in the process of being transformed into a familial institution. This became more clearly marked in later centuries, but under the Komnenoi the move in this direction acquired strong momentum. The weaknesses which were introduced into the apparatus

---

[138] An exception was the fiscal concession to Lavra in 1109 (*Lavra*, I, no. 58), but this was the culmination of a lengthy series of enquiries dating back to the late eleventh century; see below, p. 100. It is striking how little archive material granting fiscal privileges to landowners survives from the first half of the twelfth century compared with the second half of the eleventh century, another indication that the central government was more firmly in control.

[139] For Alexios's hostility to the senate, see Zonaras, III, pp. 729, 766; Lemerle, *Cinq études*, pp. 309–10; and Hendy, *Studies in the Byzantine Monetary Economy*, pp. 583–5.

[140] *Lavra*, I, no. 46. For the different types of *logisima*, see Dölger, *Beiträge*, pp. 117–18. See also Lemerle, *The Agrarian History*, pp. 211–12.

[141] *Lavra*, I, no. 51.

[142] The land which Iviron lost totalled 1,300 hectares. The confiscation probably occurred in two stages, firstly before 1095 and secondly before 1101; see Lefort, 'Une grande fortune foncière', p. 735. It would be surprising if the first confiscation occurred before 1086 when Gregory Pakourianos was still alive. It is unlikely that Alexios would have risked offending such an important supporter of his rule.

[143] Lefort, 'Une grande fortune foncière', p. 738.

Demographic growth and social relations 71

of the bureaucratic state became apparent in the late twelfth century, but for a long time they were concealed by the power and prestige of the Komnenoi rulers.[144]

By the eleventh and twelfth centuries the scale of landownership had become quite impressive. The properties of large landowners consisted of entire villages and estates. Pakourianos owned numerous villages and estates around Philippoupolis and Mosynoupolis.[145] The properties which Isaac Komnenos attributed to Kosmosotira were even more extensive, naturally enough for a member of the imperial family. The estates and villages numbered more than thirty.[146] Attaleiates' properties were fewer. He was not a particularly illustrious member of the aristocracy and did not inherit a large patrimonial property. As a result of the gains he made from service in the imperial bureaucracy, he acquired several estates. Five estates in Thrace were bequeathed to his poor-house and some others to his son.[147]

We are better informed about the estates of large monastic centres. The nucleus of Nea Mone's wealth was the property Kalothekia, which it had purchased for sixty pounds. It also received a large klasmatic property and a *chorion* in the same locality. The combined fiscal obligations of the latter properties had been forty-five *nomismata* and their extent can be estimated very approximately at 7,000 *modioi*, but the extent of the original purchase is unknown.[148] The monastery of Euergetes owned an estate *tou Theophanous* in the theme of Boleron with twelve peasants with ploughteams and another estate with sixteen peasants with ploughteams.[149]

Lavra's estates extended to over 47,000 *modioi* by the late eleventh century.[150] The only monastery on Athos which could rival it was

---

[144] See the list of such grants in Hendy, *Studies in the Byzantine Monetary Economy*, pp. 87–9. To this should be added the evidence in Lefort, 'Une grande fortune foncière', p. 738, who also emphasises the administrative functions performed by the agents of the beneficiaries of these grants. See also the summary of Kazhdan's work in Sorlin, 'Publications soviétiques sur le XIe siècle', p. 378; Oikonomides, 'L'évolution de l'organisation administrative', p. 128; and N. Oikonomides, 'Hoi authentai ton Kretikon to 1118', in *Pepragmena tou IV Diethnous Kretologikou Synedriou*, II, *Byzantinoi kai mesoi chronoi* (Athens, 1981), pp. 308–17.

[145] Gautier, 'Grégoire Pakourianos' pp. 35–7, 127–31.

[146] Petit, 'Kosmosotira', pp. 52–3.

[147] Gautier, 'La diataxis de Michel Attaliate', pp. 43–7; Lemerle, *Cinq études*, p. 102.

[148] *JGR*, I, p. 616. For the location of these lands, see Ahrweiler, 'L'histoire et la géographie de la région de Smyrne', pp. 65, 68, 100.

[149] P. Gautier, 'Le typikon de la Théotokos Évergétis', *Revue des Études Byzantines*, 40 (1982), p. 93.

[150] *Lavra*, I, nos. 50, 52.

72   Economic expansion in the Byzantine empire

Iviron, which owned twenty-six large properties in 1079, some of them *metochia* with extensive lands.[151] The Amalfitan monastery had large resources owing to its connection with the Amalfitan community in Constantinople. It had properties to the east of the Strymon, including an estate, Platanos, which it purchased for twenty-four pounds in 1081.[152] In 1089 Xenophon owned several *metochia*; three of its properties alone consisted of 2,300 *modioi*.[153] Vatopedi's lands may have been less extensive; in 1080 it owned five *proasteia*.[154]

Another form of privilege on a smaller scale was the *pronoia*.[155] Its essential feature was the attribution of fiscal revenues by the state to soldiers. It has been debated whether this included rights of ownership of the land,[156] but one of the most important features of the *pronoia* at this time was that it was not alienable by the recipient of the privilege. The institution evolved out of earlier procedures assigning fiscal revenues to landowners. The use of the term *pronoia* in the sources to describe the attribution of the Mangana to Leichoudes or the Hebdomon to Nikephoritzes, when both were actually *charistikia*, shows that the term had not acquired its technical meaning at this stage.[157] It did so in

---

[151] Dölger, *Schatzkammern*, no. 35 lines 61–79. The surface area of these properties extended to about 4,500 hectares. The subsequent confiscation of about 1,300 hectares was partly compensated for by the acquisition of the village of Radolibos; see Lefort, 'Une grande fortune foncière', pp. 728, 735–6.

[152] *Lavra*, I, nos. 42, 43; P. Lemerle, 'Les archives du monastère des Amalfitains au Mont Athos', *Epeteris Hetaireias Byzantinon Spoudon*, 23 (1953), pp. 548–66.

[153] *Xénophon*, p. 25 lines 213–28. The correct date of 1089 was pointed out by A. Hohlweg, 'Zur Frage der Pronoia in Byzanz', *Byzantinische Zeitschrift*, 60 (1967), p. 298 n. 55.

[154] Goudas, 'Vatopedi', p. 121.

[155] The fundamental studies are Ostrogorsky, *Pour l'histoire de la féodalité byzantine*, pp. 9–54; and Lemerle, *The Agrarian History*, pp. 222–41. See also H. Ahrweiler, *Byzance et la mer* (Paris, 1966), pp. 214–22; Hohlweg, 'Zur Frage der Pronoia in Byzanz', pp. 288–308; and G. Ostrogorsky, 'Die Pronoia unter den Komnenen', *Zbornik Radova Vizantološkog Instituta*, 12 (1970), pp. 41–54. The technical procedures involved in the grant of the *pronoia* in this period are not clearly elucidated in the sources. The information from the later period is clearer; see N. Oikonomides, 'Contribution à l'étude de la pronoia au XIIIᵉ siècle. Une formule d'attribution de parèques à un pronoiare', *Revue des Études Byzantines*, 22 (1964), pp. 158–75; and P. Magdalino, 'An Unpublished Pronoia Grant of the Second Half of the Fourteenth Century', *Zbornik Radova Vizantološkog Instituta*, 18 (1978), pp. 155–63.

[156] Ahrweiler, *Byzance et la mer*, p. 220 n. 3; H. Ahrweiler, 'La concession des droits incorporels. Donations conditionelles', in *Actes du XIIᵉ congrès international des études byzantines* (3 vols., Belgrade, 1964), II, pp. 110–12; Ostrogorsky, *Pour l'histoire de la féodalité byzantine*, p. 30.

[157] Lemerle, *Cinq études*, pp. 280–2; Ostrogorsky, 'Die Pronoia unter den Komnenen', pp. 42–3. For the variety of ways in which the word was used, see H. Ahrweiler, 'La "pronoia" à Byzance', in *Structures féodales et féodalisme dans l'Occident méditerranéen*

Demographic growth and social relations

the twelfth century. Nevertheless, the *pronoia* holders were not of great importance in the social structure of Byzantium at this time. Their grants were small by comparison with the privileges which had been issued to aristocratic landowners in the eleventh century and had not yet become hereditary.

The earliest grant of a *pronoia* in the sources involved a *proasteion*, Archontochorion, which three *stratiotai*, Andreas Romanos Rentinos and the brothers Theotimos and Leo Loukites, had probably received by December 1118 or 1119.[158] Another early grant of a *pronoia* had been made to an unknown member of the Synadenos family who was dead by 1136.[159] According to Choniates, Manuel was responsible for a great extension of the institution.[160] The archive material is too inadequate to test this assertion thoroughly, but it seems that land from imperial estates on Crete was assigned to soldiers as *pronoia*.[161] By 1181 a number of *pronoiai* had been established in the theme of Moglena for Kouman soldiers. At first, *paroikoi* in the village of Chostiane were attributed to six soldiers, but after Lavra claimed that they belonged to the monastery the Koumans were assigned other *paroikoi* on state land.[162] The state resorted to this system as an alternative to hiring mercenaries, but its application in the Komnenian period was not on a large enough scale to justify the great claims made by Ostrogorsky.[163]

Discussion has concentrated on the larger units of landownership because of the bias of the source material, which contains numerous instances of the grant of a village or a large estate to an individual

(*X–XIIIᵉ siècles*). *Bilan et perspectives de recherches* (Collection de l'École Française de Rome 44) (Rome, 1980), pp. 681–9. Angold, *The Byzantine Empire 1025–1204*, p. 126, has linked the grants of fiscal revenues by Alexios I to members of the imperial family with the twelfth-century grants of *pronoia* to soldiers. While both involve the transfer of fiscal revenues from the state to individuals and therefore have similarities, the scale and purpose of these grants was so different that they are best regarded as distinct phenomena for the purposes of a socio-economic analysis.

[158] *Lavra*, I, no. 64. For the date see, *ibid.*, p. 330.
[159] Gautier, 'Pantocrator', p. 117 lines 1473–4. The monastery also received three *estrateumena choria*; see *ibid.*, p. 117 lines 1476–7, p. 119 line 1493. These were probably in the possession of soldiers with fiscal or military responsibilities to the monastery. For a similar case involving two *choria* belonging to Isaac Komnenos where the *stratiotai* were *hypoteleis* (subject to fiscal burdens), see Petit, 'Kosmosotira', p. 71. See also the comments of Ahrweiler, *Byzance et la mer*, p. 220 n. 3.
[160] Nicetas Choniates, p. 208.
[161] N. Oikonomides, 'He dianome ton basilikon episkepseon tes Kretes (1170–71) kai he demosionomike politike tou Manouel I Komnenou', in *Pepragmena tou III Diethnous Kretologikou Synedriou*, III (Athens, 1968), pp. 195–201.
[162] *Lavra*, I, nos. 65, 66 lines 18–23.
[163] Ostrogorsky, *History*, pp. 371–2, 392–4.

74 Economic expansion in the Byzantine empire

landowner or, less frequently, to a group of *stratiotai*. There is also evidence of a more complicated pattern of landownership, where small scattered plots of land were held by landowners who had acquired them by purchase, exchange, inheritance or lease, but not by imperial favour. A good example of a medium-size group of properties was that partitioned by three brothers in 1110. They were not comparable with the large landowners who have already been discussed, but their properties were scattered and it can safely be assumed that they relied on the labour of others to cultivate them. They owned mills, vines and seven fields at St Thomas, to the south-east of Thessalonike, and pasture land which continued to be exploited in common after the partition. They also had a vineyard at Glyka and a small field at Hagios Hermogenes and had previously held an estate, Pinsson, which had been claimed by the state.[164]

The material from the Athos archives does not reveal the extent to which such smaller landowners survived in the Chalkidike, although there are hints that they were quite numerous. We are better informed about Boiotia. Compared with the larger estates of Thrace and Macedonia, the local elite of the Theban region appears rather petty. The image of landowners with entire villages contrasts with that of the *archontes* of Thebes and Chalkis with their shared ownership of small peasant holdings which had been acquired piecemeal. Only a few families such as the Rendakioi were more important, but they did not compare with the great aristocratic families of the empire. It is possible, of course, that some landowners did possess larger properties in other parts of the region not covered by the tax-register. Also, we do not know the extent of state properties in the region. Nevertheless, the titles which the landowners in the tax-register held (several *protospatharioi*, *spatharioi*, *kometes*, *kandidatoi* and other titles which had become greatly debased by the eleventh century) suggest that these were individuals who had considerable importance locally but no further.[165]

Many landowners in the Theban tax-register are not known in any other sources.[166] Some of the alliances within this local elite are

---

[164] *Lavra*, I, no. 59. For the reversion of the *proasteion* to the state, see below, p. 101.

[165] For the titles, see Svoronos, 'Recherches sur le cadastre byzantin', pp. 67–8; Ostrogorsky, 'La commune rurale byzantine', pp. 159–60; and Lemerle, *The Agrarian History*, p. 198. For the Rendakioi, who probably had important properties in the Peloponnesos, see Svoronos, 'Recherches sur le cadastre byzantin', p. 75. For a hint of the existence of properties belonging to the state, see *ibid.*, p. 15 line 18.

[166] For the prosopography of the tax-register, see Svoronos, 'Recherches sur le cadastre byzantin', pp. 68–76.

Demographic growth and social relations 75

suggested by the groups which owned properties jointly. Some holdings had been in the possession of the Leobachoi and their associates. They were clearly an important family in the region. Theodore Leobachos was an abbot of Hosios Loukas, but nothing else is known of the family.[167]

Some important conclusions have been drawn by Svoronos from the tax-register. He rightly emphasises the continuity of fiscal techniques. Originally, he also claimed that 'la commune "libre", comprenant une bonne proportion de paysans indépendants, reste bien vivante'.[168] This was challenged by Ostrogorsky, who pointed out that free peasants were in the minority and the tax-payers were mostly members of the local elite.[169] Lemerle has asserted that 'the commune is still composed of land-owning or lease-holding, but independent, peasants'.[170] All these historians, even Ostrogorsky, have overestimated the number of tax-payers who were also peasant producers. Some entries which Svoronos cities as cases of independent peasants retaining control of their own land[171] do not support his claim. Independent producers are almost non-existent in the tax-register. In cases where there is no indication of the social status of the tax-payer at the time of the final revision of the register, the lists of previous tax-payers are instructive. They were invariably members of the local elite. It is extremely unlikely that land which had been in their possession came into the ownership of peasant producers. In one exceptional case this may have happened. Nicolas, the son of Andreas Troulos, was designated as a *ptochos*. His property had previously been owned by successive groups of the Leobachoi. It was very small and his tax-payment amounted to only $\frac{5}{48}$ *nomisma*.[172] As landholdings became fragmented, small parcels possibly reverted to peasant ownership in isolated instances. Generally, it is reasonable to assume that, where previous landowners were members of the local elite, the landowner at the time of the last revision of the tax-register was not a peasant producer, even if nothing is known about

---

[167] J. Nesbitt and J. Wiita, 'A Confraternity of the Comnenia Era', *Byzantinische Zeitschrift*, 68 (1975), pp. 372–4. This was not necessarily the same Theodore Leobachos whose name was registered in the tax-register.

[168] Svoronos, 'Recherches sur le cadastre byzantin', p. 145. The following argument is taken from Harvey, 'Economic Expansion in Central Greece', pp. 22–4.

[169] Ostrogorsky, 'La commune rurale byzantine', pp. 158–66. See also Svoronos, 'Société et organisation intérieure', pp. 375–7.

[170] Lemerle, *The Agrarian History*, p. 199.

[171] Svoronos, 'Recherches sur le cadastre byzantin', p. 142 n. 4. He also claims that most of the tax-payers holding land by *ekdosis* were probably direct cultivators; see *ibid.*, p. 142 n. 7.   [172] *Ibid.*, p. 18 lines 66–70.

76   Economic expansion in the Byzantine empire

him. Three of the entries, which Svoronos considers to refer to independent peasants, involve property which had previously belonged to the Leobachoi. Two of the landowners were George Kampos, who is said in the register to have lived in Thebes, and Nicolas Kampos, probably a relative.[173] Some of the other examples are also doubtful. Peter and Kosmas Anemosphaktes owned land in several different fiscal units and they could not have cultivated more than a part of their property themselves if any at all.[174] The tax-register cannot be used as evidence for the continued existence of independent peasant communities. The subordination of direct producers to powerful landowners in the Theban region had been almost entirely effected by the eleventh century.

In spite of the strict regional limits of the Theban tax-register it does reflect general trends in the rural economy. Ostrogorsky has even suggested that independent producers, such as those of the Farmer's Law and the Fiscal Treatise, ceased to exist and were reduced to the status of *paroikoi* of the state.[175] Certainly, a larger proportion of the rural population consisted of *paroikoi*, either of private landowners or of the state, but there is no reason to believe that peasants who owned their own land and paid taxes for it had their status arbitrarily changed by the state.[176] Such a change may have occurred imperceptibly over a period of time in instances where the tax-revenues of independent peasants were transferred by the state to a private landowner, especially if the landowner already had *paroikoi* in the same village.[177]

There are indications of independent communities acting collectively in some regions. The inhabitants of Hierissos and the neighbouring villages resisted the claims of the Athos monasteries to the klasmatic land outside Athos fairly successfully in the 940s.[178] The inhabitants of

[173] *Ibid.*, p. 15 lines 4–9, p. 16 lines 31–6, p. 17 lines 51–5.
[174] *Ibid.*, pp. 18–19 lines 72–85. Peter Anemosphaktes was the son of Kosmas Gerasdes. In the first entry of the register another Gerasdes appears as the previous owner of one of the most substantial properties in the register and was clearly a prominent local figure; see *ibid.*, p. 11 lines 1–2.   [175] Ostrogorsky, *Quelques problèmes*, pp. 21–2.
[176] R. Morris, 'The Byzantine Church and the Land in the Tenth and Eleventh Centuries' (unpublished D. Phil. thesis, Oxford, 1978), p. 217. Ostrogorsky has rightly been criticised for not establishing clearly how the free peasant of the Farmer's Law was different from the *paroikos* belonging to the state. See J. Karayannopulos, 'Ein Problem der spätbyzantinischen Agrargeschichte', *Jahrbuch der Österreichischen Byzantinistik*, 30 (1981), pp. 207–37.
[177] For the case of Radolibos, see Lefort, 'Une grande fortune foncière', p. 736.
[178] *Prôtaton*, nos. 4–6. The representatives of the villages also supported the Athonite protest against the usurpation made by Kolobou earlier in the century; see *ibid.*, no. 2 lines 25–31.

Adrameri acted collectively when the *paroikoi* of Lavra encroached upon their land.[179] A guarantee made by the villagers of Radochosta was probably typical of numerous others which have not survived.[180] In Crete the inhabitants of the village of Menikon were able to obtain compensation for an infringement of their water-rights by Achillios Limenites, but it is significant that it took them seventeen years to do so.[181] The evidence in these cases is not absolutely conclusive. It is possible that the peasants were *paroikoi* acting collectively to defend their interests, but the documents do not mention any landowner to whom they were obligated and it would be forcing the evidence too much to assume that independent peasants had completely disappeared. The source material has another serious deficiency. It shows the villagers acting collectively, but it does not reveal the extent to which the trend towards the concentration of property in fewer hands prevailed within these communities. There is a hint of perceptible differences in wealth between the peasants at Radochosta. They all assembled from 'small to great' to draw up the guarantee for the monks of Roudaba. Most probably such economic stratification was becoming more pronounced during this period.[182]

In the western coastal regions of Asia Minor independent peasants survived on a large scale into the thirteenth century, possibly because of the great natural fertility of the alluvial lands. Some peasant families in the neighbourhood of Smyrna had been quite prosperous before 1204. The fate of the peasantry after the establishment of the empire in Nicaea reflects an intensification on a local scale of trends which had affected the peasantry of most other regions at an earlier date. Peasants were increasingly subordinated to new landowners, who had moved into the region following the fall of Constantinople. More land was brought into cultivation during the period of Lascarid rule and the gains

---

[179] *Lavra*, I, no. 37.   [180] *Ibid.*, no. 14.

[181] MM, VI, pp. 95–9; Oikonomides, 'Hoi authentai ton Kretikon to 1118', pp. 308–9. Lemerle, *The Agrarian History*, pp. 202–7, gives this and some other instances of the survival of an independent peasantry. One of these examples concerns the provisions relating to the payment of the *kanonikon* to the bishop. This, he thinks, refers to the commune of free peasants, but there is nothing in the text of Isaac Komnenos's legislation (*JGR*, I, pp. 275–6) to confirm this. The payment could just as well have been exacted from a community of dependent peasants. In 1074 Lavra needed to obtain a chrysobull to protect itself from the bishop of Kassandra's claims to exact the *kanonikon* from peasants installed on Lavra's properties; see *Lavra*, I, no. 36 lines 18–22.

[182] *Lavra*, I, no. 14 line 10. For the intensification of differences in wealth in peasant communities, see above, p. 37.

78   *Economic expansion in the Byzantine empire*

of this expansion mainly benefited the state and those landowners to whom it granted extensive privileges.[183]

Considerable regional variations are apparent in the pattern of economic development. In Asia Minor large aristocratic families were most prominent in the themes of Cappadocia, Paphlagonia and, above all, the Anatolikon. These were the areas of extensive pastoral farming on the Anatolian plateau. In contrast there is less evidence of such properties in the themes of Thrakesion, Boukellarion, Optimaton and Opsikion.[184] In the European provinces there is most evidence for the existence of aristocratic estates in Macedonia and there were also some significant large properties in Thrace. In some cases these belonged to families which had originated in the east and settled in the west in the eleventh century.[185] Elsewhere the scale of landownership was smaller and it was more fragmented. In some places free peasant communities were still fairly numerous, but probably much more stratified in economic terms than in the earlier period. The intervention of the state was the crucial factor in the development of landownership in large consolidated units. It conceded its claims on entire villages and estates to individual landowners. Where it did not make concessions on such a scale, as in the region covered by the Theban tax-register, the accumulation of property by feudal landowners occurred in a more piecemeal way, leading to a less consolidated pattern of landownership.

The development of the economic power of feudal landowners was a long process. It relied on the state to a great extent because of the rewards which were obtained from service to the state. The expansion of large properties occurred partly at the expense of peasant smallholders and was partly the result of an increase in population. The effect of sustained demographic growth on the revenues of both the state and feudal magnates must have been immense. Although it is not possible to propose a rate of increase with any accuracy, it is certain that the growth of population in this period was substantial. For instance, an average annual rate of increase of seven for every thousand would have doubled the population in a hundred years.[186]

---

[183] Angold, *A Byzantine Government in Exile*, pp. 102–4, 131–2; H. Ahrweiler, 'La politique agraire des empereurs de Nicée', *Byzantion*, 28 (1958), pp. 51–66, 135–6.

[184] Hendy, *Studies in the Byzantine Monetary Economy*, pp. 100–8; Vryonis, *The Decline of Medieval Hellenism*, p. 25 n. 132. For ecclesiastical properties in the region of Smyrna before 1204, see Ahrweiler, 'La politique agraire des empereurs de Nicée', pp. 55–6.

[185] Hendy, *Studies in the Byzantine Monetary Economy*, pp. 85–90.

[186] F. Braudel, *The Mediterranean and the Mediterranean World in the Age of Philip II* (2 vols. London, 1972–3), I, p. 402.

Consequently, the revenues of both the state and other landowners increased at the same time. A larger proportion of the rural population became dependent producers, cultivating land which they rented from a large landowner or the state. The *morte* developed into a feudal rent and the legal status of the *paroikos* was clarified. A balance was maintained between the state and the feudal aristocracy until the late eleventh century. Although the Turkish incursions into Asia Minor deprived many powerful families of their properties, the state also lost its revenues from this region. In its desperate need for the support of the most influential individuals and institutions in Byzantium it made very extensive concessions of lands and fiscal privileges. In the remaining part of the empire the economic position of the aristocracy was greatly strengthened. Some families from Asia Minor, which benefited from imperial favour, were established in Europe with very extensive lands. The most serious weakening of imperial authority was the large concessions of the state's fiscal claims to members of the imperial family. Such grants had occurred previously, but the Komnenoi extended their scope greatly. The centrifugal tendencies, which were latent in the social structure, were imported into the top of the imperial hierarchy. Although Alexios restored imperial authority quite effectively after the upheavals of the 1070s and 1080s, the balance of economic power between the state and the aristocracy had changed. This was not immediately obvious owing to the authority and prestige of the Komnenoi rulers. The continuing population increase in the twelfth century helped to maintain the state's revenues, but it also strengthened the economic basis of the dominant political position of the aristocracy.

---------------------------------- Chapter 3 ----------------------------------

Taxation and monetary circulation

The structure of the rural economy imposed limitations on the vitality of monetary circulation. The main socio-economic unit, the holding of the peasant family, produced largely for its own consumption. It engaged in commercial activity only insofar as it was constrained to do so by the fiscal pressures of the state. Part of its produce had to be alienated to raise the cash for its tax-payment. This could be done by recourse to urban markets or a direct, compulsory sale of produce to the state at rates determined by the latter. When independent peasant farmers formed a significant proportion of the rural population, commercial activity was sluggish. As variations in wealth inside village communities became greater and the properties of powerful landowners more extensive, commercial activity was intensified because of the greater resources available to these property owners.

The circulation of coinage was determined largely by the interests of the state. It issued money to make its necessary expenditure, which was predominantly military and administrative.[1] Consequently, the amount of money in circulation might vary greatly in different areas. Large quantities of money might be expected in important administrative centres, towns of strategic importance and the markets which armies used as they went on campaign. Most of the gold coinage, which was distributed in this way, returned to the treasury through tax-collections. The state required gold for most of its expenses and was not interested very much in the lower-value denominations, but these were more useful for most commercial transactions. In cases where peasant producers did not have the necessary gold coinage, they probably obtained it in exchange for their lower-value coins from wealthier

---

[1] This is a recurring theme of Hendy, *Studies in the Byzantine Monetary Economy*. See also M. Crawford, 'Money and Exchange in the Roman World', *Journal of Roman Studies*, 60 (1970), pp. 40–8; and Haldon and Kennedy, 'The Arab–Byzantine Frontier', p. 89.

Taxation and monetary circulation 81

landowners in the same fiscal unit or possibly from officials making the tax-collection. In either case they probably had to pay an unfavourable rate of exchange. The fiscal procedure provided an important mechanism for putting lower-value coinage into circulation. Before the Alexian taxation reform one gold *nomisma* was exacted when the obligation reached two-thirds of a *nomisma* and the change was given in silver or copper coinage.[2]

In addition to its main function of meeting the state's expenditure the gold coinage served other purposes. It was an ideal standard for accounting owing to its consistency of fineness, which it retained until the eleventh century.[3] Coinage was also the expression of the sovereign power of the ruler; this applied to other denominations as well as the gold, but the latter as a high-value currency carried greater prestige.[4] It was also stored as treasure. In this function it was the equivalent of precious silks and non-monetised gold and silver.[5] Consequently, the gold coinage, which the state distributed through its own expenditure, either came back to the treasury very quickly in taxation or it remained as treasure outside the sphere of monetary circulation for a very long time. The copper coinage gives a better guide to the intensity of economic activity. It served the function of a circulating medium for most everyday transactions. After the state put it into circulation, it had no further interest in recovering it (unlike the gold currency) and consequently it was available to meet commercial requirements.[6]

[2] *JGR*, I, p. 328; M. F. Hendy, *Coinage and Money in the Byzantine Empire, 1081–1261* (Dumbarton Oaks, 1969), p. 51; Svoronos, 'Recherches sur le cadastre byzantin', pp. 83–9.

[3] Haldon and Kennedy, 'The Arab–Byzantine Frontier', p. 90 n. 39. For the use of the silver *milliaresion* as a unit of account for fiscal purposes in the period between the coinage and taxation reforms of Alexios, see Hendy, *Coinage and Money*, pp. 26, 53–5.

[4] Haldon and Kennedy, 'The Arab–Byzantine Frontier', p. 89; G. Duby, *The Early Growth of the European Economy. Warriors and Peasants from the Seventh to the Twelfth Century* (London, 1974), pp. 61–70. The silver *milliaresion* probably had a ceremonial character during the first century of its existence; see P. Grierson, *Catalogue of the Byzantine Coins in the Dumbarton Oaks Collection*, III, *Leo III to Nicephorus III 717–1081* (Dumbarton Oaks, 1973), part 1, p. 63.

[5] One of the features of the wealth of the widow Danielis was the large number of precious textiles which she possessed, as well as wealth in gold and silver coins; see Theophanes Continuatus, pp. 228, 318–21. Symbatios Pakourianos spent the fifty pounds of gold which he received as his wife's dowry on silver objects; see Iberites, 'Byzantinai diathekai', p. 615. Hendy, *Studies in the Byzantine Monetary Economy*, pp. 209, 218–20, emphasises that coinage generally made up only a limited part of aristocratic movable wealth.

[6] Ostrogorsky, 'Byzantine Cities', and S. Vryonis, 'An Attic Hoard of Byzantine Gold Coins (668–741) from the Thomas Whittemore Collection and the Numismatic Evidence for the Urban History of Byzantium', *Zbornik Radova Vizantološkog Instituta*,

82   *Economic expansion in the Byzantine empire*

Another important channel through which money was distributed was the gift. Large grants of cash were made out of fiscal revenues by emperors to favoured monasteries and landowners. These grants, known as *solemnia*, took various technical forms. In the case of the *logisimon solemnion* fiscal revenues were transferred directly from the tax-payer to the beneficiary without any intervention from the state. The *parechomenon solemnion* was paid by the *dioiketes* out of the fiscal revenues of his province.[7] If these grants in cash were not simply stored away as treasure, the money might have worked its way into the rural economy, when the recipients purchased provisions, made expenditure on buildings or, in the case of monasteries, made charitable distributions. The upsurge of monastic foundations in relatively inaccessible areas in the tenth and eleventh centuries had an important effect on economic conditions in these regions.[8] Imperial generosity was a mechanism by which more money reached places which otherwise would have been on the periphery of monetary circulation.

The most generous *solemnia* which are known from the surviving documents were granted to the Athonite monasteries. Nikephoros II added four pounds of gold to the three which the community as a whole was already receiving. In 1057 Michael VI added an annual payment of ten pounds.[9] Naturally, Lavra was extremely privileged. It received an annual payment of four pounds from Nikephoros II and Tzimiskes supplemented it with a *solemnion* for the same amount paid out of the revenues of Lemnos.[10] This was followed by an annual grant of ten pounds of silver by Basil II. In 1057 Michael VI confirmed the full amount of Lavra's grants from previous emperors at eight pounds and twenty *nomismata* and he added another three pounds.[11]

The *solemnia* which had been granted to Iviron and Vatopedi

8, part 1 (1963), pp. 291–300, exaggerate and misrepresent the importance of the gold coinage for a monetary economy; see M. F. Hendy, 'Byzantium 1081–1204: An Economic Reappraisal', *Transactions of the Royal Historical Society*, 5th series, 20 (1970), pp. 31–52. For the copper coinage in the late Roman period, see Jones, *The Later Roman Empire*, I, pp. 443–4; and A. H. M. Jones, 'Inflation under the Roman Empire', *Economic History Review*, 5 (1953), pp. 293–318, reprinted in A. H. M. Jones, *The Roman Economy. Studies in Ancient Economic and Administrative History*, ed. P. A. Brunt (Oxford, 1974), pp. 187–227, esp. p. 223.

[7] Dölger, *Beiträge*, pp. 117–18. See also Ostrogorsky, 'Die ländliche Steuergemeinde', pp. 71–3.

[8] On monastic foundations, see J. Darouzès, 'Le mouvement des fondations monastiques au XI* siècle', *Travaux et Mémoires*, 6 (1976), pp. 159–76.

[9] 'Vie d'Athanase', p. 47; *Lavra*, I, no. 32 lines 29–31.

[10] 'Vie d'Athanase', pp. 47, 50; Dölger, *Schatzkammern*, no. 108 lines 13–14.

[11] *Lavra*, no. 7 lines 38–40, no. 32 lines 32–8.

Taxation and monetary circulation   83

fluctuated in the course of the eleventh century. At one time Iviron received eight pounds and sixteen *nomismata*. First, four pounds of the payment were cut off, then the remainder. In 1079 Botaneiates restored a payment of four pounds and sixteen *nomismata*.[12] Vatopedi had been granted eighty *nomismata* by Constantine IX and Michael VI. The sum was halved by Isaac Komnenos. Later, another thirty-two *nomismata* were deducted and the monks eventually conceded their claim to the *solemnion* in return for a fiscal privilege for their properties.[13]

Payments were made to ensure that monasteries in infertile localities were properly provisioned. Nikephoros III authorised the payment of a *solemnion* of sixteen *nomismata* by the *dioiketes* of the Cyclades to Arsenios Skenoures because of the adverse terrain in which his establishment was situated.[14] The monastery on Patmos received a *solemnion* of twenty-four *theotokia komnenata nomismata* from Alexios. It also received payments in grain, which Manuel replaced with the payment of two pounds in *trikephala nomismata* from the fiscal revenues of Crete. It was allowed to make purchases free of tax on the island.[15]

Alexios granted St Meletios an annual payment of 422 *nomismata* from the provincial revenues[16] and in 1160 Manuel authorised a *solemnion* for the monastery of Strymitza of thirty *nomismata trikephala* from the revenues of the theme.[17]

It is impossible to assess the importance of these payments in bringing money into the rural economy. Probably, the largest proportion of these *solemnia* went to monasteries in the main urban centres, but the spread of monastic communities to some of the more remote parts of the empire did facilitate monetary circulation. These communities also received substantial cash payments from powerful landowners. After a successful military campaign Leo Phokas provided the finance for the Athonite monks to rebuild Kareai. Nikephoros Phokas contributed six pounds for the construction of Lavra. Maria Skleraina gave Lazaros ten pounds to build a church.[18]

---

[12] Dölger, *Schatzkammern*, no. 35 lines 38–45.
[13] Goudas, 'Vatopedi', pp. 125–6.   [14] *Engrapha Patmou*, I, no. 3.
[15] *Ibid.*, nos. 8, 22. For these coins, see Hendy, *Coinage and Money*, pp. 26–7, 31–3.
[16] Vasilievskij, 'Meletios', p. 49. Perhaps this figure should be corrected to 432 *nomismata*, exactly six pounds.
[17] Petit, 'Notre Dame de Pitié', p. 31.
[18] 'Vie d'Athanase', pp. 29, 32; Seibt, *Die Skleroi*, p. 75. Similarly, when St Symeon arrived at Studion he delivered two pounds of gold to the monastery; see I. Hausherr and G. Horn, *Vie de Syméon le Nouveau Théologien (949–1022) par Nicétas Stéthatos* (Orientalia Christiana 12) (Rome, 1928), p. 18. For the links of patronage between monasteries and the aristocracy, see Morris, 'The Political Saint of the Eleventh

84   *Economic expansion in the Byzantine empire*

Another form of gift which affected the circulation of money was the charitable distribution to the poor, sick and elderly through the largesse of emperors, saints and the regular distributions of monasteries and charitable foundations. Constantinople was the most important centre of such activity. Not only did the emperor make most of his distributions there, but an enormous number of monasteries and charitable establishments were concentrated in the city. The best-known example is the Pantokrator monastery.[19] Although almsgiving was certainly carried out on a large scale in the more important towns, saints and monasteries also served a useful function in supplying cash to the more impoverished element in the countryside. Alexios I gave Cyril Phileotes five pounds of gold to distribute to the poor and another pound for his monastery, but the saint is said to have given away all six pounds in a famine.[20]

The proliferation of monastic centres in the more remote parts of the empire had important economic consequences, because money reached the more humble sections of Byzantine society through their charitable offerings. Various distributions were stipulated by Pakourianos in his *typikon*. On the anniversary of his death and that of his brother Apasios seventy-two *nomismata* were given to the poor, and after the performance of the liturgies another twenty-four *nomismata* were distributed. In addition twenty-four *nomismata* were distributed annually in memory of Pakourianos's father and a further twelve upon the death of the abbot of Bačkovo. If there was any surplus in the monastic revenues, half was to be given on the anniversary of Pakourianos's death to the poor and to the *paroikoi* and *misthioi* in the service of the monastery.[21]

Some landowners made cash payments to their followers and to their slaves. The monastery of Kosmosotira had to continue Isaac Kom-

---

Century'. In the eleventh century there was a great increase in monastic building, a clear reflection of economic expansion; see C. Mango, 'Les monuments de l'architecture du XIᵉ siècle et leur signification historique et sociale', *Travaux et Mémoires*, 6 (1976), pp. 351–65.

[19] For its charitable expenditure, see Gautier, 'Pantocrator', p. 20. The subject of Byzantine charitable works is discussed very uncritically by D. J. Constantelos, *Byzantine Philanthropy and Social Welfare* (New Brunswick, 1968). Skylitzes, p. 405, relates how distributions were made in all provinces as a result of Michael IV's illness. Generally, however, such imperial benevolence would have been confined to the capital or to the locality which the emperor was visiting.

[20] *Vie de Cyrille Philéote*, pp. 232, 235–6. Gifts of money as well as food are frequently reported in hagiographical texts, for instance 'Vita S. Lucae Stylitae', p. 204.

[21] Gautier, 'Grégoire Pakourianos', pp. 97–101.

Taxation and monetary circulation 85

nenos's payments to a converted Jewish couple; in addition to their food allowance the wife received fifteen *trachea nomismata* and the husband two *hyperpyra* annually.[22] The cash payments which Boilas made to his freed slaves in his will or earlier in his life amounted to more than sixty-two *nomismata* – not all the payments are specified in the will.[23] Kale Pakouriane's bequests were naturally more generous owing to her greater wealth. Her freed slaves received ten pounds and fifty-two *trachea nomismata* and her followers, described in the will as her men, received eight and a half pounds.[24]

Monetary circulation was governed by these political, military and social factors, but the amount of money in circulation also reflected economic trends. In this respect the copper coinage was the most important. One of the main reasons for its minting was its use as change by tax-collectors. The state's requirements for this purpose would naturally be linked to the tax-assessments in its provinces and therefore reflect economic conditions to some extent. Although it is impossible to estimate the volume of money in circulation at any time, or even the quantity of coins struck for a particular issue,[25] a general pattern of economic contraction in the early Middle Ages followed by a recovery beginning in the ninth and tenth centuries and continuing at a greater rate in the eleventh and twelfth centuries is suggested by three different factors. These are the number of mints producing copper coinage, the quantity of copper coins found on archaeological sites and the convenience of the denominations of the coinage for economic activity.

After the closing of the provincial mints in the seventh century[26] Constantinople was the centre of coin production. There was a provincial mint, probably at Thessalonike, during the ninth century,[27] and during the eleventh and the twelfth centuries one was regularly operating there. A temporary mint was probably established at Philippoupolis to produce the reformed *hyperpyra* and billon *trachea* of Alexios. The copper *tetartera* appear to have been struck at three mints – Constantinople, Thessalonike and another mint in central Greece, probably at Thebes.[28]

---

[22] Petit, 'Kosmosotira', pp. 64–5.
[23] Lemerle, *Cinq études*, pp. 26–7 lines 192–231.
[24] Iberites, 'Byzantinai diathekai', pp. 367–8.
[25] Grierson, 'Byzantine Coinage as Source Material'.
[26] See above, p. 20.
[27] There was also a less important mint in Cherson; see Hendy, *Studies in the Byzantine Monetary Economy*, pp. 424–7.
[28] *Ibid.*, pp. 434–7.

86   *Economic expansion in the Byzantine empire*

The most compelling evidence for a substantial increase in the volume of money in circulation comes from the archaeological finds. These have far more value than stray finds of hoards. The latter usually reflect political instability and can give a false impression of economic trends. Their main value is that their composition gives a good idea of the areas in which specific types of coins circulated. The best excavation results come from Athens and Corinth. Although a few hoards have been found there, these are insignificant compared with the thousands of other coins found on the sites. They consist overwhelmingly of copper coinage, which was used in everyday transactions. The finds have great value owing to the stability of the coinage over three hundred years. Long-term trends can be discerned and it can be asserted confidently that the occasional variations in the size of the *follis* would have been insufficient to affect the overall result, given the large quantities of coins at both sites.

Recovery began rather early at Corinth, probably because of its importance as an administrative centre. The increase in the number of *folleis* dates from the reign of Theophilos. About 150 coins can be attributed to this emperor compared with only twenty from the previous century. This was very modest in comparison with the finds from later reigns – over 2,000 attributed to Constantine VII and his family and several thousand to the Komnenian era.[29] At Athens coinage became more common in the tenth century. Over 1,500 anonymous *folleis* of the period from Tzimiskes to Nikephoros III have been found and copper *tetartera* of the Komnenian period have been found in vast quantities. For the reign of Manuel alone there are over 4,000 coins.[30]

Elsewhere the finds are not so large, but they do fit the same pattern. At Kenchreiai, the eastern port of Corinth, only one coin was found from the eighth and ninth centuries, while forty-four were found from the tenth to the twelfth centuries.[31] Over 700 Byzantine coins were

[29] D. M. Metcalf, 'Corinth in the Ninth Century: The Numismatic Evidence', *Hesperia*, 42 (1973), pp. 181–6. By 1939 the excavation had uncovered 4,495 coins of Alexios I and 4,106 of Manuel out of a total 17,796 Byzantine coins; see Harris, 'Coins found at Corinth', p. 153.

[30] Thompson, *The Athenian Agora*, II, pp. 4–5, 72–5. The large number of Komnenian coins may be explained by the lower value of the *tetarteron* compared with the *follis*, as coins of slight value are more readily lost in a casual way. Nevertheless, it is clear that the greater availability of coinage, evident in the eleventh century, continued in the twelfth.

[31] R. L. Hohlfelder, *Kenchreiai, Eastern Port of Corinth*, III, *The Coins* (Leiden, 1978), pp. 4, 75–7.

Taxation and monetary circulation

excavated at Sparta. Most were found singly and, apart from one coin of Justinian I, the series begins with Basil I and continues up to the reign of Manuel, which is represented by 140 coins.[32]

The evidence from other parts of Greece is not so good. At Trikala the coin sequence extends from Constantine VII to Manuel.[33] The excavation at Thasos uncovered several anonymous *folleis* of the eleventh century, but only in the twelfth century was coinage found in large quantities.[34] In the Rhodope region large quantities of copper coinage dating from Manuel's reign to the end of the twelfth century have been discovered.[35]

This evidence can be supplemented by the results of excavations on the lower Danube. Large quantities of coins from the period following the restoration of Byzantine authority have been discovered. This is not surprising in view of the strategic importance of the region as a border area. The installation of military garrisons must have been the main impetus to the monetisation of the region. At Dinogetia nearly 1,000 coins (mostly of copper) from the tenth to the twelfth centuries have been found. At Vicina just over 1,000 copper coins from the late tenth and eleventh centuries have been discovered. In spite of fluctuations in the second half of the eleventh and the twelfth centuries, the general trend was one of economic expansion. Although no coins from Manuel's reign were found at Dinogetia, they were abundant at Noviodounon, which was situated nearby. The reformed coinage of Alexios quickly penetrated into the region, and overall the largest number of coins came from Manuel's reign.[36]

[32] A. M. Woodward, 'Excavations at Sparta, 1924–5', *Annual of the British School at Athens*, 26 (1924–5), pp. 157–8.

[33] M. Karamesine-Oikonomidou, 'Nomismata ek tou mouseiou tou Bolou', *Thessalika*, 5 (1966), pp. 15–17.

[34] O. Picard, 'Trésors et circulation monétaire à Thasos du IVᵉ au VIIᵉ siècle après J.C.', *Thasiaca. Bulletin de Correspondance Hellénique*, supplement 5, pp. 411–54, esp. 451–2.

[35] C. Asdracha, *La Région des Rhodopes aux XIIIᵉ et XIVᵉ siècles. Étude de géographie historique* (Athens, 1976), pp. 226–30 and tables 2, 3. The list of hoards given in Hendy, *Coinage and Money*, pp. 325–404, shows the large scale on which Manuel's billon *trachea* penetrated into Bulgaria.

[36] E. Condurachi, I. Barnea and P. Diaconu, 'Nouvelles recherches sur le "limes" byzantin du Bas-Danube aux Xᵉ–XIᵉ siècles', in *Proceedings of the XIIIth International Congress of Byzantine Studies, Oxford 1966* (London, 1967), pp. 190, 193; P. Diaconu, 'Pacuiul lui Soare – Vicina', *Byzantina*, 8 (1976), p. 422; I. Barnea, 'Dinogetia – ville byzantine du Bas-Danube', *Byzantina*, 10 (1980), p. 274; E. Oberländer-Tarnoveanu, 'Quelques aspects de la circulation monétaire dans la zone de l'embouchure du Danube au XIIᵉ siècle', *Dacia*, 23 (1979), pp. 265–73; O. Iliescu, 'Premières apparitions au Bas-Danube de la monnaie réformée d'Alexis Iᵉʳ Comnène, *Études Byzantines et Post-byzantines*, 1 (1979), pp. 9–17.

88 · Economic expansion in the Byzantine empire

All the evidence points clearly to economic expansion in the European provinces during this period. The pattern is susceptible to local variations. Recovery began earlier in some places than in others. The large number of coins from the reign of Manuel does not mean that the late twelfth century saw the beginning of a decline, but simply that Manuel's coinage continued to circulate and had been issued in sufficiently large quantities to continue to meet requirements.

Information from Asia Minor is not so comprehensive and comparisons with Greece are complicated by differences in the pattern of distribution of the Komnenian coinage. The issue of the *tetarteron* was confined to Greece, and in Bulgaria and Asia Minor the billon *trachy* was issued. It was a larger and more valuable coin less likely to be lost casually and therefore appear on archaeological sites.[37] Even for the period preceding the coinage reform of 1092 the coins found in the excavations at Ephesos and Sardis are far less numerous than those found at Athens and Corinth and very few from the Ephesos site have been published. Nevertheless, some conclusions can be drawn. After the early medieval contraction coins became more readily available in the tenth and eleventh centuries. Unlike in the European provinces the twelfth century is represented in more scanty numbers and at Sardis there is a long gap without any coin finds from the reign of Alexios to that of Andronikos Komnenos, possibly another indication of the disruption of economic activity due to Turkish raids in the late eleventh and the twelfth centuries.[38] The difference in the pattern of distribution between Asia Minor and Greece cannot entirely explain away this gap because coinage from this period is found in large quantities in parts of the Balkans, where there was the same pattern of distribution as in Asia Minor.

The same pattern of recovery in the tenth and eleventh centuries also prevailed in the interior of Asia Minor. At Alishar the excavators were able to purchase *folleis* of the tenth and eleventh centuries.[39] Metcalf has shown that some varieties of class A of the anonymous *follis* (970–1030) are found more frequently in south-east Turkey than at Corinth or Athens, where other varieties are found in large quantities.[40]

---

[37] Hendy, *Studies in the Byzantine Monetary Economy*, pp. 434–7; Hendy, *Coinage and Money*, p. 311.

[38] Foss, *Ephesus*, pp. 197–8; Bates, *Byzantine Coins*, pp. 1–2, 85–140. At Ankara there are also more coins of the tenth and eleventh centuries, but the number involved is small; see Foss, 'Late Antique and Byzantine Ankara', p. 87.

[39] Van der Osten, *The Alishar Huyuk*, pp. 317–18.

[40] D. M. Metcalf, 'Interpretation of the Byzantine "Rex Regnantium" Folles of Class "A", c. 970–1030', *Numismatic Chronicle*, 7th series, 10 (1970), pp. 199–218.

Taxation and monetary circulation

Also, the large number of anonymous *folleis* excavated at Antioch shows that coinage was circulating in large quantities in the south-eastern part of the empire during the period preceding the Turkish conquests.[41]

Another indication of economic expansion was the increased flexibility of the monetary system during the eleventh and twelfth centuries. The rather rigid system of *nomisma, milliaresion* and *follis* was not well suited to commercial activity. The full-value *nomisma* was an inconveniently high denomination for transactions, except where a limited range of high-value products was involved. The first period of debasement in the eleventh century went unnoticed by contemporaries. It lasted to the end of Monomachos's reign, when even the most heavily debased *nomismata* were still worth about eighteen carats. This limited debasement and the increase in money in circulation was probably matched by an increase in the number of transactions. The heavily debased *nomismata* of the 1070s and 1080s were even more suitable for regular economic activity, because they could be used in a wider range of transactions.[42] The reformed coinage of Alexios was also more convenient for commerce than the old pre-debasement coinage. The electrum gold and silver alloy, the low-value billon *trachy* and the copper *tetarteron* gave the system considerable flexibility.[43]

Another problem is the extent to which the increase in the volume of money in circulation was felt in rural areas as well as the towns, where it is well attested by the archaeological results. The close interaction between a town and its rural hinterland would imply that more money did find its way into rural communities. Even where there was no strong urban demand for agricultural produce, compulsory purchases by the

---

[41] D. B. Waage, *Antioch on the Ornates*, IV, part 2, *Greek, Roman, Byzantine and Crusaders' Coins* (Princeton, 1952).

[42] P. Grierson, 'The Debasement of the Bezant in the Eleventh Century', *Byzantinische Zeitschrift*, 47 (1954), pp. 379–94; P. Grierson, 'Notes on the Fineness of the Byzantine Solidus', *Byzantinische Zeitschrift*, 54 (1961), pp. 91–7; Hendy, *Coinage and Money*, pp. 3–25. Modern monetarist theory has been used to examine the debasement; see C. Morrisson, 'La dévaluation de la monnaie byzantine au XIe siècle: essai d'interprétation', *Travaux et Mémoires*, 6 (1976), pp. 3–48. This raises several problems. The elements of her equation – the volume of money, the velocity of circulation, prices, and the number of transactions – are unknown, reducing her calculations to guesswork. For a comprehensive critique of this approach, see Hendy, *Studies in the Byzantine Monetary Economy*, pp. 3–6, 233–7.

[43] Hendy, 'Byzantium, 1081–1204: An Economic Reappraisal', pp. 31–52. Fractions of the *follis* were rarely struck in the early Middle Ages (Grierson, *Catalogue*, III, part 1, p. 16), another indication of the decrease in money in the early medieval period. For the variation in the distribution pattern of the reformed Komnenian coinage, see above, p. 88.

90　Economic expansion in the Byzantine empire

state led to some degree of monetisation. It seems fairly certain that the economic trends revealed on urban sites also held good on a more restricted scale for the rural economy. The clearest confirmation of this point of view is given by the fiscal changes of the eleventh and twelfth centuries. More money was exacted from the rural economy as a result of the developments which culminated in Alexios's taxation reform of 1106–9.

The fiscal system had been thrown into confusion by the debasement of the *nomisma* and the political upheavals of the 1070s and 1080s, which exacerbated the state's need for revenues. Fiscal obligations had to be paid in gold[44] and, as the debasement became more pronounced, the most powerful landowners were able to exploit the situation by paying in the most heavily debased currency. The problem was aggravated by the regular practice of farming out the taxes. Tax-farmers were liable to meet deficits from their own pockets and, if unable to exact enough from some landowners, they would increase the pressure on others. Kekaumenos advised very strongly against taking on the responsibility owing to the risks which were involved.[45] When John Doukas encountered a tax-collector who was going to Constantinople on the eve of the revolt of the Komnenoi, he took possession of his gold and the tax-collector was forced to abandon his intention of going to the imperial palace.[46] In 1104–5 Demetrios Kamateros undertook to double the revenues which were collected from Thrace and Macedonia, and when he failed his house near the hippodrome was confiscated. In 1105–6 the collection from these provinces was entrusted to Nikephoros Artabasdos, who actually succeeded in collecting the stipulated amount and requested responsibility for the following year's collection.[47]

The problems which had arisen owing to the debasement had made tax-collecting much more difficult. Artabasdos reported that there had been great differences in the payments made by individual villages and these variations had been established long enough to have become customary. In some villages one *nomisma* had been collected instead of

---

[44] According to C. Morrisson, 'La logarikè: réforme monétaire et réforme fiscale sous Alexis Ier Comnène', *Travaux et Mémoires*, 7 (1979), p. 442, the small tax-payer with a payment less than $\frac{2}{3}$ *nomisma* would pay in lower denomination coins, but such tax-payers were normally part of a fiscal unit and it was the total payment of the *chorion* that was collected in *nomismata*; see Svoronos, 'Recherches sur le cadastre byzantin', p. 14 line 78.

[45] Cecaumenos, *Strategicon*, p. 39.

[46] Anna Comnène, *Alexiade*, I, pp. 82–3.

[47] *JGR*, I, p. 334.

one *milliaresion*, in others one *trachy nomisma* instead of two *milliaresia*; in some villages one *nomisma* instead of three *milliaresia*, in others one *nomisma* instead of four *milliaresia*. These fluctuating rates of payment had clearly originated in the debasement of the 1070s and 1080s. Some powerful individuals and monasteries had been able to exploit the devaluation by paying their taxes in coins nominally worth twelve *milliaresia*, but in reality worth progressively less as the debasement continued. In the end they were paying only one *trachy nomisma* instead of twelve *milliaresia*.[48]

The *trachy nomisma* referred to by Tzirithon has been generally thought to have been the electrum coin of Alexios's reform.[49] Morrisson has emphasised that it referred not only to this coin, but to the debased coinage which had been minted before Alexios's reform and remained in circulation afterwards, being gradually replaced by the new coinage. Alexios's pre-reform Constantinopolitan *nomisma* was lacking in gold content and worth about three carats, not much more than the theoretical value of the *milliaresion*, whereas the best-quality *nomisma* of Michael VII was worth about fifteen carats. Therefore the value of the *trachea* in circulation even after the reform of the coinage varied greatly. If the lowest-value *nomisma* of Alexios were exacted for one *milliaresion*, the gain to the treasury would not have been substantial. Also, if landowners and monasteries were constrained to pay the better *trachy* of Michael VII instead of twelve *milliaresia*, they would have paid two-thirds of their theoretical obligation, not one-third.[50]

Her comments apply most forcefully to the years immediately after the coinage reform. The documents, which show pre-reform coins still in circulation after 1092, mostly date from the 1090s.[51] As these coins were collected in taxation, it is likely that they were replaced quickly by the new currency. Although pre-reform *nomismata* were still circulating at the time of the fiscal reform, large quantities of *aspra trachea nomismata* of the new coinage must have already entered circulation and the varying rates of taxation given in Artabasdos's report mainly involved the new electrum coin.[52] Clearly, tax-collectors were being

---

[48] *Ibid.*; Hendy, *Coinage and Money*, pp. 53–5.   [49] Hendy, *Coinage and Money*, pp. 53–4.
[50] Morrisson, 'La logarikè: réforme monétaire et réforme fiscale sous Alexis Ier Comnène', pp. 447–52.
[51] *Ibid.*, pp. 448–9. For an uncertain but possible use of the pre-reform coinage in 1112, see *Docheiariou*, no. 3. line 39.
[52] The spread of the reformed coinage into the lower Danube region seems to have gathered force around 1100; see Oberländer-Tarnoveanu, 'Quelques aspects de la circulation monétaire', pp. 269–70. Hoarding may have delayed the return of some of the old coinage to the state.

92   *Economic expansion in the Byzantine empire*

forced to accept much less from some landowners than the amount which was inscribed on the tax-registers and they were appropriating as much as possible from other landowners to make up their quotas.

The situation was not caused simply by the debasement of the currency, although the extreme fluctuations in the rates of payment obviously originated in the 1070s and 1080s. It reflected the increasing power of the landowning aristocracy and the contradiction between the state's need for greater revenues to meet the external threats to its existence and its need for the support of the most powerful sections in the empire. Consequently, the chrysobulls which were issued to the secular and ecclesiastical elite during those decades gave more extensive privileges than those of the first half of the century.[53] Although many aristocratic families lost their stronghold on the Anatolian plateau after the Seljuk invasions, everywhere else in the empire the economic position of the elite was strengthened greatly in the late eleventh century.

Not only was the state conceding its revenues more freely at this time, but it was having difficulty in collecting the nominal amounts which it was owed in taxes by some landowners. Some chrysobulls, which were issued to Lavra, show how influential landowners exploited the debasement to pay less in real value for their taxes and used their connections at court to retain land, while refusing to pay the taxes on it and therefore relinquishing it in theory.

Lavra's tax-payment had been established at $46\frac{7}{24}$ *nomismata* by Andronikos, a tax-assessor in the theme of Boleron, Strymon and Thessalonike, who had been active between 1044 and 1050.[54] He was one of three tax-assessors whose documents were reexamined in 1079 by John Kataphloron as part of an increase in the nominal tax-burden of these provinces. Lavra's fiscal liability was increased very sharply from $46\frac{7}{24}$ *nomismata* to $79\frac{3}{4}$ *nomismata*.[55] The additional properties which Lavra had acquired since the assessment of Andronikos were not substantial enough to merit such a large increase. The intention was to compensate the treasury for the debased coinage in which payments

---

[53] See above, p. 68.

[54] *Lavra*, I, no. 50 lines 2–4; P. Lemerle, 'Notes sur la date de trois documents athonites et sur trois fonctionnaires du XIe siècle', *Revue des Études Byzantines*, 10 (1952), p. 112.

[55] *Lavra*, I, no. 50. A surviving act of Kataphloron gives the higher tax-assessment which he imposed on the *metochion* of the Saviour in the region of Hierissos; see *Lavra*, I, no. 39.

Taxation and monetary circulation

were being made.[56] But even an increase of approximately 70% would have been insufficient compensation if Lavra was making its payments in the most heavily debased coinage. The *nomismata* of the reign of Constantine IX were worth $17\frac{1}{2}$ carats or more, those of Nikephoros III about eight or nine carats.[57]

Lavra was unwilling to pay this increase and a division of its properties between the monastery and the state was arranged, but it actually managed to retain the additional land. In 1088–9 Niketas Xiphilinos was instructed by Alexios to apply a rate of *epibole* of $535\frac{1}{2}$ *modioi* for each *nomisma* to Lavra's estates. The rate was based on a statement by Lavra's abbot that the monastery's lands amounted to 42,705 *modioi*. The rate of *epibole* was calculated to give a total payment of $79\frac{3}{4}$ *nomismata*, the figure established by Kataphloron. Xiphilinos was to attribute to Lavra the land which corresponded to the $46\frac{7}{24}$ *nomismata* imposed by Andronikos because the monastery was prepared to pay that much in taxation. The rest of the land, corresponding to the tax-increase which Lavra was unwilling to pay, was supposed to revert to the treasury.[58]

Xiphilinos discovered that Lavra was in possession of more land than the abbot had stated. His assessment of the estates amounted to just over 47,051 *modioi*. Consequently, he created a new rate of *epibole* based on this figure and the $79\frac{3}{4}$ *nomismata*, which Kataphloron had imposed. It worked out to 590 *modioi* and one *litra* for each *nomisma* and he used this figure to make the division of the property. He attributed $26,671\frac{1}{2}$ *modioi* to Lavra for the taxes imposed by Andronikos, approximately 1,800 *modioi* more than the figure which he would have

[56] N. Svoronos, 'L'épibolè à l'époque des Comnènes', *Travaux et Mémoires*, 3 (1968), pp. 376–7. Other factors which might have been involved in the increase were demographic expansion on Lavra's estates leading to the imposition of taxes on land which had been brought into cultivation since the previous assessment, and the suppression of *sympatheiai*.

[57] Grierson, 'The Debasement of the Bezant in the Eleventh Century', pp. 392–3; Morrisson, 'La dévaluation de la monnaie byzantine au XIe siècle', pp. 7–8.

[58] *Lavra*, I, no. 50 lines 1–14. The technical procedures involved in this operation were unusual, reflecting the exceptional wealth and power of Lavra. The rate of *epibole* was not calculated according to the standard procedure, but on the basis of all the land which Lavra held, and no account was taken of any *sympatheia*. Also, the supplementary taxes were not involved in this procedure. The choice which the tax-payer was given between making the additional payment or surrendering the land to the state also appears to have been a new departure. In the system envisaged by the Fiscal Treatise and the tenth-century legislation, the preferential rights of landowners in the same fiscal unit would have been involved, but Lavra's lands were so extensive that it had outgrown the system. See Svoronos, 'L'épibolè à l'époque des Comnènes', pp. 378, 383–95.

94   *Economic expansion in the Byzantine empire*

obtained had he adhered to Alexios's instructions about the rate of *epibole* to be applied. He attributed 20,380½ *modioi* to the treasury, which corresponded to the increase imposed by Kataphloron. As the higher rate of *epibole* had been applied equally to the monastery and to the treasury, Alexios confirmed Lavra's ownership of the surplus 1,800 *modioi* without imposing any additional tax on this land; from then onwards only the tax imposed by Andronikos was to be recorded in the tax-registers.[59]

Xiphilinos's enquiry did not settle the matter because conditions in the empire were propitious for powerful landowners to hold more than the land to which they were legally entitled by their tax-payments and privileges. A chrysobull issued to Lavra in 1094 mentions accusations that the activities of Xiphilinos were detrimental to the treasury. A new assessment was made by another tax-assessor, Gregory Xeros. Using the same rate of *epibole* as Xiphilinos had already applied, Xeros found that Lavra was holding a surplus of 11,000 *modioi*. Alexios made an unconditional donation of 8,000 *modioi*, but it seems that Lavra was able to retain all the surplus.[60]

The chrysobull also contained some clauses which reflected the uncertain conditions prevailing in the countryside at that time. Lavra's lands were not to be subjected to a new assessment unless a dispute arose which could not be settled in any other way. Even in this case only the lands in dispute were to be measured.[61] The stipulation did not have any lasting effect in practice, but it was unusual for such a clause to be inserted in chrysobulls of the eleventh century. It reflects unease at the activities of tax-officials, especially as the monks were intent on retaining all their land without paying the full tax-burden.

Lavra was of course a special case. Most other landowners lacked its influence in Constantinople and did not receive such extensive privileges. The fortunes of other Athonite monasteries in their dealings with the state at this time contrasted sharply. Docheiariou, like Lavra, effectively exploited its contacts in the capital to prevent any reduction in its properties. Xiphilinos had attempted to attribute part of its land to the state after imposing an increase in its land-tax. In particular the

[59] *Lavra*, I, no. 50; Svoronos, 'L'épibolè à l'époque des Comnènes', p. 378.

[60] *Lavra*, I, no. 52. The denunciations were probably made by the agents of the emperor's brother, Isaac, who had been granted fiscal revenues in the region of Thessalonike. They were probably attempting to increase their revenues by drawing Alexios's attention to the large quantity of surplus land which Lavra had retained; see Svoronos, 'L'épibolè à l'époque des Comnènes', p. 379 n. 16.

[61] *Lavra*, I, no. 52 lines 23–32.

Taxation and monetary circulation 95

imposition on the estate of Perigardikeia was increased by 100 *nomismata*, but after an appeal to Anna Dalassena the monastery was allowed to retain its land without paying any more tax.[62]

In 1095 the next tax-assessor of the province, Euthymios, who had been instructed to make a general enquiry into the activities of Xiphilinos and Xeros, made an assessment of the property of Esphigmenou using a very different rate of *epibole* from that applied to Lavra's lands. The monastery was assigned $412\frac{1}{2}$ *modioi* of second-quality land. The basic land-tax was established at $2\frac{3}{4}$ *nomismata*, a rate of approximately 150 *modioi* to the *nomisma*. It also had to pay $\frac{7}{24}$ *nomisma* in supplementary taxes. This was the standard technical procedure outlined in the Fiscal Treatise. Lavra's case was different. Not only was it paying a much lower rate of taxation, but that rate was calculated on the total tax-payment and there was no question of paying any supplementary taxes.[63]

In contrast, when Lavra received two estates, Asmalou and Lorotomou, in an exchange with the treasury in 1104, they had a special rate of taxation imposed on them. The monastery paid eight *aspra trachea nomismata* for $7,030\frac{1}{2}$ *modioi*, a rate of 878 *modioi* for each *aspron trachy*, strikingly high even for such a highly privileged institution as Lavra. The monastery had previously owed the same payment for the estate at Barzachanion, which it conceded to the state in the exchange. The tax on Lavra's land was paid directly to the *sekreton ton oikeiakon* in Constantinople.[64] Probably, this was one of the cases where powerful monasteries had been making payments in lower-value *trachea nomismata* instead of the full-value coins and the payments had been established long enough to be recorded as the official payment. The gains which Lavra made from imperial favour contrast sharply with the losses sustained by Iviron through the confiscation of some of its lands by the state.[65]

The instability of the fiscal system and the great variations in the rate of taxation provoked complaints about heavy taxation in the literary

---

[62] Perigardikeia's surface area extended to over 20,000 *modioi*, so the increase would have been at the rate of one *nomisma* for about 200 *modioi*, a very substantial increase considering that only a part of the land was cultivable; see *Docheiariou*, no. 2 and the notes on pp. 51–2.

[63] *Esphigménou*, no. 5; Svoronos, 'L'épibolè à l'époque des Comnènes', pp. 383ff. For the imposition of the rate of *epibole* as outlined in the Fiscal Treatise, see Dölger, *Beiträge*, p. 115 lines 2–12. See also n. 58, above.

[64] *Lavra*, I, no. 56 lines 45–53, 103–6; Svoronos, 'L'épibolè à l'époque des Comnènes', pp. 380–1.

[65] See above, p. 70.

96   *Economic expansion in the Byzantine empire*

sources. Zonaras referred to the state's lack of money in the early years of Alexios's reign and the expedients to which he resorted. He accused him of issuing a *nomisma* of copper, which he used along with the most heavily debased coinage of his predecessors to pay imperial expenses. Alexios was also charged with sending tax-assessors into the fields and villages of his subjects to make new assessments and to devise new forms of impositions. While expenses were paid in copper, taxes were collected in gold, silver and copper.[66] The quality of the coin which the tax-collector obtained depended on his ability to exact from the tax-payer a better-quality coin rather than the most heavily debased *nomisma*. A similar emphasis was placed on heavy taxation by John of Oxeia, patriarch of Antioch. He complained of the exactions of *praktores*, *phorologoi* and also *tritotai*. The latter was probably a popular term for fiscal officials who tried to increase the land-tax substantially.[67]

If the collectors had difficulty making up their full quotas, one resource open to them was to turn a blind eye to older privileges, a procedure which was the basis of Theophylaktos's complaints. The *klerikoi* of his church were, he alleged, paying twice as heavy a tax on their mills as the Bulgarian laity in spite of an earlier exemption and they were also paying more for the tax on fishing. Another accusation was that the measure of the *schoinon* had been shortened, so that the assessment of the land in *modioi* and the resulting tax-burden were increased.[68] Such rhetorical writings should not be taken automatically at face value, but for the late eleventh century they are corroborated by the more reliable evidence of the fluctuations in tax-payments and they reflect real conditions.

The confusion persisted until Alexios reformed the fiscal system in 1106–9. Owing to the different rates of payment Artabasdos asked for clarification of the procedure for the collection of 1106–7. He was instructed to collect one *palaion trachy nomisma* for every *milliaresion* from all villages and the most powerful individuals. Alexios's later *lyseis* referred to the *aspron trachy* of the reformed coinage instead of the old pre-reform *trachy*. The electrum coin became the basis of the new system and, as the earlier debased gold coinage disappeared from circulation, the rate of taxation was substantially increased. Alexios

---

[66] Zonaras, III, pp. 737–8; Hendy, *Studies in the Byzantine Monetary Economy*, pp. 516–17.

[67] P. Gautier, 'Diatribes de Jean l'Oxite contre Alexis Ier Comnène', *Revue des Études Byzantines*, 28 (1970), pp. 30–1 n. 19.

[68] Bryennius, pp. 329–33; Xanalatos, *Beiträge*, pp. 37, 43.

Taxation and monetary circulation

was institutionalising the highest rate of taxation, which had previously been extracted from the weakest part of the rural population, and it is probable that the monasteries and wealthier secular landowners were unable to avoid paying it. The few exceptions would have been the highly privileged landowners like Lavra, whose payments had already been fixed by official decrees. Many fiscal units would have been adversely affected by Alexios's decision. Those which had previously paid one *trachy* instead of three or four *milliaresia* had their basic land-tax payment trebled or quadrupled and the text does hint that some landowners found the new arrangement onerous.[69]

Another imperial *lysis* established the basis of the new system. The *charagma*, the part of the basic land-tax exacted in precious-metal coins, was to be collected in *nomismata*; the *lepta psephia*, the amount raised through the supplementary taxes and fractions of the basic taxes, were to be reckoned in copper *noumia*. The document caused some confusion. It stated that the *lepta psephia* were to be calculated at the rate of four *milliaresia* to the *nomisma*. Although it seems very clear, some officials misinterpreted it. They thought that, although the entire *nomisma* corresponded to four *milliaresia*, fractions were still to be reckoned at the old rate of twelve *milliaresia* to the *nomisma*. As the emperor was not in Constantinople, the officials decided to adopt the course which was most advantageous to the treasury and in 1106–8 the higher rate prevailed. The report by George Spanopoulos, who, as the *logothetes tou genikou*, was the head of the bureau responsible for the assessment and collection of the land-tax, admitted that the collection for these two years had proceeded to the detriment of the emperor's subjects. A further *lysis* made it clear that the fractions were to be reckoned at four *milliaresia* to the *nomisma*.[70]

The final alteration to the fiscal system concerned the supplementary taxes, which were raised with the basic land-tax. Again, the general tendency was to exact more cash for these payments. There were four supplementary taxes and under the old system they were calculated in a very awkward and complicated way. The *dikeraton* was raised at one

---

[69] *JGR*, I, p. 334; Hendy, *Coinage and Money*, p. 54; Morrisson, 'La logarikè: réforme monétaire et réforme fiscale sous Alexis Ier Comnène', pp. 450–3.

[70] *JGR*, I, pp. 335–6; Hendy, *Coinage and Money*, pp. 56–7; Morrisson, 'La logarikè: réforme monétaire et réforme fiscale sous Alexis Ier Comnène', pp. 453–5. In the old system the *charagma* had a different meaning. It was the gold coin which was exacted when the basic tax and the *dikeratohexafollon* reached $\frac{2}{3}$ *nomisma* and the change was given in low-value coinage; see Svoronos, 'Recherches sur le cadastre byzantin', pp. 78–9.

98   *Economic expansion in the Byzantine empire*

milliaresion for every *nomisma*. The *hexafollon*, in contrast, was a flat-rate tax which was exacted only when the basic tax reached $\frac{2}{3}$ *nomisma*. The *synetheia* and *elatikon* were also flat-rate taxes. The former was collected at the rate of one *milliaresion* for every *nomisma* until the basic tax reached six *nomismata*. Then one *nomisma* was collected for any amount between six and ten *nomismata*. For higher tax-payments it continued to increase in stages. Smaller amounts were exacted for the *elatikon*, which was also increased in stages.[71]

The arrangement was very anomalous. The additional burden varied greatly according to the level of the basic tax. If the latter was $\frac{1}{4}$ *nomisma*, the surcharge was twelve *folleis* or 16%. If the basic tax was $\frac{2}{3}$ *nomisma*, the additional taxes amounted to 20%. As the basic tax became higher, the surcharge generally became lower; for 100 *nomismata* it was only 14.5%. However, there were freakish exceptions. A land-tax of $10\frac{1}{2}$ *nomismata* incurred a surcharge of $4\frac{5}{48}$ *nomismata*, about 40%. The system was clearly in need of simplification.[72]

In the few documents which give the composition of the total tax-payment in practical cases the imposition of these supplementary taxes was inconsistent. When Kataphloron imposed a new rate of taxation on a *metochion* belonging to the monastery of Kaliourgou in 1079, the *dikeraton*, *hexafollon* and *synetheia* were all imposed, but not the *elatikon*.[73] There is also a peculiarity in the assessment made by Euthymios of an estate belonging to Esphigmenou. Only the *dikeraton* and the *hexafollon* were imposed, not the other two taxes.[74] It is difficult to imagine why the state did not impose its claims fully in this case. In a slightly earlier instance the monastery of Panteleemon had to pay a basic tax of $\frac{1}{2}$ *nomisma* for a property in Kassandra. The *dikeraton* was established at twelve *folleis*, the correct figure, but one *milliaresion* and twelve *folleis* were charged for the *synetheia* and the *elatikon* respectively. This was the rate when the basic tax was a full *nomisma* and it seems that the official was exacting more than he ought in this case.[75]

Alexios's reform removed the inconsistencies in the arrangement and a standard rate for the supplementary taxes was established. As the electrum coin, the basis of the new system, was worth one-third of the old full-value *nomisma*, the influential landowners, who paid their taxes

---

[71] Dölger, *Beiträge*, pp. 59–60, 122–3; Svoronos, 'Recherches sur le cadastre byzantin', pp. 81–2.

[72] *JGR*, I, pp. 327–33. See also Svoronos, 'Recherches sur le cadastre byzantin', pp. 82–3.

[73] *Lavra*, I, no. 39; Svoronos, 'Recherches sur le cadastre byzantin', p. 87.

[74] *Esphigménou*, no. 5 lines 31–2.   [75] *Pantéléèmôn*, no. 3.

Taxation and monetary circulation

directly to the administration in Constantinople, questioned the amount that they should pay for these taxes. They claimed that they should pay only ten *folleis* for the *dikeratohexafollon* instead of thirty. A new rate of fifteen *folleis* for every electrum *nomisma* was established for these taxes. The same course was taken with the *synetheia* and the *elatikon*. Eighteen *folleis* were exacted for each *aspron trachy nomisma* instead of thirty-six. Therefore the new rate for the complete surcharge was standardised at thirty-three *folleis* for each *nomisma* worth ninety-six *folleis*, a rate of 34%, which was higher than the old system except in a few anomalous cases.[76]

The correspondence which outlines the principles of the reformed system referred specifically to the provinces of Thrace and Macedonia, but it held a more general application. It brought a new stability after the period of fiscal disorder in the provinces. The series of enquiries into Lavra's estates ended at exactly the same time. The administration had made fresh attempts to exact more from the monastery, probably due to the large surplus it was holding. Taxes for the *dromos* and the fleet had been imposed on its lands. When the monks requested their abolition and the confirmation of their ownership of their properties, they conceded two of their estates, Peristerai and Tzechlianes, to the state. The new assessment, which was made on Alexios's instructions for all the monastery's properties, was caused not simply by the confusion surrounding Lavra's lands, but was part of the general restoration of order to the fiscal system.[77]

In 1107–8 the *logothetes ton sekreton* made a survey of the entire region of Thessalonike, including Lavra's estates. His instructions were to leave the monastery in complete ownership of the land which was accounted for by its tax-payments and by previous imperial donations amounting to 11,000 *modioi*, and to attribute to Lavra another 16,000 *modioi* from the surplus land which it was holding as a further imperial donation. At the same time, the contributions to the fleet and the *dromos* were exempted by a *logisimon*. The estates of Peristerai and Tzechlianes were assigned to the *orphanotropheion* (orphanage). Lavra's other properties were assessed at 51,403 *modioi* and eight *litrai*. Nearly 12,428 *modioi* were attributed to Lavra in accordance with its tax-payment of $23\frac{5}{24}$ *nomismata*, based on an *isokodikon* (a copy of an extract from a tax-register) of Andronikos (who should not be confused with

---

[76] *JGR*, I, pp. 337–8. The *follis* was, of course, used simply as a term of account; see Hendy, *Coinage and Money*, pp. 57–8.

[77] *Lavra*, I, no. 58; Svoronos, 'L'épibolè à l'époque des Comnènes', p. 381.

100   *Economic expansion in the Byzantine empire*

the tax-assessor Andronikos who was active in the 1040s). This total had been reduced from $27\frac{5}{24}$ *nomismata* because the tax of four *nomismata* on a bath and some buildings at Bryai was not taken into account. It is not known when Andronikos had established the *isokodikon*, but it was clearly after the assessment by Xeros. The monastery might have obtained the reduction in its fiscal obligation by renouncing some of its taxes, even though it was not prepared to give up the land which it was holding. The 12,428 *modioi* which the *logothetes ton sekreton* assigned to Lavra was calculated at the rate of *epibole* of $535\frac{1}{2}$ *modioi* for each *nomisma*, the rate originally established by Alexios. Its ownership of 27,000 *modioi* through imperial donations was also confirmed. Then the monks petitioned the emperor to attribute to them additional land corresponding to the $5\frac{1}{12}$ *nomismata* which they had previously paid in tax for Peristerai and Tzechlianes, and the four *nomismata* which had been the tax on the buildings at Bryai. This brought the monastery's total payment up to $32\frac{7}{24}$ *nomismata*. At the same time, the state conceded a change in Lavra's rate of *epibole* to 590 *modioi* a *nomisma*, the figure which Xiphilinos had established contrary to Alexios's instructions. He also added another donation of 1,000 *modioi*. The result of this series of enquiries was the confirmation of Lavra's ownership of 47,052 *modioi*, almost exactly the same amount of land as Xiphilinos had found in its possession in 1088–9. The other 4,351 *modioi* which it had been holding was transferred to the state.[78]

Not only had Lavra been able to avoid paying the extra tax imposed by Kataphloron, but it had succeeded in paying less than the amount established in the 1040s. One problem does arise concerning the tax-payment. The documents do not specify the coin in which the payment was made, but simply state *nomismata*. The only exception is the chrysobull relating to the estates at Asmalou and Lorotomou, whose taxes Lavra paid in *aspra trachea nomismata*.[79] As the series of chrysobulls begins before the coinage reform in 1092, it seems likely that Lavra was making its payments in *aspra trachea* rather than *hyperpyra* in 1107–8. Such an influential institution would certainly have exploited the eleventh-century debasement to make its payments in low-value *nomismata*. Consequently, payment in *aspra trachea* would have provided some continuity and, as that denomination was the basis of the new

---

[78] *Lavra*, I, no. 58; Svoronos, 'L'épibolè à l'époque des Comnènes', pp. 381–3. The Andronikos who drew up Lavra's *isokodikon* has been identified by Seibt (*Die Skleroi*, pp. 97–8) as Andronikos Skleros.

[79] *Lavra*, I, no. 56 lines 103–4.

Taxation and monetary circulation

fiscal system, it is unlikely that Lavra would have been forced to make its payments with the higher-value coin.

Some of the precautionary clauses in the chrysobull of 1109 reflect Lavra's special status. Its provisions were not to be overthrown, even though they did not conform to the general regulations by which fiscal matters were arranged. No provisions about *sympatheiai* and *klasmata* which had been made in the past could be taken into account, owing to the different way in which Lavra's rate of *epibole* was calculated.[80]

It is only because of Lavra's special status that evidence survives of the assessment of the whole of the Thessalonike region in 1107–8.[81] It throws light on an otherwise obscure passage in a charter dealing with a partition of properties between three brothers in 1110. Referring to an estate (*proasteion*), Pinsson, it says that if the emperor decided that the land, which had been assigned to the treasury, should be subjected to the land-tax two of the brothers would recover the estate and pay the tax imposed on it. Clearly, the state had taken possession of the property after the survey of 1107–8[82] and many other estates probably suffered the same fate. In the confused condition of the fiscal system at this time many landowners other than Lavra must have held lands for which they were not paying enough in tax. It was logical for the state to claim these lands at the same time that the fiscal system was being reformed, and it is a reasonable assumption that other landowners were less able than Lavra to retain the properties which they were holding illegally.

It is striking that the chrysobull of 1109 ended the uncertainty about the extent of Lavra's estates and their fiscal status.[83] As the land-tax was imposed with greater consistency, the problem of large landowners holding excess land was solved until the middle of the twelfth century. By then expansion under the impetus of demographic growth had taken place and new privileges were conceded by the state.[84]

---

[80] *Lavra*, I, no. 58 lines 62–74; Svoronos, 'L'épibolè à l'époque des Comnènes', pp. 390–4.

[81] *Lavra*, I, no. 58 lines 24–5.

[82] *Lavra*, I, no. 59 lines 75–7 and p. 307. It is possible that the estate did belong to Lavra previously, as the editors have suggested. However, it seems more likely that it had been in the possession of the brothers, but their total tax-payment did not correspond to the full extent of their lands and therefore the estate was claimed by the state. In the later period Lavra did own a large estate at Pinsson, but before 1107–8 the only evidence of its ownership of land there involves the purchase of a handful of fields from a peasant family; see *ibid.*, no. 1.

[83] After the chrysobull of 1109 the next official document from the state featured in the Lavra collection is dated to 1162.

[84] See above, p. 55.

102   *Economic expansion in the Byzantine empire*

The general effectiveness of Alexios's reform leads to some fundamental conclusions about the condition of the rural economy. Its most important result was an intensification of exploitation, which was possible only in a period of economic expansion. This was reflected in the coins which were exacted under the new system. It was easier for tax-collectors to exact the medium-value electrum coin from smaller landowners instead of the unwieldy full-value *nomisma* of the old coinage or the new *hyperpyron*,[85] although large payments were most conveniently reckoned in *hyperpyra*. Even many large landowners were unable to avoid making substantial payments in the way Lavra was able to. In 1136 the obligation of the monastery *tou Molibotou* exceeded four pounds in *hyperpyra*. The monks of Latros were paying thirty-six *hyperpyra* for one estate until they received an exemption from Manuel.[86] In cases where the state had conceded fiscal revenues to landowners, the reform still caused an increase in the payments made by the direct producers. Their obligations to the landowner were established by the state's officials, who registered their payments in the *praktika* which they delivered to the landowner. Consequently, the general effect of the reform was an intensification of surplus expropriation by both the state and the feudal landowner.

The basic land-tax (*demosion*) was only a part of the obligations of the peasantry. They were responsible for the payment of the *pakton* (rent) on land which they did not own, but leased from the state or a private landowner. The largest part of the revenues from the estates which were conceded to Andronikos Doukas consisted of the *pakton*. The amount derived from the *telos* (tax-payment) paid by the peasants on their own land was far less significant.[87]

The numerous other obligations to which peasants, free and unfree, were liable are detailed in the lengthy lists of charges for which privileged landowners received exemptions in respect of their *paroikoi*. (This, of course, did not mean that the peasants did not owe these charges, but that they were due to the landowner instead of to the state.) They included payments in cash and kind and the performance

---

[85] Hendy, *Coinage and Money*, p. 55.
[86] Gautier, 'Pantocrator', p. 123 line 1550; MM, IV, p. 320.
[87] Dölger, *Beiträge*, p. 123 lines 1–8; Karayannopulos, 'Fragmente', pp. 321, 324–5; *Engrapha Patmou*, II, no. 50, pp. 10–11; Svoronos, 'Recherches sur le cadastre byzantin', pp. 139–40; Svoronos, 'Remarques sur les structures économiques', pp. 57–9; J. W. Nesbitt, 'Mechanisms of Agricultural Production on Estates of the Byzantine Praktika' (unpublished Ph.D. thesis, University of Wisconsin, 1972), pp. 124–5; Laiou-Thomadakis, *Peasant Society*, p. 148.

Taxation and monetary circulation 103

of labour services. The role of requisitions in kind and labour services offer a sharp reminder of the limitations to the monetisation of the rural economy, at least among direct producers. Nevertheless, a study of some of the obligations which appear in the lists suggests an increase in the importance of cash payments. This is another manifestation of an increase in monetary circulation and supports the conclusions which were drawn from the increases in the basic land-tax.

The most important of the taxes which were raised in cash were the *kapnikon*, the *synone*, the *aerikon* and the *ennomion*.[88] The *kapnikon* was the hearth-tax imposed on every household. It is first mentioned in the sources when Nikephoros I imposed it on the *paroikoi* of the churches and religious houses. In the early ninth century it was exacted at a standard rate of two *milliaresia* and Michael II granted the more favourable rate of one *milliaresion* to the themes of the Opsikion and Armeniakon as a reward for political loyalty.[89] In the late Roman period the *synone* was a levy in kind, but by the Byzantine period it had become a cash payment. It was frequently associated with the *kapnikon*. Families which received a converted Arab prisoner-of-war as a son-in-law were exempted from both obligations for three years.[90] The two obligations were often bracketed together in the lists of exemptions in the eleventh-century chrysobulls.[91] They were both incorporated in the *telos* paid by the *paroikoi* and, therefore, both taxes invariably featured in the lists. The payments which were made by the *paroikoi* of Andronikos Doukas varied according to their wealth in animals. Those who did not have an ox were called *kapnikarioi*. If they also did not have donkeys, they paid $\frac{1}{4}$ *nomisma* for the *kapnikon* and the *synone*. The *kapnikarioi* with donkeys and the *boidatoi* paid $\frac{1}{2}$ *nomisma* and the *zeugaratoi* one *nomisma* each.[92] It has been assumed by Dölger, mainly because the *kapnikon* was not mentioned in the Fiscal Treatise, that it was imposed only on dependent peasants.[93] This is incorrect, because the exemption which was granted to households with Arab converts applied to independent peasants.

The *aerikon* was a judicial payment, or fine, which had become a standardised fiscal obligation by the early fourteenth century. Little is known of the procedure by which it was exacted in the earlier period,

---

[88] Dölger, *Beiträge*, pp. 51–4; Ostrogorsky, 'Die ländliche Steuergemeinde', pp. 49–52, 57–8; F. Dölger, 'Das Aerikon', *Byzantinische Zeitschrift*, 30 (1929–30), pp. 450–7.
[89] Theophanes, I, pp. 486–7; Theophanes Continuatus, pp. 53–4.
[90] Constantine Porphyrogenitus, *De Cerimoniis*, I, p. 695.
[91] To take a few examples, see *JGR*, I, p. 617 line 9; *Lavra*, I, no. 38 line 37; and *Engrapha Patmou*, I, no. 1 line 38.
[92] *Engrapha Patmou*, II, no. 50 lines 311–14.   [93] Dölger, *Beiträge*, pp. 52–3.

104   *Economic expansion in the Byzantine empire*

but the tendency to collect it in fixed lump sums from villages was already apparent in the first half of the eleventh century, when John the Orphanotrophos imposed it as a special levy varying from four to twenty *nomismata* on each village.[94]

The *ennomion*, the tax on pasture, was exacted at fixed rates from the *paroikoi* on the estates of Andronikos Doukas – one *nomisma* for every 100 sheep and one *milliaresion* for every cow, horse or donkey.[95] It was one of the most important of the supplementary impositions on the peasantry. Unlike the *aerikon*, which appeared frequently in the exemption lists, the *ennomion* was not regularly conceded to private landowners in the eleventh century.[96]

Another obligation which the state was reluctant to concede was the *zeugologion*. It was charged for the imposition of the land-tax on the *zeugarion* and its inscription in the tax-register. It was frequently mentioned in Theophylaktos's letters, because it was not included in the list of charges from which the church of Ochrid was exempted by its chrysobulls. Nor does it appear in the surviving chrysobulls of the eleventh century, but in the twelfth century it was conceded to landowners more freely.[97]

The *kanonikon* was a payment in both cash and kind which does not appear in the exemption lists because it was exacted by the church. The payment was standardised by Isaac Komnenos at one *nomisma* and two *milliaresia* together with six *modioi* each of wheat and barley, six

---

[94] Scylitzes, p. 404; Dölger, 'Das Aerikon', pp. 450–7.

[95] *Engrapha Patmou*, II, no. 50 lines 314–16. The *ennomion* was exacted specifically for the use of common or state land as pasture and it should not be confused with other obligations such as the *dekateia zoon*, a tax on animals other than the ploughing oxen. It is called the *dekatosis* by Theophylaktos; see Bryennius, p. 327 line 28. The *mandratikion* was a separate tax on the use of sheep folds in state pastures; see *Lavra*, I, no. 66 line 15. See also Xanalatos, *Beiträge*, pp. 41–2; Dölger, *Beiträge*, pp. 53–4; and Ostrogorsky, 'Die ländliche Steuergemeinde', p. 57.

[96] Apart from the case of Andronikos, other instances when the state conceded its claims to the *ennomion* are to be found in Goudas, 'Vatopedi', p. 122 line 40; *Lavra*, I, no. 48 line 36; and *Engrapha Patmou*, I, no. 6 line 48. The tax on bees, the *melissoennomion*, first appears in the privilege issued to the monastery of Strymitza in 1152; see Petit, 'Notre Dame de Pitié', p. 36 line 17.

[97] F. Dölger, 'Zum Gebührenwesen der Byzantiner', in *Byzanz und die europäische Staatenwelt* (Ettal, 1953), pp. 256–8. Xanalatos, *Beiträge*, p. 41, incorrectly describes the *zeugologion* as a tax on ploughteams. For the references to it by Theophylaktos, see A. Leroy-Molinghen, 'Prolégomènes à une édition critique des "Lettres" de Théophylacte de Bulgarie', *Byzantion*, 13 (1938), p. 256 line 17; and Bryennius, p. 331 lines 25–6. For the twelfth century, see Petit, 'Notre Dame de Pitié', pp. 29 line 19, 36 line 17; *JGR*, I, p. 366; *Engrapha Patmou*, I, no. 19; and Astruc, 'Un document inédit de 1163', p. 215 line 34. The *zeugaratikion* was a tax on *paroikoi* who worked outside the landowner's properties; see Laiou-Thomadakis, *Peasant Society*, p. 181.

Taxation and monetary circulation 105

measures of wine, one ram and thirty birds from a community of thirty households.[98] Basil II granted the archbishop of Ochrid the right to collect it from the bishoprics and towns of his diocese and from all the Vlachs in Bulgaria and the Turks at Varda.[99]

The importance of these supplementary charges, requisitions and labour services compared with the basic land-tax is incalculable, but owing to the arbitrary nature of some of the charges they were a considerable burden. It is impossible to estimate the proportion of a peasant community's produce which was expropriated in requisitions or to determine whether the compensation given by the state was adequate. These charges were sufficiently important, however, for the owners of military lands to be granted exemptions from all obligations but the land-tax and the *aerikon* in compensation for their military duties.[100]

Requisitions were made for the maintenance of visiting officials and soldiers. These payments in kind to officials are known by several different names in the sources: *paroche chreion, proskynetikion, kathisma, epithesis monoprosopon, diatrophe* and *kaniskion*. The *kaniskion* was the technical term for the provisioning of a tax-collector. It appears to have been regulated more carefully than other payments in kind, because the quantities which were owed were recorded with the fiscal payment in the documents drawn up by the tax-assessors. Three charters from the eleventh century give details of the obligation. When a property of Panteleemon was assessed for a tax-payment of $\frac{2}{3}$ *nomisma*, the *kaniskion* was established at one loaf of bread, one chicken, one *modios* of barley and a half measure of wine.[101] This was probably the standard *kaniskion* for a property of moderate size. In 1095 the same *kaniskion* was imposed on a property of Esphigmenou.[102] When John Kataphloron assessed the tax-payment of a *metochion* of the monastery *tou Kaliourgou* in 1079, the only variation from the standard rate was that seven measures of barley were required.[103] Such standardisation was natural if the tax-collector stayed only a limited time on the property, but these texts give no indication of the length of time in which he was expected to discharge his duties. Another consideration is that these charters all

---

[98] *JGR*, I, pp. 275–6.
[99] Xanalatos, *Beiträge*, pp. 38–40. For the status of peasant communities subject to the *kanonikon*, see above, chapter 2 n. 181.
[100] Migne, *Patrologia Graeca*, CVII, cols. 700, 1032; Haldon, *Recruitment and Conscription*, p. 52 n. 90.
[101] *Pantéléèmôn*, no. 3 line 31.   [102] *Esphigménou*, no. 5 lines 32–3.
[103] *Lavra*, I, no. 39 lines 7–8.

106   *Economic expansion in the Byzantine empire*

concern Macedonia in the eleventh century and the standard rate which they suggest might not have applied at other times or in other regions.

Some light is thrown on these problems by three anonymous tenth-century letters exchanged by a tax-collector and a metropolitan.[104] They have the advantage that the case is presented from both sides. Tax-collectors were always maligned by Byzantine letter-writers and usually reality is clouded by a mass of rhetoric.[105] The contentious issue was the *kathisma*, which later appeared regularly in the lists of exemptions and was clearly similar to the *kaniskion*. The tax-collector had the right to stay on the property, where he was supplied with provisions, either freely or at an artificially established price. He complained that he was expelled from an ecclesiastical property and the metropolitan had encouraged the peasants to withhold their payments in kind.[106] The metropolitan replied that the tax-collector had attempted to impose a heavy payment on the property and had stayed longer than the three days he was permitted to remain there. The tax-collector attributed his longer stay to a delay in obtaining the full payment. The prescribed time-limit of three days might have been a standard procedure for estates of a certain size, a local custom or simply the rule for this particular property. The letters are also imprecise about the conditions on which the tax-collector had to be supplied with provisions. He denied making excessive demands and claimed to have exacted only two-thirds of the barley to which he was entitled and three jars of wine. At least some of these requirements were exacted with the payment of compensation.[107]

Other impositions in kind such as the *oikomodion*, a grain surcharge linked to the basic tax, were also fairly regularised.[108] In some cases state officials might try to impose such dues on privileged estates.

---

[104] Darrouzès, *Épistoliers*, pp. 358–62.

[105] See, for instance, the complaints of Theophylaktos about tax-collectors exacting harsh *meiligmata* (Migne, *Patrologia Graeca*, CXXVI, cols. 316C, 549B), which give no indication of the reasons for their actions. The *meiligmata* were gifts to officials similar to the *kaniskion*; see Xanalatos, *Beiträge*, pp. 51–2.

[106] These contributions were called *synonai*, which is the original ancient meaning of the term, not its proper Byzantine sense; see Darrouzès, *Épistoliers*, p. 359.

[107] There are references to the *antidosis* in these letters. It is probably a technical term for the payments made to the rural population for the supplies which were requisitioned; see Darrouzès, *Épistoliers*, pp. 360–1. Such forced sales were automatically listed in the eleventh-century chrysobulls; see, for instance, *Lavra*, I, no. 48 lines 41–2.

[108] J. Bompaire, 'Sur trois termes de fiscalité byzantine', *Bulletin de Correspondance hellénique*, 80 (1956), pp. 625–31. See also Psellos, *Scripta Minora*, II, no. 73; and Weiss, *Oströmische Beamte*, p. 134.

Taxation and monetary circulation

Nicolas Mystikos complained of a 'heavy and cruel' tax called the *kokkos*. This was not a technical term, but it obviously refers to a demand for grain, which had not previously been made on the patriarch's lands.[109]

The worst burdens were the visits of army units or a high-ranking civil official, who was accompanied by a large retinue. The best-known example of the disruption which such a visit could cost is given in the writings of Michael Choniates. The entry of the *praitor* into Athens had been prohibited by a chrysobull and the town had no obligation to provide a *proskynetikion*. On one occasion he was able to compel the town to admit him, and his officials exacted, according to Choniates, 500 measures of grain a day, sheep, cows, fish, wine and fodder for the horses. Oxen were requisitioned and their owners were made to pay to recover their animals.[110]

The billeting of an army also involved an obligation on the local population to provide supplies at a low price.[111] Nicolas Mystikos attempted to exploit his influence on behalf of his widowed sister-in-law, whose estate had not been freed from the imposition of soldiers. Mystikos was probably exaggerating when he asserted that it was her only source of income and the revenues were being seriously eroded.[112] The arbitrary character of the demands from the army nevertheless made landowners very quick to use whatever influence they had to obtain exemptions from them. The lists in the chrysobulls regularly included the *aplekton*, the *mitaton*, the *diatrophe phosaton* (the provisioning of soldiers) and the arming of soldiers. They also included lists of all the different nationalities which served as mercenaries.[113] The burden on the rural population was harshest when the emperor was undertaking large-scale military operations. The contributions in kind (*syneisphorai*) were particularly onerous during the reign of Nikephoros II,[114] while Manuel's preparations for his campaigns involved the

---

[109] *Nicolas, I, Patriarch*, no. 73. For the provision of selected animals, the *epithesis monoprosopon*, see Psellos, *Scripta minora*, II, no. 82; and Weiss, *Oströmische Beamte*, p. 55.

[110] Michael Choniates, II, pp. 106–7; Stadtmüller, *Michael Choniates*, pp. 284–5; J. E. Herrin, 'The Collapse of the Byzantine Empire in the Twelfth Century: A Study of a Medieval Economy', *University of Birmingham Historical Journal*, 12 (1970), pp. 196–7.

[111] Xanalatos, *Beiträge*, pp. 49–50.   [112] *Nicolas, I, Patriarch*, no. 170.

[113] To take just two examples, see *Lavra*, I, no. 48 lines 27–9; and *Engrapha Patmou*, I, no. 6 lines 38–41. For the *aplekton* and the *mitaton*, see Dölger, *Beiträge*, pp. 60–1; and Ostrogorsky, 'Die ländliche Steuergemeinde', pp. 60–1.

[114] Scylitzes, p. 274.

108   *Economic expansion in the Byzantine empire*

requisitioning of large numbers of oxen and wagons.[115] Coastal regions and islands faced the prospect of requisitions by naval forces: the seizure of cattle and movable property by passing warships was one of the reasons offered by the monks of Gymnopelagesion to explain the abandonment of the island in the tenth century.[116]

In some cases the obligation incumbent on a property consisted largely or wholly of a payment in kind. Some peasants who made payments in cabbages to the patriarch in the tenth century had been exempted from all payments to the state.[117] In another instance payment in wax was demanded by the church, and the tone of Nicolas Mystikos's letter suggests that those who made this annual payment were actively resisting attempts by ecclesiastical officials to intensify the obligation.[118]

Occasionally payments in kind had been made by villagers to a neighbouring monastery for a specific reason and the payments had become regularised by custom. After a miracle by St Theodore had saved a vine crop which had been endangered by bad weather the villagers brought fixed measures of wine to his monastery every year. Similarly, a miracle by St Meletios ensured an annual supply of oil for his monasteries from the neighbouring villages.[119]

The other category of imposition to which the peasantry was subject was the performance of labour services. These were due either to the state or to a private landowner if he had received an *exkousseia* (exemption) transferring these obligations to him. They were generally referred to as *angareiai*, but the chrysobulls mentioned specific corvées such as work on fortifications, bridges and roads, the cutting-down and transporting of wood, and in some cases shipbuilding.[120]

Pakourianos, who was entitled to labour services from all the inhabitants of Stenimachos, freed one of the *paroikoi* from all these obligations so that he could work in the service of the hostel which Pakourianos established there.[121] Forced labour was used for large-scale

[115] *Ioannis Cinnami Epitome* (Bonn edn, 1836), pp. 199, 299. For the preparations before Manzikert, see Attaleiates, p. 151.
[116] *Lavra*, I, no. 10 lines 15–18.   [117] *Nicolas, I, Patriarch*, no. 152.
[118] *Ibid.*, no. 74.
[119] *Vie de Théodore de Sykéôn*, p. 45; Vasilievskij, 'Meletios', p. 32.
[120] For the *angareiai*, see Dölger, *Beiträge*, p. 62; Ostrogorsky, 'Die ländliche Steuergemeinde', p. 60; and A. Stauridou-Zaphraka, 'He angareia sto Byzantio', *Byzantina*, 11 (1982), pp. 23–54.
[121] Gautier, 'Grégoire Pakourianos', pp. 111–13 lines 1539–43. Isaac Komnenos's *typikon* stipulated that in the event of arson all the *paroikoi* were to be compelled by the *proestos* to do the repairs; see Petit, 'Kosmosotira', pp. 66–7.

Taxation and monetary circulation

undertakings; Romanos III imposed transportation services in equipping the monastery of Triakontophyllos.[122] In the late eleventh century the military requirements of the state were predominant. Theophylaktos regarded the *kastroktisia* (fortification building) as the most oppressive corvée. He also complained about the imposition of guard-duty.[123] In the twelfth century guard-duty in the monastery of Patmos was imposed on the *stratiotai* and other villagers from May onwards.[124]

It is impossible to assess the overall impact of these corvées on peasant communities and in particular the extent to which labour services were used in agricultural production. It is not known how many days of service peasants were expected to provide in the eleventh and twelfth centuries, but it is a safe assumption that it varied from estate to estate and from region to region. The fourteenth-century *praktika* sometimes stated the number of days' work owed to the landowner: usually twelve but sometimes twenty-four or fifty-two.[125]

By the eleventh century there are signs that obligations in kind and labour services were more frequently commuted into cash payments. Although specific instances of commutation are rare in the sources except in the case of the *strateia*, there are clear indications that money payments were demanded more often. Some obligations in the lists of exemptions indisputably come into this category. The *antikaniskion* and the *antimitatikion* were cash payments instead of the *kaniskion* and the *mitaton*. A chrysobull granted to Lavra in 1060 makes it clear that in some cases cash payments were exacted instead of the billeting of soldiers or the provision of supplies.[126] Possibly the *parangareia* was a commutation of the *angareia*. It has also been suggested that there was a tendency to commute the *kastroktisia*, the *gephyrosis* (work on bridges) and the *hodostrosia* (road-laying) because these obligations were listed in the chrysobulls next to the monetary obligations;[127] they did not, however, become regular cash payments on all estates[128] because these obligations were sometimes more useful than a straightforward money payment.

---

[122] Scylitzes, p. 384.

[123] Xanalatos, *Beiträge*, pp. 46–7, 50–1; S. Trojanos, 'Kastroktisia. Einige Bermerkungen über die finanziellen Grundlagen des Festbaues im byzantinischen Reich', *Byzantina*, 1 (1969), pp. 41–57. For the guard-duty, see Leroy-Molinghen, 'Prolégomènes à une édition critique des "Lettres" de Théophylacte de Bulgarie', p. 260.

[124] MM, VI, p. 147 lines 23–5.

[125] Laiou-Thomadakis, *Peasant Society*, p. 181.

[126] The most important phrase is *logarike eispraxis*, which implies a cash payment; see *Lavra*, I, no. 33 lines 81, 116.

[127] Dölger, *Beiträge*, p. 62 n. 4.   [128] Trojanos, 'Kastroktisia', pp. 49–50.

110   *Economic expansion in the Byzantine empire*

Sometimes the commuted payments were very high. In 1082 Vatopedi succeeded in obtaining an exemption from an *antikaniskion* of twenty *nomismata* which had been exacted from two of its estates – a higher sum than the combined land-tax of nineteen *nomismata* from these two estates.[129] In some villages the *angareiai* were all transformed into cash payments. In 1219 this was the case in Lampsakos. The obligations were commuted into fixed sums depending on the wealth of the peasants. Each *zeugaratos* and *boidatos* paid four *hyperpyra* instead of performing labour services and each *aktemon* appears to have paid one *hyperpyra*.[130] The evidence from Lampsakos can be misleading. Owing to its position as a naval port the peasants' produce could be transported easily to Constantinople and cash was probably more readily available in Lampsakos than in more unfavourably situated villages and small towns.[131] The case of Lampsakos illustrates a tendency for payments to be demanded in cash more frequently, or at least recorded in monetary terms for accounting purposes even if they were not always exacted in cash, but a complete commutation was probably not possible everywhere.

The obligation whose commutation is most regularly attested in the sources is the *strateia* (military holding). In the tenth century cash payments were demanded with greater frequency, but commutation became generalised only in the eleventh century.[132] The earliest record of commutation on a large scale comes from the reign of Leo VI, when payments were demanded in the western themes from those who chose not to perform military service. Again, in the reign of Romanos I, 100 pounds in cash and 1,000 horses were demanded from the Peloponnesos for the non-performance of military service in Italy. The rates imposed by the administration were five *nomismata* from everyone who was responsible for military service; every two *aporoi* were allowed to make the payment jointly. However, the commutation had not yet become institutionalised. Porphyrogenitos's account implies that the thematic force had an element of choice in the way it discharged its

---

[129] Goudas, 'Vatopedi', pp. 125–6.

[130] Tafel and Thomas, *Urkunden*, II, p. 209; Angold, *A Byzantine Government in Exile*, pp. 222–3 n. 86.

[131] It is impossible to accept the opinion of Dölger, (*Beiträge*, p. 62) that by the early thirteenth century the *angareiai* were universally commuted into cash payments. For some of the problems involved in an extensive commutation, see Hendy, *Studies in the Byzantine Monetary Economy*, pp. 294–9.

[132] There is little evidence to support the contention of Angold (*The Byzantine Empire 1025–1204*, p. 4) that Basil II was responsible for the generalised commutation of military service in the armies of the themes.

Taxation and monetary circulation

responsibilities, rather than having a generalised policy of commutation imposed upon it by the state.[133]

By the second half of the century the tendency towards commutation had been intensified, but it was still not universal. Cash payments appear to have been exacted for obligations to the *dromos*, navy and army. Under Nikephoros II the contributors were transferred from one obligation to another that was more onerous, a procedure which was practical only if cash payments were involved. The extent of these obligations was also widened. Peasants who had previously been outside their range were enrolled for the *dromikai strateiai*. The spread of cash payments was also encouraged by the division of the responsibility for the *strateia* among heirs or other co-contributors (*syndotai*). Nikephoros not only widened the range of these obligations, but increased the payments for them.[134]

Some chrysobulls show how extensive commutation had become. The *strateia* and the payments for the *dromos* both appeared in the lists of exemptions in association with such cash payments as the *kapnikon*, the *synone* and the *aerikon*.[135] The peasants who were installed on the estates of Nea Mone had to be free of all fiscal payments due to the state, including responsibility for the *strateia* and the *dromos*.[136] A chrysobull which Lavra received in 1104 is even more explicit. If any *strateia*, obligation to the *dromos* or other charge was imposed on the monastery's estates, the payment was to be suppressed and registered as a *logisimon* in the relevant departments.[137]

The sources give a few details of the *strateia* imposed as a cash payment on specific properties. In the middle of the eleventh century Constantine Phasoulos paid $2\frac{1}{2}$ *nomismata* as the *strateia* on land which he held in the Kassandra peninsula. His property bordered that of the monastery of Panteleemon, which encroached upon sixteen *modioi* of

---

[133] Perhaps Porphyrogenitos's figures are exaggerated. They are certainly conveniently rounded figures; see *DAI*, p. 256; Haldon, *Recruitment and Conscription*, p. 61; and Ahrweiler, 'Recherches sur l'administration', p. 14.

[134] Zonaras, III, pp. 505–6; Ahrweiler, 'Recherches sur l'administration', pp. 16–21; Haldon, *Recruitment and Conscription*, pp. 60–2 n. 107.

[135] *Lavra*, I, no. 38 lines 36–7, no. 48 lines 34–6; Lemerle, *The Agrarian History*, pp. 224–5. This is not a conclusive argument by itself, because other dues which could be raised in kind, such as the *oikomodion*, are included in the same part of the texts, but it does complement the other evidence in suggesting a general trend.

[136] *JGR*, I, p. 617 lines 5–7.

[137] *Lavra*, I, no. 56 lines 91–3. That the *stratiotes* might still be enrolled for a campaign is shown by a letter of Psellos on behalf of a poor soldier; see Psellos, *Scripta Minora*, no. 132. See also Haldon, *Recruitment and Conscription*, pp. 56–8, n. 100.

112   *Economic expansion in the Byzantine empire*

his land – the total area subject to the *strateia* is not known. The dispute was resolved by a compromise. The monastery paid ten good-quality *nomismata* to retain possession of eight *modioi*, whose fiscal obligation Phasoulos agreed to meet. Technically, the *strateia* could be alienated only with the transfer of the responsibility accompanying it, which is why Phasoulos continued to pay the tax and received such a large sum for only eight *modioi*.[138] Cash payments were imposed as *strateiai* on the peasants who were installed on Patmos by the monastery of St John. Owing to the immunity from fiscal dues which had been granted to Christodoulos, the *strateiai* were transferred from these holdings to the property on Kos which Christodoulos had conceded to the state.[139]

The same trend also applied to the maritime lands. Cash payments were usually imposed instead of personal service and they went directly to the financing of the navy until the reign of John Komnenos. Then, at the instigation of his finance minister, John Poutzes, they were paid into the treasury, which was supposed to meet future naval requirements. At this stage commutation had not been completed, but after the reform the islands no longer provided manned warships.[140]

Cash payments to finance shipbuilding were exacted from the monastery of Patmos by the *praktor* of Samos. His action was cited as a precedent by subsequent officials, who continued to demand cash payments contrary to the terms of the monastery's chrysobulls.[141] In the late twelfth century these payments were theoretically established by an assessment, but they varied in practice according to the arbitrary will of officials and the ability of the population to resist their demands. In the year before Michael Choniates's *Hypomnestikon* contributions for the *syndosiai ploimon* were exacted from the Athenians by the *praitor*, by the fleet commander Steiriones and Sgouros, a powerful regional magnate. Athens was assessed at a higher rate than the Theban region and according to Choniates the Thebans were able to avoid paying the tax. He requested that the Athenians should pay only the amount which had been fixed by the assessment of John Doukas, the *logothetes tou dromou*, and that no additional amounts should be exacted without

---

[138] *Dionysiou*, no. 1.

[139] *Engrapha Patmou*, II, no. 54; Lemerle, *The Agrarian History*, pp. 226–7; Karlin-Hayter, 'Notes sur les archives de Patmos', pp. 190–2. For the commutation of military service in Mesopotamia during the reign of Monomachos, see below, p. 113.

[140] Nicetas Choniates, p. 55. For the *baros ploimon* in Alexios's reign, see *Lavra*, I, no. 58 lines 8–9, 17–18. See also Ahrweiler, *Byzance et la mer*, pp. 212–13, 230–1.

[141] *Engrapha Patmou*, I, no. 20.

Taxation and monetary circulation   113

specific instructions from the emperor. He claimed that almost ten pounds had been exacted from the Athenians.[142]

The trend towards the commutation of obligations into cash payments was probably the main reason why the lists of exemptions in the chrysobulls became more comprehensive in the eleventh century. In the documents of the late tenth century the lists are much shorter, consisting mainly of general terms like *angareia* and *epereia*.[143] The earliest of the long, comprehensive lists in the surviving documentation date from 1044 and 1060.[144] About this time cash payments began to be demanded more regularly. It has already been suggested that the transformation of the *aerikon* into a more regularised fiscal due began about this time. The arbitrary nature of some of these cash demands made it even more important for landowners to protect themselves against tax-collectors, who could interpret the exemptions in the chrysobulls literally and impose any obligations which were not specifically mentioned.

The increase in cash payments had a sharp impact in different parts of the empire. Generally it reflected the larger quantity of money in circulation, but in some regions it provoked social unrest. In Bulgaria taxes had been raised in kind since the conquest by Basil II, who made no attempt to change the customs which had prevailed under Samuel. A peasant with one ploughteam paid one *modios* of wheat, one of millet and a measure of wine. The attempt of John the Orphanotrophos to change these obligations into cash payments contributed greatly to the widespread support which the Bulgar revolt of 1040 attracted.[145] Evidently, in Bulgaria coinage was not circulating in as large quantities as it was a century later.[146]

In Iberia and Mesopotamia the commutation of military service into cash payments in Monomachos's reign led to the dissolution of the army. Previously it had guarded the border against Arab incursions. When Leo Serblias made an assessment of the region and imposed new

---

[142] Michael Choniates, II, pp. 106–7; Stadtmüller, *Michael Choniates*, pp. 284–6; Ahrweiler, *Byzance et la mer*, pp. 276–8; J. E. Herrin, 'Realities of Byzantine Provincial Government: Hellas and Peloponnesos, 1180–1205', *Dumbarton Oaks Papers*, 29 (1975), p. 275.

[143] *Lavra*, I, no. 6 lines 21–7; Dölger, *Schatzkammern*, no. 56 lines 9–14.

[144] *JGR*, I, p. 617; *Lavra*, I, no. 33 lines 77–84, 113–20.

[145] Scylitzes, p. 412; Hendy, *Studies in the Byzantine Monetary Economy*, p. 297; J. Ferluga, 'Les insurrections des slaves de la Macédoine au XIe siècle', in *Byzantium on the Balkans* (Amsterdam, 1976), pp. 383–90. For the eleventh-century revolts provoked by fiscal practices, see Weiss, *Oströmische Beamte*, pp. 4–5.

[146] See above, p. 87.

114   Economic expansion in the Byzantine empire

taxes, the army deserted to the Arabs. The affair is represented by Skylitzes as part of the general tendency for new impositions to be devised, which he blamed on Monomachos's expensive projects like the construction of the Mangana.[147]

Several local revolts broke out in the middle of the eleventh century as a result of excessive fiscal demands. Unfortunately, the sources are uninformative about the causal factors, but the tendency towards commutation was probably one of the reasons for the discontent. The complaints of Byzantine historians about tax-collectors cannot be taken at face value automatically, but here they are supported by corroborating evidence of the intensification of cash payments from other sources and the more precise information about the effect of commutation in Bulgaria and Iberia. Attaleiates refers to the collection of unforeseen taxes and contrived arrears in the reign of Monomachos and to increases in the reign of Isaac.[148] Skylitzes connected Monomachos's need for revenues with the imposition of 'contrived taxes'. As the passage is linked with the affair in Iberia, he is probably referring to the replacement of non-monetary obligations with cash payments.[149] A revolt in Naupaktos was provoked by the imposition of novel taxes and probably also by Constantine VIII's cancellation of Basil II's remission of tax-payments.[150] In 1034 a revolt in Antioch was provoked by a tax-collector.[151] In 1040 the theme of Nikopolis (except Naupaktos) supported the Bulgar revolt for the same reason.[152]

Tax increases were also one of the grievances of the rebels in Thessaly in 1066. Nikoulitzas Delphinas, the powerful local landowner who was put in command of the rebellion against his will, advised the emperor to cancel the recent increases in order to undermine support for the revolt. It was a popular rebellion, provoked by widespread discontent not by aristocratic intrigues. The impetus came from the people of the region and the leader of the rebellion was reluctant to face the dangers. The involvement of Vlach pastoralists in the revolt suggests that the

---

[147] Scylitzes, p. 476; Attaleiates, pp. 44–5; Cecaumenos, *Strategicon*, p. 18. Zonaras, III, p. 647, says that the taxes were imposed on land which had previously paid no taxes at all. However, the holders of the *strateia* had to pay the basic land-tax; either Zonaras was misinformed or some system of *limitanei* had existed in the border region. For this affair, see also Ahrweiler, 'Recherches sur l'administration', p. 23; and Lemerle, *Cinq études*, pp. 268–9.

[148] *Ibid.*, pp. 50, 61, 77.   [149] Scylitzes, p. 476.

[150] *Ibid.*, pp. 372–3.

[151] *Ibid.*, p. 395; Zonaras, III, p. 588. For a similar revolt in Cyprus in 1042–3, see Scylitzes, p. 429.   [152] Scylitzes, pp. 411–12.

Taxation and monetary circulation 115

increases affected obligations other than the basic land-tax. Kekaumenos does not give details of the precise nature of the tax increases, but as Constantine X's reign was not marked by any further debasement of the coinage the increases were not intended to compensate for a reduction in the value of the *nomisma*. More money was being appropriated from the region and this could have been done as easily by commuting obligations into cash payments as by increasing the basic tax.[153]

These revolts vividly illustrate the limitations to monetary circulation in an economy consisting predominantly of peasant producers. Although there is no doubt that more money was in circulation than in previous centuries and the state was appropriating more in taxation, the extent to which the economy was monetised is a very different problem, complicated by regional variations. The revolts were probably symptomatic of a more widespread discontent with fiscal policies. In some regions like Bulgaria the demand for agricultural produce from urban markets was not strong enough to enable peasant producers to acquire cash easily. Even in Thessaly and the Antioch region, where coinage was circulating in larger amounts, sudden increases in taxes caused difficulties for peasants who were producing largely for their own subsistence and not for commercial purposes.

The greatest difficulty in dealing with this problem is the scarcity of evidence about the monetary resources of individual landowners and peasant producers. Skylitzes gives some rather unreliable figures for the fortunes of two ecclesiastical magnates. The metropolitan of Thessalonike is said to have had a treasure of thirty-three *kentenaria*. On the death of the patriarch Alexios in 1043 it was reported that he had stored twenty-five *kentenaria* (180,000 *nomismata*) in a monastery.[154] While these figures might be greatly exaggerated, other figures which are given in monastic *typika* underestimate the wealth of their institutions. Isaac Komnenos stipulated that Kosmosotira had to keep a contingency fund of thirty pounds of *hyperpyra*.[155] Gregory Pakourianos stipulated that Bačkovo was to maintain at least ten pounds and only a surplus above this amount was to be used for the purchase of

---

[153] Cecaumenos, *Strategicon*, pp. 66–72, esp. p. 70; Ferluga, 'Les insurrections des slaves', pp. 391–2.
[154] Scylitzes, pp. 402, 429; Hendy, *Studies in the Byzantine Monetary Economy*, p. 204. See also G. Weiss, 'Vermögensbildung der Byzantiner in Privathand. Methodische Fragen einer quantitativen Analyse', *Byzantina*, 11 (1982), pp. 77–92.
[155] Petit, 'Kosmosotira', p. 65.

116 *Economic expansion in the Byzantine empire*

properties.[156] Symbatios Pakourianos's properties were less extensive, but on his marriage he received a dowry of fifty pounds in gold coins. His wife, Kale, bequeathed fifty-four pounds to her brother Sergios in addition to her other cash bequests which totalled nearly twenty pounds.[157] Some prices which were paid for properties illustrate the resources which some landowners had at their disposal. Nea Mone spent sixty pounds on the estate of Kalothekia and the monastery of the Amalfitans paid twenty-four pounds for an estate east of the Strymon.[158] These figures all underestimate the wealth of these landowners, because cash was only one part of their total movable wealth.[159]

We are not so well informed about less illustrious landowners. A dispute between the villagers of Menikon and Achillios Limenites was resolved in 1118 with a payment of two pounds of gold to the villagers as damages. Nothing is known about the estates of Limenites. Although he was not a great aristocrat, he was a powerful landowner in Crete with substantial financial resources.[160]

In a few cases fairly substantial landowners did not have the cash resources to repay loans. A monk, George, had borrowed 132 *nomismata* to purchase the monastery *tou Pithara* at Kareai, but was unable to repay more than twenty-two *nomismata*. The remainder of the debt was paid off by Tornikios Kontoleon, who took possession of the monastery in 1024.[161] Maria Skleraina lent sixty-two pounds to a *patrikios*, Pantherios, who was probably a relative. Since he did not have the resources in movables to repay the loan, she took possession of the monastery of St Mamas in Constantinople.[162]

The extent to which peasant producers had ready cash is a difficult problem. An independent peasant farmer would have needed money to meet his fiscal obligations to the state, which was usually only interested in exacting cash. Money could have been obtained either by compulsory sales to the state at artificially determined prices or by recourse to markets. The situation of dependent peasants might have

---

[156] Gautier, 'Grégoire Pakourianos', p. 109. Lemerle, *Cinq études*, pp. 190–1, has tentatively estimated the monetary expenses of the monastery at about twenty pounds. See also Hendy, *Studies in the Byzantine Monetary Economy*, pp. 212–15.

[157] Iberites, 'Byzantinai diathekai', pp. 615; 366–8.

[158] *JGR*, I, p. 616; *Lavra*, I, no. 42.

[159] See above, p. 81; and Hendy, *Studies in the Byzantine Monetary Economy*, pp. 211, 218–20.

[160] MM, VI, pp. 97–8. [161] *Lavra*, I, no. 25.

[162] *Peira*, XV 16, *JGR*, IV, p. 54; Seibt, *Die Skleroi*, pp. 71, 86. For another crisis of this sort when the monastery established by St Nikon at Sparta did not have enough cash to meet a fiscal demand, see 'Nikon Metanoeite', pp. 191–2.

Taxation and monetary circulation

been different. Their obligations to the landowner were listed in cash in the *praktika*, but this does not necessarily mean that the landowners were paid in cash. Monetary terms may have been used as convenient units of accounts, a standard according to which payments in kind could be calculated, if it suited the landowner to exact the obligations in this way. This was probably a much easier arrangement in areas where the peasants did not have convenient access to a local market and commercial fairs were few.[163] The difficulties which some peasant communities might have had in finding even modest amounts of cash are manifest in the provisions of the tenth-century legislation concerning the repayment of the price of the land when it was restored to its previous owners. If the land had been purchased by the powerful from the poor (the *aporos* whose wealth theoretically amounted to less than fifty *nomismata*), the repayment had to be made within three years. Where the entire village community was too poor to make the repayment, the alienated land was pledged for a number of years and the price and expenses were collected from the produce of the land.[164]

The sources offer very few examples of cash payments made by peasant farmers. In 941 a peasant, Nicolas, purchased 100 *modioi* of klasmatic land in Kassandra for two *nomismata*.[165] The purchasers of the klasmatic land near Hierissos, which was sold in the same year, included peasants as well as inhabitants of the town.[166] Thirteen peasant families paid nineteen *nomismata* for 950 *modioi* at Ozolimnos, but they were unable to pay the second instalment in 956 and lost the ownership of the land.[167] Small landowners with property near towns probably had greater monetary resources owing to the proximity of a larger market. Constantine Lagoudes, who owned two vineyards near Hierissos, was not a subsistence farmer and needed to sell his produce to survive.[168] In 1097 Constantine Triphyles purchased two small plots of land contiguous to his own near Thessalonike for forty-five *trachea*

---

[163] Hendy, *Studies in the Byzantine Monetary Economy*, pp. 297–8; Haldon and Kennedy, 'The Arab–Byzantine Frontier', pp. 90–1 n. 39; Duby, *The Early Growth of the European Economy*, pp. 63–4. When Lavra made some small purchases in the late thirteenth century, the price was reckoned in monetary terms, but in some cases payment was made either wholly or partly in kind; see *Lavra* II, nos. 85, 87, 88. See also MM, VI, p. 231 line 4. For an instance of a powerful landowner preferring payment in kind rather than cash, see V. Grumel, *Les Regestes des actes du patriarcat de Constantinople*, I, *Les Actes des patriarches, fasc. III. Les regestes de 1043 à 1206* (Bucharest, 1947), no. 952.

[164] *JGR*, I, pp. 216–17.   [165] *Lavra*, I, no. 3.

[166] *Prôtaton*, nos. 4, 5.   [167] *Xéropotamou*, no. 1. See above, p. 57.

[168] *Lavra*, I, no. 18 lines 23–33, 39–41.

118   *Economic expansion in the Byzantine empire*

stauroagiodemetrata, the most heavily debased issue of *nomismata*.[169] These debased coins certainly had a wider circulation than earlier better-quality *nomismata* and came more easily into the possession of less wealthy landowners.

Angold has argued that a group of thirteenth-century documents supply evidence of the circulation of money among the peasantry. However, a different interpretation can be placed upon them. They deal with the alienation of peasant properties to monasteries and in one case to a powerful secular landowner. To show that cash circulated among the peasantry examples have to be given of peasants making purchases, not selling as they were in all these cases. Generally, they preferred to receive cash for the sales and only a few payments were made in kind. A shortage of cash was probably one of the reasons for these sales and they do not suggest that much money circulated among the peasantry in normal circumstances.[170] A similar conclusion is suggested by the evidence of peasant occupations which is derived from the names in the *praktika* of the Athonite monasteries. The villages in the Chalkidike were cohesive economic units and peasants could obtain most of their needs in the village without recourse to outside markets.[171] Consequently, the degree of monetisation was probably limited to the sale of agricultural produce in order to raise cash for fiscal obligations.

The exploitation of the direct producer was intensified by increases in the rate of the basic land-tax and also by the commutation of other obligations into cash payments. So the peasantry needed to obtain more money to meet the demands which were imposed on it. Not only was a larger proportion of the peasantry reduced to *paroikoi*, but the fiscal pressure on them was intensified. The gains which were derived from economic expansion were divided between the state and feudal landowners. The state obtained the overwhelming bulk of its revenues from the rural population. The extension of the area under cultivation added to its wealth and enabled it to increase its expenditure. The

---

[169] *Ibid.*, no. 53. For this issue, see Hendy, *Coinage and Money*, pp. 41–3, 125–6.

[170] Another possible explanation for the sales is that the land had been subdivided and fragmented to such an extent that it was uneconomic to work it; see Angold, *A Byzantine Government in Exile*, p. 107. It has been claimed, using evidence from the Nichoria excavations, that 'purchases [in rural areas] were apparently made with cash'; see W. A. McDonald, W. D. E. Coulson and J. Rosser, *Excavations at Nichoria in Southwest Greece*, III, *Dark Age and Byzantine Occupation* (Minneapolis, 1983), p. 424. Unfortunately, the finds on which this judgement is based consist of only one anonymous *follis* and one *tetarteron* from the reign of Manuel (*ibid.*, pp. 405–6), too small a number to justify such claims.

[171] Laiou-Thomadakis, *Peasant Society*, p. 126.

Taxation and monetary circulation 119

greater amount of money in circulation enabled it to impose higher rates of taxation. The weakening of imperial authority in the 1070s and the 1080s, which was mentioned in the previous chapter, is also apparent in the tax-payments which the state was able to exact at that time. The higher rates of the Alexian reform are indicative of a more general restoration of imperial control. Nevertheless, the large concessions which were made to powerful landowners in the previous decades were reinforced by the higher rates at which money was appropriated from the direct producers. Consequently, feudal landowners had larger resources in monetary wealth at their disposal to maintain their social and political position.

————————————— Chapter 4 —————————————

Agricultural production

The most serious restriction on economic growth in Byzantium was that the main unit of agricultural production, the peasant holding, was geared mainly to its own reproduction. Its resources for making improvements to its property were limited and the most obvious way of increasing production was simply to extend the area under cultivation. The peasant household's other major objective was to produce enough to meet the obligations imposed by the state or a private landowner. The larger amount of money which was being extracted from the rural economy corresponded either to a more effective exploitation of agricultural resources or to higher prices caused by a stronger demand for food from towns. Unfortunately, there is an almost complete dearth of grain and other prices during the period.[1] Any consideration of agricultural production is fraught with difficulties owing to the deficiencies of the evidence. No figures of crop yields survive from this period.[2] The only surviving treatise on agriculture is the *Geoponika*, a reworking of a sixth-century compilation, which consists of extracts from classical authorities.[3] There is no indication of any advances in agricultural technology, but it is equally important to consider how effectively agricultural resources were exploited within the limits of the technology available to the Byzantines and what effect the social trends

[1] G. Ostrogorsky, 'Löhne und Preise in Byzanz', *Byzantinische Zeitschrift*, 32 (1932), pp. 319–26. Antoniadis-Bibicou, 'Démographie, salaires et prix à Byzance au XIᵉ siècle', pp. 230–3. The evidence for urban expansion will be discussed below (see chapter 6).
[2] The evidence is also very sparse for the later period. Some figures from Cyprus in the fourteenth century give an average of between 3:1 and 4:1; see Laiou-Thomadakis, *Peasant Society*, p. 68. See also Svoronos, 'Remarques sur les structures économiques', p. 57 n. 32. These figures are too few to be of any use for statistical purposes. Some very interesting figures are available for grain yields in Palestine in the late Roman period. They give a total yield for wheat of about 7:1 and for barley of 8:1; see C. J. Kraemer, *Excavations at Nessana*, III, *Non-Literary Papyri* (Princeton, 1958), no. 82.
[3] White, *Roman Farming*, pp. 32, 45–6.

120

Agricultural production   121

of the period had on agricultural production. There has been a tendency to regard Byzantine feudalism as a negative factor leading to economic decline, but as the revenues of large landowners increased they had greater resources to make improvements to their properties. Such improvements could take the form of the acquisition of tools and ploughing animals, the construction of buildings and industrial establishments, permanent improvements such as bridges, roads, drainage and irrigation schemes, water-mills and the planting on a large scale of vines, olives and other fruit trees.[4] At the same time, demographic increase ensured that a sufficient supply of manpower was available. The absence of technological innovation should not be given an exaggerated importance. The major consideration is whether significant gains were made as a result of the social trends which were prevalent in Byzantium at this time, and in particular whether the traditional negative assessment of the economic consequences of the accumulation of extensive estates by feudal landowners is in need of revision.

The first objective of agricultural production was to achieve self-sufficiency. It was the most fundamental requirement throughout all strata of the rural economy from small peasant producers to the largest secular and ecclesiastical landowners. Self-sufficiency was presented as a virtue by the authors of saints' lives. The parents of Luke the Stylite were described as having a moderate amount of wealth, enough to cater for their own requirements.[5] Kekaumenos strongly recommended self-sufficiency for good practical reasons, particularly the creation of *autourgia* – vineyards, olives and other trees, mills and workshops – which would give an annual return with as few outlays in cash or labour as possible. A landowner needed enough oxen for ploughing and enough pigs, sheep and cattle for his herds and flocks to grow naturally and provide his consumption requirements without recourse to the market. The emphasis was on keeping expenditure down to a minimum. He also warned that the poor man should not undertake building expenses, which would put him into debt, but should concentrate on viticulture and arable cultivation. Only if he had a surplus to sell, should he spend money on buildings.[6]

---

[4] For a discussion of the limits to improvements in medieval England, see R. H. Hilton, 'Rent and Capital Formation in Feudal Society', in *The English Peasantry in the Later Middle Ages*, pp. 174–214.

[5] 'Vita S. Lucae Stylitae', pp. 199–200.

[6] Cecaumenos, *Strategicon*, pp. 36, 51; Hendy, *Studies in the Byzantine Monetary Economy*, pp. 565–8.

122   Economic expansion in the Byzantine empire

These recommendations were not simple moralising. They reflect the realities of an economy consisting mainly of small-scale peasant producers, on whom monetisation had only a limited impact. Even in modern times the main aim of many Greek farmers was to feed their own families rather than produce for the market.[7] On the large estates, too, most produce was intended for direct consumption. Besides leaving their *paroikoi* with sufficient means of reproduction, the estates had to satisfy the substantial requirements of large monasteries. In some cases these requirements were enormous: by 1045 Lavra already had 700 monks.[8] Self-sufficiency offered practical advantages to landowners. If they used wage labour, a diversity of crops spread labour requirements more evenly through the year. It also protected the landowner against the failure of individual crops, and, of course, the interaction of arable and pastoral farming helped to maintain the fertility of the soil.[9]

This emphasis on production for direct consumption does not entirely explain the stagnation of Byzantine agricultural technology compared with the medieval West. The improvements which were made in the West were less appropriate to the geographical conditions in Byzantium and, in the case of the water-mill, can also be explained by social differences between Byzantium and the West.[10]

The most fundamental innovation in western Europe was the heavy plough with a mouldboard. It was never introduced into Byzantium. The characteristic Byzantine plough remained the sole-ard, which was prevalent in the Roman period.[11] Comparisons between Byzantine and

---

[7] Admiralty, Naval Intelligence Division, *Geographical Handbook Series, Greece* (3 vols., London, 1944–5), III, p. 300.

[8] *Lavra*, I, p. 51. By 1196 there were nearly 150 monks on Patmos; see *Engrapha Patmou*, I, no. 21 line 2. For other figures, see P. Charanis 'The Monk as an Element of Byzantine Society', *Dumbarton Oaks Papers*, 25 (1971), pp. 69–71.

[9] R. Duncan-Jones, *The Economy of the Roman Empire* (Cambridge, 1974), pp. 37–8.

[10] The importance of technological developments in the West should not be exaggerated, as they have by L. White, *Medieval Technology and Social Change* (Oxford, 1962); and L. White, 'The Expansion of Technology 500–1500', in C. Cipolla (ed.), *The Fontana Economic History of Europe*, I, *The Middle Ages* (London, 1972), pp. 143–74, where he takes no account of the convincing criticisms of R. H. Hilton and P. H. Sawyer, 'Technical Determinism: The Stirrup and the Plough', *Past and Present*, 24 (1963), pp. 90–100.

[11] The only evidence about the design of Byzantine ploughs comes from artistic representations; see M. Kaplan, 'Quelques remarques sur les paysages agraires byzantins (VIème siècle–milieu XIème siècle), *Revue du Nord*, 62/244 (1980), pp. 155–76. The sole-ard survived in the post-Byzantine era; see A. A. M. Bryer, 'The Estates of the Empire of Trebizond. Evidence for their Resources, Products, Agriculture, Ownership and Location', *Archeion Pontou*, 35 (1979), pp. 395–7; and Benaki Museum, *Paradosiakes kalliergeies* (Athens, 1978), pp. 14–16.

Agricultural production

western ploughs are not entirely appropriate. The main difference between the two types is that the sole-ard throws up earth on both sides of the ploughshare without inverting it, whereas the plough with the mouldboard does make the inversion. The latter was predominant in temperate regions with heavy soils, where deep tillage and a complete inversion of the sod are necessary. The sole-ard plough scratches the surface instead of digging deep. Shallow tillage is more suitable in dryer regions such as the eastern Mediterranean. Where crops are grown in soils moistened by winter rains and the growing season is dry with hot temperatures, only a light and frequent ploughing of the surface soil is necessary. In these circumstances a heavy plough might have a disastrous effect. The lighter sole-ard is more appropriate. It also has the advantage of being much cheaper and easier to construct and of requiring only one pair of oxen. Its lighter work makes regular ploughing easier.[12] In modern times the fertile alluvial plains of Greece have given satisfactory yields with only light ploughing by the sole-ard.[13] Unfortunately, there is little evidence about the types of sole-ard plough which were in use in the Byzantine period. The most important consideration is whether the ploughshares were made of wood, or iron, which would have been more effective. References to ploughs in the sources are very scarce. There were two on the estate of Baris and iron was used for the ploughshare.[14] A twelfth-century inventory of the monastery of Panteleemon refers to four ploughshares made of iron.[15] Iron shares were found in the excavation of Dinogetia.[16] This evidence, admittedly slight, does indicate that the use of iron ploughshares was fairly common, at least on larger estates.

Discussion of the other implements which were in regular use is also hindered by lack of evidence. References to tools are scarce in the texts and descriptions are non-existent. Evidence from earlier and later periods indicates that no significant changes in farming equipment appear to have been made in the Byzantine period. The Farmer's Law mentions the tools which any peasant would normally have possessed:

[12] K. D. White, *Agricultural Implements of the Roman World* (Cambridge, 1967), pp. 126–8. In western Europe the adoption of the heavy plough was a long process, especially in the south; see G. Duby, *Rural Economy and Country Life in the Medieval West* (London, 1968), pp. 17–19, 109–12.

[13] W. M. Leake, *Travels in Northern Greece* (4 vols., London, 1835), IV, p. 444. For grain exports from these regions in the later Middle Ages, see below, p. 139.

[14] *Engrapha Patmou*, II, no. 50 lines 121–2.

[15] *Pantéléèmôn*, no. 7 line 27.

[16] G. Stefan, I. Barnea, M. Comsa and E. Comsa, *Dinogetia*, I, *Asezarea feudala timpurie de la Bisericuta – Garvan* (Bucharest, 1967), p. 392; Barnea, 'Dinogetia', p. 265.

124   *Economic expansion in the Byzantine empire*

the spade (*lisgon*), the mattock or two-pronged hoe (*dikella*), a pruning-knife (*kladeuterion*), a sickle (*drepanon*) and an axe (*pelekys*).[17] In the absence of any precise description of these tools, it is necessary to use Roman evidence. The *dikella* was a generic term for any mattock, but it also had the more specialised meaning of a two-pronged drag-hoe, which was often used in preference to the plough to turn over the soil of vineyards and to dig around olive trees. It is represented in a mosaic in the Great Palace at Constantinople, where two men are shown digging in an orchard.[18] The *lisgon* was a similar type, probably with only a single blade, and it was used for digging.[19] The sickle was commonly used; the scythe is more efficient, but the sickle leaves more stubble for pasturing animals, which explains why its use was so widespread.[20] More complete lists of tools which were available to the farmer are found in the wills of Gerontios and Theodosios Skaranos. Both lists include the *tzapion*. This term was used in the Roman period to refer to both the two-pronged hoe and the single-bladed type. Skaranos's property also included one pruning-knife, two sickles, one large axe with two cutting edges and two axes with one cutting edge.[21]

The most important factor in assessing the effectiveness of these tools is their iron content. A shortage of iron implements would have had an adverse effect on the rural economy. In western Europe during the Carolingian era many tools appear to have been wooden and it has been argued that expansion was restricted until iron became more widely used.[22] The situation in Byzantium probably never reached such a low ebb. The life of Theodore of Sykeon contains evidence that iron was used in the farming equipment of peasants. Some villagers gave up their tools so that an iron cage could be made for the saint, but they did not allow him to keep the metal permanently, presumably because the tools would have been difficult to replace.[23] In the tenth century iron was fairly readily available, but its production was kept largely under the state's control to ensure its armaments supply.[24] There are several

---

[17] Ashburner, 'The Farmer's Law', ch. 22.
[18] White, *Agricultural Implements*, pp. 49–50 and plate 3.   [19] *Ibid.*, p. 40.
[20] *Ibid.*, pp. 80–3; Bryer, 'The Estates of the Empire of Trebizond', p. 400; Boserup, *The Conditions of Agricultural Growth*, p. 85.
[21] MM, IV, p. 202; *Xéropotamou*, no. 9 lines A14–15, B20–2; Nesbitt, 'Mechanisms of Agricultural Production', p. 114; White, *Agricultural Implements*, pp. 38–40.
[22] Duby, *Rural Economy and Country Life*, p. 15; Duby, *The Early Growth of the European Economy*, pp. 13–17.
[23] *Vie de Théodore de Sykéôn*, p. 25; J. L. Teall, 'The Byzantine Agricultural Tradition', *Dumbarton Oaks Papers*, 25 (1971), pp. 51–2.
[24] The *strategoi* of the themes had to supply very large quantities of military equipment for the Cretan expedition; see Constantine Porphyrogenitus, *De Cerimoniis*, I, p. 657.

Agricultural production 125

references to the use of iron tools in agricultural production. They were used to make substantial improvements on Boilas's properties. The compiler of the *praktikon* of Patmos envisaged the clearance of 467 *modioi* with mattocks and hoes to make it suitable for arable cultivation.[25] The tools in the inventory of Panteleemon had iron fittings.[26] An iron sickle and an iron rake, which were excavated at Nemea, can be dated to the twelfth or thirteenth century.[27] Iron tools have also been found at Dinogetia.[28] Casual references by Skylitzes to agricultural equipment suggest that iron was commonly used. On one occasion the Petchenegs were said to have used axes, sickles and other iron farming equipment as weapons. On another occasion the people around Manzikert used hoes and other tools in the same way.[29] The provision of iron was included in the lists of exemptions concerning Patmos and the village of Chostiane.[30] The regularity with which the name *chalkeus* is encountered in the *praktika* of the late period confirms the availability of iron in peasant villages.[31] It has been suggested that iron was not efficiently exploited in agriculture in the Pontos,[32] but this conclusion, even if it is valid for the Pontos, cannot be applied to other regions of Byzantium.

The most difficult problem confronting Byzantine farmers was to preserve the fertility of the soil in the climatic conditions of the eastern Mediterranean, characterised by winter rains and long summer droughts. Dry farming consists essentially of making the most of a limited supply of water. It can be done by using crops which have their main period of growth during the rainy season, by weeding thoroughly to eliminate unnecessary waste of water, and by storing rain from one season for use in the next by means of stubble fallow. It was a laborious process because the fallow had to be ploughed regularly to keep it free of weeds and to ensure that the soil was receptive when the rains came.[33]

The crop rotations practised by the Byzantines probably did not correspond directly to either two- or three-field systems, but varied

[25] Lemerle, *Cinq études*, p. 22 lines 49–55; *Engrapha Patmou*, II, no. 51, p. 39.
[26] *Pantéléèmôn*, no. 7 line 27.
[27] S. G. Miller, 'Excavations at Nemea, 1973–4', *Hesperia*, 44 (1975), p. 162.
[28] Stefan *et al.*, *Dinogetia*, p. 392; Barnea, 'Dinogetia', p. 265.
[29] Scylitzes, pp. 461, 463.
[30] *Lavra*, I, no. 48 line 36; *Engrapha Patmou*, I, no. 6 line 49.
[31] Laiou-Thomadakis, *Peasant Society*, pp. 124–6.
[32] Bryer, 'The Estates of the Empire of Trebizond', p. 395.
[33] White, *Roman Farming*, p. 173 n. 3; E. C. Semple, *The Geography of the Mediterranean Region. Its Relation to Ancient History* (London, 1932), pp. 385–8; Braudel, *The Mediterranean*, I, p. 574.

126   *Economic expansion in the Byzantine empire*

according to local conditions and the requirements of the producers. The quantity of inferior grains would have varied according to the number of oxen and the size of the herd; the larger the number of animals to feed, the larger the area devoted to barley, rye and oats. On less fertile land there was likely to be a greater emphasis on lower-quality crops rather than wheat, because the yields of the latter suffered more drastically. Near towns there might have been a stronger incentive to take advantage of urban demand and concentrate more exclusively on wheat, which fetched a higher price, even if a larger area of fallow had to be left. However, diversification in crop production offered the producer greater security against fluctuations in yields. In only one case do details survive of the quantity of grain which was sown by a landowner in one year. The property which Xeropotamou received from Theodosios Skaranos in the 1270s included land which had recently been sown with thirty-one *modioi* of wheat, twenty-six *modioi* of barley and twenty-five of rye. Another eight *modioi* of dark summer wheat was ready to be used as seed. The emphasis was clearly on diversified production.[34] On the estate of Baris near Miletos there was a greater emphasis on wheat production. In 1073 the stores contained 260 *modioi* of wheat and 150 of barley and only five *modioi* of legumes.[35] About 1204 the monastery of Gerontios had a store of 130 *modioi* of wheat, of which forty-six were for seed. There is no mention in the will of inferior grains, but there were thirty-nine *modioi* of legumes, presumably fodder for the monastery's animals.[36] Generally, production on the most fertile lands, especially alluvial soils, concentrated more on wheat.

Another problem concerning crop rotations is the extent to which leguminous crops were planted. They have the merit of replacing the nitrogen which grain crops take from the soil and reducing the length of time the land has to lie fallow. It is easy to find references to legumes in the sources, but there is no indication that they were an integral part of any rotational system. They were probably grown largely in peasant gardens, which were the most effectively fertilised and intensively cultivated part of the peasant's property, while the less heavily manured arable fields needed longer fallow periods. The extent to which they were deliberately rotated with other crops cannot be ascertained, but their production was probably dictated more by the requirements of the

---

[34] *Xéropotamou*, no. 9 lines A43–4, B65–7; Nesbitt, 'Mechanisms of Agricultural Production', pp. 29, 42.
[35] *Engrapha Patmou*, II, no. 50 lines 118–19.   [36] MM, IV, p. 202 lines 17–18, 20–1.

Agricultural production 127

landowner's or the peasant's animals and the need to have some insurance against the failure of the grain crop.[37]

Fertility was also restored by frequent manuring. Roman knowledge of the quality of manure from different birds and animals was passed on to the Byzantines in the *Geoponika*. Manure from birds (apart from geese) was the most highly regarded and it does contain a significant amount of nitrogen. Donkey manure was the next most highly regarded, followed by goat and sheep manure. Both of these have a useful nitrogen content, particularly goat manure. The manure of cows, oxen and horses was less highly regarded.[38] The amount of manure which had to be applied varied according to the soil. Poor-quality land needed a substantial amount of fertiliser, good land only a moderate amount. On the best alluvial soils reasonably good returns were even obtained without any use of manure. Fresh manure is harmful to crops in a Mediterranean climate because it allows the moisture to escape, burning the crops. A compost heap has to be built to allow the manure to rot – if it is left to rot in the field, the manure loses its nitrogen content upon exposure to the sun. The *Geoponika* recommends digging a ditch to deposit the animal and human dung, urine and plants. The ditch helps to prevent the loss of moisture and water can be added to ensure that the heap decomposes properly. These recommendations are perfectly in order, but there is no indication that the compiler had any practical understanding of the subject comparable to that of some of the Roman agricultural writers.[39] A substantial heap was best obtained if the animals were kept in stables, but this depended on the availability of permanent pastures and root crops for feeding during the summer months. Stable manure has the advantage that the fertilising content of the dung is held together by the organic matter during the process of decomposition. It also absorbs the urine, which contains some useful minerals.[40]

[37] The quantity of vetch listed in the will of Skaranos shows that legumes were not cultivated on a significant scale on his land; see *Xéropotamou*, no. 9 lines A21–3, B31–3. On Gerontios's monastery the quantity of legumes was well below that of wheat; see MM, IV, p. 202. For the limited cultivation of legumes in some parts of medieval England, see J. Z. Titow, *English Rural Society 1200–1350* (London, 1969), p. 41. For their cultivation in the Roman period, see White, *Roman Farming*, pp. 121–3, but this probably presents an idealised picture.

[38] *Geoponica*, bk 2, ch. 21, pp. 60–2. Characteristically, this is a straight lift from ancient authorities; see White, *Roman Farming*, pp. 126–9.

[39] *Geoponica*, bk 2, ch. 21, pp. 60–2; White, *Roman Farming*, pp. 131–5; C. Delano Smith, *Western Mediterranean Europe. A Historical Geography of Italy, Spain and Southern France since the Neolithic* (London, 1979), p. 197. For the non-use of manure, see Leake, *Travels in Northern Greece*, IV, p. 444. [40] White, *Roman Farming*, pp. 125–6.

128   *Economic expansion in the Byzantine empire*

It is doubtful whether many peasants had sufficient permanent pastures or a large enough supply of root crops to stall feed their animals regularly. The few references to stable manure in the sources all refer to large properties. When St Niketas took refuge at the estate of Rouphinianos, across the Bosphoros from Constantinople, he had to sleep near the stables, where he did not get any rest owing to the pungent smell.[41] The working animals of Kosmosotira were pastured outside the wall of the monastery, where an official was in charge of the horses and the mules. The *paroikoi* also brought their oxen there for resting.[42] This arrangement made it easier for the dung to be used more effectively as manure. In parts of the interior of Asia Minor dung could not always be used in this way because it was also needed as fuel owing to the shortage of wood.[43]

Effective arable cultivation required a great deal of arduous work. This was especially true when it was combined with growing olive trees, which made ploughing more difficult and necessitated much laborious digging. Each successive stage of cultivation involved time-consuming operations. The fallow had to be ploughed and dug regularly to remove weeds. Manure had to be applied frequently after the winter rains. Harrowing was necessary to eliminate any lumps of earth left over after the ploughing.[44] The value of regular ploughing and effective harrowing is undeniable. Agricultural improvements in western Europe have been linked not simply with improvements in the plough, but equally with more intensive working of the land, and the latter factor also applied in Byzantium.[45]

In these circumstances the potential of the water-mill for saving both animal and human labour was very important. In the late Roman and Byzantine periods it was used more intensively than before, although the invention had been known at least from the first century BC.[46] The

[41] 'Vie du patrice Nicétas', p. 329. For stable feeding on the properties of the family of Theodore of Studium, see Teall, 'The Grain Supply of the Byzantine Empire', p. 125. In contrast, the chapters relating to pastoral farming in the Farmer's Law suggest that peasant flocks were usually kept at some distance from the village, except after harvesting when they were pastured on the stubble.

[42] Petit, 'Kosmosotira', p. 68.

[43] Darrouzès, *Épistoliers*, pp. 198–9; J. B. Tavernier, *The Six Voyages of John Baptista Tavernier, Baron of Aubonne: Through Turkey into Persia and the East Indies* (London, 1678), p. 39; R. Pococke, *A Description of the East and Some Other Countries* (2 vols., London, 1743–5), II, p. 87.

[44] White, *Roman Farming*, pp. 173–81; Bryer, 'The Estates of the Empire of Trebizond', p. 399.   [45] Duby, *Rural Economy and Country Life*, pp. 104–5.

[46] For the early history of the water-mill, see L. A. Moritz, *Grain Mills and Flour in Classical Antiquity* (Oxford, 1958), pp. 122–39.

Agricultural production   129

evidence from the Roman period is scanty, but there are clear indications of its widespread use. The regional sources give specific examples of the existence of water-mills in Byzantium, but no information about the type of water-mill in operation.

There are two basic types. The first is the less efficient horizontal wheel type. The wheel is attached to a vertical axle, which passes through the lower mill-stone and is fixed to the upper stone by a cross-bar. The whole mechanism revolves together and there is no intermediate gearing. The mill-stone turns only once with each revolution of the wheel. A mill-race is needed because the wheel turns only if water is directed against one of its sides. The more advanced Vitruvian type, which can grind about forty times as much grain as a donkey-mill each day, has a vertical wheel and a horizontal shaft. The upper stone is turned by a vertical spindle, which is geared by cog-wheels to the horizontal shaft. There are two different ways of working the vertical-wheel type, undershot as in the Vitruvian example and overshot. The undershot water-mill is turned by the force of the current without a dam or a mill-race and is suited only to fairly swift flowing rivers. In the more complicated overshot type the water has to be diverted from the river by a mill-race, stored in a mill-pond and passed through a chute. It is more appropriate than the undershot type on sluggish rivers.[47]

The basic problems concerning the water-mill are how widely it was adopted, why the more inefficient types survived, and why the most efficient overshot type was not used by the Byzantines. Diocletian's price code lists four types of mill: the horse-, donkey-, water- and hand-mills. Palladios recommended the construction of the water-mill. It was fairly familiar by the fourth century, but had not superseded the other types of mill.[48] One reason for the slow spread of the water-mill was possibly that the cost of grain was sufficiently high to keep grinding costs down to a low proportion of the total cost of bread production.[49] The late Roman evidence comes from urban centres. An inscription at Sardis, which was found on the tomb of a water-mill engineer and dated to the fourth or fifth century, indicates that water-mills were fairly common in the city and its vicinity.[50] The earliest example of the most efficient overshot type comes from Athens. It was built in the second half of the

---

[47] E. C. Curwen, 'The Problem of Early Water-Mills', *Antiquity*, 18 (1944), pp. 130–46; K. D. White, *Farm Equipment of the Roman World* (Cambridge, 1975), pp. 15–16; Bryer, 'The Estates of the Empire of Trebizond', pp. 404–11.

[48] Jones, *The Later Roman Empire*, II, pp. 1047–8.

[49] White, *Farm Equipment*, p. 16.   [50] Foss, *Sardis*, pp. 16–17, 100.

130   *Economic expansion in the Byzantine empire*

fifth century, probably in the reign of Leo I, and was destroyed in the second half of the sixth century. But this particular example was not well constructed and was probably fairly inefficient. The gears in the mill-room were not the right size. The horizontal gear wheel was too large, reducing the speed of the mill-stone.[51] The only other evidence of the vertical-wheel type comes from a mosaic in the Great Palace at Constantinople. It is dated to the early fifth century and contains a representation of the undershot Vitruvian type.[52] The late Roman adoption of the water-mill was linked to the demand for food from large urban centres.[53]

There is no evidence for the employment of the device in peasant villages until the early medieval period, when there was a greater premium on manpower. The earliest indication of its general application in the countryside is derived from the Farmer's Law. Its regulations envisaged villagers building water-mills on their own land or that of the community. The rights of other farmers whose lands were adversely affected by the diversion of water to the mill were protected by the code.[54] The Farmer's Law is particularly significant because it had a general validity for the rural economy and it concerned peasant farmers. Most other evidence involves the estates of large landowners, but the name 'miller' did occur reasonably frequently in the lists of peasant names in the fourteenth-century *praktika*.[55]

The tax-register of Thebes refers to several water-mills. Two were situated outside the *kastron* of Thebes. There were two more at Chamenai, which, Svoronos believes, lay to the south-east of the town. Another was located at the church of St Luke just south of Thebes.[56] The concentration of water-mills around the town is obvious, but owing to the fragmented condition of the text there is no clear impression of the extent to which the water-mill was used throughout the region. The tax-register does not mention animal-driven mills, but this is not

---

[51] A. W. Parsons, 'A Roman Water-Mill in the Athenian Agora', *Hesperia*, 5 (1936), pp. 70–90.

[52] G. Brett, 'Byzantine Water-Mill', *Antiquity*, 13 (1939), pp. 354–6.

[53] M. Bloch, 'The Advent and Triumph of the Water-Mill', in *Land and Work in Medieval Europe* (London, 1967), pp. 136–68, esp. 143–6, believed that the water-mill was not widely adopted until the Middle Ages. Possibly he underestimated the late Roman evidence, but he was undoubtedly right in emphasising the slow spread of the device.

[54] Ashburner, 'The Farmer's Law', chs. 81–4.

[55] Laiou-Thomadakis, *Peasant Society*, p. 120.

[56] Svoronos, 'Recherches sur le cadastre byzantin', p. 11 line 16, p. 12 line 30, p. 13 line 44, p. 14 line 67, p. 15 line 10. For the location of the place names, see *ibid.*, pp. 46–8, 53–5.

Agricultural production 131

surprising because it is a fiscal document concerned with taxable property and animal-mills were worth little.

The Lavra archives contain some evidence of water-mills owned by small monasteries and not very illustrious laymen. In the early eleventh century the monastery *ton Roudabon* purchased land near a stream in the village of Radochosta to construct mills. The monks made a payment of four *nomismata*, followed by another of two *nomismata* for a ruin, probably an old mill.[57] The properties in and around Thessalonike which were partitioned by three brothers in 1110 included two water-mills.[58] Water-mills were very common on Lavra's properties. When it received the estate at Asmalou in 1104 it contained two, which operated only in the winter. The property at Barzachanion, which it conceded to the state, contained a similar mill. In the assessment of the estates the second water-mill at Asmalou was accounted as the equivalent of one *paroikos* with a ploughteam.[59] The estates at Peristerai and Tzechlianes, which Lavra conceded to the state in 1109, included mills for which the monastery had previously been liable to pay tax (the *mylopakton*).[60] By 1184 it had possession of a mill in the fiscal unit of Mandra, which had been exempted from taxation.[61]

The construction of water-mills was no problem for large landowners with substantial financial resources. Boilas erected some when he was clearing new land in the east. Water-mills were also built on the estates of Gregory Pakourianos and were installed in some of the properties of the Pantokrator, especially those near Thessalonike.[62] The bishop of Stagoi owned two *mylostasia* and one *mylotopion* by the river Salabria. There were probably stretches of land by the river with several mills. The survey of the boundaries of the bishop's property suggests that the river was greatly used to power water-mills.[63]

It is striking that even on large properties animal-mills continued to exist. The monks of Kosmosotira used donkey-mills. Pakourianos's properties included animal-driven mills as well as water-mills. The hospital set up by the *typikon* of the Pantokrator employed a groom to

---

[57] *Lavra*, I, no. 14.   [58] *Ibid.*, no. 59 lines 9–11.   [59] *Ibid.*, no. 56 lines 51–3.
[60] *Ibid.*, no. 58 lines 83–8.
[61] *Ibid.*, no. 66 line 22. For water-mills on property belonging to Iviron, see Dölger, *Schatzkammern*, no. 35 line 64. For a water-mill belonging to Xeropotamou situated to the west of Hierissos, see *Xéropotamou*, no. 7.
[62] Lemerle, *Cinq études*, p. 22 lines 49–55; Gautier, 'Grégoire Pakourianos', pp. 43, 111; Gautier, 'Pantocrator', lines 1534–5.
[63] Astruc, 'Un document inédit de 1163', p. 214 lines 10, 11, 21. See also Psellos, *Scripta Minora*, II, no. 251.

132   *Economic expansion in the Byzantine empire*

look after the horses which were used in its two milling establishments. Vatopedi and Lavra were allowed to keep oxen inside the boundaries of Athos to grind their corn.[64] This should not automatically be dismissed as technological regression. The coexistence of animal- and water-mills was a sensible precaution. A complete dependence on water-mills involved greater vulnerability to climatic extremes – streams freezing in winter or drying up completely in summer. It was also useful for a *kastron* or a fortified monastery like Kosmosotira to have animal-mills in case of an enemy attack or siege, when the water-supply to a mill could easily have been blocked.[65]

We do not know the extent to which primitive hand-mills survived alongside the water-mill, but they were probably very common and they continued in use long after the Byzantine period.[66] It made more sense for a peasant to grind his corn by hand than to pay in cash or kind to have it done at a water-mill. The hand-mill also had the advantage that it was impossible to tax, unlike the water-mill. Consequently, the peasant family was better off remaining technologically backward, provided that it had sufficient labour available to grind corn without interfering with its other agricultural activities. Unlike in western Europe there was no seigneurial constraint on the peasantry not to use hand-mills.

The sources do not inform us which type of water-mill was in use. However, the evidence from the post-Byzantine period is decisive. The horizontal-wheel type was almost universal. It was seen in large numbers on Athos by a French traveller in the sixteenth century, in different parts of Greece and Asia Minor in the nineteenth century, and it has survived into the twentieth century.[67] The vertical-wheel type was introduced into Crete, probably during the Venetian rule, but remained far less common than the more primitive horizontal-wheel type.[68]

---

[64] Petit, 'Kosmosotira', p. 60; Gautier, 'Grégoire Pakourianos', p. 43 lines 1392–3; Gautier, 'Pantocrator', lines 999, 1049–50, 1258–60; *Prôtaton*, no. 8 lines 93–9.

[65] Bloch, 'The Advent and Triumph of the Water-Mill', p. 149.

[66] For one of the few references to corn-grinding by hand, see 'Vie du patrice Nicétas', p. 329, where the saint suffered the indignity of having to grind corn by hand in a bread shortage. For modern grinding by hand, see Benaki Museum, *Paradosiakes kalliergeies*, p. 41, no. 47; and Bryer, 'The Estates of the Empire of Trebizond', pp. 411–12.

[67] Curwen, 'The Problem of Early Water-Mills', p. 136; E. C. Curwen, 'A Vertical Water-Mill near Salonika', *Antiquity*, 19 (1945), pp. 211–12.

[68] A. E. Clutton and A. Kenny, 'A Vertical Axle Water-Mill near Drosia, Crete', *Kretologia*, 4 (1977), pp. 139–58, esp. 148.

The reasons for the non-adoption of the more advanced type were partly geographical and partly social. The horizontal-wheel type is perfectly adequate in mountainous regions, where the velocity of the stream is sufficient to power the mill. In a society of small producers it was probably more economical for individuals to construct a series of the cheaper horizontal-wheel type along the same stream than one large and more expensive vertical-wheel mill. In Crete water-mills usually occur in groups of two to six, each using the stream in turn.[69] Geographical features were not the only determining factor. Although the horizontal-wheel type is ideally suited to mountainous regions, it is easily adapted to flatter land. The important requirement is the provision of an adequate head of water, which can be achieved by a small vertical drop. Micro-relief features of the landscape can be exploited to enable the horizontal-wheel mills to operate in coastal plains and broad valley floors. This type also has other advantages, which make it more suitable in the Mediterranean climate. It has a small water requirement and is more appropriate on smaller streams. In regions where rivers dry up in summer, they remain operational longer than the vertical-wheel mills.[70]

There was an equally important social reason for the failure of the Byzantines to develop a larger and more efficient type of water-mill. The spread of the overshot mill in western Europe was closely associated with the seigneurial jurisdiction of large landowners. It was a more complicated type of mill and more expensive to construct. The greater outlay was worthwhile if the landowner had the authority to compel peasants under his jurisdiction to grind their corn at his mill.[71] This seigneurial constraint was unknown in Byzantium, where the development of feudal jurisdiction was stunted by the bureaucratic apparatus of the state. Grain was ground in much cheaper mills and in peasant households. There is evidence that some villagers took up milling as a trade. Miller was one of the names in the later *praktika*.[72] These were not cases of occupational specialisation, but of peasants who worked a plot of land obtaining an additional income. Instead of being concentrated in a smaller number of efficient mills, corn was ground in numerous smaller mills dotted along any water-supply because large landowners did not see milling as a source of revenue.

[69] *Ibid.*, p. 146.   [70] *Ibid.*, pp. 146–8.
[71] For the water-mill in western Europe, see Duby, *Rural Economy and Country Life*, pp. 16–17; and Duby, *The Early Growth of the European Economy*, pp. 187–8.
[72] Laiou-Thomadakis, *Peasant Society*, p. 120.

134   *Economic expansion in the Byzantine empire*

The availability of an abundant supply of water was of great importance for the productivity of an estate. Philaretos's properties were supposed to have been highly productive owing to their proximity to springs, which provided all the water they needed. In his will Boilas made a clear distinction between the land which was irrigated and the land which was not. Anna Komnene also emphasised the water-supply of a property belonging to Constantine Doukas near Serres.[73] Good irrigation was the most effective way to increase the productivity of relatively infertile soils. It also extended the growing season, permitting the cultivation of summer crops and enabling vegetables, which could otherwise have been grown only in moister months, to be cultivated in summer. Even some traditional Mediterranean plants, such as the vine, which are ideal for dry conditions, do give a better quality of yield if they are watered, although the quantity is less likely to be affected.[74]

Frequent disputes over water-rights reflect the importance of irrigation. A quarrel between the Athonite monasteries of Atziioannou and Kaspakos was resolved in 1012 with the decision that Atziioannou had complete rights to a stream and the monks of Kaspakos were not allowed to plant vines nor to cultivate right up to the stream.[75] A very common source of conflict was the diversion of water to a mill, leaving other land dry.[76] At the beginning of the twelfth century Achillios Limenites, the owner of an estate *tou Sempionou* in Crete, built a water-mill on the river Menikon. It diverted water which had previously been used by the villagers of Menikon for their mill and the irrigation of their lands. They had grown cotton, millet, onions, cabbages and beans, all crops in need of considerable water. In his guarantee to the villagers Limenites admitted that for seventeen years they had been deprived of these crops, and the vines and trees, which had also been irrigated by the stream, had suffered damage. He paid the villagers the substantial sum of two pounds in *theotokia nomismata* in compensation.[77]

It was possibly a favourable location that led these villagers to use irrigation so much. Generally, peasant farmers did not have the resources to undertake the large projects which the wealthy landowners might attempt. In modern times peasants who irrigated only small

---

[73] 'Vie de Philarète', pp. 113–15; Lemerle, *Cinq études*, p. 23 lines 80–4; Anna Comnène, *Alexiade*, II, p. 171.

[74] Delano Smith, *Western Mediterranean Europe*, p. 177.

[75] They were not allowed within sixteen *spithamai* of the stream; see Lavra, I, no. 17. For the *spithame*, see Schilbach, *Byzantinische Metrologie*, pp. 19–20.

[76] Ashburner, 'The Farmer's Law', ch. 83.

[77] MM, VI, pp. 95–9.

Agricultural production 135

garden plots sometimes have been unwilling to introduce more extensive schemes, regarding it as unwelcome modernisation.[78] One reason might have been the extra work involved. The higher yields which irrigation brings are obtained by a much higher input of labour per acre, but this can be spread throughout the year. Extra labour is required for watering and weeding during the growing season and for the maintenance of irrigation facilities in the dead season. The greater range of crops which can be grown also reduces the period of underemployment.[79]

As the population increased from the tenth century onwards the land had to be cultivated more intensively and there was a greater need for effective irrigation. The other crucial factor was the concentration of land in the hands of wealthy landowners. They were able to mobilise resources to implement large irrigation projects, ensuring the more effective exploitation of agricultural potential. One of the more spectacular projects was undertaken by Athanasios on Athos. Water was brought through canals from the higher parts of the mountain to Lavra to irrigate the gardens and fruit trees and provide water for the animals. Even allowing for possible exaggeration by the hagiographer, the important factor was that Athanasios had rights to the water, controlled the land through which it was channelled and had the financial resources to carry out the undertaking.[80] Psellos planned to make substantial improvements to the monastery of Medikion, including the diversion of water to its lands.[81] Boilas built canals to irrigate his property and Isaac Komnenos claimed that the construction of a water-supply for Kosmosotira had involved him in considerable expense.[82] Such activities were a positive effect of the development of feudal social relations. Although the impact of these projects cannot be quantified, they must have led to an improvement in agricultural production, not only resulting in better yields but also permitting a greater range of crops to be sown.

The agricultural potential of most lowland plains was increased during the Middle Ages by geological changes which were already

[78] Delano Smith, *Western Mediterranean Europe*, p. 178.
[79] Boserup, *The Conditions of Agricultural Growth*, pp. 34–40, 52.
[80] 'Vie d'Athanase', pp. 35–6. For his cash resources, see *Lavra*, I, p. 56.
[81] Sathas, *MB*, V, p. 264.
[82] Lemerle, *Cinq études*, p. 22 line 54; Petit, 'Kosmosotira', p. 57. Irrigated fields which were being cultivated in the twelfth and thirteenth centuries have been excavated at Nemea; see Miller, 'Excavations at Nemea, 1973–4', pp. 154–7, 162, 169; and S. G. Miller, 'Excavations at Nemea, 1975', *Hesperia*, 45 (1976), pp. 183–4.

136   Economic expansion in the Byzantine empire

under way in the Roman period and have continued in the post-Byzantine era. Upland soils were gradually eroded and deposits were carried downstream, silting up river valleys. It appears to have been a fairly general phenomenon throughout the Mediterranean, but the speed and intensity of the process varied greatly from place to place. Some evidence has been collected at archaeological sites. In the Peloponnesos the course of the Alphios river includes sediment-filled plains and is partly bordered by alluvial fans. The deposit covering Olympia extends miles up river. One of the structures covered by alluvium was an early Byzantine fortress. The deposit can be dated to the early medieval period because it formed only after coins from the late sixth century had been left on the site.[83] Elsewhere in Greece the process proceeded more slowly. The soils of Boiotia were subject to erosion only to a very limited extent.[84] Extensive erosion is more apparent on the Aegean coastline of Asia Minor. In historical times the coastland has moved inexorably westwards owing to stream deposits. The sites of some famous ports of Antiquity are now several miles inland. The valleys have been filled up with alluvium from the river and sands and gravel from the adjacent hills. The consequences of this process are alluvial fans spreading out from the hillside, a flat alluvial plain, sometimes flooded by the river about five or ten metres above the river bed, and a broad flood plain near the mouth of the river which is flooded during the winter.[85] At Sardis the eastern end of the temple of Artemis was buried in over a metre of deposits by the middle of the fourth century. As the building was probably abandoned after Christianity became the official religion of the empire or at the earliest in the third century, the silt was accumulated at a fairly rapid rate.[86] The harbour at Ephesos silted up and eventually became unusable.

---

[83] C. Vita-Finzi, *The Mediterranean Valleys. Geological Changes in Historical Times* (Cambridge, 1969), pp. 77–80. For a recent assessment of this question and its historical significance, see Hendy, *Studies in the Byzantine Monetary Economy*, pp. 58–68, 554–5.

[84] O. Rackham, 'Observations on the Historical Ecology of Boeotia', *Annual of the British School at Athens*, 78 (1983), pp. 343–4.

[85] D. Eisma, 'Stream Deposition and Erosion by the Eastern Shore of the Aegean', in W. C. Brice (ed.), *The Environmental History of the Near and Middle East since the Last Ice Age* (London, 1978), pp. 67–8. The description of the lowlands of north east Greece in Admiralty, *Geographical Handbook Series, Greece*, III, p. 106, is also relevant. It distinguishes between the lowest ground, which is flat, often marshy and consists of sand, silt or mud, and a higher zone of terraced land at the foot of the upland. The latter is composed of thick beds of weak sediments varying from gravel and sands to clays.

[86] Foss, *Sardis*, pp. 37–8.

Agricultural production 137

Already by the ninth century it was no longer adequate for the Byzantine fleet. The harbour at Miletos was constantly threatened by the Maiander in the same way.[87]

The agricultural potential of these river valleys was increased at the expense of the upland regions. Vita-Finzi has suggested that the post-classical alluvia filling the Mediterranean valley floors were smooth, loamy in texture, low enough to be irrigated easily, and at worst containing excessive moisture which could be drained away easily.[88] In modern times some parts of the river valleys were little cultivated owing to the threat of malaria. The Byzantine sources contain no evidence about the disease, but in Italy it was clearly less severe in the Middle Ages than it was from the sixteenth century. Braudel has linked this development with the introduction into Europe of a more virulent form of the disease from America and it is likely that its impact was felt in the eastern Mediterranean as strongly as in Italy.[89] These alluvial soils would have been very productive if they had been exploited properly. The crucial factors were the readiness of landowners to construct and maintain drainage schemes and the availability of an adequate labour-force to work the land effectively given the extra labour required for drainage. The documentary evidence does not permit any firm conclusions to be drawn. The combination of the expansion of large estates and demographic growth may have led to more efficient cultivation, but landowners with large flocks and herds had another alternative. Even lands which remained marshy still had considerable agricultural potential. As they dried out in the summer they provided very rich pasture at the time of the year when it was most needed. These lands could also be used to grow summer crops before they reverted back to marsh.[90]

The divergent fortunes which could befall the alluvial soils is well illustrated by the *praktikon* of Andronikos Doukas. The estate of Mandraklou consisted of two parts on each side of the river Maiander. The first had originally amounted to 185 *modioi*, but had been reduced

---

[87] Foss, *Ephesus*, p. 185; Foss, 'Archaeology and the "Twenty Cities" of Byzantine Asia', p. 477.

[88] Vita-Finzi, *The Mediterranean Valleys*, p. 119. See also Delano Smith, *Western Mediterranean Europe*, p. 323.

[89] Braudel, *The Mediterranean*, I, pp. 65–6; Delano Smith, *Western Mediterranean Europe*, pp. 384–8.

[90] R. Chandler, *Travels in Asia Minor 1764–65*, ed. E. Clay (London, 1971), p. 94; Leake, *Travels in Northern Greece*, II, p. 228; Nesbitt, 'Mechanisms of Agricultural Production', pp. 18–19.

138   *Economic expansion in the Byzantine empire*

to twenty-six *modioi* after encroachments by the river. A substantial part of the property on the other bank had also been transformed into marshland.[91] Another estate, Galaidai, in the same group of properties was more productive. It did not border the river directly, but was situated in the same region and was intensively cultivated owing to the fertility of the soil. In the absence of reliable yield figures the productivity of the estate has to be estimated roughly with some very arbitrary and hypothetical calculations. The twelve peasant households at Galaidai contained at least twenty-six people. It is certain that there were more, who were not recorded in the *praktikon*.[92] If a reasonable subsistence requirement of eighteen *thalassioi modioi* a year is assumed for each person, they would have required 468 *modioi* altogether.[93] They also had to meet a fiscal obligation of twenty-seven *nomismata*, two *milliaresia* and twelve *folleis*. If a hypothetical wheat price of ten *modioi* a *nomisma* is assumed and consideration of crops other than wheat is excluded for the moment, they would have needed to sell 272 *modioi* to meet this obligation. The estate consisted of 762 *modioi*.[94] If all the land was cultivated by *paroikoi* and a biennial crop rotation was in operation, 380 *modioi* would have been needed for annual seed. The total requirement would have been 1,120 *modioi* and a yield of about three to one would have been necessary.

Some qualifications have to be made. The fiscal burden could have been met by the sale of garden produce or non-agricultural work, but this is the smallest element in the calculation. The estate was probably cultivated by a more intensive method than biennial rotation, but the inferior grains would then have been needed as fodder for the oxen and other animals. Other factors suggest that the calculation errs on the side of caution. It entirely ignores the effect of the other obligations, apart from the *telos*, for which the *paroikoi* were liable. The most important were the requisitions in kind or forced sales at arbitrarily low prices. Also a tenth of the produce might have been owed to the landowner. The most important factor was that there were more mouths to feed

---

[91] *Engrapha Patmou*, II, no. 50 lines 270–4.

[92] *Ibid.*, II, no. 50 lines 167–75, 305–10. According to Laiou-Thomadakis, *Peasant Society*, pp. 267–9, non-registration of women and minors was not practised by the compilers of the fourteenth-century *praktika*. Her methodology has been criticised severely in a review by P. Karlin-Hayter, *Byzantion*, 48 (1978), pp. 580–5. Whatever the outcome of this difference of opinion, it is clear that there was a large degree of non-registration for Galaidai. Only a small number of male offspring were listed, presumably those old enough to work.

[93] For a discussion of diet, see below, chapter 5.

[94] *Engrapha Patmou*, II, no. 50 lines 167–75, 305–10, and for the grain price, line 318.

Agricultural production   139

than the *praktikon* records. Consequently, the amount of grain needed for subsistence was much greater than 478 *modioi*. An average yield higher than three to one was needed. The fertility of these alluvial lands enabled the region to be quite densely populated. The great agricultural potential of the Aegean coastal region is confirmed by evidence from the thirteenth century, when the region was very productive.[95]

The most important alluvial plains, on whose grain production Constantinople was dependent, were those of Thrace, Macedonia and Thessaly.[96] In later centuries they were sufficiently productive for large supplies to be exported to the west as well as transported to Constantinople. The Venetians regularly exported wheat from Thrace and Macedonia and the Bulgarian plains. The Genoese exports were mainly from the coastal areas of the Black Sea and the Thracian plain. The wheat from Thrace was considered the best quality and was more expensive than that from Gaffa. The Genoese also purchased grain in Phokaia in Asia Minor.[97] In the sixteenth century large quantities continued to be exported. When the Turks prohibited this trade, the Aegean was the scene of a lively black market in grain which was smuggled out of the mainland.[98] Later travellers often mention the great grain-producing capacity of these plains.[99] According to Leake the yields of wheat in the region of Trikkala averaged ten to one.[100] He regarded the plain around Belestinon as equal in fertility to that of Larissa and it generally gave good yields. He describes a method of cultivation – a light scratch plough pulled by a pair of oxen – which was identical to that of the Middle Ages, and there is no reason to doubt that these alluvial soils were extremely productive in earlier centuries. Their fertility enabled the rapidly increasing population to be absorbed

[95] Angold, *A Byzantine Government in Exile*, pp. 102–4. There is some evidence that peasant families around Smyrna were well-off before 1204; see *ibid.*, p. 131.

[96] Michael Choniates, II, p. 83.

[97] F. Thiriet, *La Romanie vénitienne au moyen âge* (Paris, 1959), pp. 327, 340; M. Balard, *La Romanie génoise (XIIe–début du XVe siècle)* (Rome, 1975), pp. 752–3. Another productive area, less important for the supply to Constantinople, was the plain of Arta, from which Ragusa imported large quantities of wheat in the fourteenth century; see B. Krekic, *Dubrovnik (Raguse) et le Levant au moyen âge* (Paris, 1961), pp. 88, 94.

[98] Braudel, *The Mediterranean*, I, pp. 583–4.

[99] Pococke, *A Description of the East*, II, pp. 140–3; Leake, *Travels in Northern Greece*, II, p. 218; III, pp. 428–9.

[100] Leake, *Travels in Northern Greece*, IV, p. 280. He also reported average yields of six or seven to one at Konitza, rising to ten to one in good years (*ibid.*, IV, pp. 113–14), and yields of ten to one in the plain of Elis in the Peloponnesos (W. M. Leake, *Travels in the Morea* (3 vols., London, 1830), I, pp. 13–14). While not to be taken automatically at face value, these indications do complement the other evidence that these were grain-exporting regions.

140 Economic expansion in the Byzantine empire

without any signs of economic hardship resulting from overpopulation in the eleventh and twelfth centuries. It seems that in these very fertile regions there was no great cleavage between agricultural resources and a growing population, at least before 1200.

Production on some estates was sufficient to support newly founded monasteries and charitable establishments. Some tentative calculations about grain production on the estates of Pakourianos have been made by Asdracha. The monastery owned forty-seven ploughteams and she assumed that each pair of oxen cultivated an average of 150 *modioi*, giving a total area under cultivation of 7,050 *modioi*. She assumes a yield of three to one and obtains a total production of 10,575 *modioi* or 14,000 *modioi*, depending on whether biennial or triennial rotation was in use. The consumption requirements of the monks of Bačkovo were about 1,000 *modioi* and there were additional outlays for servants and charitable distributions. The surplus at the monastery's disposal was much larger, but the *typikon* gives no indication of the number of *paroikoi* established on the estates, nor the number of oxen they owned themselves, nor the amount of land which they cultivated. Three hostels, which were established by Pakourianos, were supplied from the surplus produce of individual villages. One at Stenimachos distributed 730 *modioi* each year. The two others, provisioned by the villages of Srabikion and Prilongion, distributed the same quantity of grain between them. Asdracha estimates the surface area needed to provision the hostels at 972 *modioi* with a biennial rotation and 729 *modioi* with a triennial rotation. What proportion of the total production of these villages this amounted to is impossible to determine.[101]

The *typikon* of the Pantokrator stipulated allowances for the personnel of the hospital, the hostel and the priests of the church of Eleousa amounting to 2,569 *modioi annonikoi*, 15 *monasteriakoi modioi* and 1,232 *thalassioi modioi*.[102] If the same yield ratio of three to one is assumed, 1,478 *modioi* would have been needed with a biennial rotation. This makes no allowance for the consumption requirements of the monks in the *metochia*, the provisions for the sick in the hospital or any other expenditure in kind. The vast landed wealth of the Pantokrator – most of its properties were in the fertile areas in Macedonia, Thrace and to a lesser extent Asia Minor – no doubt ensured that its consumption requirements and those of its *paroikoi*

---

[101] Asdracha, *La Région des Rhodopes*, pp. 183–4.
[102] For the relationship between these different measures, see Schilbach, *Byzantinische Metrologie*, pp. 95–100.

Agricultural production 141

were met easily and that a substantial surplus of agricultural produce remained.[103]

Peasants who did not have enough arable land to subsist on their own grain production could compensate for the deficiency by concentrating heavily on gardening, especially if their land was situated conveniently near an urban market. The regularity with which gardens are mentioned in the charter material reflects the importance of this form of production. It was potentially very profitable because land around the peasant's house was easiest to manure and dig over regularly and it could withstand intensive cultivation. As well as being used for the continuous cultivation of legumes, enclosed gardens might have contained a few vines and fruit trees. Olive trees and vineyards were, of course, more valuable than arable land and were taxed more highly. Duby has suggested, on the basis of French evidence, that three concentric zones around the village formed the basis of agricultural activity – the intensely exploited enclosures in the village, the arable belt around the village and the more distant uncultivated belt of land which was used as pasture.[104] This representation of village production is in general corroborated by the Farmer's Law. Some chapters assume that gardens and vineyards were divided off from the property of other villagers by ditches and fences and that the owners had immunity against any claims for damages if animals were injured falling into the ditches or were impaled on the stakes.[105] The arable land was not enclosed and probably one of the greatest sources of contention in the village community was the encroachment of one farmer on the furrows ploughed by another.[106] There were also enclosed vineyards further away from the village and sometimes a guard was employed to look after them.[107]

The importance of the cultivation of legumes is obvious. Besides restoring nitrogen to the soil they reduced the risks of a production which was too dependent on grain and offered the possibility of some relief when the wheat harvest was bad. The pattern of cultivation of legumes was similar to that of cereals. They had to be furrowed after

---

[103] Gautier, 'Pantocrator', pp. 13–15.

[104] He applies this pattern to the ninth and tenth centuries, long before the level of population began to outstrip the resources of the land; see Duby, *Rural Economy and Country Life*, pp. 7, 11. For the varying rates of taxation, see Dölger, *Beiträge*, p. 56.

[105] Ashburner, 'The Farmer's Law', chs. 50, 51, 58. See also Dölger, Beiträge, p. 115 line 26; and Kaplan, 'Quelques remarques sur les paysages agraires byzantins', pp. 155–76.

[106] Ashburner, 'The Farmer's Law', ch. 1.

[107] *Ibid.*, chs. 33, 79.

142 Economic expansion in the Byzantine empire

sowing, harrowed, and then a considerable amount of time had to be spent hoeing.[108] Saints' lives abound with references to peasant vegetable plots; usually, the saint had to rescue them from some natural catastrophe.[109] Cultivation of legumes on large estates seems to have been slight. Quantities kept in storage were small compared with those of grain. The modest amounts kept on the estate of Baris and at the monastery of Hagia Marine were probably used for fodder or ploughed back into the land.[110] The most important feature of leguminous cultivation was that it was carried out mainly on peasant plots, thus mitigating the effect of economic inequalities by allowing a peasant with a small plot of land to cultivate it intensively.

Arboriculture and viticulture were equally important to the small producer. A vine and a few fruit trees were necessary for the consumption of peasant households, but any surplus was more suitable than legumes for disposal on the market or exchange. Although specific information about peasant properties is scarce, almost invariably they included at least one vineyard where geographical conditions permitted. In 897 the monastery of St Andrew bought some peasant fields, a vineyard with a press, a well to the east of Thessalonike and another enclosed vineyard.[111] In some cases the owner of a very small plot consisting of only a few *modioi* was forced to cultivate vines or fruit trees to survive. He was at a great advantage if his property was located near a town. In 1014 Constantine and Maria Lagoudes donated their entire property to Lavra. It consisted only of a courtyard (*aule*) in Hierissos and two vineyards. The only condition was that they retained them until the end of their lives because they had no other means of support.[112] The well-known case of specialised production of olives by peasant farmers in north Syria in the late Roman period is a classic example of the effect which a strong urban demand could have on agricultural production.[113] Nothing so spectacular occurred in Byzantium, but the urban revival did offer greater scope for specialisation to agricultural producers situated in convenient locations.

---

[108] White, *Roman Farming*, p. 190.

[109] *Vie de Théodore de Sykeôn*, pp. 80–1; 'Vie de patrice Nicétas', p. 335. Such passages recounting destruction by locusts or caterpillars are standard in hagiographies, but they do reflect the ubiquity of vegetable plots in peasant farms. See also *Vie de Cyrille Philéote*, p. 200.

[110] MM, IV, p. 202; *Engrapha Patmou*, II, no. 50 lines 118–19.

[111] *Lavra*, I, no. 1.   [112] *Ibid.*, no. 18.

[113] G. Tchalenko, *Villages antiques de la Syrie du Nord. Le massif du Bélus à l'époque romaine* (3 vols., Paris, 1953–8). It is possible that current work on other parts of north Syria will lead to different results; see Lemerle, *The Agrarian History*, p. 16 n. 2, p. 249.

Agricultural production 143

Vines involved a great deal of laborious work, but fruit trees did not need so much attention except in their first years. Both were considered as *autourgia* by the Byzantines because they produced revenue regularly without a great deal of working.[114] However, this oversimplifies the matter. Even after intensive care and irrigation in the early years olive trees still needed some working. A couple of ploughings a year were necessary – in summer to prevent the ground from cracking, which would expose the roots to the sun, and in autumn to form ditches from the highest to the lowest slopes. They also had to be manured in autumn and have their trunks cleared of moss. The slow rate of growth involved a substantial outlay of cash and labour and, consequently, olives were often grown in combination with grain crops. On smaller properties this was a sensible precaution, because the olive produces fruit only once every two years.[115] The olive, like the fig tree, has the great advantage that after the initial period of growth it is suited to a variety of soils. Poor soils can be perfectly adequate provided that they have good drainage.

The vine is a more difficult plant to grow. An adequate supply of manpower at different times of the year is absolutely essential for its proper cultivation. It needs moisture, but only in moderate quantities. It also needs heat to ripen properly, but the fruit can be damaged easily by dry summer winds before it is harvested. Regular digging and ploughing is necessary to ensure a proper balance between moisture and heat. The best soils for vines are stony and gravelly, allowing for proper drainage.[116] The *Geoponika* describes black, loamy soils as the best for viticulture, as long as they were not too thick, which would cause drainage problems. They were best situated near a stream. Young vines had to be planted in moist lowlands and most importantly in places protected from the wind. The *Geoponika* recommends that they should face the south or the east, but this depended on the nature of the terrain and the prevailing winds. Vines were generally planted in the summer, but in very dry places it was better to wait until the autumn.[117]

---

[114] Cecaumenos, *Strategicon*, p. 36. See also Petit, 'Notre Dame de Pitié', p. 29 lines 26–7.

[115] White, *Roman Farming*, pp. 225–7; Delano Smith, *Western Mediterranean Europe*, p. 26. The olive can be left for long periods and is the most appropriate form of cultivation if the farmer is absent for any length of time or if the plot of land is an inconvenient distance from the main holding. Nevertheless, inadequate ploughing does lead to inferior yields. See E. Y. Kolodny, *La Population des îles de la Grèce* (2 vols., Aix-en-Provence, 1974), I, p. 88.

[116] White, *Roman Farming*, pp. 229–30.

[117] *Geoponica*, bk 5, ch. 1, pp. 123–4; ch. 2, pp. 126–7; ch. 6, p. 132; White, *Roman Farming*, pp. 230–1.

144   *Economic expansion in the Byzantine empire*

The plant requires much attention. Its tendency to proliferate creates a danger that the fruit-bearing shoots will be impeded by other non-productive shoots and that its surface rootlets will weaken the root-system. The growth was curtailed with a *kladeuterion* (pruning-knife). The removal of surplus growth involves frequent work at different times of the year – pruning in autumn or spring, shaping and tying, and trimming leaves. The classical authorities recommended three diggings of the soil around the plant to allow the air to penetrate the soil to the roots and also to remove surface rootlets. The *dikella* was used to dig around the roots without causing unnecessary damage to the plant. Care had also to be taken when applying the dung. Too much could damage the roots.[118] The preparation of vineyards which had been leased on equal shares was regulated in the Farmer's Law. The lessee was responsible for the pruning of the vines and he had to dig the vineyard, fence it and dig it over again.[119]

Although vines and olives could withstand very dry conditions once they had reached maturity, they needed regular watering in the early stages until their root-systems had developed properly.[120] Vegetables were also capable of absorbing a large quantity of water. It is not surprising that many of the gardens and vineyards mentioned in the sources were situated near streams. In 1008 the monks of Roudaba received a guarantee from the villagers of Radochosta that the small property which they had purchased could be turned into gardens or *mylostasia* (properties with mills).[121] The peasant vineyard which St Andrew of Peristerai purchased in 897 was supplied with water from a well.[122]

Peasant farmers were very dependent on a favourable situation for their garden or vineyard because they lacked the resources of wealthier landowners to undertake large irrigation schemes.[123] Arboriculture and viticulture were an ideal form of specialised production for a large

---

[118] White, *Roman Farming*, pp. 237–40; White, *Agricultural Implements*, pp. 47–8. See also Delano Smith, *Western Mediterranean Europe*, p. 26.

[119] Ashburner, 'The Farmer's Law', ch. 12. For wage labour working on vines, see *Vie de Cyrille Philéote*, p. 99.

[120] When their root-systems had developed, they could be transferred to dryer permanent positions (White, *Roman Farming*, p. 225), but it is doubtful whether this happened often in practice.

[121] *Lavra*, I, no. 14 lines 24–5. For other gardens situated near streams, see *ibid.*, no. 59 lines 9–11; Svoronos, 'Recherches sur le cadastre byzantin', p. 13 A44; and Dölger, *Schatzkammern*, no. 35 lines 64–5. See also White, *Roman Farming*, pp. 153–5.

[122] *Lavra*, I, no. 1 lines 15–16.

[123] Svoronos, 'Remarques sur les structures économiques', p. 60. See also below, p. 159.

Agricultural production

landowner. Owing to the long time it takes for vines and olive trees to reach maturity, they involved a heavy outlay in cash and labour. The revival of the *Geoponika* in the tenth century possibly reflected a greater emphasis on this branch of agriculture. A quarter of the compilation was devoted to viticulture and three chapters dealt with arboriculture. In contrast, there was a very short treatment of arable farming.[124]

On some large estates there was a substantial interest in arboriculture. The monastery which St Nikon founded near Sparta soon acquired a workshop in which olives were crushed.[125] The estates of Parthenion and Temenia on Leros had over 300 cultivated olive trees in 1088 as well as small numbers of almond, pomegranate, quince, fig and pear trees and vines.[126] The monastery of St Paul on Latros owned an estate of olive trees, for which it paid a tax of thirty-six *hyperpyra*, until it received an exemption in Manuel's reign. It leased the property out for an annual payment of twenty-four measures of oil. It contained 370 trees including young ones.[127]

There are some very notable instances of large-scale expenditure on vines and olive trees by the Athonite monasteries. They had considerable cash resources owing to imperial patronage and their own extensive properties. Athanasios's irrigation project enabled Lavra to cultivate vines and fruit trees.[128] When Symeon, who was the great *droungarios* in the reign of Nikephoros III, took possession of Xenophon and restored the monastery, new vineyards and olive groves were planted. A *metochion* contained 300 olive trees and a vineyard.[129] Lavra provided the monastery of Bouleuteria with 520 *nomismata*, which was spent partly on new vineyards.[130] Upon the resolution of a dispute between Vatopedi and Philadelphiou, whose lands bordered each other, the abbot of Philadelphiou received forty-nine *nomismata* in compensation for the improvements which had been made to the disputed land – the planting of vineyards and the development of gardens.[131] A

---

[124] Teall, 'The Byzantine Agricultural Tradition', pp. 40–4, emphasises the value of the *Geoponika* to the Byzantine elite, but he exaggerates its importance. It consisted of a mixture of 'well tried practices' and 'a great deal of worthless magic'; see White, *Roman Farming*, pp. 32, 45–6. Its revival can also be regarded as an example of the cultural antiquarianism of the time of Constantine VII.

[125] 'Nikon Metanoeite', p. 203. In the twelfth century large quantities of oil were exported from this region to Italy; see Thiriet, *La Romanie vénitienne*, p. 44.

[126] *Engrapha Patmou*, II, no. 52 lines 68–9, 107c–d.

[127] MM, IV, pp. 320–2.

[128] 'Vie d'Athanase', pp. 35–6.

[129] *Xénophon*, no. 1, pp. 21–2 lines 74–80, 127–33.

[130] *Lavra*, I, no. 26 lines 1–13.   [131] Goudas, 'Vatopedi', pp. 115–16.

146   *Economic expansion in the Byzantine empire*

property near Gomatou was taken over by the monastery of Sarabaros and vines were planted there. Iviron later claimed that the land lay inside its boundaries and had simply been neglected by its officials. The cost of planting the vines is unknown, but by 1080 the land was valued at 100 *nomismata* and the wine which had been produced amounted to 124 measures.[132] In 1193 Sabas paid 300 *aspra nomismata hyperpyra* for unexploited land on Athos which he intended to plant with vines. It was situated next to a vineyard, which he had already planted, and he established a monastic cell there to ensure that the vines were properly supervised.[133]

The evidence elsewhere is more patchy. During Sabas's period as abbot on Patmos the items which the monastery purchased in Constantinople included plants. It is possible that olives and fig trees were already being grown on the island in Christodoulos's life-time.[134] One of the best illustrations of this type of activity is contained in Psellos's description of the improvements made to imperial properties by Constantine IX. In his excessively laudatory account he credits the emperor with the transformation of barren fields into productive ones, but this was done to create attractive parks by uprooting trees elsewhere and transplanting them.[135] Psellos himself was responsible for the construction of an irrigation system and the planting of vines on the land of the monastery of Medikion.[136] Similarly, Boilas built aqueducts and created gardens and vineyards on his lands.[137]

Perhaps this expenditure led to an increase in wine and oil production as a proportion of total agricultural production, but such an increase would have been relatively slight. Nevertheless, some areas did achieve some renown for their wine. Michael Choniates emphasised the importance of wines from Euboia, Chios and Rhodes for the supply of Constantinople and in the thirteenth century Nicolas Mesarites referred to the quality of wines from Lesbos and Monembasia as well as Chios and Euboia.[138] The Venetians valued wine from Crete most highly and

---

[132] Dölger, *Schatzkammern*, no. 104.   [133] *Chilandar*, no. 2.

[134] MM, VI, p. 244; Karlin-Hayter, 'Notes sur les archives de Patmos', p. 200 n. 17.

[135] Psellos, *Chronographie*, II, pp. 56–7. Possibly, he was responding to a stronger urban demand for garden produce, but the passage does not deserve the exaggerated importance attributed to it by Teall, 'The Byzantine Agricultural Tradition', p. 44.

[136] Sathas, *MB*, V, no. 29, p. 264. See also Weiss, *Oströmische Beamte*, p. 151.

[137] Lemerle, *Cinq études*, p. 22 lines 49–60.

[138] Michael Choniates, II, p. 83; A. Heisenberg, 'Neue Quellen zur Geschichte des lateinischen Kaisertums und der Kirchenunion, III. Der Bericht des Nicolaos Mesarites über die politischen und kirchlichen Ereignisse des Jahres 1214', in *Sitzungsberichte der bayerischen Akademie der Wissenschaften. Philosophisch-philologische und historische Klasse* (Munich, 1923), 3. Abhandlung, p. 21. For the significance of wine production

Agricultural production 147

it was the island's most lucrative export.[139] In later centuries many islands were dependent on the export of part of their wine because they were not self-sufficient in grain and had to import it. This was true of many of the Ionian islands, which imported grain from the mainland. It is highly improbable that geographical conditions permitted any other course of action in the Byzantine period.[140] The most important region for the cultivation of olive trees was the Peloponnesos. The Venetians exported large quantities of oil from Corinth and Sparta. The significance of the extensive cultivation of olive trees in the region around Korone was emphasised in the eyewitness testimony of Benedict of Peterborough towards the end of the twelfth century.[141] In the post-Byzantine period oil continued to be the major export from many places in the Peloponnesos, especially Mistra and Korone. On the west coast of Epiros, notably around Prebeza, olive cultivation was carried out on an extensive scale. Leake estimated the annual export of the town and its region at 70,000 litres; the trees were not intercultivated with crops because the oil was the most important produce of the area. He also estimated the total produce of Salona and its region at 500,000 litres.[142] Perhaps agricultural production in this area was less specialised during the Byzantine period, but the Venetian exports from the Peloponnesos show that in some places a significant surplus of oil was being produced.

Although the evidence for the cultivation of mulberry trees is more limited, information from later travellers can be combined with Byzantine evidence to give some general impressions. When Leake visited the region around Iznik and Bursa, it was given over extensively to mulberry cultivation. The main centres at that time for working up the silk into textiles were Istanbul and Bursa.[143] In the Byzantine period

---

in Chios in the later medieval period, see Balard, *La Romanie génoise*, II, pp. 704–5, 844; and in Monembasia, see D. A. Zakythinos, *Le Despotat grec de Morée. Vie et institutions*, 2nd edn (London, 1975), p. 249. For wine exports from Euboia in later centuries, see Leake, *Travels in Northern Greece*, II, p. 253.

[139] Thiriet, *La Romanie vénitienne*, p. 320.

[140] H. Holland, *Travels in the Ionian Islands, Albania, Thessaly, Macedonia etc., during the Years 1812 and 1813* (London, 1815), pp. 21–2, 62–3; Leake, *Travels in Northern Greece*, III, pp. 27, 65–6.

[141] Thiriet, *La Romanie vénitienne*, p. 47; *Gesta Regis Henrici Secundi Benedicti Abbatis. The Chronicle of the Reigns of Henry II and Richard I AD 1169–1192; Known commonly under the Name of Benedict of Peterborough*, ed. W. Stubbs (2 vols., London, 1867), II, p. 199.

[142] Leake, *Travels in the Morea*, I, pp. 131, 437; Leake, *Travels in Northern Greece*, I, p. 177; II, p. 589.

[143] W. M. Leake, *Journal of a Tour in Asia Minor, with Comparative Remarks on the Ancient and Modern Geography of that Country* (London, 1824), pp. 6, 13, 16; Pococke, *A Description of the East*, II, p. 120.

148 *Economic expansion in the Byzantine empire*

mulberry cultivation must have been large enough to meet much of the requirements of the textile industry in Constantinople and in the thirteenth century at Nicaea.[144] In Thessaly there were large numbers of mulberry trees on the estates of the bishop of Stagoi in the twelfth century.[145] Much later Holland saw extensive mulberry plantations on the road from Stagoi to Trikkala. At that time the silk was transported to Ioannina and Smyrna.[146] In the eleventh and twelfth centuries it is likely that large quantities were sent from Thessaly to Thebes, a major centre of textile production. The Venetians regularly exported silk from the Peloponnesos from the twelfth century and later travellers recounted the impressive quantity of production in the region.[147]

The evidence for the revenues which were derived from arboriculture and viticulture is limited. Nevertheless, some rents which were exacted for small vineyards during the later Byzantine period show how lucrative a properly tended vineyard might have been. There were twelve small vineyards around Constantinople, the largest of which was six *modioi*. There were slight variations in the payments, but the standard was one *nomisma* for three *modioi*. The total surface area of the vineyards was fractionally over forty-five *modioi*. The total rent amounted to $14 \frac{7}{24}$ *nomismata*, an average of just under one *nomisma* for three *modioi*.[148] It implies a quite lucrative exploitation of a small property. These payments were only the surplus extracted from the direct producer and there is no information about the total value of the produce of these properties. The rents suggest that even a peasant with a very small plot of land could survive if it was suitable for viticulture and situated near an urban centre. Viticulture could ameliorate the worst difficulties of small landowners as well as offer large landowners with financial resources scope for considerable expenditure on agriculture.

The only good figures for agricultural production in this period come from Byzantine Italy. An inventory drawn up by the metropolis of Reggio in the theme of Calabria lists the payments which the city

---

[144] For the industry at Nicaea, see Angold, *A Byzantine Government in Exile*, p. 109. For silk imports from Asia Minor by Italians, see Balard, *La Romanie génoise*, pp. 723–5.
[145] Astruc, 'Un document inédit de 1163', p. 214 lines 14–20.
[146] Holland, *Travels*, pp. 244–5. For silk production elsewhere in Thessaly, see Leake, *Travels in Northern Greece*, III, pp. 386–7; IV, pp. 389–90, 393–4.
[147] Thiriet, *La Romanie vénitienne*, pp. 44, 49; Leake, *Travels in the Morea*, I, pp. 131, 347–9; II, p. 50.
[148] P. Gautier, 'Le typikon de la Théotokos Kécharitôménè', *Revue des Études Byzantines*, 43 (1985), pp. 148–50.

Agricultural production 149

received from its properties and from the lands over which it exercised economic jurisdiction. Unfortunately, the rolls detailing the payments from cereal and wine production are not extant. The only surviving accounts concern mulberry trees. The tax-assessment was based on the number of bags of leaves which were used as food for the silkworms. The 8,107 mulberry trees in the text were worth 521 *nomismata* annually to the city and the text only deals with the southern part of Calabria. Guillou has estimated that the productive trees yielded 19,275 quintals of leaves, $64\frac{1}{4}$ of seed, 19,600 of moist cocoons, 6,553 of dry cocoons and $1,606\frac{1}{4}$ quintals of raw silk. The total value of the silk, based on a 1020 price from the Cairo geniza of $2\frac{1}{2}$ dinars for 328 g of silk, he estimates at approximately $1\frac{1}{4}$ million dinars. This was the produce of a cultivated area of between 1,500 and 1,900 hectares. The extent of mulberry cultivation in the whole of Calabria is unknown. Guillou has used the smallest area planted with mulberries since the sixteenth century to estimate the annual value of the production of the theme at four million dinars. These calculations are hugely speculative and probably inaccurate. In an economy where only a very limited proportion of the total production was sold in markets, such global calculations, based on price evidence from elsewhere in the Mediterranean, are bound to be distorted. Nevertheless, the document does give a useful impression of the scale of silk production. The evidence for economic expansion in the inventory is unquestionable. About a fifth of the trees were not subject to tax, presumably because they were less than ten years old. The cultivation of mulberry trees was sufficiently remunerative to encourage fresh expansion.[149]

The other major form of production is pastoral farming. It was inextricably linked with other branches of agriculture. The advantages of stable feeding to produce good fertiliser have already been emphasised. Different systems of exploitation of pastoral resources ranged from the rearing of a few animals close to the peasant household as part of a mixed farming system to the maintenance of large herds on extensive tracts of grazing land, a form of agricultural specialisation open to the wealthy landowner.

The animals which peasant families were most likely to possess were pigs, sheep and goats. The pig is the most useful for adding meat to the diet because it is cheap to raise and yields a large quantity of meat. It

[149] A. Guillou, 'Production and Profits in the Byzantine Province of Italy (Tenth to Eleventh Centuries): An Expanding Society', *Dumbarton Oaks Papers*, 28 (1974), pp. 92–5.

150   *Economic expansion in the Byzantine empire*

was the easiest animal for a poor peasant family to keep. It could be kept near the house with occasional excursions to obtain food or it could be allowed to roam freely in the woods and forests feeding on acorns. Sheep and goats need far less fodder and grazing than cattle. The goat does not need a high quality of feed and can be kept on land which could not be used for other animals or it can be given fodder which is unsuitable for other animals. In contrast, cattle required a large quantity of feed, were much more expensive and were restricted to wealthier peasant families. The variations in the animal wealth of peasant farmers or landowners involved the types of animals, their numbers, the proportion of one type to another and the balance between livestock and arable. At the bottom of the scale there was the small peasant landholding with some pigs, sheep or goats. Then there was the peasant with enough land to need ploughing animals. On larger properties there was the distinction between rearing enough animals for self-sufficiency and specialisation involving large herds and flocks kept on extensive grazing lands.[150]

The size of peasant flocks was restricted by the limitations on the amount of fodder which a peasant was able to grow and by the availability of pasture. The second factor depended on the extent of arable cultivation and partly on local conditions. Marshy land around river deltas and lakes could be used to pasture large herds. Pastoral farming figures prominently in the regulations of the Farmer's Law. The code was compiled during a period of demographic contraction and its chapters give the impression of village communities with sufficient grazing land at their disposal. The animals most frequently mentioned in the code are oxen, donkeys, sheep, rams and pigs, but the size of peasant herds and flocks should not be exaggerated. The ox was the most frequently mentioned animal in the code, but its importance was primarily for arable cultivation. The donkey was most useful as a working animal for transportation. The combined number of the peasant livestock was sometimes sufficient for a community to entrust them to hired herdsmen. In most cases they were pastured near the village – some regulations concerned animals breaking into cultivated plots. The problem of finding sufficient pasture and manure was partly met by allowing the animals to graze on the stubble after the corn had been harvested.[151]

[150] Delano Smith, *Western Mediterranean Europe*, pp. 219–29.
[151] The assertion of A. Kazhdan, 'Two Notes on Byzantine Demography of the Eleventh and Twelfth Centuries', *Byzantinische Forschungen*, 8 (1982), p. 119, that in the

Agricultural production 151

There are few precise figures for the animal wealth of peasants in this period. The *praktikon* of Andronikos Doukas lists forty-nine *paroikoi*. Altogether they owned forty-two oxen, but the peasants on some estates were much better equipped than those on others. Unfortunately, the document does not reveal the number of sheep and cows each peasant owned, but gives only the total payment for the pasture-tax. A few figures were included in the lists of *paroikoi*. Five peasants, each on a different estate, owned a combined total of thirty-nine pigs. Four mares, ten other horses and two mules were also recorded. They were all registered in the names of peasants who owned ploughing animals. Any livestock belonging to the *aktemones* (peasants without oxen) was not recorded. It is impossible to estimate the size of peasant herds and flocks, but the payments for the *ennomion* (pasture-tax) were fairly small. The limited number of pigs also suggests that the peasants were not well off for animals.[152] The animal wealth of the monk Gerontios gives a good impression of what a wealthy peasant family might have possessed. His monastery owned five working oxen, three cows, two calves and sixty-two sheep.[153] There are better figures for the early fourteenth century. In Gomatou the majority of peasant families possessed no flocks in 1300–1, but eight households owned 928 animals.[154] Owing to the inadequacy of the evidence any adverse effect which the expansion of arable cultivation might have had on the pastoral resources of peasant farmers is difficult to ascertain, but it probably had a restrictive effect in the most densely populated regions.

Pastoral farming on this scale contrasts completely with the large herds and flocks which powerful landowners maintained by extensive ranching. It has been suggested that in regions threatened by external attack pastoral farming was the safest form of agricultural activity because the herds could be led to safety in times of emergency, and that in the early Middle Ages large landowners concentrated increasingly on this sphere of activity rather than arable farming.[155] Insecurity was not the only factor involved in this choice. The scarcity of manpower, resulting from the demographic contraction of the seventh and eighth centuries, reduced the extent of arable cultivation and increased the area available for pasture. Cattle needed less manpower than cereal

---

Farmer's Law 'cattle-breeding seems to have a priority over the cultivation of the soil' ignores the important role of the oxen in arable cultivation. See also Köpstein, 'Zu den Agrarverhältnissen', p. 44.

[152] *Engrapha Patmou*, II, no. 50.   [153] MM, IV, p. 202.

[154] Laiou-Thomadakis, *Peasant Society*, pp. 30–1.

[155] Haldon and Kennedy, 'The Arab–Byzantine Frontier', pp. 100–1.

152   *Economic expansion in the Byzantine empire*

cultivation and represented the best way of building up wealth in these centuries.[156]

The most extensive grazing region was the Anatolian plateau. Consisting largely of rolling upland with sparse vegetation, it was best suited to large-scale ranching, and the sunken basins of the plateau provided winter pasture. In the post-Byzantine era the pastoral resources of the plateau were exploited largely by nomadic groups whose wealth lay in their herds, which provided them with meat, dairy products, wool and leather. Their major occupational craft was rug-weaving. They marketed part of their produce to obtain grain and other goods from villages and towns. The most prestigious wool was produced around Ankara and the Turks forbade its export before it had been worked up by the inhabitants of the area.[157] In the Byzantine period the resources of the plateau were exploited largely by the state and powerful aristocratic families. It was important to the state for grazing horses. Most of the imperial stud farms were on the plateau and its loss in the 1070s probably caused problems in the supply of horses to the army.[158] In the account of Philaretos's wealth the hagiographer gave pride of place to the herds and flocks. He is said to have possessed 600 cows, 100 pairs of oxen, 800 grazing horses, 80 mules and packhorses and 12,000 sheep.[159] Such herds would have required an enormous amount of pasture, but much of the plateau was better suited to this type of farming than to concentrated settlements. The economic power of the great magnates, who posed such a threat to the state in the tenth century, was firmly based on such extensive ranching.

Some figures for the animal wealth of large landowners in the European provinces in the eleventh century are more reliable than those for the herds of Philaretos and Leo. Gregory Pakourianos's properties included mountain pastures in the high plateaux of the Rhodope range. These lands were best suited to grazing and were populated partly by nomads who practised transhumance farming.

---

[156] Leo III's family had large flocks in Thrace. He made a gift of 500 sheep to Justinian II and in return was awarded the title of *spatharios*; see Theophanes, I, p. 391.

[157] Vryonis, *The Decline of Medieval Hellenism*, pp. 267–76; Pococke, *A Description of the East*, II, pp. 89–90.

[158] Hendy, *Studies in the Byzantine Monetary Economy*, pp. 54–6; R. Guilland, 'Les logothètes, études sur l'histoire administrative de l'empire byzantin', *Revue des Études Byzantines*, 29 (1971), pp. 71–3.

[159] 'Vie de Philarète', pp. 113–15; Köpstein, 'Zu den Agrarverhältnissen', pp. 60–4; Nesbitt, 'The Life of St Philaretos', pp. 150–8. Although these figures may be inaccurate in the specific case of Philaretos, they nevertheless give a good indication of the basis of the wealth of noblemen in the interior of Asia Minor.

Agricultural production

153

Pakourianos's animals included 110 horses and mares with their young, 15 donkeys, 4 cows for milking, 2 calves, 47 pairs of oxen, 72 cows and bulls, 238 sheep, 94 rams and 52 goats.[160] The properties of Symbatios Pakourianos in Macedonia included extensive mountain pastures, which were used for raising horses. He bequeathed eight to the emperor as a token gesture and twenty to his brother Sergios. A few years later his wife bequeathed thirteen mares to various followers.[161] Horse-rearing was an almost obligatory requirement for a member of the aristocracy with military duties, but after the loss of the grazing lands on the Anatolian plateau there was an urgent need for horses from the European provinces.

The structure of the animal wealth of Xenophon was different. Its herds had been increased by Symeon and by 1089 the monastery owned 14 pairs of oxen, 100 horses and donkeys, 130 buffaloes, 150 cows and 2,000 sheep and goats. Its lands lay in fertile areas in the theme of Kalamaria and the Kassandra peninsula, which could support quite intensive grazing. Their convenient location enabled the monastery to ship produce to Athos to meet its own consumption requirements and to send any surplus to Thessalonike for sale.[162]

A good approximation of the numbers of the livestock of the monastery at Strymitza is given by an exemption which it received in 1106. It was freed from all obligations in respect of 10 grazing horses, 40 cows and 150 sheep.[163] Pastoral farming on this scale was probably closely integrated with the monastery's arable cultivation, in contrast to the greater specialisation on the estates of Pakourianos and Xenophon. It is unlikely that the monastery produced a significant surplus of dairy produce for sale.

Elsewhere, such figures are unavailable and only general remarks are possible. There is some indication of specialisation in horse-rearing in some areas of the Peloponnesos. Several parts of the peninsula offer excellent pastoral facilities. There is ample rainfall in the western Peloponnesos, and the plain of Elis, which is watered by the Alphios and Peneus rivers, contained the best lowland pastures in the peninsula. In the plateau of Arkadia the small lake basins were liable to be flooded after the winter rains and the spring thaw. When the water-line receded during the summer drought, they offered good pasture land.[164] As part

---

[160] Gautier, 'Grégoire Pakourianos', p. 37 line 284, p. 43 lines 390–1, p. 125 lines 1755–66.
[161] Iberites, 'Byzantinai diathekai', pp. 613–18; 365–71.
[162] *Xénophon*, no. 1 lines 226–8.   [163] Petit, 'Notre Dame de Pitié', p. 29 lines 15–17.
[164] Semple, *The Geography of the Mediterranean Region*, pp. 321–2.

154   *Economic expansion in the Byzantine empire*

of the commutation of military service during Romanos's reign 1,000 horses were demanded from the theme. Only the best-quality horses would have been suited for military service and the capacity of the theme to supply so many on one occasion must have been due to an extensive raising of horses.[165] Mount Athos had great potential as an area of pastoral farming and the claims of the villagers outside the peninsula to enter it with their herds and flocks was a contentious issue. The monks were already trying to prevent them in the ninth century. In 883 Basil I issued a decree prohibiting the herdsmen of the *enoria* of Hierissos from taking cattle, sheep or other animals onto Athos.[166] At the beginning of Leo VI's reign the monks of Kolobou temporarily acquired the ownership of the peninsula by a legal contrivance. They exploited it as pasture for their own animals and allowed neighbouring villagers to use it in return for a payment until the Athonite monks were able to annul the usurpation.[167] The monks did not succeed in excluding the villagers from the mountain completely. When the boundary dispute between the two parties was settled, the right of the latter to take their animals onto Athos in the event of a foreign invasion was maintained. Limits were placed on the activities of the people of Hierissos inside Athonite territory. They had to give the monks advance warning of their entry and were not allowed to set up folds or beehives, which would have been indicative of a more permanent presence.[168]

This issue had an artificial character. The inhabitants of Hierissos and the villagers had arable lands near the boundary and found themselves deprived of some pasture owing to the special status of the Athonite community. The problem of livestock on Athos took on a new form as the community expanded. Theoretically, the monasteries were not allowed any animals on the peninsula, but by 1045 many had sheep and goats and Lavra had oxen. The other monasteries agreed to remove their animals. Lavra was able to plead a special case owing to its large number of monks and because its livestock had been brought into the peninsula fifty years earlier with the permission of the abbots. Its sheep had to be removed, but it was allowed to keep its cattle. It was also allowed to keep four pairs of oxen for grinding corn. Vatopedi was also allowed one pair and in 1082 it received imperial authorisation to maintain two pairs of oxen and cows on Athos.[169] These measures

---

[165] *DAI*, p. 256.   [166] *Prôtaton*, no. 1 lines 15–17.
[167] *Ibid.*, no. 2.   [168] *Ibid.*, no. 5 lines 55–60.
[169] *Ibid.*, no. 8 lines 78–9 and pp. 104–5; Goudas, 'Vatopedi', p. 126.

Agricultural production 155

probably had limited effectiveness. Previous regulations had not stopped the monks from maintaining flocks on the mountain and there is no reason to assume that Monomachos's *typikon* had a different result. Not only were monks keeping flocks, but *paroikoi* were also pasturing their animals on Athos.[170] The most notorious case was that of the Vlach pastoralists. Three hundred families, the women dressed like men, were established as *douloparoikoi* and they provided the monks with cheese, milk and wool until the scandal became so great that they were expelled from Athos.[171]

The availability of good pasture in the Kassandra peninsula was facilitated by the terms of the sale of klasmatic land there. All purchasers had the right to graze animals on uncultivated parts of this land and on the fallow. Outsiders were also allowed to take their animals onto the klasmatic land if there was a foreign invasion.[172]

Environmental conditions sometimes give a greater importance to pastoral farming in relation to arable cultivation. Many Aegean islands have large tracts of barren, hilly and mountainous terrain which can be used only for pasturing sheep and goats, and their economy depended heavily on these flocks. Mykonos has little cultivable land and did not produce enough wheat for the consumption of its inhabitants. Skyros has abundant pasture and Leake estimated the number of sheep and goats on the island at 15,000, of which 2,000 were exported annually. Although Paros was better off in other branches of agriculture, it also had extensive tracts of pasture. Leake reckoned its flocks amounted to about 14,000 sheep and goats.[173]

Christodoulos's properties on Leros consisted mostly of rough terrain with little arable land, and their greatest potential lay in pastoral exploitation. One estate, Parthenion, contained only 409 *modioi* of arable land and the other, Temenia, 259 *modioi*. The rest of the land consisted of pasture and mountains.[174] A dispute between the monks

---

[170] In 991 Lavra took over the property of Platys at the north-east extremity of Athos on condition that it did not usurp the bordering lands, which were used for pasture by the monasteries' *paroikoi*; see *Lavra*, I, no. 9.

[171] P. Meyer, *Die Haupturkunden für Geschichte der Athoskloster* (Leipzig, 1894), pp. 163–4. See also M. Gyoni, 'La transhumance des Vlaques balkaniques au moyen âge', *ByzantinoSlavica*, 12 (1951), pp. 29–42, esp. pp. 36–8; and G. Rouillard, 'La dîme des bergers valaques sous Alexis Ier Comnène', in *Mélanges offerts à M. Nicolas Iorga* (Paris, 1933), pp. 779–86. [172] *Lavra*, I, no. 2 lines 29–35, no. 3 lines 14–16.

[173] Leake, *Travels in Northern Greece*, III, pp. 87, 105, 108.

[174] *Engrapha Patmou*, II, no. 52 lines 65, 99; Karlin–Hayter, 'Notes sur les archives de Patmos', pp. 203–4; E. Malamut, 'Les îles de la mer Égée de la fin du XIe siècle à 1204', *Byzantion*, 52 (1982), pp. 310–50.

156   *Economic expansion in the Byzantine empire*

and the *paroikoi* of two neighbouring fields arose over the pasture land, immediately after Christodoulos received Parthenion. The *paroikoi* claimed the right to use the pasture of Parthenion, but the monks asserted that the estate with all its territory formed a separate fiscal unit from the two fields. Previously, the properties had been joined for fiscal purposes and common pasturing had been practised. When the fields were separated from Parthenion, the *paroikoi* tried to continue common pasturing. They were able to do so initially until a *periorismos* assigned the correct amount of land to each party. The total area of Parthenion was 6,050 *modioi*, of which only 409 *modioi* was in use as arable.[175] Pastoral farming was also the major activity at Temenia. Several of its buildings were used as stables. It had one place of residence for the *misthioi* and another for the *paroikoi*. There was a clear distinction between the two categories and in this context the *misthioi* must have been hired labourers. Herdsmen would have been needed to supervise the animals pastured on the estate.[176]

Pastoral production had a similar preeminence on the island *ton Neon*, which was owned by Lavra. It was very dry and unsuitable for arable cultivation. Some crops were grown, but they were probably for the consumption requirements of the novices who were trained on the island. There were also some vineyards, but the herds and flocks were more important. Lavra obtained its supply of working animals from the island. After a plague of locusts had done great damage to the supply of fodder, the goats were transferred elsewhere because they were highly valued for the quality of their wool.[177]

These properties possessed more than adequate pastoral resources of their own, but often the summer drought made the maintenance of livestock very difficult and herds had to be grazed on mountain pastures. There are two basic types of transhumance. The first occurs where sheep farmers are people from the lowlands who leave in the summer. The second, 'inverse' transhumance involved shepherds and flocks coming down from the mountains. There is also a third, less important type where the dwelling is halfway between the summer and winter pastures. Transhumance is a regulated and generally peaceful way of life involving a settled form of agriculture, villages and a specialist group of shepherds.[178] It was a common phenomenon in areas

---

[175] *Engrapha Patmou*, II, no. 52, pp. 56–7.   [176] *Ibid.*, no. 52 lines 107–107b.

[177] 'Vie d'Athanase', p. 70. For Lavra's acquisition of this island from John of Iviron, see *Lavra*, I, p. 44 n. 157.

[178] Braudel, *The Mediterranean*, I, pp. 86–7.

Agricultural production

157

where there was a lack of convenient pasture.[179] The best-known example was the Vlachs, who came down from the mountains in winter. They descended on the lowland plains to make good the deficiency in their grain supply and offered in exchange dairy and woollen products. In 1066 there was a considerable Vlach population around Larissa, when the town rebelled. They had stayed behind while their families had taken their flocks back into the mountains. They were probably intending to supplement the produce of their flocks by working on the grain harvest in Thessaly.[180]

Lavra had mountain pastures in the theme of Moglena which were used by the Vlachs. In 1184 the monastery had to resort to imperial intervention when the Koumans exploited these pastures without paying the *dekateia*. The Koumans also usurped Lavra's claims on Vlach and Bulgarian pastoralists by illegally transforming them into their own *paroikoi*. Their actions caused a shortage of pasture and the Vlachs took their animals onto state land, using two folds in the state's mountain pasture (*demosiake planena*). Both were given to Lavra with the right to exact all the payments which the users of the fold had previously made to the state.[181] In this case it is not clear whether these pastoralists were engaged in transhumance or a less rigid nomadism.

As in other spheres of production pastoral resources were more intensively exploited in this period, possibly because the extension of arable cultivation restricted the amount of pasture available in some regions. This was not the only factor. Wealthy landowners had the resources to build up large herds and flocks. The example of the monastery of Xenophon shows how rapidly this could be done. Such landowners were in a better position than peasant farmers to provide winter feed and avoid slaughtering. They were able to specialise to a certain extent according to the quality and situation of their land and to build up flocks which produced more dairy produce and wool than they needed for their own immediate requirements.

Other subsidiary activities such as bee-keeping, salt production and fishing also deserve consideration. Bee-keeping was widely practised because honey was the only sweetener available before the development of cultivated sugar-cane. Large numbers of flowers are needed to

---

[179] For the use of mountainous pasture in north-west Phrygia, see Laurent, *La Vie merveilleuse*, p. 85.

[180] Cecaumenos, *Strategicon*, pp. 68–9; Gyoni, 'La transhumance des Vlaques balkaniques au moyen âge', p. 34.

[181] *Lavra*, I, no. 66; Rouillard, 'La dîme des bergers valaques', pp. 779–86.

158   *Economic expansion in the Byzantine empire*

produce any quantity of honey and areas dominated by pastoral farming are best suited to bees. Strabo claimed that the best honey came from the slopes of mount Hymettos in Attika.[182] Philaretos engaged in bee-keeping on a fairly large scale. After his animal wealth had been reduced to a cow, a calf and a donkey, he still owned 250 bee-hives.[183] Some peasants listed in the fourteenth-century *praktika* owned hives,[184] clearly a common activity.

Little is known about salt production in Byzantium, although it must have been a very widespread activity. In the eighteenth century Pococke reported that it was exported from Nikomedia, where there was a saltworks at the eastern end of the bay.[185] Salt is found in many of the lakes on the Anatolian plateau. In Thessalonike in the fifteenth century the salt merchants were organised into a guild.[186] The best-known salt-producing region was the Ionian islands. The Venetians' major source of revenue from Corfu, amounting to about 10,000 *hyperpyra* annually, was salt.[187]

In coastal areas and near rivers and lakes fishing was a major source of food and revenue. For the peasant it offered variation from a production too dependent on grain and had a mitigating effect in years of hardship. Many *paroikoi* near the Strymon owned fishing boats in the fourteenth century[188] and presumably also in previous centuries. At Dinogetia the most commonly found occupational equipment was for fishing, a major source of revenue for the inhabitants of the lower Danube region.[189] Kosmosotira had water-rights along the river Maritza, where it obtained its supply for the monks' tables. In the monastery's *typikon* the quality of the fish caught in the river Samia

---

[182] White, *Roman Farming*, p. 331; G. Clark, 'Bees in Antiquity', *Antiquity*, 16 (1942), pp. 208–15.

[183] 'Vie de Philarète', pp. 129, 131. For bee-keeping along the Bosphoros, see *Vie de Cyrille Philéote*, p. 67.

[184] Laiou-Thomadakis, *Peasant Society*, p. 31. For bee-keeping in Cyprus in the same period, see J. Richard, 'Une économie coloniale? Chypre et ses resources agricoles au moyen âge', *Byzantinische Forschungen*, 5 (1977), p. 345.

[185] Pococke, *A Description of the East*, II, p. 96.

[186] *Dionysiou*, no. 14. For salt production in the same region in the seventh century, see Vasiliev, 'An Edict of the Emperor Justinian II, September 688', pp. 1–13; Grégoire, 'Un édit de l'empereur Justinien II, daté de septembre 688', pp. 119–24; and Spieser, 'Inventaires', pp. 156–9.

[187] F. Thiriet, 'Agriculteurs et agriculture à Corfu, au XVème siècle', *Kerkyraika Chronika*, 23 (1980), pp. 315–28.

[188] Laiou-Thomadakis, *Peasant Society*, p. 31; Nesbitt, 'Mechanisms of Agricultural Production', pp. 77–8.

[189] Stefan *et al.*, *Dinogetia*, I, p. 392; Barnea, 'Dinogetia', p. 265.

Agricultural production 159

near Neokastron was praised and the abbot warned to keep a close check on the monastery's interests there.[190] Landowners with water-rights could allow others to fish in their part of the river in return for payments. This was probably the case when St Symeon encountered a fisherman who refused to give up his catch because he had to hand it over to a *patrikios*.[191]

In all the major sectors of agriculture, production was intensified. This is most apparent in the case of wealthy landowners, but there are occasional hints of improvements by small landowners. The Farmer's Law envisages improvements by individual peasant farmers,[192] but gives no indications of combined action by a community to bring land under cultivation or to secure a reliable water-supply. Such actions were presumably undertaken, but we know nothing of this aspect of rural life. The resources available to a village community were limited and improvements were restricted in scale compared with those made by wealthy landowners.[193] Increasing differences in the wealth of members of village communities probably undermined the basis for such cooperation, but it did mean that a small number of reasonably successful landowners were able to make modest improvements to their properties. Small improvements were also made by relatively insignificant monasteries. A good example is the purchase of land by the monastery of Roudaba to build a new mill.[194] Such activities were no doubt much more common than the few chance references in the sources would indicate and had some impact on the economy.

The most dynamic element in the rural economy was the efforts made by powerful landowners to improve their properties. The case of Lavra with its imperial patronage has already been cited. When Psellos acquired the monastery of Medikion, he intended to exploit its lands more effectively by purchasing oxen and other animals, planting vines and improving the irrigation of the land by redirecting streams and bringing the water-supply in through channels. He anticipated greater yields of wheat, barley and wine. He also intended to supply oxen, cattle and sheep to the monastery *ton Mountanion*, whose *charistikarios* he had just become.[195] Boilas brought an extensive area under cultivation by

---

[190] Petit, 'Kosmosotira', pp. 50–1; Asdracha, *La Région des Rhodopes*, p. 201. See also *Vie de Cyrille Philéote*, p. 67; and Gautier, 'Pantocrator', line 1562.
[191] Hausherr and Horn, *Vie de Syméon le Nouveau Théologien*, pp. 170–2.
[192] Ashburner, 'The Farmer's Law', chs. 17, 21, 81, 82.
[193] Svoronos, 'Remarques sur les structures économiques', pp. 60–1; Teall, 'The Byzantine Agricultural Tradition', pp. 56–7.   [194] *Lavra*, I, no. 14.
[195] Sathas, *MB*, V, nos. 29, 178. See also Psellos, *Scripta Minora*, II, no. 89. For his role as *charistikarios*, see Weiss, *Oströmische Beamte*, pp. 145–52.

160   *Economic expansion in the Byzantine empire*

reducing woodland by fire and axe and creating meadows, parks, gardens, vineyards, aqueducts and water-mills. All the villages which were listed in his will were freshly colonised by Boilas. His exploits cannot automatically be regarded as indicative of economic trends in the eastern border region owing to the political reasons for his settlement there, but they are a good illustration of the impact which a landowner with considerable resources could have on the economy of a region.[196] The actions of Gregory Pakourianos demonstrate better the expansion of the rural economy in this period. He was much more wealthy than Boilas. He constructed *kastra* and monasteries and created new villages. The state conceded all its claims to revenues from his estates and any obligations arising out of the improvements which he made. A chrysobull waived the treasury's claims if his revenues exceeded the stipulated level of the *logisimon*. Unfortunately, the precise details of his activities are largely unknown. Only the bare subject matter of the privileges is listed in the *typikon*. There is no detailed discussion of the most interesting aspect of his economic activity, the creation of new villages. We are left only with a fairly general description of his estates – arable land cultivated by *paroikoi*, vineyards, fruit trees, extensive pasture land and water-mills. It seems that improvements were made in most aspects of agricultural production on his estates.[197]

Consequently, widely accepted conclusions about agricultural production in Byzantium are in need of revision. The first point is that the chronological pattern of economic development is wrong. The onset of decline or stagnation has usually been placed in the eleventh century, just when there is much evidence of expansion. Recently, Svoronos has conceded that there was some expansion in the tenth and first half of the eleventh century, but has concluded that peasants were unable, and large landowners generally unwilling, to make serious efforts to increase production substantially and, consequently, stagnation prevailed from the late eleventh century onwards.[198] Although Teall has tried to present a more optimistic view of Byzantine agriculture, the same criticism applies to his chronological pattern. He regards the ninth, tenth and the first half of the eleventh century as the great period of agricultural improvement.[199]

[196] Lemerle, *Cinq études*, p. 22 lines 49–55. See also above, p. 64.
[197] Gautier, 'Grégoire Pakourianos', p. 43 lines 387–96, p. 127 lines 1796–1800. See also above, p. 65.
[198] Svoronos, 'Remarques sur les structures économiques', pp. 60–3.
[199] Teall, 'The Byzantine Agricultural Tradition', pp. 53–9.

Agricultural production 161

The most important factor in the increase in agricultural production was the growth in population, which resulted in the expansion of the area under cultivation. The course of demographic growth is in itself sufficient to refute the standard orthodoxy that production stagnated from the eleventh century. Although there was a temporary decline in production in Asia Minor in the late eleventh and early twelfth century, the general pattern was one of an increasing amount of land being brought into cultivation.[200]

The economic consequences of the increasing predominance of large estates has also been misjudged. Large landowners had the resources to make significant improvements to their properties. They also had access to a sufficiently large supply of manpower to ensure that the land was properly cultivated. These are the main reasons for some improvements in production. The alluvial plains, which could yield very high returns, needed an adequate supply of manpower to be cultivated effectively. Their fertility enabled a growing population to be accommodated on the land without any clear sign that it was placing a great strain on agricultural resources. Large landowners had the resources to undertake extensive irrigation schemes. These activities enabled a greater range of crops to be grown. Irrigated lands needed extra labour, but this was spread more evenly throughout the year. In the sources irrigation was frequently associated with the planting of vines and olives. Production of wine and oil probably increased slightly in relation to other spheres of production. The importance of this development should not be exaggerated because most production was intended for direct consumption. Nevertheless, around towns it was possible for landowners and peasants to concentrate more heavily on viticulture and arboriculture. Although the amount of produce which was sold on the market remained marginal, it was increasing.

The nature of this economic expansion has been misinterpreted by Teall, whose arguments suffer from a serious misunderstanding of Byzantine society. He regards land as 'capital investment designed to produce returns' and believes that by the eleventh century Byzantium was facing a 'crisis of agricultural capitalism'.[201] Such terminology is completely inapplicable to Byzantium. Peasants remained in effective possession, if not ownership, of the means of production. Landowners did make some significant improvements to their properties, but their outlays on agricultural production were certainly only a limited part of

---

[200] See above, chapter 2.
[201] Teall, 'The Byzantine Agricultural Tradition', pp. 56–9.

162   *Economic expansion in the Byzantine empire*

their total expenditure. It was capital formation within the limited perspective of feudal landownership[202] and the easiest way of increasing production remained a straightforward extension of the area under cultivation.

An important consequence of economic expansion was the strengthening of the economic base of the aristocracy. Its revenues were derived only partially from its lands. It also benefited from its share in political power and gratuities from the state.[203] However, this depended on imperial favour, which was not always forthcoming. Unfortunately, little is known of the revenues which were obtained from landed wealth and what proportion they were of the total revenues of landowners.[204] This varied according to the official positions which a landowner occupied. Lavra received *solemnia* amounting to eleven pounds and twenty *nomismata* by the mid eleventh century, probably a relatively small amount compared with the revenue from its lands.[205] The total revenues from Lavra's estates cannot be calculated, but they certainly increased sharply as more peasants were installed on them and improvements were made to the land. This trend applied to feudal landowners generally and strengthened their economic position, reinforcing centrifugal tendencies in the empire.

[202] See the discussion of the problem using English evidence by Hilton, *The English Peasantry*, pp. 174–214.

[203] See the summary of Kazhdan's work in Sorlin, 'Publications soviétiques sur le XIᵉ siècle', pp. 367–80.

[204] Boilas's will suggests that his revenues were a low percentage of the total value of the estates (3.45% or 3.7%), but this possibly excludes additional payments like the *ennomion* or charges in kind; see Lemerle, *Cinq études*, p. 60. The remote situation of Boilas's properties was a disadvantage. A landowner whose estates were situated near a large town was likely to obtain larger cash revenues from his estates.

[205] *Lavra*, I, no. 32 lines 32–9. By 1089 Lavra was in possession of over 47,000 *modioi* in the theme of Boleron, Strymon and Thessalonike; see *Lavra* I, no. 50 lines 17–18. A good example of how revenues could increase sharply on one estate is provided by the village of Chostiane. When Lavra received the property there were only twelve *paroikoi*. By 1181 there were sixty-two *zeugaratoi*; see *ibid.*, no. 65. The *telos* which they paid can be estimated roughly at two pounds a year without taking into consideration all the other charges.

Chapter 5

The pattern of demand

The impact which the intensification of agricultural production had on the economy as a whole needs careful consideration. The developments which have already been outlined show that the revenues which the state and powerful landowners derived from agriculture must have increased considerably from the tenth century onwards. Their scope for expenditure was extended and an outline of their main requirements will provide a useful guide to the possibilities for the development of commodity production, the role of commercial markets in the economy and more generally its capacity for expansion. The pattern of demand in the Byzantine economy has to be defined overwhelmingly in terms of consumption. The main requirements were diet, clothing and building and, as has been mentioned already, the emphasis on self-sufficiency reflected the realities of an economy consisting predominantly of direct producers operating on a small scale and having a very restricted commercial sector. Both landowners and peasants obtained as large a proportion of their produce as possible from their own estates,[1] although wealthy landowners were also able to indulge their taste for scarcer items, which were expensive and therefore had a considerable prestige value. Investment played a very minor role. Although no precise figures are available, it is certain that the improvements made by landowners to their properties accounted for only a small proportion of their total expenditure, and their involvement in industry and

---

[1] For this emphasis on self-sufficiency, see above, p. 121. The most detailed survey of Byzantine diet is made by Ph. Koukoules, *Byzantinon bios kai politismos* (6 vols., Athens, 1948–55), V, pp. 9–135. See also Patlagean, *Pauvreté économique et pauvreté sociale à Byzance*, pp. 36–53; Kazhdan and Constable, *People and Power in Byzantium*, pp. 55–6; and M. Debinska, 'Diet: A Comparison of Food Consumption between some Eastern and Western Monasteries in the 4th–12th Centuries', *Byzantion*, 55 (1985), pp. 431–62. For broader methodological considerations, see M. Aymard, 'Pour l'histoire de l'alimentation: quelques remarques de méthode', *Annales ESC*, 30 (1975), pp. 431–44.

164   *Economic expansion in the Byzantine empire*

commerce was also very restricted.[2] Spending by the state was also heavily directed towards consumption. The main exception, and a very important economic factor, was its military expenditure. Otherwise the purpose of its spending was to run the state's bureaucracy and to maintain an extremely high level of conspicuous consumption, which acted as a model which large landowners tended to copy.

The main variations in demand were determined by regional differences in resources and by social class. The most important regional variations were those which geographical conditions imposed on agricultural production. On large parts of the Anatolian plateau wheat cultivation was restricted and the main agricultural sector was pastoral farming. This would have necessitated a certain amount of exchange to maintain the supply of wheat, at least to the most illustrious of the local population. The clearest indication is given by Leo, the metropolitan of Synnada. The area surrounding the town did not produce oil and usually did not produce wine. Conditions did not permit the cultivation of wheat, only that of barley. Other requirements had to be imported from the theme of Thrakesion, Attaleia or Constantinople.[3] Unfortunately, he does not give precise details of the items which were imported. While it is likely that the wealthier inhabitants wanted good-quality wheat, poorer landowners and peasants probably had to be satisfied with locally grown grains of inferior quality because the price of imported grain might have been prohibitively high. In some of the Aegean islands environmental constraints would also have prevented self-sufficiency in wheat production, but the effect on economic demand would have been minimal compared with that from the interior of Anatolia. Even where regional conditions did affect the need for produce, the demand was largely confined to the elite of the region.

While wealthy landowners had greater flexibility in the range of items which they could include in their diet, the peasantry was largely restricted to the produce of their locality. The diet of the peasantry is difficult to analyse because of the nature of the sources. The most detailed dietary information concerns monastic establishments, and even the provisions given to the sick and poor in charitable

---

[2] See above, p. 161, and below, chapter 6.

[3] Darrouzès, *Épistoliers*, pp. 198–9; Hendy, *Studies in the Byzantine Monetary Economy*, pp. 138–45; L. Robert, 'Les kordakia de Nicée, le combustible de Synnada at les poissons-scies. Sur des lettres d'un métropolite de Phrygie aux Xe siècle. Philologie et réalités', *Journal des Savants* (1961), pp. 137ff. For the export of corn from the empire of Nicaea to Seljuk territories in the thirteenth century, see Angold, *A Byzantine Government in Exile*, p. 116.

The pattern of demand

establishments such as Attaleiates's poor-house or the hospital of the Pantokrator reflect the relative wealth of these establishments rather than the consumption norms of the lower strata of Byzantine society. The best guide to what the peasantry consumed is what it produced. The general range of production is indicated by the items extracted from villages as payment for the *kanonikon* – wheaten flour, barley, a ram and hens. The lists of impositions in the eleventh-century chrysobulls give a greater variety of types of grain, animals and birds and include oil as well as wine.[4] The crucial problem for the peasantry was not so much the quality of the food as the quantity. This, of course, depended on the size of the peasant holding, but as has already been emphasised there is no indication that the population increase of the eleventh and twelfth centuries had reached the point where the balance between land and population had shifted enough to endanger the peasant's ability to subsist. Variety in the diet depended mainly on local environmental conditions. Peasants living near rivers or the sea could supplement their agricultural produce by catching fish, which provided useful protein. Protein was also obtained from poultry, which seems to have been ubiquitous in peasant villages, and from grazing animals where sufficient pasture was available. Vitamins were derived from the produce of the gardens around peasant houses. In fertile and well-situated localities peasants with a sufficiently large landholding would have had a reasonably healthy diet, probably more healthy than that of the poorer sections of the capital's population, who were largely dependent on the cheaper range of imported foods. Peasants in less fertile localities had to subsist on less nourishing fare.

The most important food was, of course, bread, but the sources rarely reveal the different types of grain which were cultivated in different regions. In the excavations at Dinogetia carbonised grains of wheat, barley, rye and millet were found.[5] Wheat was the predominant grain for human consumption in most areas of reasonable fertility and was the most expensive and prestigious of cereals. Usually, the other grains were cultivated for animal feed and were used for human consumption only in extreme circumstances. In 1073 the stores of the estate of Baris contained 260 *modioi* of wheat, 150 *modioi* of barley and no other type of grain. A more complete list of the range of grains cultivated by the Byzantines is included in the thirteenth-century will of Theodosios

---

[4] *JGR*, I, pp. 275–6; *Lavra*, I, no. 48. For the *kanonikon* and other obligations, see above, chapter 3.

[5] Stephan *et al.*, *Dinogetia*, I, p. 392.

166　Economic expansion in the Byzantine empire

Skaranos. In addition to ordinary wheat (*sitos*) there were also stores of dark summer wheat, barley, rye and millet.[6] The evidence from saints' lives is more fragmentary. Even when Philaretos was supposed to have been impoverished, he purchased six *modioi* of wheat; there was no consideration of economising by eating barley. Wheat was also the main grain consumed in the monasteries of St Peter of Atroa and Theodore of Sykeon. The more expensive form of white bread (*katharos artos*) was available to Theodore, but he refrained from eating it. During a shortage at Sykeon the monastery's supply was replenished by a donation of wheaten bread from Cyprus.[7]

Barley had a much lower prestige than wheat and was normally sold at about two-thirds the price of wheat.[8] Whereas the allowances for officials authorised by the *typikon* of the Pantokrator consisted of wheat, barley was used as fodder for the horses. In the *kaniskia* of the eleventh century both a loaf of bread and a quantity of barley had to be supplied, the latter no doubt for the officials' horses.[9] The lowly prestige of barley was also illustrated by complaints in the literary sources. The description of the region of Synnada, which could not support a grain crop due to lack of fertility, has already been noted. Michael Choniates alleged that the exactions of state officials had caused not only a dearth of wheat in Athens, but even a shortage of barley. Sometimes barley was consumed by saints who rejected good-quality wheat in a show of piety. Consumption was subject to regional variations and in parts of Greece and Anatolia barley consumption was probably fairly common.[10] Millet was also regarded as an inferior grain to be consumed only as a last resort.[11]

Good-quality white bread is referred to in general terms as *katharos artos* (clean bread) in the sources. In the *typikon* of the Pantokrator this term is used, but the finest bread used in the most important liturgies is called *semidalis* (or *aphraton*).[12] This was the lightest, most finely

---

[6] *Engrapha Patmou*, II, no. 50 line 119; *Xéropotamou*, no. 9 lines 43–5, B64–7.
[7] 'Vie de Philarète', p. 131; Laurent, *La Vie merveilleuse*, p. 167; *Vie de Théodore de Sykéôn*, pp. 13, 26, 83.
[8] Ostrogorsky, 'Löhne und Preise in Byzanz', pp. 319–23.
[9] Gautier, 'Pantocrator', p. 103 lines 1258–9. For the *kaniskion*, see above, p. 105.
[10] Michael Choniates, II, pp. 42–3; Teall, 'The Grain Supply of the Byzantine Empire', pp. 99–100. For later evidence, see Nesbitt, 'Mechanisms of Agricultural Production', pp. 40–1.
[11] See the comments in Anna Comnène, *Alexiade*, III, pp. 93–4. This was purely a matter of social snobbery. The so-called inferior grains are not inferior to wheat from a nutritional point of view; see Ministry of Agriculture, Fisheries and Food, *Manual of Nutrition*, 8th edn (London, 1976). [12] Gautier, 'Pantocrator', pp. 41, 81.

The pattern of demand
167

ground bread. It is also mentioned in the poetry of Ptochoprodromos, where there are clear links between categories of bread and social prestige. In one passage he distinguishes between the best quality, which he calls *aphratitzin*, and an inferior sort known as *mesokatharon* or *tes meses*, terms indicating a middle category. In these poems *semidalaton* was consumed by well-fed abbots and affluent bakers, while the poor monk and scholar had to settle for inferior breads. The lowest quality of bread, made from inferior grains, was known as *ryparoi artoi* (foul bread) or as *kibaroi*, another term also implying poor quality. They are clearly associated by Ptochoprodromos with poverty. In particular he singles out a bread called *piteraton* (made from bran), which is contrasted sharply with good-quality white bread.[13]

The general range of foodstuffs which were consumed at court and in aristocratic households is best illustrated by Constantine Porphyrogenitos's description of the provisioning of imperial expeditions. This was a great undertaking involving eighty pack animals to transport the provisions and the silver plate of the imperial table and cash was also available to cover expenses for seasoning the food. A comprehensive range of produce was transported. There were wines of various qualities, top-quality oil, beans, rice, nuts, lentils. Other foods included animal fats, cheese, salted fish and animal meat. The livestock included sheep with their lambs and cows with their calves. The imperial *kouratoreia* had to provide a quantity of carp. There were also nets for keeping birds.[14] A similar impression is derived from a letter of Leo, the metropolitan of Synnada, to Arsenios, the metropolitan of Herakleia. When the latter was visiting bishoprics in his diocese, he was alleged to

---

[13] Hesseling and Pernot, *Poèmes prodromiques*, p. 62 lines 315–16, p. 76 lines 80–1, p. 77 line 101. While the poverty of the scholar and lowly monk need not be taken literally, the connection between diet and social standing is clear. It is striking that the 'impoverished' scholar had to make do with bread of the medium quality (which in the variant manuscript readings is clearly linked with poverty). A contempt for medium-quality bread would indicate the perspective of a well-off writer. In Simeon Seth, *Syntagma de Alimentorum Facultatibus*, ed. B. Langkavel (Leipzig, 1868), p. 19, in one of the variant manuscript readings (line 13(D)), *katharos artos* is divided into two categories – *silignites*, the highest quality, and *semidalites*. The former was distinguished by the more finely ground flour. However, this is a reproduction of classical writing and the distinction is not apparent in other medieval sources. For a discussion of the term *mese*, taken to refer to medium-quality bread and not the street known as *Mese*, see Koukoules, *Byzantinon bios kai politismos*, V, pp. 19–20. I should like to acknowledge the help in interpreting this literature which I have received from Professor Margaret Alexiou.

[14] Constantine Porphyrogenitus, *De Cerimoniis*, I, pp. 463–4; Hendy, *Studies in the Byzantine Monetary Economy*, p. 305.

168   *Economic expansion in the Byzantine empire*

have demanded as hospitality old and fragrant wine, good-quality bread flavoured with saffron, a chicken, young pigs, geese, and choice, fattened pigs and sheep. He was also alleged to have rejected the fish which were offered to him and insisted on larger ones.[15] The expense of lavish banquets is illustrated by the comments attributed to Theodore of Smyrna in the *Timarion*. He says he earned large sums from the discourses which he gave at court and squandered the money on extravagant dining.[16]

More comprehensive information about diet can be obtained in the monastic *typika* of the eleventh and twelfth centuries. The example of the Pantokrator is particularly interesting, as its monks enjoyed a wide range of food owing to the establishment's great wealth. The usual regime consisted of bread, wine and, when in season, fruit and legumes. On Mondays the monks received three meals, cooked in oil with seasoning, consisting of cabbages, peas, beans, oysters and mussels. Five days a week they had eggs and cheese and on the two other days fresh or salted fish. Naturally, the allocation was more restricted during Lent. It was made up of bread, dry legumes soaked in water, brine, nuts, dried figs and, later in Lent, onions prepared in oil and dry legumes prepared with honey.[17] The *typikon* of the monastery of Mamas is not so specific, but it gives a similar impression. The monks' diet included cooked meat as well as bread. On more frugal days they received fish, cheese, dry legumes, cabbage and fruit. During Lent they had to be satisfied with boiled beans, black olives, dry legumes soaked in water, raw cabbage, walnuts and dried figs. During the same period the monks who worked in the vineyards and gardens were allowed, if necessary, to have grapes.[18]

Although religious constraints must have led to a reduction in the

[15] Darrouzès, *Épistoliers*, p. 181.

[16] *Timarione*, p. 71. For an English translation and commentary, see B. Baldwin, *Timarion* (Detroit, 1984); and for a discussion, see M. Alexiou, 'Literary Subversion and the Aristocracy in Twelfth-Century Byzantium: A Stylistic Analysis of the Timarion (chs. 6–10)', *Byzantine and Modern Greek Studies*, 8 (1982–3), pp. 29–45. While precise figures of expenditure on food in Byzantium are lacking, details of aristocratic spending elsewhere in medieval Europe are available. In England provisions for the household could account for about a third of total income; see C. Dyer, 'English Diet in the Later Middle Ages', in T. H. Aston, P. R. Coss, C. Dyer and J. Thirsk (eds.), *Social Relations and Ideas. Essays in Honour of R. H. Hilton* (Cambridge, 1983), pp. 191–2.

[17] Gautier, 'Pantocrator', pp. 55–9.

[18] S. Eustratiades, 'Typikon tes en Konstantinopolei mones tou hagiou megalomartyros Mamantos', *Hellenika*, 1 (1928), pp. 274–7. For the dietary prescriptions of the monastery of Euergetes, see Gautier, 'Le typikon de la Théotokos Évergétis', pp. 39–43.

The pattern of demand

demand for most types of meat during the major ecclesiastical festivals, social status was nevertheless very apparent in the types of meat which were consumed. This was especially the case with the consumption of fresh meat, which was relatively uncommon due to the problems of preserving the meat. Generally, the consumption of fresh meat on a large scale was the luxury of the wealthy who had sufficiently large herds and flocks, yet even the provisioning of imperial expeditions included a large quantity of preserved meat.[19] In Constantinople the poorest sections of the population had to be satisfied with salted fish. Individuals who were rather better off but by no means as wealthy as major landowners might have been able to afford salted animal meat. There is a considerable amount of evidence concerning meat-eating in the poetry of Ptochoprodromos. Like his comments about bread there are clear indications of differences in social status reflected in the quality of food which is consumed. The poverty of his stock characters, the poor monk and the impoverished grammarian, need not be taken literally, but the envious description of the meals of others can be taken as a general indication (if somewhat exaggerated for literary purposes) of what the more affluent traders and artisans of the capital were consuming in the twelfth century. The cobbler consumes tripe for breakfast, at lunch-time boiled meat followed by meat cooked in wine and finally a hot-pot. A neighbour who is a sieve-maker has roasted meat. The poet found his father cooking a slightly salted smoked meat which was well covered in fat.[20] In the *Timarion* an anonymous glutton is described devouring a meal of salted pork and Phrygian cabbage, drenched in fat. In the same text the list of items which Theodore of Smyrna wanted to be sent to him included a five-month-old lamb, two three-year-old hens fattened and slaughtered, and a young pig, clearly items which would have been mainly the preserve of wealthy landowners.[21]

A few passages in saints' lives refer to the consumption of meat, but give no impression of its extent or frequency. When Philaretos's village was visited by an imperial delegation, the meat in the meal which they were offered came from rams, lambs, hens and pigeons.[22] Generally

[19] Constantine Porphyrogenitus, *De Cerimoniis*, I, p. 464.
[20] Hesseling and Pernot, *Poèmes prodromiques*, pp. 75–80 lines 47–63, 130–3, 166–7; M. Alexiou, 'The Poverty of Écriture and the Craft of Writing: Towards a Reappraisal of the Prodromic Poems', *Byzantine and Modern Greek Studies*, 10 (1986), pp. 1–40. See also Nesbitt, 'Mechanisms of Agricultural Production', pp. 50–3.
[21] *Timarione*, pp. 65, 91.
[22] 'Vie de Philarète', p. 137.

170   *Economic expansion in the Byzantine empire*

these sources mention meat only to highlight the asceticism of the saint who scorned such food. Theodore of Sykeon was offered pieces of boiled and roasted birds. He instructed some carpenters at work in his monastery not to eat meat until they had completed their work. Usually all meats other than fish were excluded from monastic diets, but occasionally illness might lead to some relaxation of these rules.[23] Meat was, no doubt, consumed relatively infrequently in peasant households, but the situation varied according to the potential of different regions. The most accessible types of meat were poultry and, in some areas, fish. A chicken was a regular part of the *kaniskion* which a tax-collector was able to claim. A village of thirty households had to provide one ram and thirty chickens as part of the *kanonikon*. The exemption lists in the eleventh-century chrysobulls mention the provision of geese, duck, swans, cranes, peacocks and pigeons, but such a complete list reflects the landowner's concern that the privilege should encompass every eventuality rather than the range of items which might be available to peasants. For most peasants meat was a rare luxury, their flocks were usually small, and animals were kept primarily for their dairy produce.[24]

For many people the most important source of protein in their diet was fish. Its availability to peasants depended, of course, on their geographical situation. For peasants in an advantageous location fishing was an important addition to the food produced by agriculture. In some cases its economic importance might even exceed that of grain production.[25] Generally, large fresh fish featured in the diet of the wealthy, whereas the poor, at least in the towns, had to be content with salted fish. The cheapness and inferior status of salted fish is reflected in the regulations of the *Book of the Eparch*. It was sold by the grocers, while fresh fish was the province of the fishmongers. The latter were not allowed to salt fish as a precaution against its transport out of the city (unless they had large surplus stocks which would have rotted otherwise). Every market in Constantinople selling fish had an official to fix the retail price according to the price paid for the catch. The profit of the fishmonger was restricted to two *folleis* per *nomisma*, a low rate of less than 1%, which implies that they dealt in large quantities of fish to make a living. The large high-quality fish were not so common and

---

[23] *Vie de Théodore de Sykéôn*, pp. 13, 56–7.
[24] See above, p. 105. For the *exkousseia*, see *Lavra*, I, no. 48 line 33.
[25] This was clearly the case for the *paroikoi* of the village of Doxompous in the early fourteenth century, when the revenues which were owed to Lavra were largely made up of obligations relating to fishing; see *Lavra*, II, no. 104.

The pattern of demand   171

the eparch had to be informed daily of the number which was caught the previous night so that he could fix the price accordingly.[26]

Fish was an especially important part of monastic diets, which tended to exclude animal meats. Consumption fluctuated according to the time of the year. During some religious festivals the monks were not allowed to eat fish, but were only permitted shellfish or 'bloodless' fish.[27] Ptochoprodromos's poetry gives a good impression of which fish made up a prestigious diet for the wealthy and which were the fare of the poor. His stock character, the well-fed abbot, is represented as eating a very high quality diet, while the unfortunate monk is forced to subsist on the sort of fare which was the lot of the poor. The abbot's meals consisted of smaller seafood which was boiled and larger fish served in a thick sauce with spices. These included the *kephalos* (the grey mullet), the *synagrida*, one of the sea-bream family which in modern times has the maximum length of a metre, the *triglion* (another type of mullet), turbot and mackerel. Elsewhere in the same poem Ptochoprodromos describes a hot-pot which included salted swordfish, carp, sturgeon and greyfish. A well-off monk would also eat mackerel and bass. On festive days when dietary limitations were imposed the leading monks gorge themselves on lobsters, crab, boiled crawfish, fried shrimps, oysters, mussels, scallop and shellfish. In contrast the impoverished monk's status is reflected in the lowly quality of the fish which he consumes. He eats salted anchovy and salted tunny fish and mackerel. The latter might have been reputable when fresh, but here it is salted and inferior. The cellarer of the monastery is represented as denying him even a miserable sardine, bonito, mackerel, or a foul tunny fish.[28] While these lines are obviously written for literary effect, they do give a useful indication of which fish were the most expensive and prestigious and which were consumed mainly by the lower strata of the population in the capital.

---

[26] *To Eparchikon Biblion*, pp. 47–53; Nesbitt, 'Mechanisms of Agricultural Production', pp. 48–9.

[27] Gautier, 'Le typikon de la Théotokos Évergétis', pp. 39–43. In the rule of the monastery of Nicolas *ton Kasoulon* drawn up in 1160 fish are referred to continually and were obtained directly by some of the monks who were fishermen; see A. Dmitrievskij, *Opisanije liturgiceskih rukopisej*, I (Kiev, 1895), pp. 818–23, esp. ch. 25. For the impact of religious festivals in causing fluctuations in the demand for fish, see Nesbitt, 'Mechanisms of Agricultural Production', pp. 58–9.

[28] Hesseling and Pernot, *Poèmes prodromiques*, p. 52 lines 82–3, 93–9, p. 55 lines 152–4, p. 56 lines 179–80, 204–5, p. 59 line 259, p. 60 lines 275–8. See also Bryer, 'The Estates of the Empire of Trebizond', pp. 382–4; and A. Davidson, *Mediterranean Seafood*, 2nd edn (Harmondsworth, 1981).

172   *Economic expansion in the Byzantine empire*

For the less wealthy dairy produce was also an important source of protein. Most peasant families who maintained animals did so for their cheese and milk rather than for their meat. Cheese was also specified in monastic diets where meat-eating was discouraged. It featured among the food which was eaten with bread (the *prosphagion*) and it was relatively cheap. In the rule of the Pantokrator monastery, on certain days only cheese and eggs were eaten.[29] Nevertheless, some types of cheese were considered of a particularly high quality. The range of good cheeses which were available in Constantinople is indicated by the Ptochoprodromic writings, especially the account of the feast of the wealthy and gluttonous monks whose fare included Cretan and Vlach cheese and good creamy cheese. These monks bought their supplies in the Venetian quarter. The affluent cobbler featured in another poem was also eating Vlach cheese. The merits of Paphlagonian cheese were extolled by Psellos and also by Symeon Seth, who in general did not regard cheese as a particularly prestigious food.[30]

Vegetables were generally not highly regarded and had the status of fasting food. Their consumption by wealthy landowners was probably restricted and they were mainly used for flavouring rather than for substantial dishes on their own. Liudprand of Cremona describes a choice dish sent to him by the emperor. It consisted of goat richly stuffed with garlic, onions and leeks drenched in a fish sauce.[31] Apart from these the most commonly eaten vegetables were cabbages, peas, beans, lentils, carrots and lettuce. Legumes were an important element of monastic diet, especially during lenten periods. On some days of the great Lent the monks of Euergetes were restricted to boiled beans, raw green vegetables and small fruit. This was general monastic practice and on ordinary days legumes and green vegetables still made up an important part of the diet.[32] Although letters frequently attest to the sending of items of food as token gifts, vegetables – a not very splendid gift – are rarely mentioned unless the recipient was undergoing a fast.[33]

---

[29] Gautier, 'Pantocrator', pp. 55–7. For the *prosphagion*, see Koukoules, *Byzantinon bios kai politismos*, V, pp. 31f.

[30] Hesseling and Pernot, *Poèmes prodromiques*, p. 53 lines 109–10, p. 56 lines 181–2, p. 75 line 52; Simeon Seth, *Syntagma*, pp. 104–5; A. Karpozelos, 'Realia in Byzantine Epistolography X–XIIc', *Byzantinische Zeitschrift*, 77 (1984), pp. 25–6.

[31] Liudprand of Cremona, *Relatio de Legatione Constantinopolitana*, ch. 20, ed. and trans. F. A. Wright, *The Works of Liudprand of Cremona* (London, 1930), p. 247.

[32] Gautier, 'Le typikon de la Théotokos Évergétis', pp. 39–41; Nesbitt, 'Mechanisms of Agricultural Production', pp. 58–9.

[33] Karpozelos, 'Realia in Byzantine Epistolography', pp. 21–2, 26–7. Even in these cases the gifts most often consisted of bread, wine and fruit.

The pattern of demand 173

It was a standard sign of sanctity for holy men to confine themselves to legumes and to avoid other foods, even fruit in some cases. St Cyril Phileotes even went as far as to disapprove of his monks eating a concoction called *hagiozomion* (holy broth). It is described with great distaste in the Ptochoprodromic poetry. A large number of onions are thrown into a pot of boiling water, oil and aromatics are added and the broth is poured over slices of bread, which are then given to the most lowly of the monks.[34] The range of items to which a reasonably well-off Constantinopolitan might have access is also outlined in these poems. A supposedly impoverished head of a family complains that he cannot afford basic necessities. A long list of vegetables, herbs and spices follows, suggesting that the writer's perspective was not that of a person too familiar with poverty (the spices would have been the most expensive of these items). Besides the most common vegetables already mentioned, the requirements included celery, turnips, spinach, mushrooms and cucumber.[35]

Fruit was a useful source of vitamin C and nuts a source of cheap protein. The most common fruits were apples, pears, figs, cherries, grapes and olives.[36] In letters there are references to gifts of grapes, melons, figs, peaches, pomegranates and sometimes wild pears. Melon was one of the commonest and probably cheapest fruits, but was not highly regarded by medical writers.[37] Dried figs were part of the dietary regime of the monks of the Pantokrator during Lent. The fruits which were demanded by the head of the household in Ptochoprodromos's poetry included cherries from Leukate on the gulf of Nikomedia, melons and various sorts of apples. The meal of the abbot in another poem included olives, apples, dates, dried figs, walnuts and raisins from Chios.[38] The most common nuts were walnuts, almonds and hazelnuts and it has been suggested that they might have been more important than fish as a source of protein in the Pontos.[39]

In the preparation of food olive oil and animal fats were mainly used. Olive oil predominated in coastal regions with a Mediterranean climate and animal fat in more rugged inland areas, but this distinction was, of

---

[34] *Vie de Cyrille Philéote*, pp. 186–90. Hesseling and Pernot, *Poèmes prodromiques*, pp. 61–2 lines 290–306.

[35] Hesseling and Pernot, *Poèmes prodromiques*, pp. 42–5.

[36] Laiou-Thomadakis, *Peasant Society*, pp. 29–30; Bryer, 'The Estates of the Empire of Trebizond', p. 386.

[37] Karpozelos, 'Realia in Byzantine Epistolography', pp. 21–2.

[38] Gautier, 'Pantocrator', p. 57; Hesseling and Pernot, *Poèmes prodromiques*, pp. 44, 60.

[39] Bryer, 'The Estates of the Empire of Trebizond', p. 384.

174   *Economic expansion in the Byzantine empire*

course, not absolute. It was usual for expensive meat dishes to be cooked with large quantities of fat.[40] Besides its use in cooking, olive oil was also used for seasoning and was sometimes not permitted to monks during parts of religious festivals. Honey, which was used as a sweetener, and vinegar were also used for flavouring.[41]

The use of expensive spices in the preparation of meals was one of the most conspicuous features of the diet of the wealthy. The most expensive and exclusive spices were included in the items taken on the imperial baggage-train when the emperor went on campaign and the imperial *bestiarion* had the responsibility for transporting these items. These included cinnamon of first and second quality and cinnamon-wood (probably cassia or cinnamon-bark) as well as a range of other spices which were used as perfumes.[42] Cinnamon and pepper were available in Constantinople from the guild of perfumers, who also sold a range of items used for perfumery or dyeing.[43] The herbs and spices which a well-off Constantinopolitan of the twelfth century might require is vividly illustrated by Ptochoprodromos. His protestations of poverty can be ignored. The formidable list of items which were presented as essential needs for this supposedly impoverished character must have constituted a considerable expense. They included pepper, cumin and ground spices generally and herbs such as cress, dill and endive. The meal of the gluttonous abbot included a fish served with cloves, cinnamon and other spices.[44] The *Book of the Eparch* specifically mentions imports of spices from Chaldia and Trebizond. They also came through Egypt, as evidence from the geniza documents indicates. Merchants in Alexandria handled dyeing plants including saffron imported from Tunisia, medical and culinary herbs and perfumes and oriental spices. Both Byzantines and Italians were important customers for goods sold in Egypt and Syria. Byzantine traders were especially keen to acquire pepper, cinnamon and ginger. The price of pepper in Egypt fluctuated quite sharply during the eleventh century due to western and Byzantine demand. It varied from eleven or twelve to twenty-five dinars for 100 pounds, but the average price (admittedly

[40] See above, p. 169.
[41] Hesseling and Pernot, *Poèmes prodromiques*, p. 54 line 151; Nesbitt, 'Mechanisms of Agricultural Production', p. 60.
[42] Constantine Porphyrogenitus, *De Cerimoniis*, I, p. 468; J. I. Miller, *The Spice Trade of the Roman Empire, 29 BC to AD 641* (Oxford, 1969), pp. 42–7, 74–7, discusses cinnamon and cassia, but the Byzantine sources do not give any indication of what set first-quality cinnamon apart from second-quality.
[43] *To Eparchikon Biblion*, pp. 41–3, ch. 10.
[44] Hesseling and Pernot, *Poèmes prodromiques*, pp. 42, 54.

The pattern of demand   175

from limited data) was around seventeen dinars. By the time it had been transported to Sicily, the price had doubled.[45] We do not have any information about prices in Constantinople, but it is likely that transportation there from Egypt led to an increase of a similar order to that in Sicily. For anyone to build up a stock of a good range of herbs and spices was quite an expensive undertaking, especially in years when the price was fluctuating upwards.

Little is said in the sources about the varying quality of local wines. The main differentiation was by region. As has already been mentioned, Michael Choniates approved of the quality of wines from Chios, Rhodes and Euboia, and Cretan wines were generally highly regarded and were exported by the Venetians.[46] In the poetry of Ptochoprodromos the well-fed monks drank wine from Chios, Crete and Samos and sweet wine from Ganos in Thrace, while the poor monk had to make do with watered-down wine from Varna.[47] When sophisticated and educated men had to spend any length of time in the provinces, they often complained in their letters about the abysmal quality of the local wine. Michael Choniates found it difficult to cope with Athenian retsina. Nikephoros Basilakes, writing from Philippoupolis, made similar complaints, as did Gregory Antiochos in Bulgaria.[48]

Considerable problems are involved in attempting to assess the nutritional quality of the Byzantine diet. Firstly, detailed information about the quantity of food which was consumed is available in only a restricted number of cases. Secondly, the measurements which were used in the medieval period cannot be translated into modern terms with an excessive degree of confidence, but the estimates that Schilbach has proposed will be used as a rough approximation.[49] Thirdly, there is no guarantee that the nutritional content of food was the same as in

---

[45] S. D. Goitein, *A Mediterranean Society. The Jewish Communities of the Arab World as Portrayed in the Documents of the Cairo Geniza*, I, *Economic Foundations* (Berkeley, 1967), pp. 44, 153–4, 220–2.

[46] Michael Choniates, II, p. 83; Thiriet, *La Romanie vénitienne*, p. 320.

[47] Hesseling and Pernot, *Poèmes prodromiques*, p. 59 line 260, p. 60 line 285, p. 62 lines 312–13.

[48] Karpozelos, 'Realia in Byzantine Epistolography', p. 26. For the consumption of wine mixed with warm water or seasoned with spices, see Koukoules, *Byzantinon bios kai politismos*, V, pp. 122–35.

[49] Schilbach, *Byzantinische Metrologie, passim*. The problems involved are vividly illustrated by the controversy which has arisen over the quality of monastic diet in Carolingian France; see M. Rouche, 'La faim à l'époque carolingienne: essai sur quelques types de rations alimentaires', *Revue Historique*, 250 (1973), pp. 295–320; and J.-C. Hocquet, 'Le pain, le vin et la juste mesure à la table des moines carolingiens', *Annales ESC*, 40 (1985), pp. 661–90 (including rejoinders by both Rouche and Hocquet).

176   *Economic expansion in the Byzantine empire*

modern times. So at best any conclusions about dietary needs are subject to considerable qualification and should be used as only an approximate guide.

The first problem is to establish the population's calorie requirements. This is not a simple matter because these vary according to the amount of work which a person does, their physical size and age, and the climate. Fewer calories are needed in a warmer climate and the higher the proportion of children in the population the lower the calorie requirement per head of the population. The figures advanced by the FAO as calorie requirements have been criticised for being based on a European 'reference man'. The nature of work in traditional agricultural communities will lead to a reduction in the figures. Although agricultural work can be very intensive at peak periods this is counterbalanced by other periods of relative inactivity. Clark and Haswell's figures for calorie consumption in many areas of Asia and Africa show that communities were able to subsist at levels well below the FAO ideal.[50]

It is difficult to assess accurately how satisfactory the dietary regime was for most of the population in the Byzantine empire because information about the quantity of food consumed by most people is not available. The only comprehensive figures dealing in quantities of food concern monasteries and charitable foundations and therefore have to be treated with some caution. Lavra's archive includes three food allowances which the monastery provided in return for the alienation of property. They were not simply subsistence payments in kind, but compensation for the loss of revenues from these lands. Consequently, they do not give an accurate reflection of consumption needs, but vary according to the value of the land. Symeon, the abbot of the monastery of Prodromos *tou Atziioannou* received an annual allowance of thirty *modioi* of wheat, fifty measures of wine, six *modioi* of dry legumes and a payment of six *nomismata*. The allowance which Lavra gave to Athanasios of Bouleuteria was similar. In addition to the same quantity of wine, he received thirty-six *modioi* of wheat each year, two *bitinai* of oil, eight *kalikia* of cheese and eight *modioi* of legumes. His servants each received two *modioi* of wheat every month. A closer idea of basic

---

[50] In particular, the FAO recommendations for the calorie intake of children have been criticised for being too high, thereby inflating average requirements per head of population. The figure which is given for Japanese consumption, an average daily intake per person of 2,210 calories, is particularly significant because it comes from a high-income society. See C. Clark and M. Haswell, *The Economics of Subsistence Agriculture*, 4th edn (London, 1970), pp. 1–26.

The pattern of demand 177

consumption needs is given by the annual allowance made to the abbot Damianos in return for his donation of the monastery of Kalaphatou to Lavra. It consisted of twelve *modioi* of wheat, forty measures of wine, three *modioi* of legumes, twelve litres of oil, one *megarikon* of honey and four litres of wax.[51]

The conversion of these payments into a daily intake of calories presents serious problems. The texts do not state which type of *modioi* was used. It will be assumed that the monastic *modios* was involved in all three cases. This measure, equivalent to four-fifths of the *thalassios modios*, amounted to about 10.2 kg.[52] Once the wheat allowance is converted into modern measures, an estimate has to be made of the amount of grain removed in the milling process. In spite of all the qualifications it is clear that the allowances paid to Symeon and Athanasios were well above basic subsistence requirements. The thirty-six *modioi* of wheat which Athanasios received was about 368 kg and Symeon's thirty *modioi* amounted to about 307 kg a year. This works out to daily rations of 1 kg (3,320 calories) and 840 g (2,789 calories) respectively. At least 10% has to be deducted for losses during milling. Much depended on the type of bread which was expected. Although stoneground flour is suitable for traditional wheat preparation, it is not so appropriate for the production of light, white bread. The latter's production involves a great deal of sieving and a large proportion of the grain has to be discarded in this process. As these men were unlikely to have engaged in sustained physical activity, their calorie requirements would have been low and would have been exceeded by their grain provisions alone without taking into account the other items in their allowances. They obviously had a large enough surplus over basic needs to be able to indulge a taste for light, white bread if they wanted.[53] The third allowance – that given to the abbot Damianos – was a more modest affair. The annual wheat allowance of twelve *modioi* amounted to 122 kg. When a 10% loss for milling is taken into account the daily ration would have been about 300 g (996 calories). The other items in the allowance raised the calorie content considerably. The wine alone (forty measures) amounted to about $\frac{4}{5}$ litre daily (approximately 520 calories). With the addition of the legumes, honey and oil the allowance

---

[51] *Lavra*, I, nos. 19, 27, 54; R. Morris, 'The Byzantine Church and the Land', pp. 240–2.

[52] Schilbach, *Byzantinische Metrologie*, pp. 96–9.

[53] W. R. Aykroyd and J. Doughty, *Wheat in Human Nutrition* (FAO Nutritional Studies 23) (Rome, 1970), pp. 18, 86; Clark and Haswell, *The Economics of Subsistence Agriculture*, pp. 58–9; and C. Clark, *Population Growth and Land Use*, 2nd edn (London, 1977), pp. 128–30.

178   *Economic expansion in the Byzantine empire*

would have been more than adequate for a monk who probably undertook little physical activity.[54]

The payments in kind recorded in the rules of monastic and charitable foundations show a similar range and variation reflecting the wealth of the institution. The allowances listed in the Pantokrator's *typikon* illustrate its prestige as an imperial foundation. The provisions of the monks of Eleousa varied from twelve to twenty-five *thalassioi modioi* (the largest type of *modios*) and they also received cash payments. Some of the allowances for the servants in the hospital were even larger. The provisions for the sick and for the inmates of the old people's home were also quite generous. The sick each received twenty-four *thalassioi modioi* of white bread each year as well as beans and other legumes. The annual ration for the elderly was twenty *thalassioi modioi* of bread, eighteen *thalassia metra* of wine, two *thalassioi modioi* of legumes, fifty litres of cheese and one measure of oil.[55]

In all these cases the level of consumption was well above basic needs of subsistence. The recipients of charity in Attaleiates's poor-house were in a different situation because the foundation was endowed with much more restricted resources. Their allowance was twelve *annonikoi modioi* a year. The *annonikos modios* was smaller than either the *thalassios* or the *monasteriakos* and this allowance is the smallest in the *typika* of the eleventh and twelfth centuries.[56] It amounted to only 830 calories a day after milling. No doubt this was supplemented by legumes and wine, but no details are given. An extremely low allowance of five *modioi* and three *nomismata* was given by St Athanasios to an ascetic. If these *modioi* were *thalassioi*, this would have provided 524 calories a day after milling. This would of course have been inadequate for a working peasant, but might have been sufficient for an ascetic if the cash allowance was used to supplement the grain.[57]

Information derived from these allowances cannot be extended arbitrarily to apply to peasant families. In the absence of figures directly relating to the peasantry, the nutritional quality of its diet can only be considered in general terms. Nevertheless, it is clear that a diet of

---

[54] *Lavra*, I, no. 54. The calorie content for wheat is taken from Aykroyd and Doughty, *Wheat in Human Nutrition*, p. 18; that for wine from Ministry of Agriculture, Fisheries and Food, *Manual of Nutrition*, p. 108.

[55] Gautier, 'Pantocrator', p. 77 line 812, p. 79 line 823, p. 91 lines 1035–50, pp. 99–105 lines 1178–1289, p. 109 lines 1356–60.

[56] Gautier, 'La diataxis de Michel Attaliate', p. 47 lines 501–5.

[57] Svoronos, 'Remarques sur les structures économiques', p. 60 n. 38.

The pattern of demand 179

reasonable nutritional quality was available to peasants provided that they had sufficient land at their disposal. Discussion so far has been confined to needs in terms of calories. If this requirement was satisfied, the intake of protein, minerals and vitamins would generally have been sufficient. Although wheat contains less protein than other foods like eggs, meat, fish and cheese, it still has a protein content of 8–15% and, because it was consumed in such large quantities, its importance as a source of protein cannot be dismissed. Animal proteins are not essential except in very small quantities and these were obtained mainly from dairy produce, but also from poultry and, where conditions permitted, from fish.[58] Shortages of minerals and vitamins were unlikely to develop in farming communities because food was obtained directly from natural sources. Generally, the heat applied in the cooking of wheat products does not greatly affect nutritional value.[59]

It has been suggested in an analysis of diet in medieval England that upper-class consumption might have been affected by deficiencies in vitamins A and C due to the low intake of dairy products, fruit and vegetables.[60] This question cannot be resolved in regard to the Byzantine upper classes because comparable detailed evidence is unavailable. The general pattern of aristocratic diet in Byzantium seems broadly similar to that in the West. There was the same disdain for dairy produce and vegetables. However, the consequences of this attitude might have been modified by the large number of days when there were religious festivals. Any wealthy landowner who took the dietary prescriptions for these occasions seriously might have consumed considerable quantities of low-status foods such as cheese, eggs, fruit and legumes and at least partly compensated for this deficiency. This problem would, of course, have been less serious for peasants, for whom the cheaper types of food were a more regular part of their diet. Their diet was probably sufficiently nutritious as long as they were able to produce enough food, and that depended on the amount of land available to them and its fertility.

[58] Aykroyd and Doughty, *Wheat in Human Nutrition*, pp. 17–19; Clark and Haswell, *The Economics of Subsistence Agriculture*, pp. 3–6. Diets that are heavily based on wheat are not totally adequate; for the most important dietary deficiencies, see Aymard, 'Pour l'histoire de l'alimentation: quelques remarques de méthode', p. 439. The significant place of fruit, vegetables and dairy products in the diet of the Byzantine peasantry would have offered protection against such deficiencies.

[59] Clark and Haswell, *The Economics of Subsistence Agriculture*, p. 4; Aykroyd and Doughty, *Wheat in Human Nutrition*, pp. 34–5.

[60] Dyer, 'English Diet in the Later Middle Ages', pp. 195–6.

180   *Economic expansion in the Byzantine empire*

It is very difficult to estimate the amount of land necessary to maintain a peasant family, but a hypothetical assessment can provide a useful rough approximation. A peasant family of four might have needed about 6,400 calories daily.[61] If the estimate is restricted to grain consumption, a loss of around 10% through milling has to be taken into account. So grain amounting to 7,100 calories would be needed daily, which was equivalent to an annual requirement of 780.57 kg or sixty-one *thalassioi modioi*. If an annual grain yield of three to one is assumed, a yield of $91\frac{1}{2}$ *modioi* would provide for subsistence and the seed for the following year's crop. Therefore about $30\frac{1}{2}$ *modioi* would have to be sown and some land left fallow. Several qualifications have to be made, however. If wine or fruit was produced for sale, grain could be purchased and a smaller area of land could support the household. Also, the calorie requirement would have been partly met by foods other than cereal products, although the latter would have been the most important single item. The area needed to produce enough wine and fruit for consumption was relatively small, only a few *modioi* of vines and a limited number of fruit trees, which might have been intercultivated with the arable. On the other hand some land might have been needed to cultivate lower-quality grains as fodder for oxen and other animals. The other crucial factor in estimating the minimum holding necessary for subsistence was the amount of produce extracted by either the state or a landowner. This cannot be estimated with any confidence.[62] On land of moderate fertility a tentative approximation of the minimum holding necessary for the subsistence of a household with four members would be fifty to sixty *modioi* (ten to twelve acres).[63] This

[61] This figure is approximate. It would have been affected by the age of the children. Younger children need a much smaller intake of calories; see Clark and Haswell, *The Economics of Subsistence Agriculture*, p. 16.

[62] Our information about grain prices is so inadequate that it is difficult to convert tax-payments into grain equivalents. In any case such a procedure is open to criticism on methodological grounds because the great bulk of grain production was geared to direct consumption. The amount of grain sold for cash was very small in the context of the total volume of production, and the application of the scanty evidence for prices beyond the relatively small proportion of grain which was sold for cash would very likely create a distorted result.

[63] The figure of twenty *modioi* has been suggested as generally sufficient for a peasant household without ploughing animals; see Nesbitt, 'Mechanisms of Agricultural Production', pp. 91ff. This ignores the possibility that these households supplemented the produce of their land by labouring on the land of others or by non-agricultural activities. The figure corresponds to four or five acres, which was considered a very small holding in western Europe even in the period of greatest population pressure; see R. H. Hilton, *A Medieval Society. The West Midlands at the End of the Thirteenth Century* (London, 1966, reprinted Cambridge, 1983), pp. 114–15, 121–3; and Hilton,

The pattern of demand 181

would be subject to variation according to the number of animals which were kept and their fodder requirements. Naturally, in the most fertile regions less land was needed, especially where fiscal obligations could be met by selling wine or oil, of which a surplus could be produced from a smaller area.

Food was the basic need of the population and the area in which the requirement of self-sufficiency applied most strongly. Constantinople, however, was a major source of demand for foodstuffs, a demand which was intensified by the urban revival of the eleventh and twelfth centuries, and this encouraged trade in basic provisions in coastal ports.[64] But it was the other elements of demand, notably clothing and building, which provided scope for greater artisanal specialisation in towns. First, the relative importance of the requirements of wealthy landowners and the peasantry needs some consideration. Naturally, the stimulus given to commodity production by feudal landowners was much greater than that given by peasant producers. The latter, whose first concern was subsistence, probably obtained most of their requirements from village craftsmen unless the village was situated very close to a town. The most pressing compulsion on peasants to trade in towns was the state's fiscal pressure. Taxation acted as an extra-economic constraint on the direct producer to alienate part of his produce to meet his obligations. In some cases this was done by forced sales to the state. Otherwise it had to be effected by sale at a market. The exaction of larger amounts of cash from the direct producers in the eleventh and twelfth centuries could have been achieved only if commercial exchange had increased and the demand for agricultural produce intensified. However, taxation stimulated commerce in only one direction, the movement of produce from the countryside to the towns. The extent to which peasants also purchased goods from urban markets varied according to fluctuations in the harvest. In a bad year prices would rise and a smaller amount of produce needed to be sold to meet fiscal demands (if the peasant was unable to go into arrears for that year), but the remainder of the crop would be needed for the

---

The English Peasantry, p. 197. For viticulture and olive yields, see Morris, 'The Byzantine Church and the Land', pp. 244–6. In the 1950s the villagers of Vasilika in Boiotia considered forty *stremmata* (about ten acres) the minimum to maintain a decent standard of living for a household with four members (E. Friedl, *Vasilika. A Village in Modern Greece* (New York, 1962), pp. 32–3), but this is quite a recent development and is due to the application of better farming techniques. Previously a much larger holding was required; see *ibid.*, p. 37.

[64] See below, chapter 6.

182   *Economic expansion in the Byzantine empire*

subsistence of members of the household and its animals. The quantity of produce set aside for the household remained fairly constant in spite of fluctuations in the yield of the harvest. The amount of produce which was sold to obtain industrial goods was, in contrast, very elastic. In a bad year a peasant would have scant resources for the purchase of goods from urban artisans. The volume of produce sold at a market was liable to much more drastic fluctuations than the total yield from the harvest.[65]

The same was partly true of sales of produce by feudal lords. Their requirements for consumption would have been great if they maintained large retinues. The amount of produce which they marketed would have been considerably less in a bad year. Whether high prices would have compensated for the smaller volume of sales is impossible to determine, but they were still in a better position than peasants to exploit fluctuations in prices. Their demand for urban products was more constant than the peasant's and it extended over a wider range of products. It could stimulate the more expensive long-distance trade in luxuries and could generate a certain amount of urban commodity production and marketing activity.

Besides food, the most important material requirements were, of course, clothing and housing and the most important medieval industrial occupation was textile production, which ranged from the most prestigious silk cloths produced in imperial workshops to the most basic items made up by villagers. The most highly prized cloths were the purple silks most closely associated with imperial authority. On great occasions the halls of the palace were decorated with rich tapestries and precious silks.[66] Owing to the symbolic importance of these cloths their distribution depended on non-economic factors. They were used as diplomatic gifts to foreigners and as gifts of favour to prominent associates of the emperor. Among the equipment taken on imperial expeditions were decorated and undecorated woven wares. These included various garments which were worn in the imperial household. There were also decorated woven wares, including tunics with double borders of eagles and imperial symbols and laces to match each tunic, shorter military tunics, thin and thick cloaks, garments made of purple of the first, second and third qualities, belts of different kinds of purple

---

[65] W. Kula, *An Economic Theory of the Feudal System. Towards a Model of the Polish Economy 1500–1800* (London, 1976), pp. 62–82.

[66] R. Guilland, 'Quelques termes du livre des cérémonies de Constantin VII Porphyro-génète', *Revue des Études Grecques*, 62 (1949), p. 336.

The pattern of demand 183

and imitation purple (priced variously at one *nomisma* four *milliaresia*, at one *nomisma* and at eight *milliaresia*), and also travelling-boots. These were intended for the important refugees and leading foreigners whose favour the state courted. Garments were also taken for distribution to prominent Byzantines. The *Book of Ceremonies* indicates that the *strategoi* were to receive silks with triple borders, the tourmarchs silks with two borders and various other officers of lower rank silks with one border. In addition, officials of inferior ranks received lower-quality items which the administration had acquired by purchase in markets.[67]

The importance of the demand for cloth in Constantinople is indicated by the space given to the regulation of textile production and trade in the *Book of the Eparch*. The silk dyers were not permitted to make up the most prestigious garments, which were on the prohibited list, for there were strict restrictions that sought to prevent these cloths from being sold to foreigners without the approval of the eparch. Purchasers of the most expensive cloths (*ta blattia*) had to declare them to the eparch. When these goods were exported there was a considerable demand for them. Evidence from the Cairo geniza shows that the products of the Byzantine silk industry were greatly appreciated in other Mediterranean countries. The regulation of the industry involved clear limitations on the activities of each guild. There was a single guild for merchants of manufactured cloths imported from Syria. They were forbidden to buy cloths other than those of a Syrian origin and those which were imported from Seleukia and its region. The imports were stored in a warehouse where they were divided up among the members of the guild, which had to buy the whole consignment of Syrian cloths arriving in the capital, the inferior quality as well as the superior. One of the main purposes of the regulations was to curtail private production of expensive items by powerful individuals. This must have been difficult when it was possible for them to produce the raw silk on their estates. Consequently, scope was given for a limited amount of private trading. Prominent officials and dignitaries were permitted to make purchases directly from the importers of Syrian wares, provided that it was strictly

[67] Constantine Porphyrogenitus, *De Cerimoniis*, I, pp. 469–71, 486; Hendy, *Studies in the Byzantine Monetary Economy*, pp. 307–8; Guilland, 'Quelques termes du livre des cérémonies de Constantin VII Porphyrogénète', pp. 328–50; R. S. Lopez, 'The Silk Industry in the Byzantine Empire', *Speculum*, 20 (1945), pp. 1–42. The translation of Greek terms follows that of Hendy, but, as he emphasises, a precise translation is often very problematical. However, this is not important for the purposes of this chapter, which is concerned more with the broader issues of economic demand. For a general survey of Byzantine clothing, see Koukoules, *Byzantinon bios kai politismos*, VI, pp. 267–94.

184   *Economic expansion in the Byzantine empire*

for their household requirements only. The administration was more concerned to prevent them from producing cloths. They were not allowed to import raw silk through the agency of the dealers in raw silk. Restrictions were also imposed on the dressers of raw silk to ensure that surplus stocks were not sold off to wealthy individuals.[68]

The demand for such cloths can also be accounted for partly by their ecclesiastical uses. Many landowners adorned their churches with expensive silk cloths[69] and they also served as treasure to be accumulated along with cash and precious objects. The importance of imperial favour for the acquisition of some of these items is apparent in the *typikon* of Pakourianos. The cloths listed there included imperial tunics given him by Alexios and other similar precious items given him both by Alexios and his brother Isaac as rewards for his services. He also possessed valuable undecorated tunics. In the will of Symbatios Pakourianos there are also references to garments of various kinds.[70] Attaleiates's *typikon* also gives a list of the valuable cloths with which he endowed his foundation. These were mainly silk cloths of various types which were used for ecclesiastical purposes. At the end of the *typikon* there is also a list of items bequeathed to the monastery by a monk. They included several cloths: three silk cloths with three borders, one of which had a style associated with the products of Attaleia, and an embroidered linen cloth of Arab origin.[71] The way in which silk cloths and precious objects were accumulated as wealth is clearly illustrated by the dowry given by a Jewish resident of Seleukia. Besides paying $4\frac{1}{2}$ pounds in gold coin he also handed over the equivalent of 200 dinars in the form of a pound of silver, a brocade robe, two silk robes, two woollen garments, two Greek pounds of ornaments, other items of silk and cotton, carpets, blankets and silverware.[72]

---

[68] *To Eparchikon Biblion*, pp. 26–38; Lopez, 'The Silk Industry in the Byzantine Empire', pp. 13–23. For the demand for these cloths outside the Byzantine empire, see Goitein, *A Mediterranean Society*, I, p. 103.

[69] A good example is the church of Eustathios Boilas; see Lemerle, *Cinq études*, p. 24 lines 124–30.

[70] Gautier, 'Grégoire Pakourianos', p. 43; Hendy, *Studies in the Byzantine Monetary Economy*, pp. 210, 213. Undecorated tunics would still have been of value if they had been made of high-quality silk. There are no figures available for the cost of production, but evidence from the Cairo geniza is suggestive. One eleventh-century account puts the cost of the silk at about two-thirds of the total cost, with about one-quarter spent on the dyeing; see Goitein, *A Mediterranean Society*, I, p. 107.

[71] Gautier, 'La diataxis de Michel Attaliate', pp. 97–9, 129.

[72] S. D. Goitein, 'A Letter from Seleucia (Cilicia) dated 21 July 1137', *Speculum*, 39 (1964), p. 299; Hendy, *Studies in the Byzantine Monetary Economy*, pp. 216–17.

The general range of clothing which a moderately prosperous resident of Constantinople would need is suggested by the requirements of the head of a family in one of the Ptochoprodromic poems. He wanted a *kontosphiktouron* – a large cloak with a belt for protection against the cold – furs for his children, a cloak for his wife and also linen and cotton items.[73] There was a considerable demand for linen clothing. The state did not impose any restrictions on the purchase of the raw material by the guild of linen merchants; they were allowed to buy it freely anywhere, but notably in the Strymon region and the Pontos.[74]

There are no surviving accounts detailing expenditure by landowners or anyone else on clothing. Clearly, large sums could have been spent where an element of conspicuous display of status was involved, but for most of the population the consideration was purely practical. Some indication of the outlay involved can be derived from the payment of *rogai* which were made to the monks of Bačkovo every Easter. They were intended to cover the monks' needs, of which clothing and shoes were the most important. The abbot received thirty-six *trachea nomismata*. The monks were divided into three categories: fifteen received twenty *nomismata* each; the fifteen in the second category received fifteen *nomismata* each, and the twenty monks in the third category ten *nomismata* each. The total payment was 761 *nomismata* and its payment coincided with a fair held at the monastery to prevent the monks from making long journeys in search of their requirements.[75]

Little is known about the clothes worn by the peasantry. They were likely to have been functional and basic, produced in the villages and very rarely purchased at urban markets. The craft names which appear in the *praktika* of the fourteenth century suggest that the production of clothing was a regular activity in peasant villages. Among the most common of these names were tailor and weaver. There is also evidence of the regular cultivation of flax in the fourteenth century, when a tax was imposed wherever flax was washed (*linobrocheion*).[76] Although the evidence is not so good for earlier centuries, there are indications that its cultivation was important in the tenth and eleventh centuries. Its production in the Strymon region and the Pontos has already been

---

[73] Hesseling and Pernot, *Poèmes prodromiques*, pp. 42–3.
[74] *To Eparchikon Biblion*, pp. 39–40.
[75] Gautier, 'Grégoire Pakourianos', pp. 67–9; M. F. Hendy, 'The Gornoslav Hoard, the Emperor Frederick I, and the Monastery of Bachkovo', in C. N. L. Brooke, I. Steward, J. G. Pollard and T. R. Volk (eds.), *Studies in Numismatic Method Presented to Philip Grierson* (Cambridge, 1983), pp. 179–91.
[76] Nesbitt, 'Mechanisms of Agricultural Production', pp. 30–1.

186   *Economic expansion in the Byzantine empire*

mentioned. In some eleventh-century chrysobulls the forced purchase of flax was one of the charges from which the beneficiaries' estates were spared.[77] Acorns and a range of plants available locally could be used for dyeing cloth.[78] In regions with a strong pastoral regime peasants would have been able to produce their own woollen garments.[79] Peasant demand for clothing probably fluctuated considerably. In difficult years new acquisitions could be postponed and garments repaired and patched up until conditions became more favourable and some spare cash or surplus produce was available.

Consequently a large section of the population contributed very little to the volume of clothing purchased in markets. The main element of demand was the purchases of powerful landowners in the capital and in the major urban centres, and the more modest purchases of less important landowners who made up local elites based around provincial towns. The needs of large monastic foundations and other ecclesiastical institutions were also substantial, as the example of Bačkovo shows. Demand for textiles was not restricted to clothing, but also included cloths made for ecclesiastical purposes, and the regularity with which churches featured on the property of wealthy landowners and the general upsurge in monastic building in the eleventh century[80] ensured that this was a substantial element in the demand for high-quality textiles. In areas like southern Greece, where mulberry cultivation was extensive, landowners might have met many of their needs by having the silk produced on their own properties and manufactured on their own initiative,[81] but for the most prestigious items they were likely to have relied on imperial favour or to have purchased directly from urban manufacturers. Their requirements were an important factor in stimulating production.

The other major sphere of economic activity was building work. It

---

[77] *Lavra*, I, no. 48; *Engrapha Patmou*, I, no. 6 line 55. The place name Linobrochi on the island of Leros suggests that it might have been the site of flax-washing; see *ibid.*, II, no. 52 line 62. Flax production was, however, a minor activity on the estate of Baris; see *ibid.*, II, no. 50 lines 119–20.

[78] R. Walpole (ed.), *Memoires relating to European and Asiatic Turkey and Other Countries of the East* (London, 1812), pp. 236ff.

[79] Numerous instances of the production of woollen items in later centuries can be obtained from travellers' accounts; for instance, see Pococke, *A Description of the East*, II, pp. 89–90; and Leake, *Travels in the Morea*, I, p. 18.

[80] See below, p. 188.

[81] The clearest example is the description of the wealth of the widow Danielis; see Theophanes Continuatus, pp. 228, 318–21. This is a ninth-century case and there is no evidence of any similar occurrence in the eleventh or twelfth centuries. For urban textile production in southern Greece during these centuries, see below, p. 219.

The pattern of demand 187

provided a significant outlay for the revenues accumulated by the state and wealthy individuals and although much has been written about Byzantine architecture there has been little discussion of its importance from the perspective of the economic historian.[82] This can be attributed partly to inadequate sources, which make precision impossible; nevertheless, some attempt has to be made to assess the demand for construction work and its economic consequences. Outlays on construction can be divided into domestic housing, ecclesiastical building and work on fortifications and communications. Little is known of the housing of the mass of the population and attention in the sources is focused on the larger projects which were undertaken by emperors and powerful landowners and involved the mobilisation of large resources in cash and labour. Generally, there was a significant increase in construction in the period covered by this study. It reflected the greater resources made available by expansion in the rural economy, but it remains to be determined how productive this building was as a means of exploiting these resources. It did influence economic life by providing employment and an outlay for the expenditure of surplus revenues. Whether such expenditure had a negative impact as largely unproductive conspicuous expenditure depends on the alternative options for expenditure which were open to the state and wealthy landowners. It has already been argued that spending on agricultural improvements was restricted by a stagnant technology, and qualitative improvements (as opposed to a simple extension of the cultivated area) were limited to expenditure on irrigation channels, where necessary, and a greater specialisation in more easily transportable and marketable produce like wine and oil.[83] The scope for productive investment in a modern sense was limited. Therefore the negative view that conspicuous expenditure on building diverted resources from other potentially more productive possibilities should be regarded with some caution.[84]

The most extensive projects, which could create a large demand for labour and help put cash into circulation, were those undertaken by individual emperors. In the ninth century a large number of churches were restored and others newly built in the imperial palace. The tenth-century emperors did add extra buildings to the palace, but their

---

[82] A point emphasised by Mango, 'Les monuments de l'architecture du XIe siècle'.
[83] See above, chapter 4.
[84] For a discussion of these questions using evidence from medieval England, see H. T. Johnson, 'Cathedral Building and the Medieval Economy', in *Explorations in Entrepreneurial History*, 2nd series, IV (1966–7), pp. 191–210 (but for criticisms of his methodology and on points of detail, see the debate in vol. VI).

188   *Economic expansion in the Byzantine empire*

activities were on a smaller scale. From the eleventh century emperors started to spend large sums on the construction of monasteries in Constantinople.[85] Psellos gives a rather tendentious account of their activity and accuses emperors of wasting large quantities of revenues on their favourite projects. Romanos III is accused of wasting resources in building the monastery of Peribleptos and equipping it as if it were a court with thrones, sceptres and purple cloth. Michael IV was responsible for the construction of the church of the Anargyroi and he also built a poor-house on which considerable sums were expended. The work which was most strongly criticised was the construction of the Mangana by Constantine Monomachos, who was alleged to have pulled down the church originally standing on the site; Psellos describes at length the luxurious fittings, the gold leaf on the roof and the precious stones set into the floors and walls.[86] The equally lavish construction of the orphanage (*orphanotropheion*) of Alexios Komnenos is well known due to the account of Anna Komnene.[87] These accounts have until recently distracted attention from the way in which these institutions functioned as economic organisations administering extensive areas of state land,[88] but the main consideration here is the economic consequences of their construction. They were clearly major undertakings, but the suggestion that they were responsible for emptying the imperial coffers should not be taken too seriously. Large numbers of skilled craftsmen would have been needed, but the duration of employment and the rates of pay are unknown. Also, large numbers of unskilled workers would have been needed for the transportation of materials. This may have been achieved through the state's claims to impose labour services on the population, which may have gone some way to reducing expenses, but large sums must have ended up in the hands both of the skilled craftsmen (many of whom may have been exclusively in imperial employment)[89] and of the labourers of the capital and its immediate hinterland.

Aristocratic status was displayed by an imposing house which demonstrated the owner's social position. Normally a house on an estate would include a church, hall, bath-house, storehouses and

---

[85] Mango, 'Les monuments de l'architecture du XIe siècle', pp. 352–5.

[86] Psellos, *Chronographie*, I, pp. 42–4, 71–2, 74–5; II, pp. 61–3; Mango, 'Les monuments de l'architecture du XIe siècle', p. 355.

[87] Anne Comnène, *Alexiade*, III, pp. 214–17.

[88] This has now been set out by Lemerle, *Cinq études*, pp. 272–85.

[89] For imperial workshops, see N. Oikonomides, *Les Listes de préséance byzantines des IXe et Xe siècles* (Paris, 1972), p. 317.

The pattern of demand 189

separate apartments for members of the family and guests. An estate belonging to Constantine Doukas near Serres had a sufficient number of buildings to receive the emperor and his entourage in some style. The house on the estate at Baris given to Andronikos Doukas in 1073 included a church, a hall with four chambers opening off it and a bathhouse. Although it was more modest than the house near Serres, it served the needs of a landowner visiting the group of properties around Baris. Depending on the wealth and interest of the owner, a house might have been adorned with gold mosaic, coloured marble and other luxurious fittings.[90] Often the church or monastery which a landowner had founded on his property featured strongly in his concerns. Eustathios Boilas was responsible for the construction of a church of the Theotokos and a half of his estate, Bouzina (valued at twenty pounds), was bequeathed to the church to maintain it. Attaleiates envisaged that his monastery and poor-house would use half of the surplus revenues from its lands to maintain its properties and buildings.[91] The construction work of more highly privileged landowners was naturally more extensive, especially when their lands were situated in provinces where considerations of defence were well to the fore. Pakourianos's expenditure on building was directed towards the monastery of Bačkovo and the construction of houses and fortifications. In his *typikon* he claims that the monastery with its churches and its cells was built at considerable personal expense because he did not resort to arbitrary impositions and forced labour services from the peasants on his estates. He also built two *kastra* at the nearby village of Stenimachos and houses on land which he purchased in Mosynoupolis.[92]

The concentration of economic power in the hands of the imperial family under Alexios Komnenos was reflected in the grandeur of their buildings. Zonaras likened their domestic residences to imperial palaces.[93] In the *typikon* of Kecharitomene Irene speaks in general terms of the luxurious buildings which she constructed in the monastic complex. There were two courtyards with buildings which were occupied by Irene, her children and servants, as well as the monastic cells. There was also a church of St Demetrios equipped with two bathhouses.[94] The monastery of Kosmosotira was also a large undertaking,

[90] P. Magdalino, 'The Byzantine Aristocratic Oikos', in Angold, *The Byzantine Aristocracy, IX to XIII Centuries*, pp. 95–6.
[91] Lemerle, *Cinq études*, p. 23 lines 98–101; Gautier, 'La diataxis de Michel Attaliate', p. 73.
[92] Gautier, 'Grégoire Pakourianos', pp. 35–7.   [93] Zonaras, III, p. 767.
[94] Gautier, 'Le typikon de la Théotokos Kécharitôménè', pp. 137–9.

190   *Economic expansion in the Byzantine empire*

but its location in the provinces meant that considerations of defence were also involved in its construction. It functioned as a fortification as well as a monastery. The complex included a hospital, a hostel for the aged, bath-houses, a cistern and bridges, all of which had been built by Isaac Komnenos and were the responsibility of the monastery to maintain. Again, no details of the cost of the work is provided, but clearly it was an expensive undertaking.[95]

Major monastic centres were also responsible for extensive building activity. Athanasios, who had received six pounds of gold from Nikephoros Phokas, undertook the construction of a hermitage and chapel and then a church of the Theotokos, work involving a considerable effort clearing woodland and levelling out rough ground. The Theotokos was the principal church and was later flanked by two smaller churches built alongside it. A complex of monastic cells was also built around the church. Then Athanasios built a hospital and a hostel with a bath-house. The construction of additional cells and hermitages in Lavra's dependent monasteries followed and the growth of the monastery led him to undertake the construction of a harbour nearby.[96]

Occasionally the sources give some impression of the sums involved in building expenditure. All the expenses made on improvements to the monastery of Bouleuteria – work on the church, monastic cells and other buildings, as well as the planting of vineyards – amounted to 520 *nomismata* and were met by Lavra. The precise amount spent on the buildings is unknown, but it is likely to have been a considerable proportion of the total expenditure.[97] However, the documents usually do not give any indications of the amounts spent on building. In his testament the abbot of Docheiariou, Neophytos, describes how he had built up the wealth of the monastery. He constructed additional buildings and cells and he first demolished and then rebuilt more lavishly the church of St Michael.[98] By 1169 the monastery of Thessalonikeos had fallen into decline and was amalgamated with the monastery of Rossikon, whose monks were to restore it and encircle it with a fortification.[99]

There was a considerable increase in building in towns during this period (see the discussion of the urban revival in the next chapter). The

---

[95] Petit, 'Kosmosotira', pp. 17–77; Asdracha, *La Région des Rhodopes*, p. 126.
[96] 'Vie d'Athanase', pp. 33–6, 47.
[97] *Lavra*, I, no. 26.
[98] *Docheiariou*, no. 6.
[99] *Pantéléèmôn*, no. 8. For expenditure by Xeropotamou on the renovation of an old church in Hierissos, see *Xéropotamou*, no. 4.

The pattern of demand

191

state's main concern was the maintenance of fortifications and communications, and construction work inside provincial towns reflected the economic situation of landowners and townsmen. Unfortunately, there is little evidence relating to the residences of leading figures in towns or the economic aspects of such building work.[100] A recently published document does give details of a complex of seven workshops on two storeys. It was situated in the quarter of Kataphyge in Thessalonike and was obtained by Nikephoros Bourtzes in an exchange of property with the monastery of Docheiariou. The two houses on the north side, constructions made out of stone with marble columns, were probably fairly old. The buildings on the west and south sides, made of stone and brick with wooden columns and wooden stairs, were very likely newer. The older construction had probably been a mansion which was subsequently reconstructed, possibly in the eleventh century, and converted into a more lucrative complex with workshops and domestic residences.[101]

Archaeological evidence does give some general impressions of urban building. It was intended to meet needs as they arose without any deliberate planning. Materials from ancient ruins were often reused and the general quality of building was not very high. Houses often consisted of a series of small and irregularly shaped rooms around a small courtyard and were made at least partly of two storeys. The ground floor would have been used for the storage of agricultural produce.[102] Many houses were even more modest. At Sardis by the eleventh century most houses consisted of one or more rooms of about five square metres.[103] The very basic quality of much provincial urban housing is revealed by the excavations at Dinogetia on the lower Danube, where a large number of very modest houses have been unearthed. Some were based on stone foundations and in places the walls were made of materials taken from ancient ruins and held in place by clay. However, most of the population lived in huts. They were either rectangular or square in shape with sides of three to five metres and were well sunk into the ground. Several stakes at the corners of the ditches and sometimes a post in the middle were used to support the roof and above ground the walls were made of planks covered by clay. There

---

[100] The most useful overall surveys are by C. Bouras, 'Houses in Byzantium', *Deltion tes Christianikes Archaiologikes Hetaireias*, 11 (1982–3), pp. 1–26; and Bouras, 'City and Village: Urban Design and Architecture', pp. 611–53.

[101] *Docheiariou*, no. 4.

[102] Bouras, 'Houses in Byzantium', pp. 1–26.

[103] Foss, *Sardis*, p. 70.

192   Economic expansion in the Byzantine empire

were also a number of more modest houses which did not have foundations; only a few vestiges of these have survived.[104]

These dwellings were quite similar to those of the peasantry. In Europe, generally, peasant houses were makeshift constructions made from whatever materials were locally available. Wood was the main building material, supplemented by earth, clay and straw.[105] Evidence relating to Byzantine peasant houses is very scarce. Some references in the monastic archives show how rough and ready these constructions could be. A tax-assessment of property belonging to a *metochion* of the Saviour refers tersely to worthless houses inside the *kastron* of Hierissos. These were probably occupied by the cultivators of the lands of the monastery. A clearer example concerns a land dispute between Lavra and a neighbouring *pronoia* holder. When *paroikoi* belonging to the latter were found settled on the property of Lavra, they were transferred along with their houses to the land of the *pronoia* holder. These constructions must have been no more than very rudimentary huts to have been moved so easily.[106] The archaeological record is also inadequate. However, a peasant house excavated in Elis in the western Peloponnesos was a more solid building. It consisted of three small rooms with an outside shelter (which may have been used as a kitchen).[107] Generally, the simple construction of peasant houses, the sites of which were easily ploughed over, has ensured that survivals are very scarce.[108] The same general considerations apply to other structures erected by the peasantry. The chapel found at Nichoria in the south-west Peloponnesos is notable for its modest size and casual construction. It is likely that the labour and the costs were met by the local villagers. The building seems to have been an isolated chapel rather than a proper church and its construction would suggest that the walls were not even laid out by a local mason, but were haphazardly put up by the local inhabitants.[109]

---

[104] Barnea, 'Dinogetia', pp. 259–61.

[105] W. Minchinton, 'Patterns and Structure of Demand 1500–1750', in C. Cipolla (ed.), *The Fontana Economic History of Europe*, II, *The Sixteenth and Seventeenth Centuries* (London, 1974), p. 136; F. Braudel, *Civilisation and Capitalism 15th–18th Century*, I, *The Structures of Everyday Life. The Limits of the Possible* (London, 1981), pp. 272–7.

[106] *Lavra*, I, nos. 39, 64.

[107] J. E. Coleman, 'Excavation of a Site (Elean Pylos) near Agrapidochori', *Archaiologikon Deltion*, 24 (1969), pp. 155–61.

[108] This is reflected in the contrast between the large numbers of churches which survive in the Peloponnesos and the scarcity of remains of complementary domestic architecture; see McDonald, Coulson and Rosser, *Excavations at Nichoria in Southwest Greece*, III, p. 354.   [109] *Ibid.*, p. 376.

The greater part of the population met their housing requirements without significant recourse to commercial transactions, and self-sufficiency was again a serious concern. Consequently, any effect which construction work had in stimulating a greater specialisation in economic activity came from the larger projects which were initiated by the state and powerful landowners. Demand was greatest in Constantinople, which contained the greatest concentration of the most highly skilled craftsmen who worked with gold and other precious materials and many of whom were directly in the pay of the state. In the *Book of the Eparch* there are references to contractors such as carpenters, plasterers, marble masons, locksmiths, painters and others.[110] Such groups of workers were doubtless found in smaller numbers in other towns and also in rural areas where large landowners were undertaking extensive projects into which they were putting much of their prestige as well as cash. Nevertheless, such activity is likely to have had only a limited effect in producing a greater specialisation within the labour-force.

Housing, clothing and diet formed the main components of economic demand, but there are some other elements which deserve consideration. A large portion of aristocratic wealth took the form of jewellery and plate. Symbatios Pakourianos used the fifty pounds of gold coins which his wife brought him as her dowry to purchase items made of silver. His wife bequeathed large items of gold and silver. When a large landowner established a church he usually endowed it with substantial quantities of liturgical objects made of precious metals and stones. Gregory Pakourianos passed on to his monastery manufactured objects such as crosses and icons, often decorated with precious stones, goblets, lamp-holders and other items made of silver. Documents detailing the accumulated movable wealth of monasteries and aristocratic landowners have a certain uniformity in listing precious objects such as these, and of course the most extensive accumulation of such wealth belonged to the emperor.[111] The economic 'spin-off' of such accumulation was very limited. The craftsmen occupied in the

[110] Oikonomides, *Les Listes de préséance byzantines*, p. 317; *To Eparchikon Biblion*, pp. 61–3, ch. 22.

[111] In addition to the cases of Pakourianos and Boilas outlined by Hendy, *Studies in the Byzantine Monetary Economy*, pp. 209–14, see Gautier, 'La diataxis de Michel Attaliate', pp. 89–91; C. Astruc, 'L'inventaire – dressé en septembre 1200 – du trésor et de la bibliothèque de Patmos. Édition diplomatique', *Travaux et Mémoires*, 8 (1981), pp. 20–2; and *Pantéléèmôn*, no. 7. For the imperial accumulation of such wealth, see Hendy, *Studies in the Byzantine Monetary Economy*, pp. 306ff.

194   *Economic expansion in the Byzantine empire*

production of such items must have been few in relation to the value of the demand for these objects.

There was a more general demand for metalwork of everyday use. Archaeological excavations have uncovered quantities of bowls, jugs and other vessels, liturgical objects, furniture fittings, locks and other metal objects.[112] Metal-working was a basic requirement in most localities, as was glass production to a lesser degree. This is reflected in the considerable quantities of jewellery uncovered on archaeological sites. At Dinogetia and Vicina numerous pearls and glass bracelets of various colours, copper and bronze bracelets and semi-circular pendants have been found. At Sardis the range of material includes an assortment of rings, bracelets, earrings and pendants.[113] The demand at the top of the social scale for prestigious and highly ornate objects, manufactured by skilled craftsmen in a limited number of centres, was matched among the less wealthy sections of Byzantine society by a demand for similar items made out of cheaper materials by local craftsmen, and this was one area which did permit a modest amount of more specialised economic activity.

In the list of items with which monasteries were endowed by their founders books appear quite frequently. They were fairly exclusive items, whose ownership was restricted to wealthier individuals and scholars. Generally, books were expensive and hard to obtain. There are also indications that parchment was sometimes in short supply, but this might have been a seasonal factor, with the situation improving in spring after the slaughter of animals. The evidence for the prices of books is limited, but it does suggest that prices generally varied from thirteen to twenty *nomismata*. Private libraries were usually small, rarely containing more than twenty volumes.[114] This scarcity is confirmed by evidence from letters indicating that books circulated around literary circles on loan and were not sent as gifts because of the expense.[115] However, a landowner who established a church on his property might have been in an advantageous position to commission the copying of books by clerics and to obtain them at a lower cost. This

---

[112] J. C. Waldbaum, *Metalwork from Sardis. The Finds through 1974* (Cambridge, Massachusetts, 1983); McDonald, Coulson and Rosser, *Excavations at Nichoria in Southwest Greece*, III.

[113] Diaconu, 'Pacuiul lui Soare – Vicina', pp. 421–2; Barnea, 'Dinogetia', pp. 266, 278–80; Waldbaum, *Metalwork from Sardis*, pp. 109ff.

[114] N. G. Wilson, 'Books and Readers in Byzantium', in *Byzantine Books and Bookmen* (Dumbarton Oaks, 1975), pp. 1–15.

[115] Karpozelos, 'Realia in Byzantine Epistolography', pp. 31–3.

The pattern of demand 195

possibly explains why Eustathios Boilas was able to build up a large library of over fifty volumes.[116] Books were a commodity whose production and distribution often had little to do with commercial markets.

There was a much more extensive demand for candles. On imperial expeditions the *eidikos* (the head of the *eidikon*, a repository of imperial wealth) was responsible for, among many other things, the provision of 300 candles of one pound each.[117] The superintendent (*nosokomos*) of the hospital of the Pantokrator was allocated 100 pounds of wax, and a small chapel by the monastery's cemetery received twelve pounds annually.[118] Some churches and monasteries were engaged in production. Hagia Sophia had workshops, and candles were manufactured inside the monastery of Kecharitomene in sufficient quantities for its own lighting. The *typikon* stipulated that if there were an excess of wax, 500 pounds was to be retained for the monastery's own needs and the remainder sold.[119] There was also a significant ecclesiastical demand for items like frankincense and myrrh, which were used for liturgical and also for medical purposes, along with spices such as cinnamon, pepper, cloves and ginger. The *nosokomos* of the hospital of the Pantokrator was allocated two pounds in *hyperpyra* annually to purchase medicines, plasters and other items. The hospital's *meizoteros* (administrative official) received thirty-six *hyperpyra* annually for myrrh, incense, mastic and other medical needs. Other more basic requirements, like oil and honey, were provided in kind, no doubt directly from the monastery's own properties.[120]

The major area of demand still to be considered was the military needs of the state. These affected the rural population mainly in the form of levies on its agricultural produce and on the natural resources of the localities which were affected. Constantine Porphyrogenitos's description of the preparations for the Cretan expedition of 949 lists the large quantities of wheat, barley, wine and animals which different provinces had to supply; the theme of Thrakesion alone was responsible

---

[116] Lemerle, *Cinq études*, p. 39. The poor spelling in the note accompanying Boilas's will would suggest that the copyist did not have to possess high literary qualities.
[117] Hendy, *Studies in the Byzantine Monetary Economy*, p. 310.
[118] Gautier, 'Pantocrator', pp. 95, 107.
[119] *To Eparchikon Biblion*, pp. 43–5, ch. 11; Gautier, 'Le typikon de la Théotokos Kécharitôménè', pp. 65–7.
[120] Gautier, 'Pantocrator', pp. 93–9. For a discussion of Byzantine medical substances, see J. Stannard, 'Aspects of Byzantine Materia Medica', *Dumbarton Oaks Papers*, 38 (1984), pp. 205–11.

196 _Economic expansion in the Byzantine empire_

for the provision of 20,000 _modioi_ of barley, 40,000 _modioi_ of wheat, 30,000 measures of wine and 10,000 animals.[121] In this respect large-scale expeditions only intensified the burdens which the rural population already bore for the provisioning of officials in the normal course of their duties. Any positive economic 'spin-offs' from the state's military activities must have been very restricted. It is certain that arms production was closely supervised in imperial workshops. In the late Roman period arms factories had existed in some of the larger cities, but arms production remained carefully controlled. It is likely that these factories were closed down in the seventh century, when political and military conditions made their continued operation impossible, and afterwards production was based predominantly in Constantinople. Large quantities of weapons were produced for the Cretan expedition in workshops where iron was smelted and forged, but due to the pressing need this had to be supplemented by weapons produced in the provinces, a procedure for which the generals in the themes were responsible.[122] The range of obligations to which rural communities could be subjected were intended to cover most of the state's basic requirements. In addition to work on fortifications, bridges and roads, communities could be liable for the provision of iron and charcoal, the equipping of soldiers, the cutting-down and transportation of wood and the construction and equipping of boats. In the eleventh century these claims on rural communities were increasingly transferred to powerful landowners, notably those like Pakourianos and Kephalas who served the state in military capacities.[123] Most of the military requirements of the state and its military commanders were obtained through state-controlled workshops or impositions on the rural population and it is likely that only a limited amount was obtained through commercial transactions.

The general pattern of demand set out above suggests that there were strict limits to the possibilities for expansion in the Byzantine economy even in a period when the revenues of the state and of landowners were increasing. The provisioning of Constantinople would have encouraged mercantile activity in the coastal regions of the empire. The areas of industrial production which were most affected by an increase in demand were textile production, construction work and metal-working

---

[121] Constantine Porphyrogenitus, _De Cerimoniis_, I, p. 658.

[122] J. F. Haldon, _Byzantine Praetorians. An Administrative, Institutional and Social Survey of the Opsikion and Tagmata, c. 580–950_ (Berlin, 1984), pp. 318–22, 591–4.

[123] _Lavra_, I, no. 48; _Engrapha Patmou_, I, no. 6. See also above, p. 108.

The pattern of demand 197

(ranging from expensive luxury products to more basic everyday needs), but their impact on the economy as a whole was reduced by the wide-ranging emphasis on self-sufficiency which restricted the opportunities for commercial transactions. These observations, based on the general pattern of demand and its economic implications, need to be developed further in the light of the evidence relating to towns and their interaction with the rural economy.

Chapter 6

Interaction between town and country

The history of Byzantine towns has been discussed too often in isolation from the broader social context which links town and country closely. Towns were very sensitive to developments in the rural economy affecting agricultural production. They cannot be defined as independent entities outside the economy and society of which they were a part.[1] A precise definition of a town cannot be given easily owing to the multiplicity of functions which it could perform – as a religious centre, a judicial centre, a fortified place for defence, a market, a central place offering services to a rural hinterland.[2] A purely economic definition would stress occupational specialisation in crafts and industry, a role which separated an urban population from rural agricultural producers.[3]

It is impossible to postulate with confidence any minimum population for an urban centre because towns are defined by function rather than size. Many towns in medieval Europe were smaller than large villages, but they were distinguished from them by their non-agricultural activities. Before 1500 the vast majority of towns in the west had less than 2,000 inhabitants. Braudel estimates the average population of the 3,000 settlements with civic status in Germany at 400.[4] Figures for Byzantine towns are lacking. We do know that there were at least 163 adult males in Lampsakos in 1219, which suggests a likely population of 600–750 if the entire adult population was recorded.[5] However, it

---

[1] P. Abrams, 'Towns and Economic Growth: Some Theories and Problems', in P. Abrams and E. A. Wrigley (eds.), *Towns in Societies. Essays in Economic History and Historical Sociology* (Cambridge, 1978), pp. 9–33.

[2] For additional functional criteria, see J. L. Nelson, 'Charles the Bald and the Church in Town and Countryside', in D. Baker (ed.), *The Church in Town and Countryside* (Oxford, 1979), p. 103.

[3] Hilton, *A Medieval Society*, pp. 168–9; Hilton, *The English Peasantry*, pp. 80–1.

[4] F. Braudel, *Civilisation and Capitalism 15th–18th Century*, I, p. 482.

[5] Angold, *A Byzantine Government in Exile*, p. 110.

198

Interaction between town and country

will be argued later that Lampsakos is not a good case from which to generalise.

Figures from the Ottoman period show how limited the population of towns might have been. Serres was the site of various representatives of the Porte supervising the fiscal administration, coinage-minting and economic activities. In 1464–5 it had a population of about 6,000. In the same year Zichna had a population of about 2,600 and Drama less than 1,450.[6] A survey of urban centres in Anatolia in the sixteenth century (a time of rapid population increase) attempts to encompass as small towns all settlements with more than 400 tax-payers. A medium-sized town was assumed to hold 1,000 tax-payers (3–4,000 inhabitants) and big cities were defined as places with 3,500 tax-payers or more (10,500–14,000 inhabitants). Most administrative divisions contained at least one medium-sized town, usually its capital. Among the larger towns were Kayseri (8,251 tax-payers in 1584), Ankara (5,344 tax-payers in 1571–2), Tokat (3,868 tax-payers in 1574–5) and Konya (3,764 tax-payers in 1584). The largest town in Anatolia was Bursa with 13,000 tax-payers in 1580.[7] These figures provide a useful indication of the possible size of the largest Byzantine towns. As they concern the later part of a century which witnessed a considerable increase in population, it is unlikely that their Byzantine counterparts were as large. An attempt to 'read back' Ottoman evidence into the Byzantine period would emphasise the small size of most towns, probably no more than 1–2,000 inhabitants and in most cases only several hundred.

Towns form a hierarchy of central places, each with its own hinterland, from which farmers or intermediaries bring produce to the market and the towns provide goods or services which are uneconomical to produce in the surrounding villages. The hinterland of large towns consists of a number of smaller central places, each of which has its own commercial and administrative functions and its own agricultural hinterland. Towns with large populations serve a broader region of towns and villages and need a large hinterland to secure their

---

[6] P. S. Nasturel and N. Beldiceanu, 'Les églises byzantines et la situation économique de Drama, Serres et Zichna aux XIVᵉ et XVᵉ siècles', *Jahrbuch der Österreichischen Byzantinistik*, 27 (1978), pp. 271–3. See also N. Beldiceanu and I. Beldiceanu-Steinherr, 'Recherches sur la Morée (1461–1512)', *Südostforschungen*, 39 (1980), pp. 17–74.

[7] L. T. Erder and S. Faroqhi, 'The Development of the Anatolian Urban Network during the Sixteenth Century', *Journal of the Economic and Social History of the Orient*, 23 (1980), pp. 265–303.

200   *Economic expansion in the Byzantine empire*

food supply. Consequently, the situation of a town in the urban hierarchy was usually linked closely to the size of its population.[8]

Owing to inadequate evidence it is impossible to show any direct link between the size of Byzantine towns and their administrative or economic functions. Nevertheless, it is clear that Constantinople was several times larger than even the largest provincial towns. The most important of these were the capitals of the themes. They probably had the largest provincial markets to meet the requirements of the officials and landowners resident there. In some administrative sub-divisions it is likely that the main settlement, even if the site of a bishopric, contained no more inhabitants than a large village. In purely economic terms the hierarchy of towns probably followed the administrative hierarchy fairly closely.

There has been a tendency to emphasise the rural character of Byzantine towns and the large proportion of their inhabitants engaged in agriculture even in large towns.[9] Certainly, at the bottom of the urban hierarchy there was not a clear distinction between towns and villages. This is reflected in the terminology which Byzantine writers applied to towns. In the sixth century the designation *polis* had been used to distinguish them from fortifications and villages. From the end of the sixth century the distinction between a *polis* and a *kastron* became blurred.[10] The terminological confusion is well illustrated by Anna Komnene's references to Tzouroulon, a fortified town in Thrace. Usually it is described as a *polichnion*, in one passage it is a *kome*, in another a *polis*. The town was a bishopric in the eighth century. A ninth-century inscription shows that it was a small administrative centre with a *basilikos kourator* of Tzouroulon in charge of the imperial estates in the area. It was a high fortified site on top of a hill overlooking a plain and it seems likely that most of its inhabitants were agriculturalists.[11] The term *kastron* had three meanings – a simple castle, the citadel of a town or the whole of a fortified town. Some *kastra*, which were intended mainly as places of refuge for the rural population in case of attack, had room for only a very restricted permanent population. When the

---

[8] *Ibid.*, pp. 269–70. See also F. Braudel, *Civilisation and Capitalism 15th–18th Century*, II, *The Wheels of Commerce* (London, 1982), pp. 114–20.

[9] A. A. M. Bryer, 'The Late Byzantine Monastery in Town and Countryside', in D. Baker (ed.), *The Church in Town and Countryside* (Oxford, 1979), pp. 221–2.

[10] Dölger, 'Die frühbyzantinische und byzantinisch beeinflusste Stadt', pp. 72–3.

[11] Anna Comnène, *Alexiade*, I, p. 73 line 10, p. 81 line 15; II, p. 123 line 12; I Sevcenko, 'Inscription Commemorating Sisinnios, "Curator" of Tzurulon (AD 813)', *Byzantion*, 35 (1965), pp. 564–74.

Interaction between town and country 201

monastery of Patmos received land on Leros, there were already two *kastra* on the island. One of them was given to the monks. It contained six houses, three cells, two other smaller cells and one cistern. Its economic value was minimal and it served purely as a refuge.[12] *Kastra* which were no more than fortified villages were very common and the administration treated them as essentially rural communities. In 1044 the *anagrapheus* of Boleron, Strymon and Thessalonike was instructed to impose the land-tax on all the *kastra* and villages which were not paying it. *Kastra* and *choria* were subjected to the same technical fiscal procedure because there was no substantial economic difference between them.[13] A clear instance of a *kastron* being no more than a fortified village was Adrameri to the east of Thessalonike. A large number of the inhabitants of the *kastron* were peasant landowners who acted together in the same way that members of a village community did in matters of common interest. The names of the inhabitants of Adrameri give no indication of any non-agricultural activity except in the case of Kalotas Amaxa, who might have been a wagon-maker but certainly owned some land. Adrameri was essentially an agricultural community.[14]

Nevertheless, the emphasis on the rural character of Byzantine towns should not be overdone. Many small towns existed because of the slowness of transport overland and in the interior of Asia Minor, especially, were connected with military routes. Their main purpose was the provision of supplies and services and this did differentiate them from surrounding villages to a certain extent, even if their population also included agriculturalists.[15] Byzantium was not distinct from the rest of Europe in having farmers living in urban settlements. It was a general phenomenon throughout Europe up to the eighteenth century for urban residents to engage in agriculture. Shepherds, agricultural workers and vinegrowers were housed in towns, even in Paris. Usually, towns had an area of gardens inside and outside the walls and also fields further away. At harvest time artisans left their trades and went into

[12] *Engrapha Patmou*, II, no. 52; N. Oikonomides, 'The Donations of Castles in the Last Quarter of the 11th Century', in *Polychronion. Festschrift F. Dölger* (Heidelberg, 1966), pp. 413–17.

[13] *Pantéléèmôn*, no. 3.　　　　　　　　　　[14] *Lavra*, I, no. 37.

[15] The economic role of small towns in the Middle Ages is a subject that has not been intensively researched and in the Byzantine case the inadequacy of the evidence is a serious problem. For work based on English evidence, which offers some interesting insights, see R. H. Hilton, 'Small Town Society in England before the Black Death', *Past and Present*, 105 (1984), pp. 53–78; and R. H. Hilton, 'Medieval Market Towns and Simple Commodity Production', *Past and Present*, 109 (1985), pp. 3–23.

202 *Economic expansion in the Byzantine empire*

the fields. This was true even of Flanders in the sixteenth century.[16] In the early nineteenth century Leake described the trade of Serres as based on cloth and raw cotton, but its walls also enclosed a large space occupied by gardens and even meadows where cattle grazed.[17] Therefore brief references in the sources to agricultural work performed by townsmen should not lead to the hasty conclusion that the 'ruralisation' of towns was a phenomenon more prevalent in Byzantium than in medieval Europe generally.

Byzantine towns, like their late Roman predecessors, were centres for the consumption of surplus wealth appropriated from the rural economy. Landowners who resided in the towns lived off the produce of their properties either by direct consumption or indirectly through exchange at markets to secure their non-alimentary needs. The notion of a 'consumer-city' is not vitiated by the existence of petty commodity production by independent craftsmen to meet local needs. The important consideration is that the economic power of the dominant class was derived from rents and taxes on landed property, and commercial and industrial activity was largely a response to the demands of this class.[18] It is significant that Niketas Choniates's general description of prosperous towns emphasises the buildings with high roofs, decorated with works of art, the pleasures of the bath-houses, the fertility of wheat fields, vineyards, meadows and gardens, and says nothing about artisanal or mercantile activity.[19] The emphasis on consumption rather than production is well illustrated by evidence from earlier and later periods. In the range of occupations of the inhabitants of the late Roman town of Korykos the most frequently encountered sector was that of service. The next most common category was dealers in consumption items; they were intermediaries, tavern-keepers, oil and wine merchants. The latter were able to engage in a more highly developed form of commerce because the value of their products made long-distance transportation more feasible. Korykos is a very instructive example because it was well situated to take part in long-distance trade. Linen was imported and worked up in the town. Nevertheless, the impact of this more spectacular economic activity on the commercial structure of the town was limited. Exported products were relatively few. Most occupations reflected the existence of consumers and were

---

[16] Braudel, *Civilisation and Capitalism 15th–18th Century*, I, p. 487.

[17] Leake, *Travels in Northern Greece*, III, pp. 200–1, 207.

[18] M. I. Finlay, 'The Ancient City: From Fustel de Coulanges to Max Weber and Beyond', *Comparative Studies in Society and History*, 19 (1977), pp. 305–27.

[19] Nicetas Choniates, p. 634.

Interaction between town and country

not economically very productive. The dominant element in Korykos, as elsewhere, was landed wealth. Merchants and craftsmen played a subordinate role.[20] The same lack of industrial dynamism can be seen in the occupational structure of Serres in the late fifteenth century. Artisanal activity was confined to such basic occupations as smith, tailor, weaver, dyer, carpenter, shoemaker and other comparable trades. The only exception was the preparers and sellers of silk, who catered for the needs of the town's elite. The town contained a large number of shops, and some inhabitants were engaged in agriculture and market gardening. Commodity production was generally restricted to meeting only very basic needs.[21] The emphasis on consumption rather than production reflected the dominance of landed wealth in the towns; this leads to the inevitable conclusion that the most important factor in the economic decline or expansion of towns was the condition of the rural economy.

We are best informed about the range of artisanal and commercial specialisation in Constantinople. The *Book of the Eparch* details the main guilds which existed in the capital by about 900 and the regulations to which they were subject. Several of them were involved in provisioning the city, and the main industrial guilds, as has already been mentioned, were involved in textile production and distribution. The prices of basic necessities were subject to restrictions which were intended to promote price stability. The profit which the bakers were authorised to make was limited. They were theoretically allowed a surcharge of two *milliaresia* and twelve *folleis* on every *nomisma*, two *milliaresia* to cover costs and twelve *folleis* as profit. Difficulties caused by fluctuations in the price of grain had to be resolved by a direct approach to the eparch, who fixed the price of bread according to that of wheat.[22] Information about price levels is inadequate. Some passages in the historians suggest that a reasonable level for wheat prices in normal times was eight or ten *modioi* a *nomisma*. During shortages the price in the capital rose to one *nomisma* for four *modioi* or even for one *modios*.[23] The eparch fixed the

---

[20] Patlagean, *Pauvreté économique et pauvreté sociale à Byzance*, pp. 158–70; Haldon and Kennedy, 'The Arab–Byzantine Frontier', pp. 87–8.

[21] Nasturel and Beldiceanu, 'Les églises byzantines et la situation économique de Drama, Serres et Zichna aux XIVe et XVe siècles', p. 272.

[22] *To Eparchikon Biblion*, pp. 53–4, ch. 18; A. Toynbee, *Constantine Porphyrogenitus and his World* (London, 1973), p. 206.

[23] Theophanes Continuatus, pp. 479, 759; Attaleiates, p. 203. On this last passage, see J. Karayannopulos, 'Ho hyposis tes times tou sitou epi Parapinake', *Byzantina*, 5 (1973), pp. 106–9. See also Ostrogorsky, 'Löhne und Preise in Byzanz', pp. 319–23; Teall, 'The Grain Supply of the Byzantine Empire', pp. 114–16; and Antoniadis-Bibicou, 'Démographie, salaires et prix à Byzance au XIe siècle', pp. 215–46.

204　Economic expansion in the Byzantine empire

price of wine as supplies were brought into the city and regulated the price of fish daily.[24] The butchers were divided into two guilds, those who dealt in sheep and cattle and the pork butchers. The former purchased cattle in Constantinople after paying a tax of one *nomisma* to the eparch. They were allowed to buy sheep outside the city if the sellers were bringing their flocks over great distances. They were supposed not to wait for the sellers at towns like Nikomedia, but to cross the Sangarios to obtain lower prices. Sheep owners were permitted to sell their animals only to specified buyers and were theoretically not allowed to hinder peasants bringing their sheep to Constantinople for sale. The regulation implies that the owners of large flocks which were sold in Constantinople were pressurising peasants, who were understandably reluctant to travel too far from their land, to sell at low prices and were reselling in Constantinople. The pork butchers were restricted to the Tauros market square for their purchases of pigs. Those who bought their pigs outside the city beyond the supervision of the eparch were liable to severe penalties. One of the eparch's main concerns was to prevent price increases by the activities of intermediaries. One contrivance to overcome his efforts was to bring animals into aristocratic houses to be sold secretly; another was the retention of supplies until times of scarcity.[25]

The restrictions which were imposed on the different guilds involved in the trade in textiles have already been discussed.[26] Other industrial occupations which were regulated by the eparch catered to the basic requirements of the population of the capital; there were special guilds for the saddlers, soap-makers, wax-chandlers and perfumers. There was also an important service sector. The eparch exercised control over notaries, bullion-dealers, money-lenders, bankers and moneychangers. The range of their activities was strictly limited. The bullion-dealers had to confine their purchases to gold, silver and precious stones. They were not allowed to buy copper, linen, or any other articles which came within the sphere of other traders. The emphasis was very much on the careful regulation of the supply of the capital's needs as a centre of consumption, not the accumulation of merchant capital.[27]

These traders were part of the city's middle stratum, known in the sources as the *mesoi*, which included well-off property owners, teachers

[24] *To Eparchikon Biblion*, p. 55, ch. 19. For the regulation of the trade in fish, see above, p. 170.
[25] *Ibid.*, pp. 50–2, chs. 15, 16.　　　　[26] See above, p. 183.
[27] *To Eparchikon Biblion*, pp. 13–63; H. G. Beck, 'Konstantinopel. Zur Sozialgeschichte einer frühmittelalterlichen Hauptstadt', *Byzantinische Zeitschrift*, 58 (1965), p. 23.

Interaction between town and country   205

and doctors as well as traders and craftsmen with their own workshops. They differed from the aristocracy in that they did not have titles or offices. Some were landowners who lived off the rents from their properties in the provinces or the immediate vicinity of the city, but they were probably a small part of the middle stratum. Most of this section were artisans and merchants. Their workshops were not simply places of production, but were also used for retail sales.[28] The importance of these groups increased in the eleventh century. They took a more direct role in the political life of the empire and made inroads into the senatorial ranks.[29] Possibly this was a consequence of economic growth. If the revenues which the Constantinopolitan aristocracy and ecclesiastical institutions derived from their lands were increasing, their demands for industrial goods was likely to have increased. Nevertheless, the more immediate cause of their elevation in status was political. It was only in the tenth and eleventh centuries that the provincial aristocracy as a group was able to challenge the authority of the central government. As political power was more delicately balanced, the commercial and industrial class in the capital was able to wield greater influence until the resolution of this political tension with the establishment of the Komnenian dynasty. The reduction in the political importance of the commercial class in the following century should be attributed to political conditions and not used as an indicator of economic decline in Constantinople. The ideological bias of the Komnenoi against the merchants and craftsmen of the capital ensured that their political role was a subordinate one. As soon as imperial authority began to weaken in the 1180s, members of the guilds started to play a more assertive role again, once more purchasing important honours.[30]

Constantinople also contained large numbers of journeymen, whose economic situation was far less favourable. They were hired by employers for specific jobs and were not allowed to transfer to any other employer before they had completed their work. An exception was

[28] Beck, 'Konstantinopel', pp. 20–1.
[29] Psellos, *Chronographie*, I, p. 132; Hendy, *Studies in the Byzantine Monetary Economy*, pp. 570–82.
[30] There is also the evidence of the Ptochoprodromic literature, which is clearly exaggerated for effect but would have been devoid of impact if its image of the prosperity of the craftsmen of the capital had been totally out of touch with reality; see Hendy, *Studies in the Byzantine Monetary Economy*, pp. 582–90. For the view that Constantinople's economy was in decline in the twelfth century, see Kazhdan and Cutler, 'Continuity and Discontinuity in Byzantine History', pp. 468–9.

206   *Economic expansion in the Byzantine empire*

made only if the employer was slow in supplying the necessary materials.[31] The less skilled of these workers probably led a precarious existence, going from one job to another.

Many inhabitants of the capital obtained their food supply not by commercial exchanges but through the charitable distributions of pious establishments. If the large numbers of these institutions in the city are taken into account, large quantities of wheat and wine must have been involved. The importance of these distributions reinforces the impression that commercial structures still had a limited impact on large sections of Byzantine society even in a period of economic expansion. The quantities of grains distributed by religious houses varied greatly. The resources of Attaleiates's monastery in Constantinople were very limited and its annual distribution was very modest.[32] The scale of the resources of houses established by imperial patronage was very different. When Alexios restored the *orphanotropheion* (orphanage), he attributed properties to it by grants of chrysobulls. Its estates were located in regions accessible to the capital to facilitate the supply of provisions.[33] The Pantokrator distributed large quantities of agricultural produce through its charitable houses. Its hospital was intended to care for fifty people and it had additional beds available for emergencies; the annual outlay on all fifty inmates was about 1,200 *thalassioi modioi*. The monastery also administered an old people's home which catered for twenty-four; 480 *thalassioi modioi* of bread and 432 measures of wine were allocated to them annually.[34]

The number of inhabitants who were dependent on charity cannot be estimated; nor can the size of any other social groups in the capital. The absence of any regular food distributions by the state suggests that the unskilled lower class was not as numerous as in the late Roman period. Jacoby has suggested that the total population of Constantinople never exceeded 400,000 and his criticisms of the earlier larger estimates are justified.[35] The city's demand for basic agricultural produce probably

---

[31] *To Eparchikon Biblion*, pp. 60–3, ch. 22.

[32] It amounted to 216 *annonikoi* and 52 large *modioi*; see Gautier, 'La diataxis de Michel Attaliate', p. 47 lines 491–505. For the nutritional content of the allowances, see above, pp. 176–8. See also R. Volk, *Gesundheitswesen und Wohltätigkeit im Spiegel der byzantinischen Klostertypika* (Munich, 1983), pp. 85–91.

[33] Anna Comnène, *Alexiade*, III, pp. 213–18; Lemerle, *Cinq études*, pp. 283–5.

[34] Gautier, 'Pantocrator', pp. 91, 109.

[35] D. Jacoby, 'La population de Constantinople à l'époque byzantine: un problème de démographie urbaine', *Byzantion*, 31 (1961), pp. 81–109. In the eleventh century, when refugees came from the east, it was the administration's policy to send them back with financial incentives rather than allow the overcrowding of the capital; see Scylitzes, p. 386.

Interaction between town and country 207

increased substantially in the eleventh and twelfth centuries. The presence of the court and administration ensured a regular demand for large quantities of agricultural and industrial products. The greater prosperity of the capital doubtless caused an increase in demand for prestigious items like high-quality meat and wine and would have been a significant stimulus to industrial production. Another factor in increasing demand for agricultural produce in the capital was the presence of Italian merchants in large numbers in the twelfth century.

In the provinces recovery from the contraction of the seventh and eighth centuries was a much more protracted process. Towns which had survived in the early Middle Ages began a very slow and uneven expansion and in the Balkans an increasing number of towns are mentioned in the sources from the ninth century onwards.[36] The most salient feature of the early stage of the urban revival was the imperial role in founding towns in the eighth and ninth centuries,[37] reflecting the dominance of the state apparatus in Byzantium at this time. Its military and administrative activities encouraged urban development by putting money into circulation. The presence of a provincial governor and his retinue created a demand for agricultural and industrial products. In border regions the military factor was of major importance and the presence of garrisons acted as a stimulus to agriculture and petty commodity production. The economic demand of the state's officials was reinforced by those of the church, whose administrative hierarchy ran parallel to that of the state. Therefore urban development was generally a reflection of the administrative hierarchy of the state and church, but the lay aristocracy played a more important role as their economic power and fiscal privileges increased. They not only contributed to the economic development of towns which were already in existence, but they built *kastra* and monasteries which in some cases developed into towns. Here defence was not the only consideration. The *kastra* were probably also centres for the administration of their lands. The importance of the feudal aristocracy in promoting the development of towns is most apparent in the eleventh and twelfth centuries, a consequence of the development of feudal social relations. An external factor which contributed to economic expansion

[36] For the history of towns in one region, see Avramea, *He Byzantine Thessalia*, pp. 119–84. Most of the new towns developed on hilltops using the materials from ancient *akropoleis*. Many had Slav names. See A. Avramea, 'Les villes et les agglomérations urbaines de la Thessalie byzantine jusq'en 1204', *Collection de la maison de l'Orient méditerranéen*, VI (Série Archéologique 5) (Lyons, 1979), pp. 281–91. For another region, see Asdracha, *La Région des Rhodopes*, pp. 93ff.

[37] Frances, 'La ville byzantine et la monnaie aux VIIe–VIIIe siècles', p. 14.

208   *Economic expansion in the Byzantine empire*

also deserves mention. The cities of north Italy were becoming more populous and agricultural produce and textiles were shipped there in large quantities in the eleventh and twelfth centuries, resulting in an intensification of commercial activity in some towns, mainly in Greece.

At the lower level of the urban hierarchy the distinction between small towns and large villages was not always clear. In most villages some peasant farmers were also engaged in basic artisanal activities. Occupational specialisation in towns was more developed in the European provinces. Towns in Asia Minor increased in size from the tenth century without achieving the same degree of economic growth as some European towns like Thebes and Corinth. This may have been due to adverse agricultural conditions in the late eleventh and the first part of the twelfth century, when the upward demographic trend in Asia Minor was temporarily halted. The effect of this significant fluctuation on the incomes of landowners would have caused a reduction in demand for urban products. Geographical factors were also involved. Greater proximity to Constantinople ensured that goods could more easily be obtained from the capital and there was less need for specialised local industry. It was not accidental that the most intensive industrial activity occurred in southern and central Greece. These regions were well removed from the dominating influence exerted over the Byzantine economy by Constantinople and were advantageously situated on the sea routes from north Italy to the Middle East.

The impact of proximity to Constantinople is well illustrated by the economic activities of towns in north-west Asia Minor. The relative ease of contact with the capital did give these towns a certain commercial importance, but it also stifled artisanal activity because industrial products were easily obtained from Constantinople. Agricultural produce and livestock passed through Nikomedia, Prousa and Nicaea on its way to Constantinople. Nikomedia was also an official reception-point for travelling merchants. Coastal towns like Abydos, Kyzikos and Pylai owed their importance to their location on routes to Constantinople. Abydos, which was strategically placed on the Dardanelles straits, was an important point for the collection of the *kommerkion*. Pylai had official reception-points for merchants, and large quantities of livestock were transported from there to Constantinople.[38] More detail is available

---

[38] Vryonis, *The Decline of Medieval Hellenism*, pp. 11–13. For Abydos, see R.-J. Lilie, *Handel und Politik zwischen dem byzantinischen Reich und den italienischen Kommunen Venedig, Pisa und Genua in der Epoche der Komnenen und der Angeloi (1081–1204)* (Amsterdam, 1984), pp. 145–6.

Interaction between town and country 209

about the naval port of Lampsakos, which is sometimes cited as an example of the 'ruralisation' of Byzantine towns. It is not a good case from which to generalise because easy access to the capital made industrial activity unnecessary and it is not surprising that most of the town's inhabitants were agriculturalists. In 1219, 113 out of the 163 tax-payers were primarily farmers and were classified in the standard way as *zeugaratoi, boidatoi, aktemones* and *aporoi*. We do not know the occupations of the other fifty tax-payers, but their payments were very low by comparison with those engaged in agriculture. They paid only $51\frac{1}{2}$ *hyperpyra* out of a total of $581\frac{1}{2}$ *hyperpyra* from all the tax-payers. Even the revenues from the harbour, which had some strategic value in the thirteenth century, were relatively small – 261 *hyperpyra* – far less than the revenues extracted from the agricultural producers.[39]

The towns of the Aegean coast of Asia Minor served as an outlet for the produce of the region and as central places for their immediate hinterland. There is no indication that any of these towns had any industrial importance beyond the provision of the requirements of its locality. The literary evidence is very fragmentary and the archaeological evidence is essential for any assessment of the urban economy. Unfortunately, before the thirteenth century little is known about Smyrna, one of the most important towns in the region, and this deficiency is unlikely to be rectified because the modern city stands directly on the medieval site.[40] Ephesos was an administrative centre and it was included in the list of ports of Alexios's chrysobull for the Venetians. The monks of Galesion went there occasionally to make purchases. As its harbour silted up, the inland fortified site of Ayasuluk became the focal point of the settlement. Considerable building activity took place in the twelfth and thirteenth centuries. The new constructions around the church of St John were usually small rooms, some with commercial or industrial functions. To the south-east of the church there have been found the remains of a mill, an oven and several large storage jars. A neighbouring building produced tiles. The atrium of the church was built over with small houses, shops and workshops. These buildings also extended from the church to the entrance of the fortress, a reflection of the increasingly crowded

---

[39] Tafel and Thomas, Urkunden, II, pp. 208–9; Angold, *A Byzantine Government in Exile*, pp. 222–3.

[40] Bouras, 'City and Village: Urban Design and Architecture', p. 635. For the thirteenth century, see Angold, *A Byzantine Government in Exile*, pp. 108–9, who emphasises that the manufactured products of the Nicaean empire were intended mainly for local consumption.

210 *Economic expansion in the Byzantine empire*

conditions inside the fortification. From the eleventh century onwards the settlement also spread beyond the walls. The evidence found so far clearly indicates that the town was becoming more densely populated, but this expansion was not accompanied by a pronounced degree of industrial activity. The workshops inside the fortifications were fairly unimpressive, but the considerable building activity of the twelfth and thirteenth centuries indicates a modest prosperity.[41]

Other less important towns in the region functioned as small central places for a limited area and also enjoyed a moderate prosperity during these centuries. At Pergamon the settlement, which had been confined to the citadel in the early Middle Ages, spread beyond the walls. Most of the remains consist of houses from the eleventh century or later. These were mostly small and made from reused stones laid in mud. The town's population was largest in the twelfth and thirteenth centuries. Excavations have found large quantities of pottery and coins from this period as well as beads, glass arm-rings, and metal objects like buckles, nails and knives. A few lime-kilns have been found and pieces of iron in some rooms indicate the production of metal work, but generally the development of commodity production was very restricted.[42] We are also well informed about Sardis. The area within the walls began to be rebuilt in the tenth century and by the eleventh constructions had proliferated. The houses were small and closely packed together, covering all the available land. Settlements had also developed in the plain beneath the *akropolis* and on the site of the old temple of Artemis. The latter settlement was quite large and needed a new water-supply for the first time since the seventh century. Numerous houses have been dated by coin and pottery finds to the tenth, eleventh and twelfth centuries. Lime-kilns were found there. Another complex on the gymnasium also contained the remains of lime-kilns, suggesting that it was used as a quarry for building materials. Some large brick furnaces were probably connected with the manufacture of glazed pottery. Another settlement at the eastern end of the town revealed some indications of pottery manufacture and the roasting of iron ores. Possibly glass was also manufactured in this part of the town. The glass bracelets found there have been dated from the tenth to the thirteenth centuries. The settlements around the *akropolis* were similar to villages.

[41] Foss, *Ephesus*, pp. 116–37.
[42] See the archaeological reports in successive issues of *Anatolian Studies* from 1974 onwards; see also Foss, 'Archaeology and the "Twenty Cities" of Byzantine Asia', pp. 479–81.

Interaction between town and country

Each was probably fairly self-sufficient. Some industrial activity developed as the town expanded – the building industry, pottery and glass manufactures and iron-working. Only parts of the town have been excavated. It is possible that there were other industries, but so far the evidence indicates that production was limited to the needs of the immediate region of the town.[43] Miletos was a much poorer town. There was some recovery from the early medieval contraction, with some rebuilding in the tenth and eleventh centuries when small houses were erected over the ancient ruins, but little evidence has been found to distinguish the town from a large village in terms of economic functions.[44]

In the interior of Anatolia trading points were needed at regular intervals along the major routes owing to the slowness of the overland transport of bulky items. Also, the rugged terrain of much of the plateau necessitated the import of some basic necessities. It is possible that some of the major administrative and strategic towns were significant centres of consumption, but the evidence relating to towns in the interior of the peninsula is very sketchy. The literary sources refer to commerce in the tenth and eleventh centuries much more frequently than in the early Middle Ages, but these references are very anecdotal and difficult to assess.[45] They give no indication of the importance of traders in the social structure of these towns and it is, of course, impossible to estimate the importance of the revenues which the state derived from trade. Where archaeological evidence is available, it offers a check on the literary sources. At Ankara there are a few indications of recovery from the ninth century onwards. The church of St Clement was built outside the town's fortifications. Finds of coins and pottery in the Roman baths, which had been deserted since the seventh century, suggest a reoccupation around the beginning of the tenth century. This evidence is restricted and nothing is known of any industrial activity in the town in spite of its importance as a military and administrative centre.[46] Euchaita was a less important town with a more agrarian character, except when its annual fair was held. John Mauropous, its bishop in the middle of the eleventh century, wrote enthusiastically of its wealth in gold and silver and especially in livestock. In his writing there is a

---

[43] Foss, *Sardis*, pp. 66–76.
[44] Foss, 'Archaeology and the "Twenty Cities" of Byzantine Asia', pp. 477–8.
[45] Vryonis, *The Decline of Medieval Hellenism* pp. 17–24. Vryonis's account probably exaggerates the importance of commerce by his use of this anecdotal source material.
[46] Foss, 'Late Antique and Byzantine Ankara', pp. 83–4.

212 · Economic expansion in the Byzantine empire

contrast between the well-populated town and the poverty of the countryside, where it was difficult to grow wheat, olives and vines. Clearly some basic items had to be imported and the fundamental export of the region was livestock and its produce, a situation which gave rise to the town's annual fair.[47] Some towns had important commercial functions owing to their situation on overland routes. In the early tenth century Theodosioupolis was a focal point for the caravan trade with the Georgians. Nearby Artze, an unwalled town, was inhabited by Greek, Syrian and Armenian merchants in the first half of the eleventh century. After its destruction by the Turks a large part of its population went to Theodosioupolis, which was well fortified.[48] The town retained its importance in later centuries, when it was a transit-place for silks, cottons and cloths from Aleppo and Baghdad.[49] Such commercial importance was rare. Even Dorylaion was noted more for the fertility of its surrounding region rather than for its industry or commerce.[50] The economic role of most towns was as a market for the agricultural produce of their regions, and their industrial activities were restricted in most cases to fairly basic occupations. Perhaps the most important manufacture in Anatolia was that of woollen cloths,[51] a logical consequence of the grazing of large flocks on the plateau. Manufactures probably increased on a modest scale in the towns of the interior of Anatolia in the tenth and eleventh centuries, just as they did in the western coastal region; economic dislocation occurred in the later eleventh century, followed by recovery in the twelfth and renewed expansion in the thirteenth century in both Byzantine and Seljuk territories.[52]

Several ports on the Pontos were important because grain and wine were exported from them to Constantinople and Cherson, and Sinope

---

[47] P. de Lagarde, *Johannis Euchaitorum Metropolitae quae in Codice Vaticano 676 supersunt* (Göttingen, 1882), pp. 82, 160; Hendy, *Studies in the Byzantine Monetary Economy*, pp. 140–2; Svoronos, 'Remarques sur les structures économiques', pp. 63, 67. For the *panegyris*, see S. Vryonis, 'The Panegyris of the Byzantine Saint: A Study in the Nature of a Medieval Institution, its Origins and Fate', in S. Hackel (ed.), *The Byzantine Saint* (Studies Supplementary to Sobornost 5) (London, 1981), p. 202. For details of the little that is known of other towns in the northern part of the Anatolian plateau, see Vryonis, *The Decline of Medieval Hellenism*, pp. 21–2.

[48] *DAI*, pp. 208, 214; Scylitzes, pp. 451–2.

[49] M. Tournefort, *A Voyage into the Levant* (2 vols., London, 1718), II, pp. 195–6.

[50] *Ioannis Cinnami Epitome*, pp. 294–5.

[51] Vryonis, *The Decline of Medieval Hellenism*, p. 23 n. 126, pp. 238–9.

[52] *Ibid.*, pp. 216–23, gives details of the recovery of the twelfth and thirteenth centuries in both the Byzantine and Seljuk parts of Anatolia.

Interaction between town and country

was a significant naval port.[53] The major port of the region was Trebizond, which was a major commercial centre. It owed its importance to its position on trade routes between Constantinople and Syria, the Caucasus and central Asia. Byzantine textiles were exported through Trebizond to Arab lands and high-value spices and perfumes came into the empire along the same route.[54] On the southern coast of Anatolia the most important town was Attaleia, the outlet for the produce of a very fertile region. It was a major naval base and a stopping-place for merchants and travellers on the route from the Aegean to Cyprus and Syria. The revenues which the state obtained from the *kommerkion*, the tax on commercial transactions, was considerable at Attaleia and Trebizond. A tenth-century Arab writer states that 300 pounds of gold were exacted at Attaleia and 1,000 pounds of gold at Trebizond. There is of course no way of checking the accuracy of these figures, but the high revenues from both towns can be explained by their situation as places of entry for high-value luxury items from the Arab world.[55] Even in these cases the importance of trade in the total volume of revenues from the region should not be exaggerated. In the later period the empire of Trebizond was still deriving the largest part of its revenues from agriculture.[56] In the twelfth century the prosperity of Attaleia may have been partly undermined by the town's isolation following the Turkish occupation of the interior of Anatolia. During the second crusade the inhabitants of the town were unable to exploit its agricultural hinterland and grain had to be imported. Traders did continue to call at the port, but unstable political conditions did make this a more precarious activity and it is likely that the town's commercial life did suffer.[57]

In contrast to Anatolia some major urban centres in the Balkan provinces experienced a sustained economic expansion. The intensification of agricultural production gave a greater importance to many coastal towns, which served as outlets for the produce of their region, and in some towns of south and central Greece industrial production was not confined to meeting the needs of the immediate region, but

[53] *DAI*, p. 286; Vryonis, *The Decline of Medieval Hellenism*, pp. 14–17.
[54] Vryonis, *The Decline of Medieval Hellenism*, pp. 15–16.
[55] *Ibid.*, pp. 13–14. The figures are discussed in Hendy, *Studies in the Byzantine Monetary Economy*, p. 174.
[56] Bryer, 'The Estates of the Empire of Trebizond', pp. 370–1.
[57] Vryonis, *The Decline of Medieval Hellenism*, pp. 151–2; Lilie, *Handel und Politik*, pp. 149–53.

214   *Economic expansion in the Byzantine empire*

extended to the production of prestigious luxury items. In the Peloponnesos the beginning of the urban recovery can be traced to the ninth century.[58] A distinct hierarchy of towns developed. In the tenth century forty places in the peninsula were considered as towns.[59] The most important economically was Corinth, followed by Sparta, both sites of notable industrial activity. At the next level of the hierarchy were towns like Patras, Methone, Argos and Nauplion, ports from which agricultural produce was exported and which were consequently functionally distinct from the villages of the interior. The minor towns of the peninsula might have offered some modest artisanal services for the surrounding countryside, but most were probably little more than fortified settlements, hardly distinct in economic terms from large villages.

The economic life of Corinth is relatively well known owing to the combination of literary and archaeological evidence.[60] As the town began to recover from the early medieval decline, there are signs of a commercial revival in the ninth and tenth centuries.[61] The peak of its economic prosperity came in the eleventh and twelfth centuries when the central part of the town, which has been excavated, was a commercial and industrial quarter. It is unlikely that many of the structures were domestic houses. The excavated area has revealed traces of four pottery workshops. One was adjacent to the church of St Paul, with which it possibly had some connection. The earliest of the kilns went out of use in the late eleventh century; the others were functioning in the twelfth century. The quantity of pottery which has been found indicates a substantial increase in production during these two centuries. Two glass factories, probably dating from the late eleventh century, were located within a short distance of each other in the *agora*.[62] One quarter in the centre of the town was probably connected with building supplies. An elaborate lime-kiln was found north of the market area, and near the kiln there were extensive traces

---

[58] Zakythinos, *Le Despotat grec de Morée*, pp. 160–3.

[59] *Constantino Porfirogenito De Thematibus. Introduzione, testo critico, commento*, ed. A. Pertusi (Rome, 1952), p. 90.

[60] Scranton, *Corinth*, summarises the archaeological evidence. The literature is reviewed by J. H. Finlay, 'Corinth in the Middle Ages', *Speculum*, 7 (1932), pp. 477–99. He places the peak of the town's prosperity in the tenth century, which is earlier than the archaeological evidence suggests. For its trading contacts with Italy, see Lilie, *Handel und Politik*, pp. 195–8.

[61] Metcalf, 'Corinth in the Ninth Century: The Numismatic Evidence', pp. 203–12.

[62] Scranton, *Corinth*, pp. 67–8; C. H. Morgan, *Corinth*, XI, *The Byzantine Pottery* (Harvard, 1942), pp. 7, 12–21 and appendix 1; G. R. Davidson, 'A Medieval Glass Factory at Corinth', *American Journal of Archaeology*, 40 (1944), pp. 297–324.

Interaction between town and country 215

of settling basins in which lime was slaked.[63] There is also evidence of metal-working. A complex of apartments contained scoriae of iron and bronze, fragments of small crucibles, parts of moulds for casting metal objects and partly finished pieces of bronze. The structure clearly contained a metal-working factory.[64] Corinth, like Thebes, was best known for the quality of its silks. An inscription of a Jewish dyer in the town has survived, and textile workers were among the craftsmen who were carried off to Sicily in 1147.[65] Some shops in the commercial quarter in the centre of the town were established by the proprietors of industrial workshops as retail showrooms. A row of shops was connected to the glass and pottery factories. Others had only their shop space and there is no indication of any links with a factory or any other precise function. Others had considerable storage space and were probably general retail establishments selling food and other basic necessities. Some shops on the north side of the market place may have been larger wholesale establishments. A large twelth-century hoard of gold coins buried in front of the street suggests a more substantial accumulation than a small retailer might have managed to acquire. To the south a large structure contained a wine-press and two others were found nearby. The building was obviously geared to a strong urban demand for wine. In some shops large jars were kept below the floor level and could have been used for the storage of oil, wine and cereals.[66] The increasingly diversified economic structure of the town in the eleventh and twelfth centuries was reflected in the large number of retail establishments catering for an increased demand for agricultural produce. Another aspect of economic growth at Corinth was the revival of its harbour facilities. Niketas Choniates described Corinth as a wealthy town with two harbours. In one boats from Asia anchored, in the other boats from Italy. The trading place was nearby.[67] Although this may sound derivative from classical sources,[68] it fits in with other evidence. The archaeological results suggest that the port was hardly

---

[63] Scranton, *Corinth*, pp. 80–1.

[64] H. S. Robinson and S. S. Weinberg, 'Excavations at Corinth, 1959', *Hesperia*, 29 (1960), pp. 227–30.

[65] J. Starr, 'The Epitaph of a Dyer in Corinth', *Byzantinisch-Neugriechische Jahrbücher*, 12 (1935–6), pp. 42–9; J. Starr, *The Jews in the Byzantine Empire 641–1204* (Athens, 1939), pp. 28–9. In the second half of the twelfth century the town had a Jewish population of about 300; see Benjamin of Tudela, p. 47. For the sack of Corinth by Roger of Sicily, see Nicetas Choniates, pp. 74–6. See also Bon, *Le Péloponnèse byzantin*, pp. 87, 128–31.

[66] Scranton, *Corinth*, pp. 60, 73–5, 123–5.   [67] Nicetas Choniates, pp. 74–5.

[68] As suggested by Hohlfelder, *Kenchreiai. Eastern Port of Corinth*, III, p. 5 n. 18.

216　　　*Economic expansion in the Byzantine empire*

used from the seventh to the ninth century. Only a few pieces of pottery and a few coins have been dated to this period. In this case the archaeological evidence is not decisive, but it would not be surprising if the port had fallen into disuse owing to the decline of Corinth at the same time. The pottery and the coins both became more frequent from the tenth century.[69] Commercial activity at Corinth and its harbours was greatly stimulated by the Venetians. It was the commercial centre in Greece which they most regularly frequented. Their presence is attested from 1088 and their major exports were silk and oil.[70]

Commercial activity at Sparta is not so well documented, but coin finds suggest that the period from the late ninth to the twelfth century was one of increasing economic prosperity. Occupation became quite extensive at this time. By the twelfth century expansion outside the walls had occurred on the southern side, where houses and a bath have been excavated.[71] The main literary source for the tenth century is the life of St Nikon. When an epidemic was raging, a delegation from the town asked for his intercession. He insisted that the town would be spared only if its Jewish population was expelled. The Jews played an important part in textile manufacture and there was some opposition to the saint's instructions. One resident smuggled a Jew, whom he employed in finishing the textiles, back into the town. The text gives no indication of the organisation of the work, whether it was in a workshop or in a putting-out system. Nor is there any information about the quantity or quality of articles produced, whether they merely satisfied the local demand or were sold further afield. All that can be concluded with any certainty is that Jews were involved in the textile industry in the tenth century.[72] The life also shows how the *archontes*, who were made up from the most notable landowning families in the

[69] The coins have not been found in large quantities, but they do conform to the usual pattern; see Hohlfelder, *Kenchreiai. Eastern Port of Corinth*, III, pp. 4–5, 74–7, 92. The dating of the pottery was done through comparison because there were no building remains or deposits with which to associate the pottery; see B. Adamsheck, *Kenchreiai. Eastern Port of Corinth*, IV, *The Pottery* (Leiden, 1979), pp. 82, 100. See also the review by K. S. Wright, *American Journal of Archaeology*, 84 (1980), pp. 547–9.

[70] Thiriet, *La Romanie vénitienne*, pp. 44, 47–8.

[71] Woodward, 'Excavations at Sparta, 1924–5', p. 157; Bouras, 'City and Village: Urban Design and Architecture', p. 622; J. M. Cook and J. V. Nicholls, 'Laconia', *Annual of the British School at Athens*, 45 (1950), p. 284.

[72] 'Nikon Metanoeite', pp. 162–3, 165–6; Starr, *The Jews in the Byzantine Empire*, pp. 28, 167–8. The assertion of S. Runciman, *Byzantine Civilisation* (London, 1933), p. 172, that Sparta was exporting carpets to Italy by the tenth century is unproven. For an isolated example of the presence of Italian traders in Sparta, see 'Nikon Metanoeite', p. 215. The text gives no hint of the merchandise which they were trading, but it is possible that silk was involved. For silk-workers in the Peloponnesos in the early tenth century, see *DAI*, p. 256.

Interaction between town and country 217

town, exercised a great deal of influence over events in the town. They were responsible for the invitation to Nikon, and their assistance was essential for him to build his church in the town.[73] In the twelfth century Sparta, like Corinth, was frequented regularly by Venetian merchants and oil was its principal export.[74]

Expansion in the rural economy contributed directly to the increasing importance of the ports in the peninsula, from which the produce of the region was exported. The list of ports in the chrysobull issued to the Venetians in 1198 included Patras, Methone, Argos and Nauplion. They also visited Korone frequently.[75] Patras was a fairly substantial town. Its *kastron* was separate from the fortified settlement, which probably extended as far as the harbour. The main exports from Patras were primary produce such as wine, wheat and oil. Its commercial role was linked to the agricultural exploitation of its hinterland and it was not economically a very developed town.[76] Generally the archaeological evidence for these ports is slight and uninformative, but Monembasia is an exception. In the early medieval period the settlement was probably confined to the *kastron*, but by the eleventh century it had expanded to include the narrow strip of land on the southern side, and this area later became very densely populated. Its location might have led a larger proportion of its inhabitants to take up seafaring than at other ports in the peninsula whose commerce was directly related to the prosperity of the agriculture of their immediate hinterland. However, there is no significant evidence of any extensive trading activity by the town's inhabitants until the second half of the thirteenth century. In 1284 Andronikos II confirmed a privilege previously conceded to them by Michael VIII exempting them from the *kommerkion* on all transactions which took place in the town. A subsequent chrysobull, whose authenticity is questionable, refers to their trading activity in Constantinople and the towns of Macedonia and Thrace. Whatever the doubts about its authenticity, it is unlikely that it gives a totally false impression of the commercial activity of the townspeople, whose maritime skills were used by the state in its naval campaigns. The town was also frequented by western merchants from the thirteenth century.[77]

---

[73] Angold, 'The Shaping of the Medieval Byzantine "City"', p. 17.
[74] Thiriet, *La Romanie vénitienne*, pp. 44, 47–8.
[75] Bon, *Le Péloponnèse byzantin*, pp. 83–4.
[76] Bouras, 'City and Village: Urban Design and Architecture', pp. 619–20; Saranti-Mendelovici, 'À propos de la ville de Patras aux 13e–15e siècles', pp. 219–32.
[77] Bouras, 'City and Village: Urban Design and Architecture', p. 620; MM, V, pp. 154–5, 165–8. On the doubts about the authenticity of the chrysobull of 1316, see F. Dölger, *Regesten der Kaiserurkunden des Oströmischen Reiches von 565–1453* (5 vols.,

218   *Economic expansion in the Byzantine empire*

Elsewhere in Greece the most important towns showed signs of economic expansion. Athens became more densely populated in the eleventh and twelfth centuries and a new wall was built in the eleventh century to protect the settlements closest to the *akropolis*.[78] Information about its economic life is limited because the excavated area was mainly a residential quarter in the Middle Ages. It has been suggested on the basis of numismatic evidence that there was some commercial activity there. The coin finds certainly indicate a steady increase in commerce from the tenth century.[79] It is likely that commercial quarters were situated outside the excavated area, but it is doubtful that there was as much commodity production as at Corinth. The town expanded over a wide area. A recently published *praktikon* refers to three quarters inside the walls. The most interesting information concerns the quarter Kogchylarion to the south of the *akropolis*. The name suggests an area in which purple dye was produced. Additional evidence is provided by an inscription of 1061 which refers to a *kogchylarios*.[80] At a distance from the centre of the town, settlements were based on soap production and tanneries – occupations which needed a plentiful water-supply.[81] Production was mainly for local needs and although the town is listed in Alexios's chrysobull for the Venetians, no evidence survives of individual Venetian traders active in Athens.[82] Michael Choniates, probably exaggerating Athens's decline at the end of the twelfth century, spoke in glowing terms of the trade which he claimed the town had enjoyed not long before.[83]

The most significant town in central Greece was Thebes. It owed its importance partly to its administrative functions as the capital of a theme and partly to its position as the focal point of a fertile and densely populated agricultural region. Unfortunately, archaeological evidence is fragmentary due to the lack of a systematic excavation, but enough

---

Munich, Berlin, 1924–65), IV, no. 2383. See also Zakythinos, *Le Despotat grec de Morée*, pp. 117–18, 174, 249; and, for the lack of twelfth-century evidence, Lilie, *Handel und Politik*, p. 202.

[78] Bouras, 'City and Village: Urban Design and Architecture', p. 626.

[79] D. M. Metcalf, 'Bronze Coinage and City Life in Central Greece AD 1000', *Annual of the British School at Athens*, 60 (1965), pp. 11–12; Thompson, *The Athenian Agora*, II, pp. 4–5; Setton, 'The Archaeology of Medieval Athens', pp. 227–58; H. A. Thompson, 'Activities in the Athenian Agora: 1956', *Hesperia*, 26 (1957), p. 101.

[80] E. Granstrem, I. Medvedev and D. Papachryssanthou, 'Fragment d'un praktikon de la région d'Athènes (avant 1204)', *Revue des Études Byzantines*, 34 (1976), pp. 25–8, 33–5, A2 lines 6–28. See also I. N. Travlos, *Poleodomike exelexis ton Athenon* (Athens, 1960), pp. 149–62.

[81] Bouras, 'City and Village: Urban Design and Architecture', p. 627.

[82] Thiriet, *La Romanie vénitienne*, p. 39.   [83] Michael Choniates, II, p. 99.

Interaction between town and country

material is available to make out a general impression. After the settlement had contracted to the Kadmeian hill in the early medieval period, it had become densely populated by the twelfth century. By this time there were major areas of settlement outside the walls on the surrounding hills such as Kastellia, Ampheion and Ismenion. The excavations have also uncovered a bath, an aqueduct and sections of two roads. Recently, the remains of seven churches inside and outside the Kadmeian hill have been uncovered to add to the four which were already known.[84] These indications are supported by literary evidence of the town's importance as an industrial centre. When Niketas Choniates wrote of the traditional wealth and fame of the town, it was not simply the rhetoric of the historian. In 1147 Roger of Sicily captured the town and carried off gold, silver, gold-lined cloth and some of the town's leading industrial craftsmen.[85] The sack of Thebes did not have any drastic long-term consequences. The town continued to thrive in the second half of the century. Later, in Manuel's reign, Benjamin of Tudela visited the town and found 2,000 Jews there, whom he described as the most renowned manufacturers of silk and purple cloth in Greece.[86] In the reign of Alexios III the town's high-quality silk cloths were used as diplomatic gifts. It was one of Michael Choniates's constant complaints that the Thebans were treated more leniently than the Athenians by tax-collectors although Athens was not as famous as Thebes or Corinth for the quality of its cloth manufactures.[87] Thebes was sufficiently important for the Venetians to frequent it in spite of its inland location.[88] Chalkis was the most convenient port for access to Thebes and was the main outlet for the produce of Boiotia. Its harbour facilities, which had both military and commercial functions, acquired a greater importance as the agricultural production of the region and the industrial production of Thebes intensified and it was one of the

[84] Bouras, 'City and Village: Urban Design and Architecture', pp. 624–5.
[85] Nicetas Choniates, p. 74; Starr, *The Jews in the Byzantine Empire*, pp. 29, 223.
[86] Benjamin of Tudela, p. 47. His figures are reasonably reliable. He was mainly interested in the Jewish communities of the places he visited and certainly obtained first-hand information. It is clear from his comments about other towns that Thebes had by far the largest Jewish population in Greece.
[87] Nicetas Choniates, p. 461; Michael Choniates, II, p. 83; J. Koder and F. Hild, *Tabula Imperii Byzantini*, I, *Hellas und Thessalia* (Vienna, 1976), pp. 65, 270. See also P. A. M. Leone (ed.), *Ioannes Tzetzae Epistulae* (Leipzig, 1972), no. 71. Four members of a religious confraternity in central Greece in the late eleventh or early twelfth centuries were called Blatas, a trade name implying that the family was engaged in the manufacture or sale of silk cloth; see Nesbitt and Witta, 'A Confraternity of the Comnenian Era', p. 366 line 109, p. 367 lines 126, 136, p. 368 line 165, pp. 377–8.
[88] Lilie, *Handel und Politik*, pp. 210–13.

220   Economic expansion in the Byzantine empire

ports listed in the Venetians' privileges.[89] The archaeological evidence reveals, by the twelfth century, the usual pattern of a densely packed settlement with narrow streets and the reuse of earlier materials.[90]

Elsewhere in Greece the archaeological evidence is fragmentary, even for the most important towns, and greater reliance has to be placed on isolated literary evidence to demonstrate the economic revival of this period. By about 900 Thessalonike had become a much more densely populated town. The Arab Harun-Ibn-Yahya described it as a 'huge and large city'.[91] Kameniates gives a more complete picture of the town at this time. Its well-protected harbour made the town very accessible to the large numbers of trading ships which anchored there. Thessalonike had become a town which drew its food supplies from a very extensive and densely populated hinterland. The town also had trading contacts with the Slavonic tribes of the interior, some of which had not yet been subjugated by the Byzantines.[92] In the reign of Leo VI the trade with the Bulgars was briefly transferred from Constantinople to Thessalonike.[93] The upsurge in building activity in the town from the eleventh century is an indication of economic growth.[94] The evidence of industrial activity is modest owing to the deficiency of the source material. In 1097 the witnesses of an act of sale included three laymen. Two were furriers and the other was the head of the guild *ton*

---

[89] Koder and Hild, *Tabula Imperii Byzantini*, I, pp. 156–7; J. Koder, *Negroponte. Untersuchungen zur Topographie und Siedlungsgeschichte der Insel Euboia während der Zeit der Venezianerherrschaft* (Vienna, 1973), pp. 43–4. The town became vitally important to the Venetians in the thirteenth and fourteenth centuries; see Thiriet, *La Romanie vénitienne*, pp. 93–4, 337–41; and G. Morgan, 'The Venetian Claims Commission of 1278', *Byzantinische Zeitschrift*, 69 (1976), pp. 411–38.

[90] Bouras, 'City and Village: Urban Design and Architecture', p. 628.

[91] A. Vasiliev, 'Harun-Ibn-Yahya and his Description of Constantinople', *Seminarium Kondakovianum*, 5 (1932), p. 162.

[92] *Ioannis Caminiatae De Expugnatione Thessalonicae*, ed. G. Böhlig (Corpus Fontium Historiae Byzantinae IV) (Berlin, 1973), pp. 5–8. This account has been called into question by Kazhdan, who argues that its author was inspired by the town's difficult situation in the fifteenth century and that this evidence is of little applicability to the tenth century; see A. P. Kazhdan, 'Some Questions Addressed to Scholars Who Believe in the Authenticity of Kameniates' "Capture of Thessalonica"', *Byzantinische Zeitschrift*, 71 (1978), pp. 301–14. This view has in turn been persuasively challenged by Christides, who regards the text as a fifteenth-century reworking of an earlier record which retains its usefulness for tenth-century history; see V. Christides, 'Once again Caminiates' "Capture of Thessaloniki"', *Byzantinische Zeitschrift*, 74 (1981), pp. 7–10.

[93] The harsh exaction of the *kommerkion* was the reason for the outbreak of hostilities between the two states; see Theophanes Continuatus, p. 853.

[94] R. Krautheimer, *Early Christian and Byzantine Arhitecture* (Harmondsworth, 1965), p. 270.

Interaction between town and country

kamalaukadon, possibly makers of hoods and caps. These activities were probably carried on in the quarter of the church of Asomatoi, where the sellers owned property.[95] In later centuries associations of salt-makers, perfumers, sailors and construction workers existed in the town.[96] In the twelfth century the town contained 500 Jews, most of whom obtained their living from artisanal activities.[97] The fair of St Demetrios was a trading event which, according to a twelfth-century writer, attracted merchants from well beyond the frontiers of the empire, yet the town was not frequented by western merchants as often as Corinth, Sparta, Thebes or Constantinople.[98] There were still gardens inside the walls of the town and in the fourteenth century the main exports from Thessalonike to Venice were agricultural products; so perhaps the town's main commercial function was as an outlet for the primary produce of a large and fertile region.[99]

In Thessaly there was an interesting contrast between Larissa and the ports of Demetrias and Halmyros. In the sources Larissa is referred to as a *kastron* and a *polis*. It was an administrative centre and a fortified town of some strategic importance, but owing to inadequate evidence nothing is known of the vitality of its commerce. It was best known for the agricultural wealth of its region and its residents were able to live comfortably off the land. If Kekaumenos was right, the townsmen produced a large surplus, which enabled them to resist Bulgar attacks for a few years. During the revolt of Nikoulitzas Delphinas in the 1060s the inhabitants were still working in agriculture in large numbers. One of Delphinas's arguments in his unsuccessful attempt to dissuade them from putting him at the head of the revolt was that it was already June and such unstable conditions would have made it impossible to collect the harvest.[100] However, many of these townsmen might have

---

[95] *Lavra*, I, no. 53 lines 33–40.

[96] N. Oikonomides, *Hommes d'affaires grecs et latins à Constantinople (XIIIᵉ–XVᵉ siècles)* (Paris, Montreal, 1979), pp. 111–12.   [97] Benjamin of Tudela, pp. 49–50.

[98] *Timarione*, pp. 53–5. See the recent assessment of this source by Alexiou, 'Literary Subversion and the Aristocracy in Twelfth Century Byzantium'. For the activities of western merchants, see Lilie, *Handel und Politik*, pp. 213–16.

[99] O. Tafrali, *Topographie de Thessalonique* (Paris, 1913), p. 140. According to Palamas, a large number of the inhabitants in the fourteenth century were engaged in agriculture; see O. Tafrali, *Thessalonique au quatorzième siècle* (Paris, 1913), p. 29. For the town's exports, see Thiriet, *La Romanie vénitienne*, p. 340.

[100] Cecaumenos, *Strategicon*, pp. 65, 68. For the wealth of the region, see L. G. Westerink (ed.), *Nicétas Magistros. Lettres d'un exilé (928–946)* (Paris, 1973), p. 113. Edrisi describes Larissa as a large town surrounded by vineyards, fig trees and cultivated fields; see J.-A. Jaubert (trans.), *La Géographie d'Edrisi* (2 vols., Paris, 1836–40), II, p. 292. While this description fits in with the other evidence, it is also a stereotype which

222 *Economic expansion in the Byzantine empire*

worked in the fields only in peak seasons and have been craftsmen or traders at other times. Demetrias and Halmyros were noted for their commerce, which was very dependent on the productivity of the region. The fertility of Thessaly is reflected by occasional references to grain exports. In 667 Thessalonike, besieged by the Slavs, obtained grain from the Belegezitai tribe in the Pagasetikon gulf. In the late twelfth century Michael Choniates reminded the inhabitants of Constantinople that they benefited from the wheat production of Thessaly.[101] These examples are anecdotal, but they are supported by our information about commercial activity in the ports. Both Kameniates and Kekaumenos describe Demetrias as a densely populated town. In the latter's account of its sack by the Arabs the town's commercial function is apparent and later the Venetians traded there. Its excellent communications with the hinterland enabled produce to be brought to the market relatively easily.[102] In the case of Halmyros the evidence is more conclusive. In the twelfth century it was a thriving port, frequented by Venetians, Pisans and Genoese. Already in 1112 an emissary of the doge appeared in the town. The Venetians were not confined to a restricted colony in one quarter, but owned property in the whole town. The chrysobulls granted to the Venetians do not mention the town specifically until 1198, but several Venetian documents bear unequivocal testimony to the regularity of their commercial activities there. The earliest evidence of Pisan activity in Halmyros dates from 1108. By 1157 there was also a Genoese presence. In 1171–2 they helped to defend the town against the reprisals following the arrest of the Venetians in the empire. The attraction of the port for the western merchants was the wealth of agricultural produce, which they purchased in order to resell at Constantinople and elsewhere.[103]

The evidence of economic expansion is greater for the towns of Greece

Edrisi often uses, which raises doubts about the quality of his information. See also Koder and Hild, *Tabula Imperii Byzantini*, I, p. 198–9; and Avramea, *He Byzantine Thessalia*, pp. 124–32.

[101] Lemerle, *Les plus anciens recueils*, I, p. 214 lines 9–19, p. 218 lines 1–3; Michael Choniates, II, p. 83.

[102] *Ioannis Caminiatae De Expugnatione Thessalonicae*, ed. G. Böhlig (Corpus Fontium Historiae Byzantinae IV) (Berlin, 1973), p. 15; Cecaumenos, *Strategicon*, pp. 33–4; Avramea, *He Byzantine Thessalia*, pp. 136–41.

[103] Avramea, *He Byzantine Thessalia*, pp. 166–73; Lilie, *Handel und Politik*, pp. 184, 187–90; Thiriet, *La Romanie vénitienne*, pp. 44–5, 52 n. 4; P. Schreiner, 'Untersuchungen zu den Niederlassungen westlicher Kaufleute im byzantinischen Reich des 11. und 12. Jahrhunderts', *Byzantinische Forschungen*, 7 (1979), pp. 178–9. For the thirteenth century, see Morgan, 'The Venetian Claims Commission of 1278', pp. 427–32.

Interaction between town and country 223

than for those in Asia Minor. This has already been linked with the more sustained increase in agricultural productivity in the European provinces in the eleventh and twelfth centuries. However, the economic stimulus given by the requirements of wealthy landowners, the ecclesiastical hierarchy, and in the larger towns by state officials, was supplemented by the demands of Italian merchants. Owing to the expansion of the towns of north Italy at this time, they frequented the markets of Byzantium to purchase agricultural produce and textiles. Although Alexios's chrysobull names ports in Asia Minor as well as Europe, their trade with the European provinces was on a larger scale. Constantinople apart, Corinth was the market to which the Venetians resorted most frequently. In the Venetian documents Thebes, Sparta, Halmyros and Dyrrachion are also mentioned with great regularity. After 1150 they began to extend the range of their activity and visited Asia Minor, Crete and Cyprus more often, but even then the ports of Greece were still used more frequently. In 1135 Dobramiro Stagnario exported large cargoes of oil from Sparta to Alexandria and from Corinth to Venice. The most active Venetian merchant, Romano Mairano, was trading at Sparta and Halmyros in 1153–4; after he had established himself at Constantinople in 1155 his activities were extended to Asia Minor and as far as Alexandria. As the value of their commerce increased, Venetian merchants became resident in Greek towns, where they were able to keep a close check on Venetian interests and act as intermediaries for wealthier merchants with more extensive interests.[104] In the later twelfth century Genoese trade with Byzantium increased greatly. They profited from the expulsion of the Venetians, but Manuel did not grant them privileges as extensive as those enjoyed by the Venetians.[105] The concessions to the Venetians and later the Pisans and Genoese have often been represented as an unmitigated economic disaster for Byzantium.[106] The stimulus given to economic activity by the Italians has been ignored. The Venetian export of textiles must have encouraged production in Constantinople, Corinth and Thebes. They

---

[104] Thiriet, *La Romanie vénitienne*, pp. 43–9. The first Italian town to establish a permanent colony in Constantinople was Amalfi, which also had interests in Dyrrachion, Halmyros and Antioch, but during the period of its preeminence the trade between Italy and Byzantium was not as large as in the twelfth century. For the development of Amalfitan commercial relations with Byzantium, see M. Balard, 'Amalfi et Byzance (X^e–XIIe siècles)', *Travaux et Mémoires*, 6 (1976), pp. 85–95.

[105] G. W. Day, 'Manuel and the Genoese: A Reappraisal of Byzantine Commercial Policy in the Late Twelfth Century', *Journal of Economic History*, 37 (1977), pp. 289–301.

[106] Vryonis, *The Decline of Medieval Hellenism*, pp. 79–80; Mango, *Byzantium. Empire of New Rome*, p. 58; Lemerle, *Cinq études*, pp. 305–7.

224 Economic expansion in the Byzantine empire

also wanted primary produce, and this increase in demand coincided with the intensification of agricultural production in Byzantium. The landowners who profited from the Venetian trade had greater resources for their own expenditure on commodities, which might have stimulated a greater amount of artisanal specialisation.[107] However, the reaction against the traditional negative view of the role of the Italian merchants should not be taken to the other extreme. This trade remained a relatively minor element in the context of the economy as a whole, which continued to be dominated by landed wealth.[108]

Elsewhere the momentum behind economic growth was provided by the state's military considerations or by the initiatives of aristocratic landowners. Military considerations were dominant in border provinces. When the lower Danube region was incorporated into the theme of Paristrion following Tzimiskes's victory at Silistra in 971 and the stabilisation of Byzantine rule after 1000, many late Roman fortifications were repaired or rebuilt. In spite of attacks economic activity increased in the eleventh century and appears to have reached a peak in the reign of Alexios. The excavations at Dinogetia and Pacuiul lui Soare have revealed large numbers of coins of all denominations, large quantities of pottery, and metal ornaments. Some of the property was of local provenance and some imported from Constantinople or the coast of the Black Sea. At Pacuiul lui Soare evidence of naval construction has been found, not surprisingly in view of the island's strategic position. Metal ornaments were made locally. Excavation finds include reject buckles, pearls, and bracelets of copper and bronze. The site was abandoned in 1094 after a Kouman attack, but on other sites,

---

[107] E. Frances, 'Alexis Comnène et les privilèges octroyés à Venise', *ByzantinoSlavica*, 29 (1968), pp. 17–23. It has been suggested that the purpose of Alexios's chrysobull of 1082 for the Venetians was to draw the luxury trade in spices and oriental goods back to Byzantium; see A. R. Gadolin, 'Alexius I Comnenus and the Venetian Trade Privileges. A New Interpretation', *Byzantion*, 50 (1980), pp. 439–46. The article exaggerates the importance of the luxury trade in relation to that in agricultural produce and ignores the emphasis on trade in produce from Greece. The state had nothing to gain from the redirection of this trade because it had already exempted the Venetians from paying the *kommerkion*. The date of the chrysobull has been disputed, but it was clearly issued in 1082; see Lilie, *Handel und Politik*, p. 8 n. 19. Kazhdan and Constable, *People and Power*, p. 42 have attempted to explain the establishment of Italian commercial interests in terms of social psychology; the Byzantines' 'fear of the sea' is proposed as a reason for their eventual loss of control of the maritime trade. But the situation they describe was common to seafarers in the Mediterranean as late as the sixteenth century; see Braudel, *The Mediterranean*, I, pp. 103–8. The rise of Italian maritime activity has instead to be explained in terms of the interests and needs of the Italian cities.

[108] Hendy, *Studies in the Byzantine Monetary Economy*, pp. 590–602.

Interaction between town and country

225

such as Dinogetia and Isaccea, there was continuity in the twelfth century. At Dinogetia there were two areas of habitation – the fortification and the suburb. The higher part was the most intensively inhabited. It contained the most powerful figures in the town – imperial and ecclesiastical representatives – and also merchants. The most valuable treasures – gold, silver and precious jewels – were found there. The lower zone had artisanal workshops with less valuable contents.[109]

Elsewhere urban expansion resulted from the development of feudal social relations. Most towns were effectively under the control of their leading *archontes*, who came from prominent local landowning families connected to the state's administrative system. Their power rested on their landed wealth and their grip on the offices of the provincial administration. It was a largely informal network which exercised authority over towns and from time to time threw up a local 'strong man' during periods of imperial weakness in the eleventh and twelfth centuries.[110] New settlements were established by the initiatives of Pakourianos and Isaac Komnenos, a reflection of the growing economic power and independence of the feudal aristocracy. The creation of new villages by Pakourianos has already been discussed.[111] The intensification of agricultural production was accompanied by the development of towns and an increase in trade. Pakourianos was entitled to the revenues from some commercial fairs. Stenimachos, where he built two *kastra*, acquired some urban characteristics and Bačkovo derived revenues from its fair which was held outside the monastery at Easter when the monks received their *rogai*. As these amounted to 761 *nomismata*, the fair was likely to have attracted merchants from considerable distances.[112] One of the motives behind the construction of *kastra* was, of course, defence and some *kastra* remained no more than fortifications, but other considerations should not be ignored. They might also have been intended as administrative centres for the

---

[109] Condurachi, Barnea and Diaconu, 'Nouvelles recherches sur le "limes" byzantin du Bas-Danube aux Xe–XIe siècles'; N. Oikonomides, 'Recherches sur l'histoire du Bas-Danube aux Xe–XIe siècles: la Mésopotamie de l'Occident', *Revue des Études Sud-Est Européennes*, 3 (1965), pp. 57–79; Diaconu, 'Pacuiul lui Soare–Vicina', pp. 419–24; Barnea, 'Dinogetia', pp. 259–71.

[110] M. Angold, 'Archons and Dynasts: Local Aristocracies and the Cities of the Later Byzantine Empire', in Angold, *The Byzantine Aristocracy*, pp. 236–53.

[111] See above, p. 65.

[112] Gautier, 'Grégoire Pakourianos', p. 35 lines 272–3, p. 69 lines 840–5, p. 131 line 1842; Asdracha, *La Région des Rhodopes*, pp. 162–6, 221; Lemerle, *Cinq études*, p. 190.

226   Economic expansion in the Byzantine empire

supervision of Pakourianos's properties and the control of his *paroikoi*.[11]
The impact which the foundation of a monastery by a powerful
landowner could have on urban development is also illustrated by the
example of Kosmosotira. Bera, further inland along the Hebros from
Ainos, began to be populated only after Kosmosotira's foundation. Isaac
Komnenos referred to the monastery indiscriminately as an *asty* (town)
and a *kastron*. It had legal rights to the proceeds of the fairs which were
held several times a year at one of its neighbouring properties,
Neokastron. By the end of the twelfth century Bera was the focal point
of a group of settlements in the area.[114]

As towns expanded, the revenues which landowners and the state
received from urban rents must have increased. The importance of
these revenues cannot be estimated easily, but they were probably very
slight in comparison with the revenues from agriculture. Constantinople
was obviously a special case. The Venetians received *ergasteria*
(workshops) in the city from Alexios I and all the Amalfitans who
owned workshops in Constantinople had to pay a tax to the church of
St Mark in Venice.[115] Benjamin of Tudela estimated the tribute of the
city at 20,000 pounds of gold a day from rents and the *kommerkion*.[116]
Although the figure is obviously exaggerated, it reflects the impressive
extent of the Constantinopolitan trading quarters to a casual observer.
Owing to the sparse evidence extra value must be attached to the unique
information about five tenth-century establishments. The rents and tax-
payments of these *ergasteria* were recorded with the names of the
current and previous owners. The text, which was compiled in 959 or
soon afterwards, has the same form as a fiscal cadaster. In four of the
five cases the fiscal revenue had been conceded to religious establishments. The owners of these workshops were mostly officials or
titleholders. Only one of the nine current or previous owners was a
trader.[117] The general pattern is of rentiers leasing their properties to

---

[113] This consideration was often the major factor behind the process of *incastellamento* in
Italy; see C. J. Wickham, 'Historical and Topographical Notes on Early Medieval
South Etruria: Part II', *Papers of the British School at Rome*, 47 (1979), pp. 87–8; and
C. J. Wickham, *Early Medieval Italy. Central Power and Local Society 400–1000*
(London, 1981), pp. 163–7, 174. However, for late eleventh-century Bulgaria it is not
possible to exclude defence considerations altogether.

[114] Petit, 'Kosmosotira', pp. 19, 52 lines 13–14; Asdracha, *Le Région des Rhodopes*, pp.
124–30. For the growth of urban settlements around monasteries and the castles of
the feudal nobility in the west, see Duby, *The Early Growth of the European Economy*,
pp. 235–6.

[115] Anna Comnène, *Alexiade*, II, p. 54; Tafel and Thomas, *Urkunden*, I, p. 52.

[116] Benjamin of Tudela, pp. 53–4.

[117] N. Oikonomides, 'Quelques boutiques de Constantinople au Xᵉ siècle: prix, loyers,
imposition (Cod. Patmiacus 171)', *Dumbarton Oaks Papers*, 26 (1972), pp. 345–56.

Interaction between town and country

urban craftsmen or traders. The modest position of traders and craftsmen in the economic structure of Byzantium compared to wealthy landowners is apparent. These properties were categorised as *autourgia* because their owners had to make no outlays in cash or labour to secure their revenues.[118] The workshops and rents from private houses provided landowners with a useful supplement to the revenues which they exacted from their estates. Attaleiates's property in Constantinople included a bakery and a perfume factory, which were leased out for twenty-four and fourteen *nomismata* respectively, buildings which were leased to a doctor for five *nomismata* and a house for which he received thirty-six *nomismata* in rent. He also had properties at Raidestos and Selymbria. Although he had received no large patrimonial lands and had built up his wealth in imperial service in the capital, the most important part of his property nevertheless consisted of the estates in Thrace.[119] In the late thirteenth century Goudeles Tyrannos received an annual rent of 200 *hyperpyra* for four workshops selling cloth and a tower containing a bakery and another workshop, but as the revenues from his estates are not known it is impossible to calculate the proportion of his income which was derived from urban properties.[120] Whatever variations there might have been in individual instances, in general terms the great bulk of landowners' revenues continued to be extracted from the rural economy.

The estates of large landowners were concentrated in certain regions where they also had urban properties. Often they possessed rights to the revenues from markets and harbours. These properties formed a complex with an intimate link between rural estates and urban centres. Such a group of properties was much easier to administer. In 1216 Basil Gabalas sold a number of fields at Phygella. He found it difficult to collect the revenues from them because they were too far from his residence in Ephesos to be supervised properly. He intended to purchase properties near the town instead.[121] A concentration of properties around a town also enabled the landowner to exploit the increasing urban demand for agricultural produce. Large landowners were clearly in the best position to take advantage of short-term economic fluctuations. They had greater flexibility in disposing of surplus produce than the peasant, whose main concerns were subsistence and meeting his fiscal obligations, and they were able to sell at the most favourable

---

[118] Cecaumenos, *Strategicon*, p. 36 lines 13–16.
[119] Gautier, 'La diataxis de Michel Attaliate', pp. 43–7, 99–101; Lemerle, *Cinq études*, pp. 109–11.
[120] Angold, 'Archons and Dynasts', p. 239.   [121] MM, VI, pp. 174–5.

228   *Economic expansion in the Byzantine empire*

time of the year. They were often based in the most important towns of their region. The richer landowners of Attika lived in the *kastron* of Athens. Some of the landowners in the Theban tax-register were residents of Thebes and Chalkis.[122] Their commercial dealings were probably restricted to these local markets. The most powerful landowners, who had maritime privileges, were able to transport their produce to the more lucrative markets and obtain larger revenues from the produce of their estates.

There were extensive monastic properties around Thessalonike. The most important monasteries, like Lavra, Iviron and the Pantokrator, had *metochia* in the town which presumably functioned as administrative centres supervising the exploitation of these estates. Thessalonike offered a convenient outlet for produce to be shipped to the monasteries and there was a substantial urban market if the monks chose to sell large quantities of surplus produce. Most of Lavra's lands near Thessalonike were derived from its *metochion*, St Andrew, at Peristerai, thirty kilometres east of the town. Later Lavra transferred the administrative functions of the *metochion* to Thessalonike, presumably for convenience in administering its properties, and Peristerai became simply another of Lavra's estates.[123] When Iviron was founded it received the monastery of Prodromos in Thessalonike as a *metochion*. This monastery had already received privileges in 945–6 and by 1079 the *metochion* was the focal point of a large complex of properties in and around Thessalonike, including other monasteries, buildings in the town, vineyards and a large extent of land.[124] The Pantokrator acquired a complex of properties around Thessalonike. Its agricultural land consisted of an *episkepsis* and the estate of Hagia Galaktere. It also had the rights to a stream which flowed into the town and activated watermills in Thessalonike. Its urban properties consisted of a plot of land

---

[122] Svoronos, 'Recherches sur le cadastre byzantin', pp. 11–16 lines A1, 38, 73, 77, B19, 31. Some previous landowners were described as Athenians or from Chalkis (pp. 11–14 lines A43, 54, 64, 71). See also J. E. Herrin, 'The Social and Economic Structure of Central Greece in the Late Twelfth Century' (unpublished Ph.D. thesis, Birmingham University, 1972), pp. 114, 228.

[123] *Lavra*, I, nos. 1, 33 and pp. 58–9.

[124] Dölger, 'Ein Fall', pp. 6–7 lines 3–7; Dölger, *Schatzkammern*, no. 35 lines 77–8. Among Iviron's other properties in the area was an *agridion* at Pinsson; see Dölger, *Schatzkammern*, no. 35 lines 76–7. The monastery of Prodromos is probably to be identified with the monastery *tou Leontiou* in Basil II's chrysobull of 979–80; see Dölger, 'Ein Fall', p. 7 line 14; and G. I. Theocharides, 'Mia exasphanistheisa megale mone tes Thessalonikes, he mone tou Prodromou', *Makedonika*, 28 (1978), pp. 1–26. For the properties of Xenophon in Thessalonike and the theme of Kalamaria, see *Xénophon*, no. 1 lines 222–4.

Interaction between town and country

with a house inside the *kastron* and a poor-house with two baths, rented properties and other unspecified property rights.[125]

There are scattered pieces of information about less substantial secular landowners who lived in Thessalonike and possessed land near the town. The three brothers whose properties were partitioned in 1110 had two *aulai* (courtyards), one in the quarter of Asomatoi, the other in the quarter at Kataphyge. They also owned a workshop which they leased for an annual payment. Their rural properties consisted of water-mills, arable fields and vineyards, mostly to the immediate south-east of the town. A much smaller property was the subject of an act of sale in 1097. A brother and sister living in the district of Asomatoi owned two tiny plots of land, a vineyard of about three *modioi*, and two *modioi* of uncultivated land with only a few fruit trees. The land was situated on the road which led to Thessalonike from the south-east. The purchaser already had land bordering these plots. They were also adjacent to the land of the sellers' cousin, Nicolas Stribos, a *klerikos*, and the land of a *geitonarchon* (the head of a neighbourhood). The latter certainly lived in Thessalonike, as did the sellers and possibly Stribos. Some of the inhabitants of the town were deriving at least part of their income from land in the immediate vicinity of the town.[126]

Most Athonite monasteries acquired property in Hierissos. The most important town in the vicinity of the mountain, it was a fortified site and the centre of a small administrative subdivision.[127] It also had some importance in the ecclesiastical hierarchy and a bishopric was established there sometime between 942 and 982.[128] Information about commercial and industrial activity in the town is completely inadequate. A few peasants installed on Lavra's lands around the town in the tenth century had names which suggest basic artisanal or commercial

---

[125] Gautier, 'Pantocrator', p. 121 lines 1532–41. In 1149 the monastery's properties around Thessalonike were administered by John Smeniotes; see *ibid.*, p. 63 n. 10.

[126] *Lavra*, I, nos. 53, 59.

[127] For fiscal purposes Hierissos was the focal point of an *enoria* in the *dioikesis* of Thessalonike and Serres in 1079; see *Lavra*, I, no. 39 line 5. For the *dioikesis*, see Dölger, *Beiträge*, p. 70; and Svoronos, 'Recherches sur le cadastre byzantin', pp. 55–7. In 942–3 the land dispute between the monks of Athos and the inhabitants of the *kastron* revolved around the technical meaning of the term *enoria*; see *Prôtaton*, no. 5 lines 18–30. The term *kastron* could also be used for an administrative subdivision; see Dölger, *Schatzkammern*, no. 56 lines 4–9; *Prôtaton*, no. 5 line 1; and *Lavra*, I, no. 39 lines 4–6. In a patriarchal act Lavra's *metochion*, Gomatou, is described as in the *kastron* of Hierissos; see *Lavra*, I, no. 8 lines 8–10.

[128] M. Zivojinovic, 'Sur l'époque de la formation de l'évêché d'Hiérissos', *Zbornik Radova Vizantološkog Instituta*, 14–15 (1973), p. 158; D. Papachryssanthou, 'Un évêché byzantin: Hiérissos en Chalcidique', *Travaux et Mémoires*, 8 (1981), p. 374.

230   *Economic expansion in the Byzantine empire*

activity (builder, smith, butcher and sugar-seller), but this implies a lack of economic specialisation at that time.[129] The town's coastal situation was favourable for the development of harbour facilities. In the fourteenth century Iviron had a claim to half of the revenues from the harbour.[130] The evidence is lacking for the earlier period, but it is likely that the harbour began to function at the latest when the Athos monasteries acquired substantial properties in the region. Economic expansion in Hierissos was severely restricted by the major role which the Athonite monasteries played in the region's economic life. Their basic needs were catered for by monks performing artisanal tasks, and more expensive requirements could be obtained from further afield. It can be surmised that only a very small part of the revenues which they obtained from their estates around Hierissos was actually spent on products made in the town. For the monasteries the main importance of Hierissos was as an outlet for the produce of the eastern Chalkidike. The surpluses from their properties could have been transported to Athos for the consumption of the monks or shipped to a larger, more lucrative market for sale. The acquisition of *metochia* in the town helped to ensure a careful administration of the estates and the appropriation of revenues from them. When Iviron gained control of Kolobou in 979–80, it acquired a large amount of property in the vicinity of Hierissos. Although Kolobou had earlier been deprived of some land there owing to the settlement of Bulgars, it had received a grant of forty *paroikoi* in compensation. Some were established inside the *kastron*, others around it. By 1079 Iviron had acquired a *metochion* of Prodromos in Hierissos. The properties attached to it included a church, a bath, buildings which were leased out, vineyards and agricultural land.[131] By 974 Lavra had property at Hierissos and in 1014 it was given an *aule* inside the town and two vineyards.[132] The monastery actively consolidated its properties in the area. In 1018 it exchanged lands in the vicinity of Longos for a vineyard and field at Sykeai and a field at Praulaka, close to land which it already owned. Both places are near Hierissos and the steward (*oikonomos*) of the *metochion* in Hierissos was mentioned in the act of exchange.[133]

Some residents of Hierissos were quite wealthy, owning substantial amounts of land in the region. They had the resources to bring new

---

[129] *Lavra*, I, no. 6 lines 16–19.
[130] Dölger, *Schatzkammern*, no. 9 line 41.
[131] Dölger, 'Ein Fall', p. 7 lines 10–13; Dölger, *Schatzkammern*, no. 35 lines 65–7, no. 56.
[132] *Lavra*, I, nos. 6, 18.   [133] *Ibid.*, no. 24.

Interaction between town and country

land under cultivation. In 941–3 they contested the sale of klasmatic land with Kolobou and the Athonite monasteries with some success. The terminology of the documents is vague. Sometimes the residents of Hierissos were referred to as *choriatai*, sometimes as inhabitants of the *kastron*.[134] Another text is more specific. In 982 some lands belonging to Iviron were leased for twenty-nine years to the inhabitants of Hierissos in exchange for land in the vicinity of Longos and the payment of 100 *nomismata*.[135] Their ability to find such a large sum of cash strongly suggests that they were of a higher social status than peasants. In 1180 residents of the town unsuccessfully disputed the ownership of some land with Vatopedi. The *periorismos* of this land shows that the property in the area was divided up among several Athonite monasteries, the bishop of Hierissos and the residents of the town.[136] The ability of the wealthier inhabitants of Hierissos to expand their lands was very limited owing to the large area in the ownership of the monasteries. Therefore the development of a landowning elite in the town, stimulating commodity production by its demands, was restricted. Nevertheless, the market at Hierissos was quite strong, more likely because of the shipment of produce out of Hierissos than because of the demand created by any artisanal specialisation in the town. Consequently, the owners of small plots of land were able to survive by producing for the market. Constantine and Maria Lagoudes owned only an *aule* in the town and two vineyards and had no other means of support. Without any land given over to arable cultivation they must have supplemented the rents from the *aule* by the sale of wine in order to subsist.[137] The case illustrates the increased range of possibilities open to owners of small plots of land if they were conveniently located near an urban centre.

The interaction between town and country is apparent in the lists of properties belonging to the Pantokrator and Bačkovo. Most of the Pantokrator's lands were concentrated in Thrace and Macedonia, usually near ports so that produce could be shipped easily to Constantinople. Its complex of properties around Thessalonike has already been mentioned.[138] Elsewhere its properties were concentrated in clusters around markets or ports or near *metochia*. It possessed two

---

[134] *Prôtaton*, nos. 4, 5, 6.
[135] G. Soulis, 'On the Slavonic Settlement in Hierissos in the Tenth Century', *Byzantion*, 23 (1953), pp. 67–72.
[136] M. Goudas, 'Byzantiaka engrapha tes en Atho hieras mones tou Batopediou', *Epeteris Hetaireias Byzantinon Spoudon*, 4 (1927), pp. 213–14.
[137] *Lavra*, I, no. 18 lines 23–33, 39–41.   [138] See above, p. 228.

232   *Economic expansion in the Byzantine empire*

houses and hostels in Raidestos and cultivated fields and vineyards outside the *kastron*.[139] It had properties in other towns around the sea of Marmara. Inside the *kastron* of Panion, near Raidestos, it owned two *aulai*. At Koila, a port on the Dardanelles near Abydos, it owned the entire Jewish quarter and was entitled to a tenth on wine sales. At Madytos it owned the whole *emporion* (trading place).[140] In eastern Macedonia the monastery's wealth included a house in Chrystoupolis with its vineyards and a large building with rented properties around it.[141] In Asia Minor its most important properties were centred around Smyrna. This complex of properties, connected to an *emporion*, included gardens, a bath, rented properties, five estates and two villages.[142] It is impossible to estimate what proportion of the revenues in kind was consumed directly and what was sold commercially. The monastery had considerable expenses in cash and kind,[143] but the enormous number of its estates must have covered these needs easily and enabled it to sell large quantities of agricultural produce in Constantinople or at other markets.

Pakourianos's properties in the theme of Boleron were mostly concentrated around Mosynoupolis and Peritheorion. His estate, Zaoutze, was situated near Mosynoupolis, and his other properties were connected to the monastery of St George on mount Papikion, which had a *metochion* inside the town. The only direct evidence of economic expansion in Mosynoupolis is derived from Pakourianos's activities. He had properties inside the *kastron*, where he purchased several plots of land and spent money on the construction of new houses. The *typikon* gives an impression of a town largely dominated by Pakourianos, but this is possibly a distortion resulting from the absence of other evidence.[144] Peritheorion was a rather more important town. Pakourianos owned an estate outside and an *aule* inside the town. Vatopedi had a *metochion* in the town and an estate nearby. Peritheorion was probably the main urban centre of its region, but its commercial importance remained localised. Although it was included in the list of markets in Alexios's chrysobull for the Venetians, it was not frequented by Italian merchants in the twelfth century.[145]

[139] Gautier, 'Pantocrator', p. 115 lines 1455–7 n. 6.
[140] *Ibid.*, p. 117 lines 1465–6, p. 119 lines 1485–7.
[141] *Ibid.*, p. 121 lines 1525–7.   [142] *Ibid.*, p. 119 lines 1488–95 n. 19.
[143] For these outlays, see *ibid.*, pp. 12–21.
[144] Gautier, 'Grégoire Pakourianos', p. 37; Asdracha, *La Région des Rhodopes*, pp. 104–9.
[145] Gautier, 'Grégoire Pakourianos', p. 37; Goudas, 'Vatopedi', p. 121 lines 13–14. Little is known of the town before the late eleventh century except that it had become a bishopric by the ninth or tenth century; see Asdracha, *La Région des Rhodopes*, pp.

Interaction between town and country 233

Isaac Komnenos had property in the port of Ainos and many of his lands were situated in the vicinity of the town. They included several estates and villages and two *kastra*. He also owned an *emporion* in which *paroikoi* and tenants were installed and which also contained a warehouse for storing produce from the estates. Ainos was a very convenient outlet for this produce. Its importance as a port had already been established in 1045 when Constantine IX permitted the Athonite monasteries to sell their surplus there but no further east. Komnenos had boats to transport goods elsewhere. His *typikon* also gives evidence of commercial activity in Ainos. The abbot of Kosmosotira was advised to look for a suitable time to purchase oil cheaply and to buy it directly from the ships which were importing it, not from intermediary merchants. The existence of the latter implies that substantial quantities were being imported, not simply for the town but for the region around it. The abbot also had to buy fish and wine, although Komnenos did envisage that the monastery might produce enough wine of its own. The monastery had some flexibility in the disposal of its surplus. It could take advantage of a fairly active market in Ainos or it had the boats to transport it to Constantinople. It also had the option of purchasing the produce of other landowners in Ainos and reselling it in Constantinople.[146]

There are also scattered references in the sources to landowners with property in Traianoupolis, Chrystoupolis and Chrysoupolis. Leo Kephalas had buildings inside the *kastron* of Traianoupolis, some of which he leased out. Outside the *kastron* he owned arable and pasture land and vineyards. Isaac Komnenos also had land in the town.[147] At Chrystoupolis the empress Maria and the Pantokrator had property.[148] Lavra received an exemption from Basil II for twenty-five houses in Chrysoupolis. By 1080 Vatopedi had acquired an estate near the town and a *metochion* in the town. Its *enoikoi* and *eleutheroi* numbered twenty-four. A recent survey of Chrysoupolis has revealed the phases of

---

98–104. Pakourianos also had properties in the themes of Serres and Thessalonike, including some *kastra* of limited importance. As these properties were near Chrysoupolis there was no incentive for the development of another urban centre in the area. It seems that Pakourianos did not undertake any great expenditure in the area except for the construction of a church and monastery; see Gautier, 'Grégoire Pakourianos', p. 39; and Lemerle, *Cinq études*, p. 179.

[146] Petit, 'Kosmosotira', pp. 50–3; *Prôtaton*, no. 8 lines 65–7; Asdracha, *La Région des Rhodopes*, pp. 120–4, 224–6.

[147] *Lavra*, I, no. 60 lines 35–7; Petit, 'Kosmosotira', p. 53 line 4; Asdracha, *La Région des Rhodopes*, pp. 118–20.

[148] Anna Comnène, *Alexiade*, II, p. 171; Gautier, 'Pantocrator', p. 121 lines 1525–7.

234   *Economic expansion in the Byzantine empire*

development of the town's fortified area. The initial fortification probably dates to the reestablishment of Byzantine control in the region and by the mid fourteenth century a new wall had been erected which quadrupled the defended area. The precise chronology of the town's development cannot be ascertained, but a general pattern of expansion is doubtless partly reflected in the extension of the fortified area. Unfortunately it is not possible to make any precise link between this expansion and the development of the properties of large landowners around the town. There is also no detailed information about agricultural production on these properties, but there are, not surprisingly, references to viticulture. The proximity of a town could affect the agricultural pattern, encouraging a greater emphasis on viticulture or arboriculture and distinguishing the immediate vicinity of the town from areas where production was more heavily geared to immediate consumption requirements.[149]

The extent to which the market penetrated the rural economy should not be exaggerated. It offered peasant producers the means to raise cash to meet their fiscal obligations, which were increasing in this period. Otherwise in many instances they hardly needed to go beyond the village for their basic requirements. An example of the limitations on occupational specialisation was the case of the tenth-century *klerikos*, David, who owned a brickworks as well as agricultural land.[150] For more systematic evidence it is necessary to turn to the fourteenth-century *praktika*. The occupational names in these lists suggest that there were enough craftsmen in the village for recourse to urban markets to be generally unnecessary. The craftsmen most commonly represented by names were shoemakers, tailors, smiths, potters and weavers. Other rather less common names included carpenter, miller, barrel-maker, butcher, wine-seller, fisherman and wagon-maker. These craftsmen owned land and occupational differentiation in many villages was not pronounced.[151] A geographical breakdown of the villages where occupational names were most common might lead to interesting results. They would probably be less frequently encountered in the

---

[149] Dölger, *Schatzkammern*, no. 108 lines 23–4, 32–7; Goudas, 'Vatopedi', p. 121 lines 15, 18–19, p. 127 lines 40–2; A. W. Dunn, 'The Survey of Khrysoupolis and Byzantine Fortifications in the Lower Strymon Valley', *XVI Internationaler Byzantinistenkongress. Akten II/4, Jahrbuch der Österreichischen Byzantinistik*, 32/4 (1982), pp. 605–14.   [150] *Lavra*, I, no. 4 lines 3–6.

[151] The possibility that these designations had become fixed names rather than indicators of peasant crafts by the fourteenth century is not important here. Even as formalised names they certainly reflect earlier realities; see Laiou-Thomadakis, *Peasant Society*, pp. 120–7.

Interaction between town and country

villages nearer to Thessalonike. In a twelfth-century *praktikon* from Athens few occupational names are found, probably because the peasants had immediate access to the products of artisans working in the town.[152] Occupational specialisation is likely to have become more uncommon with distance from urban centres.

There is also some evidence of artisanal activities on large estates. This was in keeping with the general need to ensure the greatest possible degree of self-sufficiency. In the ninth century the retinue of the widow Danielis is supposed to have included female embroiderers. Although the account may be greatly exaggerated, it seems likely that larger landowners had control over some skilled workers in this field.[153] Textile production on large estates probably declined, at least in the Peloponnesos, as the urban economy expanded and production was concentrated in the towns. We have more reliable information about the activities of the monks of Athos. Athanasios installed workshops on Athos and the community had its own carpenters, boat-builders, masons and smiths. In 1154 monks were also working as weavers, barrel-makers, fishermen, tailors and shoemakers.[154] Such a concentration of artisanal activity was also partly the consequence of the peculiar situation of the Athonite community.

Even if allowance is made for the extent of rural self-sufficiency, there is no doubt that markets were becoming more important by the tenth century. As fairs were held more frequently and became more lucrative, the rights which landowners could claim if they were held on their land became a very contentious issue needing imperial regulation. Basil II's legislation restricted the circumstances in which a fair could be transferred to another site. In a dispute over the location, priority had to be given to the site with the oldest claim to the fair. There was one exception to this general rule. If the fair was transferred from the land of the 'non-powerful' to that of the powerful, it had to be done with the unanimous consent of the participants and the new site also required a valid claim of greater antiquity than the other site. This decree has to be seen not only in the context of the legislation concerning the powerful and the weak, but also as an indication of economic expansion.[155] As landowners were contesting the location of fairs, it is

[152] Granstrem, Medvedev and Papachryssanthou, 'Fragment d'un praktikon de la région d'Athènes (avant 1204)', pp. 38–41.
[153] Theophanes Continuatus, p. 318.
[154] 'Vie d'Athanase', pp. 53, 67, 76; *Lavra*, I, no. 63 and p. 59.
[155] *JGR*, I, p. 271. For this legislation, see above, chapter 2. This law was still in force in the eleventh century; see *Peira*, LVII, *JGR*, IV, p. 228.

236 Economic expansion in the Byzantine empire

possible that some were also creating fairs to supplement their revenues. Very little information about individual fairs survives. The sources generally ignore this aspect of the rural economy. Apart from urban fairs, like those at Ephesos, Thessalonike and Euchaita, or just outside the town walls at Adrianople, they were often situated near monasteries, but the sources give a one-sided picture.[156] Occasional markets were organised in special circumstances, notably to ensure the supplies of the crusading armies. Although these markets did not reflect economic trends, they at least show that some regions produced substantial surplus produce and were capable of meeting temporary increases in demand without the state resorting to requisitioning.[157]

The greatly increased commerce in agricultural produce strengthened the economic position of feudal landowners. The gains which the state obtained from this commerce were limited because it was often unable to supervise it effectively. It made unsuccessful attempts to do so in the eleventh and twelfth centuries, but these ended in failure, a consequence of the growing power of the aristocracy. One such effort was the imposition of the grain monopoly at Raidestos in the 1070s. The town was an ideal outlet for agricultural produce from Thrace and the market was frequented by monasteries, Hagia Sophia, local landowners and peasants.[158] Attaleiates's estates were concentrated around Raidestos and he was directly affected by the administration's attempt to regulate the grain trade there. Consequently, his informative account of the affair has to be treated with a certain amount of caution.

There is no evidence that the trade at Raidestos had been subject to any state regulation before Nikephoritzes, the chief minister, attempted to impose his monopoly. The town's proximity to Constantinople provided sufficient stimulus for producers to sell grain without any need for the administration to take special measures to secure the capital's supply. Nikephoritzes obtained an imperial letter granting him the rights to the monopoly and he set up a warehouse just outside the town. All the sellers bringing their grain to the town had to sell directly to the warehouse and all purchases had to be made from it. In his invective against Nikephoritzes, Attaleiates stresses how buyers and sellers had

---

[156] Vryonis, 'The Panegyris of the Byzantine Saint', pp. 202–6. For Adrianople, see Scylitzes, p. 346; Asdracha, *La Région des Rhodopes*, pp. 221–2; and Angold, *A Byzantine Government in Exile*, p. 109 n. 109. For the fair at Bačkovo, see above, p. 225. The bishop of Dryinopolis received the revenues from the market at Pelakon from Alexios I; see Dölger, *Regesten der Kaiserurkunden*, no. 1111.

[157] Asdracha, *La Région des Rhodopes*, pp. 222–3.

[158] Attaleiates, p. 201.

Interaction between town and country 237

previously made individual agreements and buyers were able to go from cart to cart until they found a suitable price. Nikephoritzes had a force of 100 armed men under his authority. Consequently, he was able to prevent anyone from purchasing from the carts and seamen from transporting grain to Constantinople. Everyone had to go to the warehouse, where the superintendent imposed duties on the transactions. If any corn was sold in a producer's house, his property was liable to be confiscated. The strident tone of Attaleiates's account implies that the monopoly was rigorously imposed not only on small producers but on large landowners. The steep increase in the price of grain which Attaleiates blamed on the monopoly – from eight or ten *modioi* to one *modios* a *nomisma* – is not altogether impossible. It is likely that aggrieved landowners reacted to the monopoly by holding back as much grain as they could store and shortages arose. As the demand for grain was inflexible, any shortages in the supply would have caused a dramatic fluctuation in price.[159]

Concern for the grain supply of Constantinople was certainly not the cause of the establishment of the monopoly. Attaleiates's account suggests that the market was already very active and important. Nikephoritzes's motive was to exact all possible revenues from the trade. It was far easier to tax the transactions if they were made at the warehouse. Attaleiates complains about the impositions exacted by the superintendent of the warehouse, but the only tax he specifically mentions is the *kommerkion*, which was perfectly legitimate in spite of his fulminations. The monopoly was lucrative and Nikephoritzes was able to lease the rights to it for sixty pounds.[160] In view of the revenues which were at stake it is not surprising that a vigorous attempt was made to impose the monopoly. Inevitably, it clashed with the vested interests of large landowners, merchants and small agricultural producers. The hostility which it provoked was aggravated by the personal stake of Nikephoritzes in the affair. Consequently, the warehouse associated with the monopoly was destroyed during the

---

[159] Attaleiates, pp. 201–4. It has been argued plausibly that this passage does not mean that the price had been eighteen *modioi* for a *nomisma* before the monopoly, but eight to ten *modioi*; see Karayannopulos, 'He hypsosis tes times tou sitou epi Parapinake'. Lemerle's assertion (*Cinq études*, p. 301) that the regulation of the market probably did not lead to a price increase seems an overreaction to the bias of Attaleiates's account. Another factor which might have had a temporary effect on prices was the Petcheneg incursion; see Attaleiates, pp. 204–6, 208–9.

[160] Attaleiates, pp. 203–4. Apart from the reference to the *kommerkion* he only uses such vague expressions as *kainotomeisthai*.

238   *Economic expansion in the Byzantine empire*

confusion following Bryennios's rebellion.[161] The affair demonstrated the economic importance of Raidestos as an outlet for the produce of Constantinople's Thracian hinterland.[162] Trade was brisk enough for an attempt to exact the full amount of revenues to seem worthwhile. The episode was a consequence of a more intensive agricultural production and a greater urban demand for grain, but the effectiveness of the monopoly was limited to a short period of a few years. It provoked too much powerful opposition to last long and its eventual failure was an indication of the weakness of the central government in the 1070s.

The strengthening of the economic situation of the aristocracy was reflected in the proliferation of maritime privileges, which facilitated its commercial activities. It is often said that the growing role played by Venetian merchants after they had received fiscal concessions from Alexios was due to a fiscal discrimination which gave them an advantage over Byzantine merchants.[163] This ignores the relatively subordinate place of the mercantile class in Byzantium. Powerful landowners gradually acquired trading privileges comparable with those of the Venetians. Early maritime privileges were restricted to exemptions from the impounding of boats for purposes of state, but by the twelfth century exemptions from the *kommerkion* and the *dekateia* were being granted. By the tenth century Hagia Sophia had received maritime privileges.[164] The Athonite monasteries were already selling surplus produce at this time. Tzimiskes attempted to restrict commercial exchanges on Athos, allowing wine to be sold to laymen only in exchange for supplies which the monks were lacking,[165] but soon the monks began to sell wine and other produce in Constantinople and other major towns. The attempts by different emperors to restrict this trade is a certain indication of its growing volume. Basil II tried unsuccessfully to limit the size of their boats. He also restricted the sale of the monks' surplus produce to Thessalonike and the ports on the way.[166] The force of these restrictions was limited by the chrysobulls which some monasteries were granted. Lavra received an exemption from Basil for a boat with the capacity of 6,000 *modioi*, but it already had enough boats and it transferred the privilege to Iviron.[167] Another

---

[161] *Ibid.*, pp. 248–9.
[162] The town was important enough for the Venetians to acquire property there in the twelfth century; see Thiriet, *La Romanie vénitienne*, p. 45. See also Balard, *La Romanie génoise*, p. 752, for later Genoese activity there.
[163] Vryonis , *The Decline of Medieval Hellenism*, pp. 79–80; Lemerle, *Cinq études*, p. 307.
[164] Darrouzès, *Épistoliers*, p. 117.   [165] *Prôtaton*, no. 7 lines 95–100.
[166] *Ibid.*, no. 8 lines 53–65.   [167] Dölger, *Schatzkammern*, no. 108 lines 22–4.

Interaction between town and country 239

attempt to impose restrictions on the monks' activities was made by Constantine IX in 1045. He limited the capacity of the Athonite boats to 300 *modioi* and they were allowed to sail as far west as Thessalonike and as far east as Ainos, but only to sell their surplus and return to Athos with the monks' requirements. In theory they were not allowed to engage in unfettered commerce, buying up produce for resale elsewhere. The restrictions on the capacity of the boats did not apply to those to which the monasteries were already entitled by previous chrysobulls, nor to the boat which Vatopedi operated with the consent of the *protos* and abbots. A special exemption was made for the monastery of the Amalfitans. They were allowed to send one boat to Constantinople to obtain supplies from the Amalfitan community there, but they were not permitted to use it for general trading purposes. It is, of course, unknown how closely they adhered to this stipulation.[168] Detailed information about the maritime privileges of the Athonite monasteries in the eleventh century is unavailable because the chrysobulls do not survive. Before 1102 Lavra had been entitled to seven boats with a total capacity of 16,000 *modioi*, but its privileges had been infringed by various imperial decrees. A new chrysobull allowed it to operate four boats, each with a capacity of 1,500 *modioi*.[169] The monastery was exempted from all charges and impositions on its boats. The great risk facing landowners with boats was that the state might impound them for its own purposes. This exemption was probably a standard feature in chrysobulls at that time, but the exemption from the *dekateia* and the *kommerkion*, which the monastery also received, was not frequently given until later.[170] Alexios made a less extensive grant to the monastery of Patmos for one boat of 500 *modioi*. It was freed from all *epereiai*, such as forced transportation, and was permitted to operate in any part of the empire, but it was not exempted from the *dekateia* and the *kommerkion*.[171] The evidence of secular landowners receiving such privileges is scarce, but this can reasonably be attributed to the poverty of the surviving source material. Isaac Komnenos did receive an exemption for twelve boats with a total capacity of 4,000 *modioi*.[172]

---

[168] *Prôtaton*, no. 8 lines 65–77, 99–101, and p. 105; Lemerle, 'Les archives du monastère des Amalfitains au Mont Athos', p. 552. The monastery of Xylourgou was also operating boats in the mid eleventh century, but their size and fiscal status are not known; see *Pantéléèmôn*, no. 4.

[169] *Lavra*, I, no. 55 lines 1–24. The monks' declaration that they possessed only two or three small boats should not be taken at face value.

[170] *Ibid.*, I, no. 55 lines 24–50; Svoronos, 'Les privilèges de l'Église', p. 384.

[171] *Engrapha Patmou*, I, no. 7.   [172] Petit, 'Kosmosotira', p. 53 lines 5–7.

240   *Economic expansion in the Byzantine empire*

The volume of the commerce carried in these boats should not be exaggerated. Even boats of 1,500 *modioi* were little more than a small yacht.[173] A boat which was excavated at Serçe Liman off the Turkish coast and has been dated to the eleventh century, was very small, only seventeen metres in length.[174] The cargoes of the boats which were owned by major landowners consisted predominantly of agricultural produce, and the importance of the maritime privileges lay not so much in the volume of the traffic but in the inability of the state to derive gains from this upsurge in commerce, however limited in scope. By the late twelfth century grants of maritime privileges had proliferated, an indication of the greater involvement of landowners in trade. The initial entitlement to one boat of 500 *modioi*, made by Alexios I to the monastery of Patmos, was extended by later emperors. By 1186 it possessed three boats of this size; they were allowed to come to Constantinople once a year. Isaac II extended their exemption to include the *dekateia*.[175]

As landowners benefited from more extensive maritime privileges, the potentially greater revenues resulting from increasing commercial activity were not exacted by the state. Its weakness in relation to feudal landowners was illustrated by the desperate, but unsuccessful, measures taken by the hard-pressed administration of Alexios III. It revoked all previous chrysobulls and *prostagmata* concerning maritime privileges on the grounds that they had become so numerous as to infringe the state's fiscal interests.[176] The assertion may have contained some truth if the extension of Patmos's exemption to include the *dekateia* was not an isolated instance. However, the monastery quickly obtained another chrysobull making it a special case. Besides the confirmation of its previous chrysobulls and *prostagmata* it was allowed another boat of 500 *modioi*. In 1203 its boats were replaced by one larger boat of 2,000 *modioi*.[177] These texts frequently refer to the *dekateia oinarion*. This was not mere form, but indicates that wine was the most important item transported in the monastery's boats.[178] If the monastery of Patmos was

---

[173] Schilbach, *Byzantinische Metrologie*, gives modern equivalents for measures of capacity, but given the problems involved in such calculations it is perhaps unwise to seek extreme precision in this matter.

[174] R. W. Unger, *The Ship in the Medieval Economy* (London, 1980), p. 104.

[175] *Engrapha Patmou*, I, no. 9.   [176] *Ibid.*, no. 11 lines 1–3.

[177] *Ibid.*, I, no. 11; II, no. 59. See also P. Lemerle, 'Notes sur l'administration byzantine à la veille de la IVe crusade d'après deux documents inédits des archives de Lavra', *Revue des Études Byzantines*, 19 (1961), pp. 258–72.

[178] *Ibid.*, pp. 271–2.

Interaction between town and country 241

able to resist the attempts by the state to revoke its maritime privileges, it is likely that other powerful landowners also exploited their influence to this end. Lavra overcame an attempt by the administration to hinder its commercial activities. In order to overturn the chrysobull of 1102 the administration used the pretext that the monastery had not been exempted from the *dekateia oinarion*, because that obligation had not been specifically mentioned in the document. When the boats entered Constantinople, the tax was imposed on the merchandise. The case came before a court which had been established by the *megas logariastes* and *logethetes ton sekreton* John Belissariotes. The *sekreton thalasses* (maritime department) justified its action on the grounds that only the *kommerkion* and the *dekatismos* were mentioned in the chrysobull, not the *dekateia oinarion*. It had received a *prostagma* ordering that all charges which were not specifically listed in the maritime privileges were to be imposed. It also produced a *prostagma* concerning the imposition of the tax on wine which was brought to Constantinople. It was to be exacted at a rate of one measure in every ten. The court ruled that the exemption from the *dekatismos* in Alexios's chrysobull included the exaction of the tax on wine just as on any other item and that the two *prostagmata* did not conflict with the chrysobull.[179] We have already seen that there is evidence of considerable expenditure on viticulture by the Athonite monasteries and the preoccupation of the administration with the tax on wine rather than any other produce shows that it was the most important cargo shipped to Constantinople by Lavra. However, the state continued to grant new maritime privileges to powerful landowners. In 1199 the newly founded monastery of Chilandar, which had already spent large sums on its landed property, was granted a complete exemption for a boat of 1,000 *modioi*, which was allowed to operate along the coast of the themes of Boleron, Strymon and Thessalonike.[180] The administration's attempt to exact greater revenues from commercial traffic was ephemeral and unsuccessful. Its failure emphasised the effect of economic expansion in strengthening the position of powerful landowners in relation to the state.

Owing to the close interaction between town and country the course of urban history reveals close parallels to that of the rural economy. The condition of the rural economy was the prime factor underlying the decline or expansion of towns. After the early medieval contraction,

[179] *Lavra*, I, nos. 67, 68.
[180] *Chilandar*, no. 5. For the monastery's expenditure on landed property, see *ibid.*, no 2 lines 7–25, 48–52.

242   *Economic expansion in the Byzantine empire*

recovery in the rural economy and the gradual intensification of agricultural production were important preconditions for urban expansion. Besides making available a greater supply of food for the towns, it led to an increase in the revenues of both the state and private landowners and consequently stimulated demand for industrial goods. The development of feudal relations of production was vital for the expansion of provincial towns, and the role of landowners like Pakourianos in establishing new urban sites deserves consideration. Generally, the economic functions of towns were restricted to serving the needs of their immediate regions, and the upsurge in commodity production, though perceptible, remained modest. A notable feature of the urban revival of the eleventh and twelfth centuries and the upsurge in commerce was the strong link with trade in primary produce. Many towns which increased in importance, especially in the European provinces, owed their greater prominence to their roles as outlets for the produce of their region. Agricultural produce made up the greater part of the cargoes acquired by Italian merchants and was also the main item marketed by major landowners. The more rapid development of the European towns was partly due to an expansion in agricultural production which was more sustained than in Asia Minor. Nevertheless, very few towns were industrial centres of more than local importance. One reason for this was the overblown importance of the capital. Outside Constantinople the most significant industrial production was located in south and central Greece. This was due partly to the flourishing agrarian economy of the region, but at least two other factors were also involved. Its remoteness from Constantinople gave greater scope for production than in other provinces, where goods were more readily obtained from the capital. The proximity of the region to the towns of northern Italy and its convenient location on the trade routes from Italy to the Middle East ensured that Italian merchants frequented its major towns with considerable regularity. The economic expansion of these centuries has not always been fully appreciated owing to the emphasis which has incorrectly been placed on economic stagnation or decline by many historians.[181] This interpretation is based partly on the mistaken view that agricultural production was no longer increasing. It is also based on the concessions made by Alexios to the Venetians, whose economic consequences have often been misrepresented – at least for the eleventh and twelfth centuries. The pessimistic

---

[181] Svoronos, 'Remarques sur les structures économiques', pp. 62–3, 67; Lemerle, *Cinq études*, pp. 305–9; Mango, *Byzantium. Empire of New Rome*, p. 58.

Interaction between town and country 243

view of the economy can also be attributed to the image of a *société bloquée*, which has been used to describe Byzantium in the Komnenian era.[182] However, this does not do justice to the continued vitality of the Byzantine economy in the twelfth century, only to the limited gains which the state was able to derive from this expansion. Economic growth greatly reinforced the power of feudal landowners. In contrast, the position of the mercantile class remained relatively modest. The dominant position of the landowners was reflected in their involvement in trade. They would conduct this trade in relatively favourable conditions owing to the privileges which they could obtain from the state. Consequently, much of the wealth which was created evaded the grasp of the state and reinforced the centrifugal tendencies at work in Byzantium.

[182] Lemerle, *Cinq études*, pp. 309–12.

Conclusion

The pattern of economic development which has been presented here differs from the standard orthodoxy of Byzantine agrarian history and corresponds in general terms to that of the medieval west much more closely than has usually been allowed. Although the limitations of the surviving source material do not permit the more detailed analysis of economic trends which is possible elsewhere, the upsurge in economic activity in the eleventh and twelfth centuries is unmistakable. The major factor which has encouraged historians to differentiate Byzantine economic history from that of western medieval Europe is the emphasis on the role of the state. To some extent this is understandable because many of the documents surviving in the monastic archives were issued by the state and Byzantine writers viewed events with a Constantinopolitan perspective. Indeed, the important functions of the state in putting coinage into circulation and in stimulating economic demand through its expenditure should not be minimised. Nevertheless, a tendency to work out the chronology of Byzantine economic history within a framework determined by the political fortunes of the state has led to a much greater emphasis on the eleventh century as a turningpoint in Byzantine economic fortunes than the evidence warrants. This interpretation originated in attempts to explain the political reverses of the 1070s and 1080s by a corresponding economic decline. In particular, the debasement of the coinage, which was the consequence of the financial difficulties of the central government, has usually been linked with broader economic difficulties. However, the eleventh century is most notable for a steady expansion, which continued in the twelfth century and affected all aspects of economic activity.

These centuries experienced a sustained demographic growth. This was especially important because the most immediate way of increasing productivity was to extend the cultivated area, and the consequent growth of revenues derived from agriculture was a major stimulus to

244

Conclusion 245

other spheres of the economy. The density of population and the chronology of its increase varied considerably from region to region, although the source material offers only a general perspective. The coastal areas which had been longest under firm Byzantine control were the most densely populated. In the Chalkidike peninsula the growth of population was already under way in the tenth century, when large numbers of peasants were established on the estates of powerful landowners, and was sustained through the eleventh and twelfth centuries. In Boiotia peasant holdings had become quite small by the later eleventh century, but in parts of Bulgaria there was still scope for extensive colonisation.[1] This general trend of expansion in the European provinces, which has been based on documentary evidence, has received additional support from the results of archaeological survey work. This has given a general perspective on the relative density of settlement during different periods in regions for which no documentary evidence survives. Work on the Greek mainland and islands reveals a broadly similar general pattern; very little evidence of settlements has been found for the early medieval period, and a great deal for the eleventh and twelfth centuries. Survey work in Boiotia and Crete has already been mentioned.[2] Similar results have also been obtained at Palaipaphos in Cyprus, the island of Keos and the Argolid.[3] It is possible that improvements in knowledge of Byzantine pottery might refine the overall picture somewhat and lead to a slightly less desolate view of the so-called 'dark ages', but the evidence for a sustained increase in population in the eleventh and twelfth centuries is overwhelming. While the documentary evidence offers glimpses of short-term localised fluctuations, the general trend of expansion applied in the European provinces. There was an important contrast, however, between Europe and Asia Minor, where there was probably a major fluctuation in the demographic trend in the late eleventh and early twelfth centuries owing to the Turkish invasions. The upward trend in the western part of Anatolia was resumed in the mid twelfth century and continued in the thirteenth century.

[1] For the details of this process, see above pp. 47–67.
[2] See above, pp. 18, 66 n. 123.
[3] D. W. Rupp and R. H. King, 'Canadian Palaipaphos Survey Project', in D. R. Keller and D. W. Rupp, *Archaeological Survey in the Mediterranean Area* (Oxford, 1983), pp. 323–7; J. L. Davis, J. F. Cherry and E. Mantzourani, 'An Archaeological Survey of the Greek Island of Keos', *National Geographical Society. Research Reports*, 21, pp. 109–16; T. H. Van Andel, C. N. Runnels and K. O. Pope, 'Five Thousand Years of Land Use and Abuse in Southern Argolid Greece', *Hesperia*, 55 (1986), pp. 103–28.

246   *Economic expansion in the Byzantine empire*

While only a general trend of expansion in the cultivated area can be discerned in Byzantium, the greater quantity of documentation in the west does allow different phases of the extension of the arable to be outlined. In Duby's first phase lords merely tolerated expansion and in his second they took charge of land reclamation. The first, the most immediate form of reclamation, seems to have begun by the tenth century and involved a steady enlargement of the cultivated area immediately around the settlement. It was very much a piecemeal process, not as spectacular as some of the more extensive reclamation programmes, but probably more significant in the long run. In the second phase most of the new villages which were established resulted from the deliberate acts of powerful lords or the communes in north Italy. These new villages provided an extension of the political and jurisdictional authority of the lords as well as additional sources of revenues. The magnates who profited most came from the higher ranks of the aristocracy. Naturally, the expense involved in recruiting men, moving their households and providing them with equipment was considerable, but leading magnates were also able to offer enticements granting peasants favourable terms to settle in new villages.[4] The first of these two processes, the gradual extension of the cultivated area around already existing settlements was unquestionably the more significant in Byzantium. It is likely that the privileges which landowners received entitling them to the revenues from additional peasants established on their properties were usually a response by the landowners to the gradual increase in population on their property, rather than the reflection of a conscious drive by these landowners to extend the cultivated areas on their estates. Cases of the foundation of new villages by powerful landowners are few and the circumstances were special. Boilas's activities were a product of his exile and cannot be regarded as in any way indicative of general economic trends. Pakourianos's initiatives followed the transfer of his base from the eastern part of the empire to Bulgaria, but unlike Boilas he benefited from imperial favour and it is likely that his activities were part of a movement towards a more intensive exploitation of the region by powerful landowners.[5]

No precise chronology for land reclamation in Byzantium can be established, but it is clear that the eleventh and twelfth centuries did see a considerable extension of the cultivated area. In many parts of the

---

[4] Duby, *Rural Economy and Country Life*, pp. 72–81.
[5] See above, p. 65.

Conclusion 247

west reclamation proceeded most intensively around the middle of the twelfth century and thereafter slowly abated. As it ceased in the course of the thirteenth century the pressure of increasing population on landed resources became acute. It is well known that peasant holdings became fragmented through repeated division among heirs and had to support a growing population, leading eventually to higher mortality rates among the poorest strata of rural society. As arable cultivation was extended by necessity to less fertile soils, the area available for pasturing animals was reduced, cutting down the manure available for fertilising the land.[6] There has been little discussion of these issues in relation to Byzantium. This is partly because of the limitations of the Byzantine evidence. The most detailed source material from the eleventh, and to a lesser extent the twelfth, century is contained in the archives of the monasteries of mount Athos, but they do not contain any significant evidence from the first part of the thirteenth century. Material dating from throughout this century is found in the archives of Patmos and Lembiotissa. The indications of expansion on Patmos's estates on Leros around the middle of the thirteenth century have already been mentioned.[7] For western Asia Minor there is considerable evidence of an intensification of agricultural production in the thirteenth century. There is literary evidence that villages were rebuilt and new ones founded and that the Nicaean emperors gave concessions to landowners to install peasants on their properties in order to resettle the countryside after the political upheavals of the late twelfth and early thirteenth centuries.[8] The Lembiotissa archives confirm the more general literary evidence. The restoration of the monastery was confirmed by a chrysobull of 1228. Imperial favour ensured that it was well endowed with landed wealth, and the conditions on which peasants could be installed on its properties were regulated by the state. They were normally described as outsiders (*xenoi*) and unknown to the treasury (not recorded in any of its tax-registers).[9] As in previous centuries these concessions were intended to ensure that the expansion on landowner's properties did not encroach upon the state's own claims to revenues. Details of this procedure are unavailable except for one of the monastery's properties, Baris. The *paroikoi* on that estate in 1235

---

[6] Duby, *Rural Economy and Country Life*, pp. 119–25; E. Miller and J. Hatcher, *Medieval England. Rural Society and Economic Change 1086–1348* (London, 1978) pp. 53–63.

[7] See above, pp. 53–4.

[8] Angold, *A Byzantine Government in Exile*, pp. 103–4, 108.

[9] MM, IV, pp. 5, 25, 145.

248 *Economic expansion in the Byzantine empire*

are recorded by name. In the main list there were fifteen households, some including married children. Then there was a supplementary list of 'outsiders' who had recently been established there. There were six families, all with under-age children, and they were clearly recent settlers on the estate, which also contained two abandoned peasant holdings.[10] The revenues which landowners were entitled to draw from their estates were, of course, recorded in their *praktika*, but during a period of expansion these documents could become outdated. A good indication of the steady increase in revenues in the thirteenth century is given by an imperial *prostagma*, which was probably issued in 1261. The revenues which Lembiotissa was obtaining from its estates were found to be in excess of the amount to which it was entitled according to its privileges. The official who made the assessment of its properties, John Syropoulos, was instructed to allow the monastery fifteen *hyperpyra* from this surplus and the rest was to be sent to the imperial treasury.[11]

There is no detailed and reliable evidence concerning the size of peasant holdings on these estates, which would enable the impact of population increase on the condition of the peasantry to be assessed accurately, but there are some indications that the economic situation of the peasantry deteriorated in the later thirteenth century. A dispute arose between the monastery and the villagers of Neochorion, who encroached upon the monastery's property in their village and brought it under cultivation. Following an official investigation the peasants were expelled from the land and ordered to pay the *morte* for the period in which they had occupied the fields. However, according to the guarantee drawn up in 1293 the monks relinquished their claims to the *morte* because of the poverty of the peasantry. Although the amount to which it had been entitled is not stated, it is unlikely that a powerful landowner, whose claims had been vindicated by an official enquiry, would have conceded the *morte* without good reason.[12] There are also indications of discontent among the *paroikoi* of Lembiotissa, although it is uncertain how this was affected by their economic situation. Some time before 1274 the inhabitants of Baris refused to make the payments which they owed to the monastery. The *paroikoi* who had been longest established persuaded the more recent settlers to withhold their payment

[10] MM, IV, pp. 13–14; Angold, *A Byzantine Government in Exile*, p. 104 n. 61.
[11] MM, IV, p. 254. For the dating of the document, see Ahrweiler, 'L'histoire et la géographie de la région de Smyrne', p. 148 n. 100.
[12] MM, IV, pp. 231–2.

Conclusion 249

and they also refused to perform the *angareia*, which was fixed by customary practice, and in general did not meet the obligations which were imposed upon them as *paroikoi*. Another of the monks' grievances was that they had loaned their *paroikoi* fifty-five *exagia hyperpyra*, an indication that the peasants might have faced economic difficulties, and that this had not been repaid.[13] Another option open to the peasantry was to flee from their properties. Precise details are not available, but the monks did complain to the emperor that *paroikoi* were fleeing from their estates; some went to Nymphaion, others to various places, and the monastery was deprived of revenues to which it was legally entitled. It received an imperial *prostagma* ordering the officials of the theme of Thrakesion to take the necessary measures to ensure that the monastery's *paroikoi* were restored to it. No doubt such a course of action would have led to resistance both from the peasants and from other landowners who might have benefited from the situation, but we have no information about the outcome of the operation.[14]

There are a few indications of peasant poverty in the land sales of the later thirteenth century, but they are not numerous enough to permit firm conclusions. Some of the sales involved very small parcels of land, which might have been the result of the division of holdings through successive inheritances.[15] The evidence of prices cannot be used to measure the variation in demand for land during the century because the quantity of surviving documents is inadequate, information about the quality of land is lacking and the sales took place between parties which were socially unequal and could be determined by other than purely economic factors.[16] It is possible that the extension of the cultivated area led to a serious reduction in the amount of pasture which was available to landowners and peasants in some areas, but again the evidence is patchy. In the late thirteenth century a serious dispute arose between Lembiotissa and Michael Branas over lands at Baris and Palatia. Branas claimed that the monks entered mountainous land, to which he had rights of pasture and collecting wood, but it was found that the land lay within the boundary of the monastery's lands as outlined in its documents. Some neighbouring *paroikoi*, presumably

[13] MM, IV, pp. 255–6.
[14] MM, IV, p. 262. For the theme of Thrakesion in the thirteenth century, see Ahrweiler, 'L'histoire et la géographie de la région de Smyrne', pp. 137–8.
[15] MM, IV, pp. 127, 131–2, 164–5, 226, 269–70.
[16] Kazhdan and Constable, *People and Power*, pp. 46–8. The situation was also complicated by the debasement of the *hyperpyron* in the thirteenth century; see Hendy, *Coinage and Money*, pp. 247–8.

250   *Economic expansion in the Byzantine empire*

belonging to Branas, from the village of Mourmounton entered their animals into the monastery's land during the harvest season. Previously, both parties had reciprocal rights to pasture their animals on each other's land, but the *paroikoi* were infringing this arrangement by attempting to expropriate the monastery's land for their exclusive use.[17] In 1293 Constantine Cheilas had to make a clear delimitation of the pasture land next to the lands of Branas and the monastery so that both sides could exploit it but neither had any right to cultivate it.[18] Early in the fourteenth century *paroikoi* belonging to John Nestongos entered their animals on pasture land of Lembiotissa, one of a series of infringements against the rights of the monastery.[19] While these incidents suggest there might have been less pasture land available in the region of Smyrna by the end of the thirteenth century, they are by no means conclusive. Nevertheless, they do fit into the clearly established pattern of more intensive agricultural production in the region in the thirteenth century.

There are some indications of peasant poverty in Thessaly, where the Maliassenos family acquired several small pieces of peasant property for their monastic foundation of Nea Petra in the 1270s. The acts of sale make several references to impoverishment. In some cases the reason for the sale was given as a severe shortage of grain and the seller needed the money to buy food. Two other sellers needed the money to buy oxen to work their land. The precise causes of this situation cannot be determined. No doubt adverse climatic conditions had contributed to the grain shortage. It is possible that the fragmentation of peasant properties had also been a factor, but there are no details of their size, only measurements of the small vineyards which were sold.[20]

The best evidence of the amount of land available to peasants comes from the Athos archives and dates from the early fourteenth century. It shows that the population increase in Macedonia during the eleventh and twelfth centuries had been sustained, doubtless with many local fluctuations which are undocumented, and in certain areas settlements had become very dense. For some estates details survive of the assessment of the surface area, particularly the amount of arable land

---

[17] MM, IV, pp. 273–84; Ahrweiler, 'L'histoire et la géographie de la région de Smyrne', pp. 152–3. The *paroikoi* of Mourmounton belonged to another powerful landowner, Komnenos Angelos; see MM, IV, p. 279.

[18] MM, IV, p. 181.

[19] MM, IV, pp. 257–8.

[20] MM, IV, pp. 399–414. Most of the vineyards consisted of one *holokotinarea*, the equivalent of one *modios*; see Schilbach, *Byzantinische Metrologie*, pp. 60–1.

Conclusion   251

under cultivation, and also the number of *paroikoi* recorded in the *praktika*. Usually the land listed directly under the name of the *paroikos* was restricted to small plots of garden or vineyard without any reference to large amounts of arable land. There were some exceptions, like the estates belonging to Esphigmenou, where the allocation of land, in most cases either fifty or twenty-five *modioi*, to individual peasants was recorded in the *praktika*. However, the list of peasant holdings was generally followed by a bald statement of the quantity of the land and the revenues which the landowner derived from them, usually at a rate of one *nomisma* for every fifty *modioi* unless the land was of an inferior quality. The uniformity of this rate indicates some sort of short-term leasing arrangement, but the specific details of the allocation of this land are not given. Any assessment of the size of peasant holdings on these estates cannot be totally precise, but it gives a useful overall perspective.[21] The purpose of this discussion is not to provide a detailed analysis of the demographic trends of the early fourteenth century,[22] but simply to show that by this time the region was more densely populated than it had been in earlier centuries, the result of a period of sustained population increase which was already under way in the later tenth and the eleventh centuries. The pattern that is obtained is a very varied one. On many estates the average size of peasant holdings was small and on others there is no sign of any land shortage caused by high population levels. Although these variations are apparent within the same administrative region, there is also a broader pattern. In the western Chalkidike there were estates where the peasantry was not under any great pressure because of land shortages and others where many households might have struggled for a standard of living much above subsistence level. In other parts of the peninsula there were areas where relatively little arable land was available to the peasantry. Another particularly densely settled area was the Strymon region, where on many estates most peasants had to be content with small holdings.

The region which shows the widest variation in the density of settlement was the district of Kalamaria in the western part of the Chalkidike peninsula. Two estates from this region, Lorotomou and

---

[21] It can be argued that the effects of a dense settlement on any estate could be offset by peasants working outside their landowner's property. However, if they did so they were liable to pay the landowner the *zeugaratikion*; see Laiou-Thomadakis, *Peasant Society*, p. 181. There is little evidence that this obligation raised very much cash for the Athonite landowners.

[22] See Laiou-Thomadakis, *Peasant Society*, pp. 223–98.

252   *Economic expansion in the Byzantine empire*

Asmalou (known as Loroton and Hagia Euphemia in the fourteenth century) have been discussed in an earlier chapter. In both cases the peasant population on the estates had multiplied between 1104 and 1321. At Loroton the balance between peasant holdings and arable land worked out to an average of thirty-two *modioi* (approximately six or seven acres) for each *paroikos*, and at Hagia Euphemia to fifty-nine *modioi* for each *paroikos*.[23] By 1321 some other estates were notable for the small size of their peasant holdings. At Gournai twenty-nine *paroikoi* held an average of forty-eight *modioi* each; at Genna there were nineteen *paroikoi* with an average holding of twenty-three *modioi* and at Panagia twenty-nine with an average holding of thirty-five *modioi*.[24] Only these average figures are available. The realities of landholding must have been much more complicated. It is inevitable that some peasants, especially those who owned oxen, held more than the average figures on these estates and that the poorer peasants had to manage with a smaller amount of land. On these estates it is likely that a significant proportion of the peasantry had to survive on a very meagre holding and may have been scarcely above the subsistence level.[25] On one other of Lavra's estates in this region, Karbeos, the average holding was below 100 *modioi*,[26] but in four other cases and Esphigmenou's property at Portarea it was between 100 and 150 *modioi* for each *paroikos*.[27] Again the precise details of the exploitation of the land are unknown and it is possible that some *paroikoi* had lands which were much smaller than the average holding, but it is unlikely that there was a significant number of smallholders on these estates. Only on one estate, Sarantarea, was there a great abundance of land.[28]

Elsewhere in the Chalkidike there are clear indications of the proliferation of peasant smallholdings. On Lavra's estate at Ptelea in the Kassandra peninsula the average amount of land available to each *paroikos* was just under twenty *modioi* and on the monastery's properties in the Longos peninsula the average figure was just below fifty *modioi*.[29] Some of the most intensive exploitation of arable land

[23] *Lavra*, II, no. 109 lines 133–265, 948–9, 950–1. See also above, pp. 51–3.
[24] *Ibid.*, lines 20–45, 320–39, 397–417, 941–2, 960–1, 968–9.
[25] For the amount of land necessary to ensure the reproduction of the peasant household, see above, p. 180.   [26] *Lavra*, II, no. 109 lines 296–319, 959.
[27] *Ibid.*, lines 93–132, 265–96, 339–89, 417–50, 944–5, 957, 964–5, 969–70; *Esphigménou*, no. 14 lines 134–76, 214–15.
[28] *Lavra*, II, no. 109 lines 45–93, 943. It is very uncertain that the assessment of this estate was accurate; see Lefort, *Villages de Macedoine*, I, p. 168. Even on the lowest possible figure, however, there was clearly more than enough land for its *paroikoi*.
[29] *Lavra*, II, no. 109 lines 472–89; IV, pp. 85, 110.

Conclusion 253

occurred in the eastern Chalkidike around the village of Gomatou. In 1300 Lavra's estate there was assessed at 6,167 *modioi*, of which only 500 *modioi* were cultivated. The rest was mountainous, stony and generally unsuitable for cultivation. Another estate, Debelikeia, which was attributed to the *metochion* at Gomatou, was assessed at 4,551 *modioi*, of which only 450 was cultivated. Again the rest was mountainous and not fit for cultivation. Although the precise number of *paroikoi* on the estates at this time is uncertain because of gaps in the *praktikon*, it is likely that there were at least ninety-five *paroikoi* belonging to Lavra in the village. In 1321 the monastery possessed 104 *paroikoi* there.[30] So by 1300 Lavra's peasants had very limited arable land available to them, although the rough terrain did offer scope for pastoral farming. It was probably this situation which prompted the monks of Lavra to usurp neighbouring land, install their *paroikoi* there and cultivate it.[31] The peasant holdings on Iviron's estate at Gomatou were also small. There were 1,900 *modioi* of arable land under cultivation and fifty *paroikoi* – thirty-eight *modioi* for each *paroikos* – and all the land was described as second and third class, producing revenues lower than the standard rate of one *nomisma* for fifty *modioi*.[32] On some properties around Hierissos the pressure on resources was not so intense. Iviron's thirty-six *paroikoi* held an average of eighty-five *modioi*[33] and on Xeropotamou's properties the figure was just under 100 *modioi* (approximately twenty acres).[34]

The Strymon region was quite densely populated in many places. On Esphigmenou's estate at Krousovo in 1318 the 817 *modioi* of arable land was divided among twenty-six *paroikoi*. Although the average figure was thirty-one *modioi*, six paroikoi held fifty *modioi*, one had thirty, three were allocated twenty-five *modioi* and two others had twenty and twelve *modioi*. The precise allocation of the remaining 380 *modioi* is unknown.[35] Normally, small holdings of about thirty *modioi* might not have proved adequate to maintain a peasant household, but in the Strymon region the situation might have been different for two reasons. Firstly, the alluvial soils would have been very fertile, where

---

[30] *Lavra*, II, no. 90 lines 292–312, no. 91, no. 109 lines 520–642.

[31] *Chilandar*, no. 19.

[32] F. Dölger, *Sechs byzantinische Praktika des 14. Jahrhunderts für das Athoskloster Iberon* (Munich, 1949), pp. 37–40.

[33] *Ibid.*, pp. 40–6. This does not take into account 600 *modioi* of land which is described in the *praktikon* as unsuitable for cultivation.

[34] *Xéropotamou*, no. 18 pp. 154–6.

[35] *Esphigménou*, no. 14 lines 76–113, 199–200.

254   *Economic expansion in the Byzantine empire*

they were not too marshy and, secondly, many villagers possessed boats and fishing was a major element of the peasant economy. In 1333 properties at Chantax and Nesion on the Strymon river were given to Michael Monomachos. The *praktikon* lists the land which each *paroikos* held. Most of them had received between twenty-four and thirty-six *modioi* of arable land, but out of a total of twenty *paroikoi* four had less than twenty *modioi*. However, there was also 400 *modioi* of land which had not been allocated to individual *paroikoi*, but no doubt they cultivated it, reducing the effect of the small size of their holdings. It was very significant that every *paroikos* also possessed a small boat for fishing. Similarly, at Nesion six of the seven *paroikoi* also had boats. There the pattern of landholding was different. Three peasants held seventy *modioi* each, a very substantial holding, one had thirty-six and the other three had only three *modioi* each. The estate also included another 150 *modioi*, of which only 50 *modioi* was cultivated because the remainder was marshy. Although it was not formally allocated to any *paroikos*, it was certainly worked by the three *paroikoi* with insufficient arable resources.[36] We have no information about the relative importance of arable cultivation and fishing in the economy of the peasants of Chantax and Nesion, but more detailed evidence is available for the village of Doxompous in 1317. The land was assessed at 4,300 *modioi*, of which 3,000 was cultivated; possibly some sort of three-fold crop rotation was practised. The *praktikon* recorded 121 *paroikoi*; in some cases they possessed more than one building and it is possible the actual number of households was higher. The average holding of arable land, including the fallow, was thirty-five *modioi* (about seven acres), but it is likely that the peasants with oxen cultivated more and some of the others rather less. While these holdings were very small, the breakdown of the revenues from this estate shows that arable cultivation was not predominant in Doxompous unlike in most villages. The revenues exacted from the peasants for their houses, animals, gardens and vineyards, the tax on the pasture of their animals and the revenues from the arable land came to just over 275 *hyperpyra*, while the payments exacted from the fishing (including the landing and sale of the catch) amounted to 350 *hyperpyra*. This diversity in economic activity, besides considerably improving the diet of the peasantry, permitted a dense settlement without reducing some of the peasantry to the subsistence level.[37]

The increase in the population of the village of Radolibos between

[36] *Zographou*, no. 29.   [37] *Lavra*, II, no. 104.

Conclusion   255

1103 and 1316 has already been mentioned.[38] It is a very clear illustration of how the expansion of the cultivated area led to the maximum possible exploitation of the resources of the village. The increase in population led to new land clearances, which cut down the area available for pasture, and by the end of the thirteenth century occupation had spread to the mountainous area.[39]

In 1342 some properties around Serres and Zichna were transferred to John Margarites. There was a considerable diversity in the size of the peasant holdings, but several had fairly small properties. At Topolia some peasants held just under twenty *modioi* and Michael Melokates had twenty-five *modioi*, but neither of his brothers had any land at all. At Gostompous the peasants had amounts varying from twenty to thirty-six *modioi*, but one had a very extensive vineyard of forty *modioi*, and was obviously able to produce commercially. At Gornobitza, near Zichna, most of the arable holdings were about twenty to thirty *modioi*, except for one very large holding of sixty-four *modioi* of arable and forty-nine *modioi* of vineyard, again enough for commercial production.[40]

This evidence from different regions is admittedly fragmentary, but it does indicate that by the early fourteenth century settlement had become denser, which could only have been the result of a steady increase in population during the previous centuries. A difficult problem to resolve is the extent to which this population growth was affected by inheritance customs. In Byzantium the provisions of Roman law ensured that partible inheritance was the norm. Theoretically, strict partible inheritance should ensure a high frequency of nuclear family households, early marriage and low emigration, implying a rapid rate of increase, but inheritance customs were flexible and could be adapted to changing situations.[41] The structure of Byzantine rural society suggests that the inheritance system did not have any important

---

[38] See above, p. 50.

[39] Lefort, 'Radolibos: population et paysage', *Travaux et Mémoires*, 9 (1985), pp. 195–234.

[40] P. Lemerle, 'Un praktikon inédit des archives de Karakala (janvier 1342) et la situation en Macédoine orientale au moment de l'usurpation de Cantacuzène', in *Charisterion eis Anastasion K. Orlandon* (4 vols., Athens, 1965–8), I, pp. 278–98.

[41] L. K. Berkner and F. F. Mendels, 'Inheritance Systems, Family Structure and Demographic Patterns in Western Europe, 1700–1900', in C. Tilly (ed.), *Historical Studies of Changing Fertility* (Princeton, 1978), pp. 209–23. For a critique of attempts to determine different population densities in medieval England by different inheritance customs, see Z. Razi, *Life, Marriage and Death in a Medieval Parish. Economy, Society and Demography in Halesowen 1270–1400* (Cambridge, 1980). The fullest discussion of inheritance practices in Byzantium is Laiou-Thomadakis, *Peasant Society*, pp. 186–203.

256   *Economic expansion in the Byzantine empire*

consequences in this respect. On most of the estates for which good
evidence is available the property listed directly under the *paroikoi*
included gardens and vineyards, but not arable land. The latter was
listed separately in most cases and, as has been mentioned already, we
do not have precise information about its allocation. It is likely that it
was leased or share-cropped on a short-term basis according to the
resources of the peasant family in manpower and oxen, a factor liable
to considerable temporal variation. Only in a few cases was land listed
in the *praktika* directly under the peasant household. Consequently, the
peasant property which was divided up among heirs did not form the
total basis of a peasant family's means of reproduction. In the
documents partible inheritance appears as the dominant practice,
although forms of extended households (vertically and laterally) are
also in evidence.[42] The properties whose transfer to heirs can be
followed were mainly vineyards and gardens, not arable land. It is
possible that on most large estates the impact of population increase
and the pressure which it put on agricultural resources did not have a
dramatic effect on inheritance practices, precisely because the owner
oversaw the allocation of the land. Of course, most of the evidence
relates to the properties of large monastic estates, where there was a
continuity of ownership and administration. On some other estates,
given as *pronoiai* to lay landowners, ownership was more precarious.
When Margarites and Monomachos received their *pronoiai*, a large
proportion of the arable was listed directly under the peasant household
and there are signs of different inheritance practices on these estates. On
Margarites's properties there are instances of unequal divisions between
heirs, which took the form of a preferential system of partible inheritance
whereby some relatives held small plots of land around their houses
while one member of the family retained the bulk of the holding.[43] In
contrast, at Chantax there was a broad uniformity in the size of the
holdings and indications of fairly equal divisions among heirs, even
though only modest amounts of arable land were involved.[44] There is a
possible economic explanation of these divergent practices. At Chantax
fishing was an important part of the village's economy owing to its
location near the Strymon. The pressure on agricultural resources was
relieved by this alternative source of livelihood, but no such option was

[42] Laiou-Thomadakis, *Peasant Society*, pp. 196–203.
[43] Lemerle, 'Un praktikon inédit des archives de Karakala', p. 282 lines 8–11, pp.
284–5 lines 33–5.
[44] *Zographou*, no. 29 lines 8–20.

Conclusion 257

available to the peasants near Zichna, where the impact of pressure on agricultural resources must have been greater.

The extension of the cultivated area owing to the growth of population was accompanied by some limited improvements in agricultural production. It was not a question of technological innovation, but the more effective exploitation of agricultural potential within the limits of the technology available to the Byzantines. Comparisons with the west are not totally appropriate because the advances made there, notably the spread of the heavy plough and the overshot water-mill, were largely unsuitable for Mediterranean farming conditions. The greater availability of iron for agricultural implements in the west from the eleventh century has been attributed considerable importance by Duby, especially in relation to the plough, whose blade was regularly reinforced with iron by the twelfth century.[45] Although the evidence is fragmentary there is no indication of any serious shortage of iron implements in Byzantium.[46] Another significant tendency in the west was towards a three-fold crop rotation, but it needed good-quality soil. While common on the alluvial soils of the Paris basin, its spread elsewhere was haphazard, and usually the sequence of crops was irregular. This was probably true too for Byzantium. Where soils were fertile and the population sufficiently high to necessitate a more intensive exploitation, some sort of triennial rotation might have occurred. This was possibly the case at Doxompous in the early fourteenth century.[47] No firm conclusions can be drawn owing to lack of evidence, but generally Mediterranean conditions would have permitted only a biennial rotation in most places. One factor which probably did lead to some improvements in production was the greater availability of labour, because dry farming is a very arduous and time-consuming process, needing regular ploughing and weeding. The other significant factor was the greater resources available to large landowners. While it is unlikely that expenditure on agricultural improvements ever made up a large proportion of their total expenditure, they did have the cash to spend when it was needed and the sources do reveal numerous instances of improvements made by landowners. There does not appear to have been any clear distinction in this respect between lay and ecclesiastical properties, although more is known about the latter. In particular, the monasteries,

---

[45] Duby, *Rural Economy and Country Life*, pp. 107–9.
[46] See above, pp. 124–5.
[47] See above, pp. 126, 254.

258   *Economic expansion in the Byzantine empire*

which in later centuries acquired a reputation as inefficient landlords, did make improvements to their lands. The efforts of these landowners were directed to the improvement of irrigation facilities and the planting of cash crops. Some irrigation schemes, notably that of Athanasios of Lavra, were quite extensive. In the absence of precise figures it is only possible to speculate as to whether they led to a significant increase in productivity. They required greater inputs of labour, but this was spread through the year, reducing seasonal under-employment. It is also possible that some of the potentially very fertile alluvial lands were more effectively exploited, but some references in the sources to flooding would suggest some caution on this point. They would have needed good drainage to avoid this danger and a significant amount of manpower was required for this purpose. The population of Constantinople was greatly dependent on the produce of the alluvial plains of Thrace, Macedonia and Thessaly for its grain supply. Some landowners spent considerable sums on olive trees and viticulture. In some cases this might have been due to greater consumption requirements (especially in the early years of a monastic foundation when the number of monks might increase sharply), but the important stimulus to this form of production was the relative ease with which the products could be transported to urban markets. Once consumption needs had been met – and large estates could cover these easily – landowners had more scope for concentrating on specific crops. The regularity with which vineyards were situated near streams or linked to irrigation works reflects the importance of the produce in boosting the cash revenues of large landowners. The overall impact of these improvements is difficult to assess, but a comparison with developments in northern Italy is suggestive. There the organisation of flood control, drainage and irrigation was taken over by the urban communes and carried out much more extensively than such projects were by individual landowners in Byzantium. Yet evidence of crop yields would indicate a normal yield in most parts of Italy of three- to six-fold. This suggests that medieval farming there was more successful in extending the cultivated area than in improving yields, although an increase in the range of crops planted might have resulted from the improvements.[48] It is likely that the improvements made by Byzantine landowners were most significant in increasing the quantities of produce like wine, which was

---

[48] See the chapter on Italy by P. Jones in M. M. Postan (ed.), *The Cambridge Economic History of Europe*, I, *The Agrarian Life of the Middle Ages*, 2nd edn (Cambridge, 1971), esp. pp. 358–60, 376–7.

Conclusion   259

relatively easily marketed, thereby augmenting the revenues which they derived from agriculture.

A problem which deserves some consideration is the relative effectiveness of large and moderate-sized landowners in exploiting their properties. It has received some discussion in relation to other parts of medieval Europe. English evidence[49] suggests that smaller landowners often invested a larger proportion of their total income in maintaining and improving their properties than larger landowners, but one reason for this was that they could not exact labour services to do the work. The personal involvement of landowners in running their estates might have led to improvements in efficiency (unless the landowner was inefficient, in which case the effect would have been the opposite). This is an area where the Byzantine evidence is particularly inadequate. The case of Skaranos, who seems to have run his properties quite efficiently, suggests that production on smaller properties did not vary significantly from that on larger estates,[50] although there was less scope for specialisation and larger landowners had important advantages in terms of flexibility in marketing their produce.

There are parallels between Byzantium and the west in the general pattern of growth in monetary circulation and commercial exchange. By the eleventh century payments in cash were becoming more common in most parts of Europe although the chronology of the process varied greatly from region to region and in some places, like the mountainous region of Provence, money continued to be rare even in the thirteenth century.[51] In Byzantium the increase in the resources available to the state led to larger amounts of money being put into circulation. The growth in the quantity of money is best reflected in the archaeological finds on urban sites and in the fiscal developments of the eleventh and twelfth centuries. The higher rates of taxation incumbent on the direct producers after Alexios's fiscal reform and the increasing commutation of non-monetary obligations into cash payments compelled the peasantry to raise larger sums through the sale of part of their produce. Provided that the increases were not too steep and abrupt, the higher rates could be exacted in many regions where money was circulating in large quantities, but several times in the eleventh century,

[49] Hilton, *The English Peasantry*, p. 200; Miller and Hatcher, *Medieval England*, p. 228; R. H. Britnell, 'Minor Landlords in England and Medieval Agrarian Capitalism', *Past and Present*, 89 (1980), pp. 3–22.

[50] See the discussions of Skaranos's will in Nesbitt, 'Mechanisms of Agricultural Production', pp. 28–30, 36, 42–4.

[51] Duby, *Rural Economy and Country Life*, pp. 130–1.

260   *Economic expansion in the Byzantine empire*

when the trend towards commutation into cash payments was very marked, fiscal demands provoked discontent and isolated instances of localised revolts,[52] an indication of the limited extent to which the peasant economy was monetised in spite of the greater volume of money in circulation. Although cash passed through the hands of the peasants when they needed it for their tax-payments, it is likely that little remained in the peasant economy. The clearest evidence that commercial activity in villages was very sluggish comes from the details in the *praktika* of the obligations of *paroikoi* to their landowners. These payments reflected the range of economic activity in the peasant communities and sometimes included the proceeds of commercial fairs held in the village. These fairs were usually very unproductive compared to the total revenues to which the landowner was entitled. In the village of Brasta in 1318 the commercial fair produced revenues of $\frac{1}{4}$ *nomisma* out of total revenues of 168 *nomismata* and not surprisingly this fair had disappeared altogether from the records by 1321.[53] This is an extreme case, but others lead to similar conclusions. The revenues from the market at Stephaniana fluctuated between 4% and 6% of the total revenues.[54] Lavra's revenues from its estate at Pinsson totalled 209 *nomismata* in 1321, but only six *nomismata* came from the proceeds of the fair.[55] Similarly at Hierissos in 1301 Iviron's revenues totalled sixty-three *nomismata*, but only two *nomismata* were obtained from the fair.[56] There is one partial exception to this argument. The village of Doxompous was distinct from most peasant communities in that it was not totally dominated by agricultural production. Although revenues from the commercial fair amounted to only 1.5% of the total payments, other obligations imposed on the transportation and sale of fish pushed the exactions relating to commerce up to nearly 10% of the total, substantially higher than in the other villages. However, this case shows that even in a village with a relatively diversified economy commercial activity took place within very restricted limits. In a peasant economy geared essentially to meeting subsistence requirements, there was little scope for commerce. This was also a reflection of the dominant role of agricultural production in the Byzantine economy as a whole.

The development of towns also fits into the general pattern of a

---

[52] See chapter 3. [53] *Esphigménou*, no. 14 line 194.
[54] *Ibid.*, no. 14 lines 121–34, 205–10; no. 16 lines 57–67, 77–80.
[55] *Lavra*, II, no. 109.
[56] Dölger, *Sechs byzantinische Praktika*, pp. 41–2 lines A153–60.

Conclusion 261

limited economic expansion. The course of urban history offers a useful parallel to that of agrarian history owing to the close interaction between town and country. In the seventh and eighth centuries there had been a dramatic contraction of urban sites in both Asia Minor and the Balkans and the position of Constantinople as an urban centre became almost monopolistic. In these centuries the state played a major role in establishing new urban sites, and military and administrative factors were preeminent in giving towns importance. However, the upsurge of new urban sites and the expansion of older sites from the tenth century onwards was made possible only by a substantial increase in agricultural production. Not only did this ensure a secure food supply for a larger population engaged in non-agricultural activities, but the increase in revenues from agriculture stimulated a greater demand for urban products. Nevertheless, the extent of urban expansion should not be exaggerated. It was of course nowhere near as pronounced as in parts of Italy, where already in the tenth century cities like Milan and Lucca were thriving commercially on a scale unknown in Byzantium outside Constantinople,[57] but the general pattern of expansion in the eleventh and twelfth centuries does follow the general course of urban development in medieval Europe.[58]

There was one very significant difference between Byzantine towns and their counterparts in many regions of the medieval west. In Byzantium towns were so dominated by the landowning elite that the mercantile and industrial groups were never able to gain firm control of the towns and the long-running struggles for power between townsmen and their feudal overlord, so familiar in the west,[59] did not occur in Byzantium. Urban vitality in Byzantium was most notable in the European provinces. Possibly towns in Asia Minor suffered from the adverse impact of the Turkish incursions on agricultural production, and economic expansion was retarded, at least until the thirteenth century.[60] Certainly there is strong evidence that commercial activity there was sluggish and commodity production was generally limited to the provision of basic requirements. Even in the European provinces towns like Thebes and Corinth, which were important industrial centres, were the exception. More commonly, towns acted as a local market centre with only a modest amount of simple commodity

[57] Wickham, *Early Medieval Italy*, pp. 85, 91.
[58] E. Ennen, *The Medieval Town* (Amsterdam, 1978).
[59] Duby, *The Early Growth of the European Economy*, pp. 244–8.
[60] For the thirteenth-century evidence, see Angold, *A Byzantine Government in Exile*, pp. 108–11.

production, but even this was a considerable change from the situation in the early Middle Ages. In the eleventh and twelfth centuries many coastal towns which were outlets for the agricultural produce of their regions increased in economic importance. Industrial production was still limited in these towns, but their commercial functions clearly distinguished them from their agricultural hinterlands. Even where town dwellers were also agricultural producers, the proximity of a market gave their agriculture a different character from that of a peasant producing mainly for subsistence. There was greater scope for specialisation in cash crops, because a larger part of the produce could be sold. The increasing revenues of large landowners gave some stimulus to industrial and commercial activity in the provincial towns and some towns were founded through individual initiatives by landowners. The growing power of the feudal aristocracy was reflected in the greater vitality of these towns in the eleventh and twelfth centuries, a sharp contrast with the seventh and eighth centuries.

As this interpretation differs from standard accounts, it necessitates some consideration of the impact of these economic trends on the political history of these centuries. Usually, the political problems of the empire have been connected to economic decline. Historians have generally passed negative judgements on the development of feudalism and have not made any connection between feudal social relations and economic expansion. A reexamination is necessary in view of the evidence of economic growth and is best done by assessing the impact which the changes outlined above had upon the state and the main social classes, the landowning aristocracy, the peasantry and the commercial and artisanal population.

Economic expansion increased the resources available to the state as well as the wealth of feudal landowners. Demographic increase was an important and generally neglected factor in the growth of large properties. Independent peasant farmers gradually became a less important social group than they had been in the seventh and eighth centuries. Peasant communities were restricted by territorial limits and population increase must have led to a fragmentation of landholdings, especially if the existence of neighbouring estates belonging to powerful landowners prevented any expansion of a community's territory. Large estates benefiting from imperial privileges expanded more rapidly and the proportion of independent peasants in the rural population was reduced as *paroikoi* of the state and private landowners became more numerous. This was not the result of a straightforward policy of the

Conclusion 263

state aimed at transforming free peasants into *paroikoi*. Doubtless, peasants were constrained to sell out to large landowners as the state's fiscal pressure increased, but the absorption of large numbers of landless peasants on large estates was probably a more important cause of the change in the relative proportions of free peasants and *paroikoi* in the rural population. Not only was a greater part of the peasantry subordinated to large landowners, but the cash demands on the peasantry were increasing, providing the state and feudal landowners with greater revenues. Generally, the privileges which landowners received did not detract from the resources of the state because they were restricted to the installation of landless peasants, who owed no obligations to the state, and the administration was generally able to enforce the conditions of these privileges. The expansion of large estates was linked with the increase in the number of direct producers. It coincided with the greater importance which the state attached to the direct exploitation of its own estates compared with the exaction of tax-payments from independent peasants, because imperial estates, like those of powerful landowners, could be cultivated more intensively due to the larger supply of labour.

While land was being cultivated more intensively, the area directly under the state's control diminished in the late eleventh century. It is difficult to determine the extent to which territorial loss was compensated for by more intensive agricultural production in the remaining lands. The loss of south Italy was probably of limited importance for the imperial finances. Although it was quite a lucrative region, it is unlikely that large sums were finding their way back to Constantinople. The distance involved probably gave the provincial administrators there a much greater degree of autonomy than that possessed in other provinces. The loss of the interior of Asia Minor was more serious, but it consists predominantly of rugged land of limited productivity outside the sunken basins of the plateau and it had been dominated by powerful provincial magnates. Bulgaria, which had been subjugated by Basil II, was probably at least as lucrative and the regions which remained under Byzantine control were generally more productive than the interior of Anatolia. In the Komnenian period the territorial resources available to the state were easily comparable to the resources at the disposal of tenth-century emperors before the defeat of the Bulgarian state. In the eleventh and twelfth centuries these resources were exploited much more intensively and, if only because of the greater number of direct producers, must have yielded larger

264   *Economic expansion in the Byzantine empire*

revenues. An exceptional phase was, perhaps, the 1070s and 1080s, when the dislocation caused by territorial loss and pressing military expenses created financial problems, but this was temporary and ceased with the firm establishment of the Komnenian dynasty. The general trend in this period was towards an increase in the revenues available to the state.

The state's wealth increased, but the structure of its expenditure remained unchanged. The most important outlays were on military, administrative and diplomatic expenses and on conspicuous consumption. The verdict of historians on the conspicuous expenditure of the emperors of the mid eleventh century has usually been unfavourable. It sees them squandering the state's resources rather than responding to the increase in revenues by increasing expenditure. The most notable increase in military expenditure can be attributed to the much more regular hiring of mercenaries, especially from the reign of Monomachos onwards.[61] It was a particularly onerous burden during some of Manuel's more ambitious expeditions and was supplemented by considerable naval expenditure. Another expensive and related outlay involved diplomatic payments. These increased during periods of military activity, when the need to secure the neutrality of other foreign rulers was most pressing. Outlays on fortifications must also have increased greatly from the late eleventh century. The Seljuk invasions in Asia Minor created a need to protect areas which had previously been far removed from the dangers of incursions. Recovery from the impact of their raids was clearly linked with the construction of extensive new lines of fortifications in the twelfth century.[62] The greater resources at its disposal enabled the state to extend the range of its military and diplomatic activities in the twelfth century and to pursue an ambitious and expensive foreign policy.

At the same time as the state's wealth was increased, its internal authority was being slowly undermined by a gradual process of social change. The most important contradiction in the Byzantine social formation was that by service in the state's military and administrative apparatuses feudal landowners were able to accumulate social and economic power and eventually pose a threat to the state's ability to control the provinces. In the early Middle Ages the state's authority had been strong, even though the resources available to it were restricted by extensive economic contraction. The old senatorial aristocracy was in

[61] Oikonomides, 'L'évolution de l'organisation administrative', p. 144.
[62] Vryonis, *The Decline of Medieval Hellenism*, pp. 216–20.

decline and the new provincial aristocracy based in the themes was beginning to build up its power. Only in the tenth century did it become a serious threat to the state.

In the late eleventh century the power of many feudal landowners was significantly strengthened. Although many aristocratic families lost their patrimonial estates in Asia Minor, some settled in the European provinces with extensive privileges. In the 1070s and 1080s the pattern of concessions by the state to landowners changed, partly because of the political crisis resulting from the Seljuk invasion of Asia Minor and the Norman attacks in the Balkans. The state was prepared to purchase the support of a powerful but restricted group of landowners at a high price. The privileges which it granted in these decades were generally more far-reaching than those which had usually been given previously. It granted revenues, which it had previously collected, to these landowners, instead of simply allowing them to establish landless peasants (whose names were not recorded in the administration's records) on their estates. At the same time, powerful landowners were exploiting the devaluation of the gold coinage. The clearest indication of the power of the most influential landowners was the ability of Lavra to retain land illegally in the decades preceding Alexios's fiscal reform. After Alexios had established his authority securely, the proliferation of generous privileges ceased. The strengthening of central control resulted in administrative change and the reform of the coinage and later the taxation system. At the same time the reestablishment of imperial authority left some weaknesses in the administrative apparatus. The highest posts in the administration, especially in the military sphere, became the preserve of the imperial family and the clan of related families to the exclusion of other aristocratic lines. Alexios's brothers were the beneficiaries of the most far-reaching fiscal concessions. The state granted them the taxes from extensive areas, and the responsibility for their collection lay with the beneficiaries personally, not with the state. It was clearly a partial abdication of administrative authority over quite large areas. This system of '*appanages*', which was to become more widespread under the Palaiologoi, contained its own centrifugal tendencies. Initially, this arrangement helped the new Komnenian dynasty to establish its authority securely, but in the long term it marked an intensification of the contradiction between the centralised, bureaucratic state and the developing feudal social relations.

The growing political power of the aristocracy was reinforced by the consolidation of its economic resources. The pattern of spending by the aristocracy, like the state's spending, probably did not change greatly as its wealth increased. The proportion of revenues used to make improvements to properties was usually fairly small. The outlays on conspicuous expenditure, buildings, military purposes and the maintenance of retinues were much greater. Conspicuous expenditure may have been most notable among landowners whose interests were most closely tied to the imperial bureaucracy in Constantinople. The expenditure of prominent members of the provincial aristocracy turned more towards military considerations, in particular the construction and upkeep of fortifications. Their increasing revenues in both cash and kind also gave them the resources to maintain imposing retinues, a clear symbol of prestige and power. The aristocracy remained the dominant social group in Byzantium in spite of the expansion of urban commodity production.

Agricultural production continued to be the most important factor in the Byzantine economy and the revenues which landowners derived from urban rents were of limited significance compared with those from their rural estates. Although mercantile and artisanal activity increased, the mercantile class did not become strong enough to challenge the social position of the landowning aristocracy. A significant proportion of commerce was undertaken by wealthy landowners with maritime privileges (not to mention the Italian merchants). An increasingly large proportion of the wealth created by economic expansion was going into the hands of these landowners. There were isolated instances when the state seemed to recognise this and attempted to impose some control and increase its revenues from trade, but these efforts were short-lived and unsuccessful.

The development of feudal relations of production was an integral part of the economic expansion of these centuries, which was stronger and more sustained than has usually been admitted. The decline in the authority of the central government was not the result of economic stagnation or decline. Instead, the centrifugal tendencies in the provinces were greatly reinforced by economic growth. They were concealed to a certain extent by the power of the Komnenian rulers because the state's resources also increased, but the rapid increase in the wealth of the aristocracy had important social and political consequences. Although landowners did derive great gains from service in the administration, this had made them more dependent on the vicissitudes of imperial favour, but as their economic power-base was strengthened they acquired some degree of protection from this

Conclusion   267

dependence. The provinces had become much more lucrative regions, which at the end of the twelfth century were maintaining local rulers who were *de facto* independent of Constantinople. The disintegration of the Byzantine empire in the final decades of the twelfth century is best illustrated by the gaps in the *Partitio Romaniae*, a document which was almost certainly based on Byzantine fiscal documents. It deals with the division of the conquered empire by the crusaders after the capture of Constantinople in 1204, but extensive areas which had nominally been part of the empire did not figure in the document because they had passed out of effective imperial control.[63] Although some rebels did display some pretensions of imperial authority by issuing their own coinage,[64] they were generally concerned more with consolidating their local authority. This process of disintegration had already started in the 1180s when Isaac Komnenos usurped power in Cyprus and ruled the island independently of Constantinople, maintaining his regime by the collection of taxes which had previously been paid to the capital. Then a revolt in Bulgaria led to the creation of the second Bulgarian empire. The events were connected closely to political intrigues, but in other cases rebels were local landowners whose power-base was in the regions which they usurped. In 1188 Philadelphia became the centre of a revolt by Theodore Mankaphas, who assumed the imperial title and minted his own coins. The imperial offensive against him was interrupted by the approach of the third crusade and a compromise was agreed whereby Mankaphas renounced all his imperial pretensions but retained control of Philadelphia. In 1193 he was forced to flee to Ikonion after he lost power in Philadelphia and, although he was handed over to the emperor by the sultan, he was again the local ruler in Philadelphia by the time of the fourth crusade. In southern Greece Leo Sgouros carved out a substantial independent territory of his own. A magnate from Nauplion, Sgouros had already conquered Argos before 1202. He successfully resisted an imperial fleet, imposed his authority on Corinth and unsuccessfully attacked Athens. Later in 1204 he captured Thebes and advanced into Thessaly, but was eventually defeated by the crusaders. By April 1204 Trebizond had been occupied by Alexios, the grandson of Andronikos Komnenos, who founded the dynasty of the Grand Komnenoi. Attaleia was under the

---

[63] N. Oikonomides, 'La décomposition de l'empire byzantin à la veille de 1204 et les origines de l'empire de Nicée: à propos de la "Partitio Romaniae"', in *Actes du XV*e *congrès international d'études byzantines. Athènes, septembre 1976*, I, *Histoire*, pp. 1–28.
[64] Hendy, *Studies in the Byzantine Monetary Economy*, pp. 438–9.

268 *Economic expansion in the Byzantine empire*

control of Aldebrandinos, a Byzantine of Italian extract. Rhodes had also escaped from the authority of the administration in Constantinople and was probably under the control of a member of the Gabalas family. Manuel Maurozomes and Sabas Asidenos had established themselves as independent rulers in the Maiander valley and at Sampson, near Miletos, respectively. Unfortunately, nothing is known of the situation in these places before 1204 and it is not certain how long they had been independent of Constantinople.[65]

The greater wealth of the provinces made them attractive regions in their own right without reference to Constantinople. This was emphatically confirmed by the prosperity of the Lascarid empire in the thirteenth century. The conflict of interests between Constantinople and the provinces had reached a higher level of intensity than in previous centuries. In the years preceding the fourth crusade Byzantium was a state disintegrating from within, a process accelerated by the Latin conquest in 1204. It was the result of the conflict between the bureaucratic apparatus of the imperial state, which had survived from Antiquity, and rapidly developing feudal relations of production. Unlike in the west, where ancient social relations had dissolved more quickly and feudalism exercised a more positive function, the constraints placed upon its development in Byzantium by the centralised state gave it a more negative, destructive aspect as a factor contributing to the political decline of the empire. As the economy expanded in the provinces, state control gradually weakened. By the end of the twelfth century upsurge in economic activity contrasted sharply with the weakness of the state.

[65] Oikonomides, 'La décomposition de l'empire byzantin à la veille de 1204'; C. M. Brand, *Byzantium Confronts the West 1180–1204* (Harvard, 1968); J. Hoffman, *Rudimente von Territorialstaaten im byzantinischen Reich (1071–1210)* (Munich, 1974); Ostrogorsky, *History*, p. 426. For Choniates's description of the division of the empire among many local rulers after 1204, see Nicetas Choniates, pp. 638–9.

Bibliography

PRIMARY SOURCES

Anna Comnène. *Alexiade*, ed. B. Leib (3 vols., Paris, 1967).

Ashburner, W. 'The Farmer's Law', *Journal of Hellenic Studies*, 30 (1910), pp. 85–108; 32 (1912), pp. 68–95.

Asher, A. (ed. and trans.) *The Itinerary of Rabbi Benjamin of Tudela* (New York, 1840).

Astruc, C. 'Un document inédit de 1163 sur l'évêché thessalien de Stagi', *Bulletin de Correspondance Hellénique*, 83 (1959), pp. 206–46.

'L'inventaire – dressé en septembre 1200 – du trésor et de la bibliothèque de Patmos. Édition diplomatique', *Travaux et Mémoires*, 8 (1981), pp. 15–30.

Beckh, H. *Geoponica sive Cassiani Bassi de Re Rustica Eclogiae* (Leipzig, 1897).

Bompaire, J. *Actes de Xéropotamou* (Archives de l'Athos III) (Paris, 1964).

Branouse, E. L. *Byzantina Engrapha tes Mones Patmou*, I, *Autokratorika* (Athens, 1980).

Brooks, E. W. 'The Campaign of 716–718 from Arabic Sources', *Journal of Hellenic Studies*, 19 (1899), pp. 19–33.

Cameron, Averil and Herrin, J. (eds.). *Constantinople in the Early Eighth Century. The Parastaseis Syntomai Chronikai* (Leiden, 1984).

Cecaumeni Strategicon, ed. B. Wassiliewsky and V. Jernstedt (St Petersburg, 1896, reprinted Amsterdam, 1965).

Constantine Porphyrogenitus, *De Administrando Imperio*, 2nd edn ed. G. Moravcsik and R. J. H. Jenkins (Washington, 1967).

Constantini Porphyrogeniti Imperatoris De Cerimoniis Aulae Byzantinae Libri Duo, ed. J. J. Reiske (2 vols., Bonn, 1829).

Constantino Porfirogenito De Thematibus. Introduzione, testo critico, commento, ed. A. Pertusi (Rome, 1952).

Darrouzès, J. *Épistoliers byzantins au Xe siècle* (Paris, 1960).

Delahaye, H. 'Vita S. Lucae Stylitae', *Les Saints stylites* (Subsidia Hagiographica 14) (Brussels, 1923), pp. 195–237.

Dmitrievskij, A. *Opisanije liturgiceskih rukopisej, hranjastihsja v bibliotekah pravoslavnogo volstoka*, I, *Typika* (Kiev, 1895).

269

270   *Bibliography*

F. Dölger, *Regesten der Kaiserurkunden des Oströmischen Reiches von 565–1453* (5 vols., Munich, Berlin, 1924–65).

Beiträge zur Geschichte der byzantinischen Finanzverwaltung besonders des 10. und 11. Jahrhunderts (Leipzig, Berlin, 1927).

Aus den Schatzkammern des heiligen Berges (Munich, 1948).

Sechs byzantinische Praktika des 14. Jahrhunderts für das Athoskloster Iberon (Munich, 1949).

'Ein Fall slavischer Einsiedlung im Hinterland von Thessalonike im 10. Jahrhundert', *Sitzungsberichte der bayerischen Akademie der Wissenschaft. Philosophisch-historische Klasse* (1952), pp. 3–28.

Downey, G. 'Nikolaos Mesarites: Description of the Church of the Holy Apostles at Constantinople', *Transactions of the American Philosophical Society*, 47 (1957), pp. 855–924.

Dujčev, I. (ed.). *Cronaca di Monemvasia. Introduzione, testo critico, traduzione e note* (Palermo, 1976).

Dvornik, F. *La Vie de saint Grégoire le Décapolite et les slaves macédoniens au IXe siècle* (Paris, 1926).

To Eparchikon Biblion. The Book of the Prefect. Le Livre du préfet, with an introduction by I. Dujčev (London, 1970).

Eustratiades, S. 'Typikon tes en Konstantinopolei mones tou hagiou megalomartyros Mamantos', *Hellenika*, 1 (1928), pp. 245–314.

Festugière, A.-J. *Vie de Théodore de Sykéôn* (Subsidia Hagiographica 48) (Brussels, 1970).

Fourmy, M. H. and Leroy, M. 'La vie de S. Philarète', *Byzantion*, 9 (1934), pp. 85–170.

Gautier, P. 'Diatribes de Jean l'Oxite contre Alexis 1er Comnène', *Revue des Études Byzantines*, 28 (1970), pp. 5–55.

'Le typikon de Christ Sauveur Pantocrator', *Revue des Études Byzantines*, 32 (1974), pp. 1–145.

'La diataxis de Michel Attaliate', *Revue des Études Byzantines*, 39 (1981), pp. 5–143.

'Le typikon de la Théotokos Évergétis', *Revue des Études Byzantines*, 40 (1982), pp. 5–101.

'Le typikon du sébaste Grégoire Pakourianos', *Revue des Études Byzantines*, 42 (1984), pp. 5–145.

'Le typikon de la Théotokos Kécharitôménè', *Revue des Études Byzantines*, 43 (1985), pp. 5–165.

Gesta Regis Henrici Secundi Benedicti Abbatis. The Chronicle of the Reigns of Henry II and Richard I AD 1169–1192; known commonly under the Name of Benedict of Peterborough, ed. W. Stubbs (2 vols., London, 1867).

Goudas, M. 'Byzantiaka engrapha tes en Atho hieras mones tou Batopediou', *Epeteris Hetaireias Byzantinon Spoudon*, 3 (1926), pp. 113–34; 4 (1927), pp. 211–48.

Bibliography 271

Granstrem, E., Medvedev, I. and Papachryssanthou, D. 'Fragment d'un praktikon de la région d'Athènes (avant 1204)', *Revue des Études Byzantines*, 34 (1976), pp. 5–44.

Grégoire, H. 'Un édit de l'empereur Justinien II, daté de septembre 688', *Byzantion*, 17 (1944–5), pp. 119–24.

Halkin, F. 'La vie de saint Nicéphore, fondateur de Médikion en Bithynie (†813)', *Analecta Bollandiana*, 78 (1960), pp. 396–430.

Hausherr, I. and Horn, G. *Vie de Syméon le Nouveau Théologien (949–1022) par Nicétas Stéthatos* (Orientalia Christiana 12, no. 45) (Rome, 1928).

Heisenberg, A. 'Neue Quellen zur Geschichte des lateinischen Kaisertums und der Kirchenunion, III. Der Bericht des Nicolaos Mesarites über die politischen und kirchlichen Ereignisse des Jahres 1214', in *Sitzungsberichte der bayerischen Akademie der Wissenschaften. Philosophisch-philologische und historische Klasse* (Munich, 1923), pp. 3–96.

Hesseling, D.-C. and Pernot, H. *Poèmes prodromiques en grec vulgaire* (Amsterdam, 1910).

Iberites, I. 'Ek tou archeiou tes en hagio orei hieras mones ton Iberon. Byzantinai diathekai', *Orthodoxia*, 5 (1930), pp. 613–18; 6 (1931), pp. 364–71.

Ioannis Caminiatae De Expugnatione Thessalonicae, ed. G. Böhlig (Corpus Fontium Historiae Byzantinae IV) (Berlin, 1973).

Ioannis Cinnami Epitome, ed. A. Meineke (Bonn, 1836).

Ioannis Scylitzae Synopsis Historiarum, ed. J. Thurn (Corpus Fontium Historiae Byzantinae V) (Berlin, 1973).

Ioannis Zonarae Epitome Historiarum, ed. M. Pinder and T. Büttner-Wobst (3 vols., Bonn, 1841–97).

Jaubert, J. A. *La Géographie d'Edrisi* (2 vols., Paris, 1836–40).

Jenkins, R. J. H. and Westerink, L. G. *Nicolas I, Patriarch of Constantinople. Letters* (Dumbarton Oaks, 1973).

Karayannopulos, J. 'Fragmente aus dem Vademecum eines byzantinischen Finanzbeamten', in *Polychronion. Festschrift F. Dölger* (Heidelberg, 1966), pp. 318–34.

Lagarde, P. de. *Johannis Euchaitorum Metropolitae quae in Codice Vaticano 676 supersunt* (Göttingen, 1882).

Lampros, S. *Michael Akominatou tou Choniatou ta Sozomena* (2 vols., Athens, 1879–80).

'Ho bios Nikonos tou Metanoeite', *Neos Hellenomnemon*, 3 (1906), pp. 129–228.

Laurent, V. *La Vie merveilleuse de saint Pierre d'Atroa* (Subsidia Hagiographica 29) (Brussels, 1956).

Lefort, J. *Actes d'Esphigménou* (Archives de l'Athos VI) (Paris, 1973).

Lemerle, P. *Cinq études sur le XIe siècle byzantin* (Paris, 1977).

Les Plus Anciens Recueils des miracles de saint Démétrius et la pénétration des Slaves dans les Balkans, I, *Le texte*, II, *Commentaire* (2 vols., Paris, 1979, 1981).

272 Bibliography

'Un praktikon inédit des archives de Karakala (janvier 1342) et la situation en Macédoine orientale au moment de l'usurpation de Cantacuzène', in *Charisterion eis Anastasion K. Orlandon* (4 vols., Athens, 1965–8), I, pp. 278–98.

Lemerle, P., Dagron, G. and Ćirković, S. *Actes de Saint-Pantéléèmôn* (Archives de l'Athos XII) (Paris, 1982).

Lemerle, P., Guillou, A., Svoronos, N. and Papachryssanthou, D. *Actes de Lavra, I, Des origines à 1204* (Archives de l'Athos V), (Paris, 1970).

Actes de Lavra, II, De 1204 à 1328 (Archives de l'Athos VIII) (Paris, 1977).

Actes de Lavra, IV, Études historiques. Actes serbes. Compléments et index (Archives de l'Athos XI) (Paris, 1982).

Leone, P. A. M. (ed.). *Ioannis Tzetzae Epistulae* (Leipzig, 1972).

Leroy-Molinghen, A. 'Prolégomènes à une édition critique des "Lettres" de Théophylacte de Bulgarie', *Byzantion*, 13 (1938), pp. 253–62.

Liudprand of Cremona, *Relatio de Legatione Constantinopolitana*, ed. and trans. F. A. Wright, *The Works of Liudprand of Cremona* (London, 1936).

Magdalino, P. 'An Unpublished Pronoia Grant of the Second Half of the Fourteenth Century', *Zbornik Radova Vizantološkog Instituta*, 18 (1978), pp. 155–63.

Meyer, P. *Die Haupturkunden für die Geschichte der Athoskloster* (Leipzig, 1894).

Michaelis Attaliotae Historia, ed. I. Bekker (Bonn, 1853).

Michaelis Pselli Scripta Minora, ed. G. Kurtz and F. Drexl (2 vols., Milan, 1936–41).

Michel Psellos. *Chronographie ou histoire d'un siècle de Byzance (976–1077)*, ed. E. Renauld (2 vols., Paris, 1926–8).

Migne, J.-P. *Patrologiae Cursus Completus, Series Graeca* (Paris, 1857–).

Miklosich, F. and Müller, J. *Acta et Diplomata Graeca Medii Aevi* (6 vols., Vienna, 1860–90).

Nesbitt, J. and Wiita, J. 'A Confraternity of the Comnenian Era', *Byzantinische Zeitschrift*, 68 (1975), pp. 360–84.

Nicephori Archiepiscopi Constantinopolitani Opuscula Historia, ed. C. de Boor (Leipzig, 1880).

Nicephori Bryennii Historiarum Libri Quattuor, ed. P. Gautier (Corpus Fontium Historiae Byzantinae IX) (Brussels, 1975).

Nicetae Choniatae Historia, ed. J. A. van Dieten (Corpus Fontium Historiae Byzantinae XI) (Berlin, 1975).

Nystazopoulou-Pelekidou, M. *Byzantina Engrapha tes Mones Patmou, II, Demosion Leitourgon* (Athens, 1980).

Oikonomides, N. *Actes de Dionysiou* (Archives de l'Athos IV) (Paris, 1968).

Les Listes de préséance byzantines des IXe et Xe siècles (Paris, 1972).

Actes de Docheiariou (Archives de l'Athos XIII) (Paris, 1984).

'Contribution à l'étude de la pronoia au XIIIe siècle. Une formule d'attribution de parèques à un pronoiare', *Revue des Études Byzantines*, 22 (1964), pp. 158–75.

Bibliography 273

'Quelques boutiques de Constantinople au Xe siècle: prix, loyers, imposition (cod. Patmiacus 171)', *Dumbarton Oaks Papers*, 26 (1972), pp. 345–56.

Papachryssanthou, D. *Actes du Prôtaton* (Archives de l'Athos VII) (Paris, 1975).

'Un confesseur du second iconoclasme: la vie du patrice Nicétas (†836)', *Travaux et Mémoires*, 3 (1968), pp. 309–51.

Petit, L. *Actes de Xénophon* (Actes de l'Athos I), *Vizantijskij Vremennik*, 10 (1903), supplement 1.

Actes de Chilander, I, *Actes grecs* (Actes de l'Athos V), *Vizantijskij Vremennik*, 17 (1910), supplement 1.

'Le monastère de Notre Dame de Pitié en Macédoine', *Izvestija Russkogo Arheologičeskogo Instituta v Konstantinopole*, 6 (1900), pp. 1–153.

'Vie de St Michel Maléinos, suivie du traité ascétique de Basile le Maléinote', *Revue de l'Orient Chrétien*, 7 (1902), pp. 543–603.

'Vie de Saint Athanase l'Athonite', *Analecta Bollandiana*, 25 (1906), pp. 5–89.

'Typikon du monastère de la Kosmosotira près d'Aenos (1152)', *Izvestija Russkogo Arheologičeskogo Instituta v Konstantinopole*, 13 (1908), pp. 17–77.

Regel, W., Kurtz, E. and Korablev, B. *Actes de Zographou* (Actes de l'Athos IV), *Vizantijskij Vremennik*, 13 (1907), supplement 1.

Romano, R. *Pseudo-Luciano, Timarione* (Naples, 1974).

Sargologos, E. *La Vie de saint Cyrille le Philéote, moine byzantin (†1110)* (Subsidia Hagiographica 39) (Brussels, 1964).

Sathas, K. N. *Mesaionike Bibliotheke* (7 vols., Athens–Paris, Venice–Paris, 1872–94).

Sevcenko, I. 'Inscription Commemorating Sisinnios, "Curator" of Tzurulon (AD 813)', *Byzantion*, 35 (1965), pp. 564–74.

Simeon Seth. *Syntagma de Alimentorum Facultatibus*, ed. B. Langkavel (Leipzig, 1868).

Spieser, J. M. 'Inventaires en vue d'un recueil des inscriptions historiques de Byzance, I. Les inscriptions de Thessalonique', *Travaux et Mémoires*, 5 (1973), pp. 145–80.

Stadtmüller, G. *Michael Choniates, Metropolit von Athen* (Orientalia Christiana Analecta 33) (Rome, 1934).

Starr, J. 'The Epitaph of a Dyer in Corinth', *Byzantinisch-Neugriechische Jahrbücher*, 12 (1935–6), pp. 42–9.

Svoronos, N. 'Recherches sur le cadastre byzantin et la fiscalité aux XIe et XIIe siècles: le cadastre de Thèbes', *Bulletin de Correspondance Hellénique*, 83 (1959), pp. 1–145.

Tafel, G. L. F. and Thomas, G. M. *Urkunden zur älteren Handels- und Staatsgeschichte der Republik Venedig* (3 vols., Vienna, 1856–7).

Theophanes Continuatus, Ioannes Cameniata, Symeon Magister, Georgius Monachus, ed. I. Bekker (Bonn, 1838).

Theophanis Chronographia, ed. C. de Boor (2 vols., Leipzig, 1883–5).

Vasiliev, A. 'An Edict of the Emperor Justinian II, September 688', *Speculum*, 18 (1943), pp. 1–13.

274   *Bibliography*

Vasilievskij, V. G. 'Nikolaou ek Methones kai Theodorou tou Prodromou syngrapheon tes ib' hekatontaheteridos bioi Meletiou tou neou', *Pravloslavnyi Palestinskij Sbornik*, 17 (1886), pp. 1–69.

Weiss, G. 'Die Entscheidung des Kosmas Magistros über das Parökenrecht', *Byzantion*, 48 (1978), pp. 477–500.

Westerink, L. G. (ed.). *Nicétas Magistros. Lettres d'un exilé (928–946)* (Paris, 1973).

Wilson, N. and Darrouzès, J. 'Restes du cartulaire de Hiéra-Xérochoraphion', *Revue des Études Byzantines*, 26 (1968), pp. 5–47.

Zepos, J. and Zepos, P. *Jus Graeco-Romanum* (8 vols., Athens, 1931–62).

MODERN WORKS

Abrams, P. 'Towns and Economic Growth: Some Theories and Problems', in P. Abrams and E. A. Wrigley (eds.), *Towns in Societies. Essays in Economic History and Historical Sociology* (Cambridge, 1978), pp. 9–33.

Adamsheck, B. *Kenchreai. Eastern Port of Corinth*, IV, *The Pottery* (Leiden, 1979).

Admiralty, Naval Intelligence Division. *Geographical Handbook Series, Greece* (3 vols., London, 1944–5).

Ahrweiler, H. *Byzance et la mer* (Paris, 1966).

'La politique agraire des empereurs de Nicée', *Byzantion*, 28 (1958), pp. 51–66, 135–6.

'Recherches sur l'administration de l'empire byzantin aux IXe–XIe siècles', *Bulletin de Correspondance Hellénique*, 84 (1960), pp. 1–109.

'La concession des droits incorporels. Donations conditionelles', in *Actes du XIIe congrès international des études byzantines* (3 vols., Belgrade, 1964), II, pp. 103–14.

'L'histoire et la géographie de la région de Smyrne entre les deux occupations turques (1081–1317) particulièrement au XIIIe siècle', *Travaux et Mémoires*, 1 (1965), pp. 1–204.

'Charisticariat et les autres formes d'attribution de fondations pieuses aux Xe–XIe siècles', *Zbornik Radova Vizantološkog Instituta*, 10 (1967), pp. 1–27.

'La "pronoia" à Byzance', in *Structures féodales et féodalisme dans l'Occident méditerranéen (X–XIIe siècles). Bilan et perspectives de recherches* (Collection de l'École Française de Rome 44) (Rome, 1980), pp. 681–9.

Alexiou, M. 'Literary Subversion and the Aristocracy in Twelfth-Century Byzantium: A Stylistic Analysis of the Timarion (chs. 6–10)' *Byzantine and Modern Greek Studies*, 8 (1982–3), pp. 29–45.

'The Poverty of Écriture and the Craft of Writing: Towards a Reappraisal of the Prodromic Poems', *Byzantine and Modern Greek Studies*, 10 (1986), pp. 1–40.

Anderson, P. *Lineages of the Absolutist State* (London, 1974).

Passages from Antiquity to Feudalism (London, 1974).

Bibliography

Angold, M. *A Byzantine Government in Exile. Government and Society under the Laskarids of Nicaea (1204–61)* (Oxford, 1975).
   (ed.). *The Byzantine Aristocracy IX to XIII Centuries* (Oxford, 1984).
   The Byzantine Empire 1025–1204. A Political History (London, 1984).
   'Archons and Dynasts: Local Aristocracies and the Cities of the Later Byzantine Empire' in M. Angold (ed.), *The Byzantine Aristocracy IX to XIII Centuries* (Oxford, 1984), pp. 236–53.
   'The Shaping of the Medieval Byzantine "City"', *Byzantinische Forschungen*, 10 (1985), pp. 1–37.
Antoniadis-Bibicou, H. 'Villages désertés en Grèce: un bilan provisoire', in *Villages désertés et histoire économique, XIe–XVIIIe siècles* (Paris, 1965), pp. 343–417.
   'Démographie, salaires et prix à Byzance au XIe siècle', *Annales ESC*, 27 (1972), pp. 215–46.
   'Mouvement de la population et villages désertés: quelques remarques de méthode', in *Actes du XVe congrès international d'études byzantines, Athènes – septembre 1976*, IV, *Histoire. Communications* (Athens, 1980), pp. 19–27.
Asdracha, C. *La Région des Rhodopes aux XIIIe et XIVe siècles. Étude de géographie historique* (Athens, 1976).
Avramea, A. P. *He Byzantine Thessalia mechri tou 1204. Symbole eis ten historiken geographian* (Athens, 1974).
   'Les villes et les agglomérations urbaines de la Thessalie byzantine jusqu'en 1204', in *Collection de la maison de l'Orient méditerranéen*, VI (Série Archéologique 5) (Lyons, 1979), pp. 281–91.
Aykroyd, W. R. and Doughty, J. *Wheat in Human Nutrition* (FAO Nutritional Studies 23) (Rome, 1970).
Aymard, M. 'Pour l'histoire de l'alimentation: quelques remarques de méthode', *Annales ESC*, 30 (1975), pp. 431–44.
Bakirtzis, C. 'He agora tes Thessalonikes sta palaiochristianika chronia', in *Praktika tou 10ou Diethnous Synedriou Christianikes Archaiologias*, II (Thessalonike, 1984), pp. 5–19.
Balard, M. *La Romanie génoise (XIIe–début du XVe siècle)* (Rome, 1975).
   'Amalfi et Byzance (X^e–XIIe siècles)', *Travaux et Mémoires*, 6 (1976), pp. 85–95.
Barnea, I. 'Dinogetia – ville byzantine du Bas-Danube', *Byzantina*, 10 (1980), pp. 239–86.
Bates, G. E. *Byzantine Coins. Archaeological Explorations at Sardis*, I (Cambridge, Massachusetts, 1971).
Beck, H. G. 'Konstantinopel. Zur Sozialgeschichte einer frühmittelalterlichen Haupstadt', *Byzantinische Zeitschrift*, 58 (1965), pp. 11–45.
Beldiceanu, N. and Beldiceanu-Steinherr, I. 'Recherches sur la Morée (1461–1512)', *Sudöstforschungen*, 39 (1980), pp. 17–74.
Benaki Museum, *Paradosiakes kalliergeies* (Athens, 1978).

276 *Bibliography*

Berkner, L. K. and Mendels, F. F. 'Inheritance Systems, Family Structure and Demographic Patterns in Western Europe, 1700–1900', in C. Tilly (ed.), *Historical Studies of Changing Fertility* (Princeton, 1978), pp. 209–23.

Bintliff, J. L. and Snodgrass, A. M. 'The Cambridge/Bradford Boeotian Expedition: The First Four Years', *Journal of Field Archaeology*, 12 (1985), pp. 123–61.

Blackman, D. and Branagan, K. 'An Archaeological Survey of the Lower Catchment of the Ayiofarango Valley', *Papers of the British School at Athens*, 72 (1977), pp. 13–84.

Bloch, M. 'The Advent and Triumph of the Water-Mill', in *Land and Work in Medieval Europe* (London, 1967), pp. 136–68.

Bompaire, J. 'Sur trois terms de fiscalité byzantine', *Bulletin de Correspondance Hellénique*, 80 (1956), pp. 625–31.

Bon, A. *Le Péloponnèse byzantin jusqu'en 1204* (Paris, 1951).

Boserup, E. *The Conditions of Agricultural Growth* (Chicago, 1965).

Bouras, C. 'City and Village: Urban Design and Architecture', *XVI Internationaler Byzantinistenkongress. Akten, Jahrbuch der Österreichischen Byzantinistik*, 31/1 (1981), pp. 611–53.

  'Houses in Byzantium', *Deltion tes Christianikes Archaiologikes Hetaireias*, 11 (1982–3), pp. 1–26.

Brand, C. M. *Byzantium Confronts the West 1180–1204* (Harvard, 1968).

Braudel, F. *The Mediterranean and the Mediterranean World in the Age of Philip II* (2 vols., London, 1972–3).

  Civilisation and Capitalism 15th–18th Century, I, *The Structures of Everyday Life. The Limits of the Possible* (London, 1981), II, *The Wheels of Commerce* (London, 1982).

Bréhier, L. 'Les populations rurales au IXe siécle d'après l'hagiographie Byzantine', *Byzantion*, 1 (1924), pp. 177–90.

Brett, G. 'Byzantine Water-Mill', *Antiquity*, 13 (1939), pp. 354–6.

Britnell, R. H. 'Minor Landlords in England and Medieval Agrarian Capitalism', *Past and Present*, 89 (1980), pp. 3–22.

Bryer, A. A. M. 'The Estates of the Empire of Trebizond. Evidence for their Resources, Products, Agriculture, Ownership and Location', *Archeion Pontou*, 35 (1979), pp. 370–477.

  'The Late Byzantine Monastery in Town and Countryside', in D. Baker (ed.), *The Church in Town and Countryside* (Oxford, 1979), pp. 219–41.

Chandler, R. *Travels in Asia Minor 1764–65*, ed. E. Clay (London, 1971).

Charanis, P. 'The Monastic Properties and the State in the Byzantine Empire', *Dumbarton Oaks Papers*, 4 (1948), pp. 53–118.

  'The Significance of Coins as Evidence for the History of Athens and Corinth in the Seventh and Eighth Centuries', *Historia*, 4 (1955), pp. 163–72.

  'The Transfer of Population as a Policy in the Byzantine Empire', *Comparative Studies in Society and History*, 3 (1961), pp. 140–54.

'Observations on the Demography of the Byzantine Empire', in *Proceedings of the XIIIth International Congress of Byzantine Studies, Oxford 1966* (London, 1967), pp. 445–63.

'The Monk as an Element of Byzantine Society', *Dumbarton Oaks Papers*, 25 (1971), pp. 63–84.

Christides, V. 'Once again Caminiates' "Capture of Thessaloniki"', *Byzantinische Zeitschrift*, 74 (1981), pp. 7–10.

Clark, C. *Population Growth and Land Use*, 2nd edn (London, 1977).

Clark, C. and Haswell, M. *The Economics of Subsistence Agriculture*, 4th edn (London, 1970).

Clark, G. 'Bees in Antiquity', *Antiquity*, 16 (1942), pp. 208–15.

Clutton, A. E. and Kenny, A. 'A Vertical Axle Water-Mill near Drosia, Crete', *Kretologia*, 4 (1977), pp. 139–58.

Coleman, J. E. 'Excavation of a Site (Elean Pylos) near Agrapidochori', *Archaiologikon Deltion*, 24 (1969), pp. 155–61.

Condurachi, E., Barnea, I. and Diaconu, P. 'Nouvelles recherches sur le "limes" byzantin du Bas-Danube aux Xe–XIe siècles', in *Proceedings of the XIIIth International Congress of Byzantine Studies, Oxford 1966* (London, 1967), pp. 179–93.

Constantelos, D. J. *Byzantine Philanthropy and Social Welfare* (New Brunswick, 1968).

Cook, J. M. and Nicholls, J. V. 'Laconia', *Annual of the British School at Athens*, 45 (1950), pp. 261–98.

Crawford, M. 'Money and Exchange in the Roman World', *Journal of Roman Studies*, 60 (1970), pp. 40–8.

Curwen, E. C. 'The Problem of Early Water-Mills', *Antiquity*, 18 (1944) pp. 130–46.

'A Vertical Water-Mill near Salonika', *Antiquity*, 19 (1945), pp. 211–12.

Darrouzès, J. 'Le mouvement des fondations monastiques au XIe siècle', *Travaux et Mémoires*, 6 (1976), pp. 159–76.

Davidson, A. *Mediterranean Seafood*, 2nd edn (Harmondsworth, 1981).

Davidson, G. R. 'A Medieval Glass Factory at Corinth', *American Journal of Archaeology*, 40 (1944), pp. 297–324.

Davis, J. L., Cherry, J. F. and Mantzourani, E. 'An Archaeological Survey of the Greek Island of Keos', *National Geographical Society. Research Reports*, 21, pp. 109–16.

Day, G. W. 'Manuel and the Genoese: A Reappraisal of Byzantine Commercial Policy in the Late Twelfth Century', *Journal of Economic History*, 37 (1977), pp. 289–301.

Debinska, M. 'Diet: A Comparison of Food Consumption between some Eastern and Western Monasteries in the 4th–12th Centuries', *Byzantion*, 55 (1985), pp. 431–62.

Delano Smith, C. *Western Mediterranean Europe. A Historical Geography of Italy, Spain and Southern France since the Neolithic* (London, 1979).

278 *Bibliography*

Diaconu, P. 'Pacuiul lui Soare – Vicinia', *Byzantina*, 8 (1976), pp. 409–47.

Ditten, H. 'Zur Bedeutung der Einwandlung der Slaven', in H. Winkelmann et al., *Byzanz im 7. Jahrhundert. Untersuchungen zur Herausbildung des Feudalismus* (Berlin, 1978), pp. 73–160.

Djuric, I. 'La famille des Phocas', *Zbornik Radova Vizantološkog Instituta*, 17 (1976), pp. 189–296.

Dölger, F. 'Das Aerikon', *Byzantinische Zeitschrift*, 30 (1929–30), pp. 450–7.

'Zum Gebührenwesen der Byzantiner', in *Byzanz und die europäische Staatenwelt. Ausgewählte Vorträge und Aufsätze* (Ettal, 1953), pp. 232–60.

'Die frühbyzantinische und byzantinisch beeinflusste Stadt (V.–VIII. Jahrhundert)', in *Atti del 3° Congresso Internazionale di Studi sull'Alto Medioevo, 1956* (Spoleto, 1959), pp. 65–100.

'Ist der Nomos Georgikos ein Gesetz Justinians II', in *Paraspora. 30 Aufsätze zur Geschichte, Kultur und Sprache des byzantinischen Reiches* (Ettal, 1961), pp. 241–62.

Duby, G. *Rural Economy and Country Life in the Medieval West* (London, 1968).

The Early Growth of the European Economy. Warriors and Peasants from the Seventh to the Twelfth Century (London, 1974).

Duncan-Jones, R. *The Economy of the Roman Empire* (Cambridge, 1974).

Dunn, A. W. 'The Survey of Khrysoupolis and Byzantine Fortifications in the Lower Strymon Valley', *XVI Internationaler Byzantinistenkongress. Akten II/4, Jahrbuch der Österreichischen Byzantinistik*, 32/4 (1982), pp. 605–14.

Dyer, C. 'English Diet in the Later Middle Ages', in T. H. Aston, P. R. Coss, C. Dyer and J. Thirsk (eds.), *Social Relations and Ideas. Essays in Honour of R. H. Hilton* (Cambridge, 1983), pp. 191–216.

Eisma, D. 'Stream Deposition and Erosion by the Eastern Shore of the Aegean', in W. C. Brice (ed.), *The Environmental History of the Near and Middle East since the Last Ice Age* (London, 1978), pp. 67–81.

Ennen, E. *The Medieval Town* (Amsterdam, 1978).

Erder, L. T. and Faroqhi, S. 'The Development of the Anatolian Urban Network during the Sixteenth Century', *Journal of the Economic and Social History of the Orient*, 23 (1980), pp. 265–303.

Evert-Kappesova, H. 'Une grande propriété foncière du VIIIe siècle à Byzance', *ByzantinoSlavica*, 24 (1963), pp. 32–40.

Favory, F. 'Validité des concepts marxistes pour une théorie des sociétés de l'Antiquité. Le modèle impérial romain', *Klio*, 63 (1981), pp. 313–30.

Le Féodalisme à Byzance. Problèmes du mode de production de l'empire byzantin, *Recherches Internationales à la Lumière du Marxisme*, 79 (1974).

Ferluga, J. 'Les insurrections des slaves de la Macédoine au XIe siècle', in *Byzantium on the Balkans. Studies on the Byzantine Administration and the Southern Slavs from the VIIth to the XIIth Centuries* (Amsterdam, 1976), pp. 379–97.

Finlay, J. H. 'Corinth in the Middle Ages', *Speculum*, 7 (1932), pp. 477–99.

Bibliography

Finlay, M. I. 'The Ancient City: From Fustel de Coulanges to Max Weber and Beyond', *Comparative Studies in Society and History*, 19 (1977), pp. 305–27.

Foss, C. *Byzantine and Turkish Sardis* (Harvard, 1976).

Ephesus after Antiquity. A Late Antique, Byzantine and Turkish City (Cambridge, 1979).

'The Persians in Asia Minor and the End of Antiquity', *English Historical Review*, 90 (1975), pp. 721–47.

'Archaeology and the "Twenty Cities" of Byzantine Asia', *American Journal of Archaeology*, 81 (1977), pp. 469–86.

'Late Antique and Byzantine Ankara', *Dumbarton Oaks Papers*, 31 (1977), pp. 29–87.

Frances, E. 'La ville byzantine et la monnaie aux VIIe–VIIIe siècles', *ByzantinoBulgarica*, 2 (1966), pp. 3–14.

'Alexis Comnène et les privilèges octroyés à Venise', *ByzantinoSlavica*, 29 (1968), pp. 17–23.

Friedl, E. *Vasilika. A Village in Modern Greece* (New York, 1962).

Gadolin, A. R. 'Alexius I Comnenus and the Venetian Trade Privileges. A New Interpretation', *Byzantion*, 50 (1980), pp. 439–46.

Godelier, M. *Rationality and Irrationality in Economics* (London, 1972).

Perspectives in Marxist Anthropology (Cambridge, 1977).

Goitein, S. D. *A Mediterranean Society. The Jewish Communities of the Arab World as Portrayed in the Documents of the Cairo Geniza*, I, *Economic Foundations* (Berkeley, 1967).

'A Letter from Seleucia (Cilicia) dated 21 July 1137', *Speculum*, 39 (1964), pp. 298–303.

Gomulka, G. 'Bemerkungen zur Situation der spätantiken Städte und Siedlungen in NordBulgarien und ihrem Weiterleben am Ende des 6. Jahrhunderts', in H. Köpstein and F. Winkelmann (eds.), *Studien zum 7. Jahrhundert in Byzanz. Probleme der Herausbildung des Feudalismus* (Berlin, 1976), pp. 35–42.

Grierson, P. *Catalogue of the Byzantine Coins in the Dumbarton Oaks Collection*, III, *Leo III to Nicephorus III 717–1081* (Dumbarton Oaks, 1973).

'The Debasement of the Bezant in the Eleventh Century', *Byzantinische Zeitschrift*, 47 (1954), pp. 379–94.

'Notes on the Fineness of the Byzantine Solidus', *Byzantinische Zeitschrift*, 54 (1961), pp. 91–7.

'Byzantine Coinage as Source Material' in *Proceedings of the XIIIth International Congress of Byzantine Studies, Oxford 1966*. (London, 1967), pp. 317–33.

Grumel, V. *Les Regestes des actes du patriarcat de Constantinople*, I, *Les Actes des patriarches, fasc. III. Les regestes de 1043 à 1206* (Bucharest, 1947).

Guilland, R. 'Quelques termes du livre des cérémonies de Constantin VII Porphyrogénète', *Revue des Études Grecques*, 62 (1949), pp. 328–50.

Bibliography

'Les logothètes: études sur l'histoire administrative de l'empire byzantin', *Revue des Études Byzantines*, 29 (1971), pp. 5–115.

Guillou, A. 'Production and Profits in the Byzantine Province of Italy (Tenth to Eleventh Centuries): An Expanding Society', *Dumbarton Oaks Papers*, 28 (1974), pp. 91–109.

Gyoni, M. 'La transhumance des Vlaques balkaniques au moyen âge', *ByzantinoSlavica*, 12 (1951), pp. 29–42.

Hadjinicolaou-Marava, A. *Recherches sur la vie des esclaves dans le monde byzantin* (Athens, 1950).

Haldon, J. F. *Recruitment and Conscription in the Byzantine Army, c. 550–950. A Study of the Origins of the Stratiotika Ktemata* (Vienna, 1979).

Byzantine Praetorians. An Administrative, Institutional and Social Survey of the Opsikion and Tagmata, c. 580–950 (Berlin, 1984).

'Some Remarks on the Background to the Iconoclast Controversy', *ByzantinoSlavica*, 38 (1977), pp. 161–84.

'Some Considerations on Byzantine Society and Economy in the Seventh Century', *Byzantinische Forschungen*, 10 (1985), pp. 75–112.

Haldon, J. F. and Kennedy, H. 'The Arab–Byzantine Frontier in the Eighth and Ninth Centuries: Military Organisation and Society in the Borderlands', *Zbornik Radova Vizantološkog Instituta*, 19 (1980), pp. 79–116.

Harris, J. M. 'Coins found at Corinth', *Hesperia*, 10 (1941), pp. 143–62.

Harvey, A. 'Economic Expansion in Central Greece in the Eleventh Century', *Byzantine and Modern Greek Studies*, 8 (1982–3), pp. 21–8.

Havlik, L. E. 'The Genesis of Feudalism and the Slav Peoples', in V. Vavrinek (ed.), *Beiträge zur byzantinischen Geschichte im 9.–11. Jahrhundert* (Prague, 1978).

Hendy, M. F. *Coinage and Money in the Byzantine Empire, 1081–1261* (Dumbarton Oaks, 1969).

Studies in the Byzantine Monetary Economy c. 300–1450 (Cambridge, 1985).

'Byzantium 1081–1204: An Economic Reappraisal', *Transactions of the Royal Historical Society*, 5th series, 20 (1970), pp. 31–52.

'The Gornoslav Hoard, The Emperor Frederick I, and the Monastery of Bachkovo', in C. N. L. Brooke, I. Steward, J. G. Pollard and T. R. Volk (eds.), *Studies in Numismatic Method Presented to Philip Grierson* (Cambridge, 1983), pp. 79–91.

Herrin, J. E. 'The Social and Economic Structure of Central Greece in the Late Twelfth Century' (unpublished Ph.D. thesis, Birmingham University, 1972).

'The Collapse of the Byzantine Empire in the Twelfth Century: A Study of a Medieval Economy', *University of Birmingham Historical Journal*, 12 (1970), pp. 188–203.

'Realities of Byzantine Provincial Government: Hellas and Peloponnesos, 1180–1205', *Dumbarton Oaks Papers*, 29 (1975), pp. 253–84.

Bibliography 281

Hild, F. *Das byzantinische Strassensystem in Kappadokien* (Vienna, 1977).

Hilton, R. H. *A Medieval Society. The West Midlands at the End of the Thirteenth Century* (London, 1966, reprinted Cambridge, 1983).

The English Peasantry in the Later Middle Ages (Oxford, 1975).

(ed.). *The Transition from Feudalism to Capitalism* (London, 1976).

'Rent and Capital Formation in Feudal Society', in *The English Peasantry in the Later Middle Ages* (Oxford, 1975), pp. 174–214.

'Agrarian Class Structure and Economic Development in Pre-industrial Europe: A Crisis of Feudalism', *Past and Present*, 80 (1978), pp. 3–19.

'Small Town Society in England before the Black Death', *Past and Present*, 105 (1984), pp. 53–78.

'Medieval Market Towns and Simple Commodity Production', *Past and Present*, 109 (1985), pp. 3–23.

Hilton, R. H. and Sawyer, P. H. 'Technical Determinism: The Stirrup and the Plough', *Past and Present*, 24 (1963), pp. 90–100.

Hindess, B. and Hirst, P. Q. *Pre-capitalist Modes of Production* (London, 1975).

Hocquet, J.-C. 'Le pain, le vin et la juste mesure à la table des moines carolingiens', *Annales ESC*, 40 (1985), pp. 661–90.

Hoffmann, J. *Rudimente von Territorialstaaten im byzantinischen Reich (1071–1210). Untersuchungen über Unabhängigkeitsbestrebungen und ihr Verhältnis zu Kaiser und Reich* (Munich, 1974).

Hohlfelder, R. L. *Kenchreiai, Eastern Port of Cornith, III, The Coins* (Leiden, 1978).

Hohlweg, A. 'Zur Frage der Pronoia in Byzanz', *Byzantinische Zeitschrift*, 60 (1967), pp. 288–308.

Holland, H. *Travels in the Ionian Islands, Albania, Thessaly, Macedonia etc., during the Years 1812 and 1813* (London, 1815).

Hrochova, V. 'La place de Byzance dans la typologie du féodalisme européen', in V. Vavrinek (ed.), *Beiträge zur byzantinischen Geschichte im 9.–11. Jahrhundert* (Prague, 1978), pp. 31–45.

Hunger, H. *Die hochsprachliche profane Literatur der Byzantiner* (2 vols., Munich, 1978).

Huxley, G. L. 'The Second Dark Age of the Peloponnese', *Lakonikes Spoudes*, 3 (1977), pp. 84–110.

Iliescu, O. 'Premières apparitions au Bas-Danube de la monnaie réformée d'Alexis 1er Comnène', *Études Byzantines et Post-byzantines*, 1 (1979), pp. 9–17.

Jacoby, D. 'La population de Constantinople à l'époque byzantine: un problème de démographie urbaine', *Byzantion*, 31 (1961), pp. 81–109.

'Une classe fiscale à Byzance et en Romanie latine: les inconnus du fisc, eleuthères ou étrangers', *Actes du XIVᵉ congrès international des études byzantines, Bucharest 1971* (2 vols, Bucharest, 1974–5), II, pp. 139–52.

Janin, R. *Les Églises et les monastères des grands centres byzantins* (Paris, 1975).

Johnson, H. T. 'Cathedral Building and the Medieval Economy', *Explorations in Entrepreneurial History*, 2nd series, IV (1966–7), pp. 191–210.

282 Bibliography

Jones, A. H. M. *The Later Roman Empire 284–602. A Social, Economic and Administrative Survey* (2 vols., Oxford, 1964).

The Roman Economy. Studies in Ancient Economic and Administrative History, ed. P. A. Brunt (Oxford, 1974).

'Inflation under the Roman Empire', *Economic History Review*, 5 (1953), pp. 293–318.

'The Roman Colonate', *Past and Present*, 13, (1958), pp. 1–13.

Kaplan, M. 'Quelques remarques sur les paysages agraires byzantins (VIème siècle–milieu XIème siècle)', *Revue du Nord*, 62/244 (1980), pp. 155–76.

'Les villageois aux premiers siècles byzantins (VIème–Xème siècles): une société homogène?', *ByzantinoSlavica*, 43 (1982), pp. 202–17.

'Remarques sur la place de l'exploitation paysanne dans l'économie rurale byzantine', *XVI Internationaler Byzantinistenkongress. Akten II, Jahrbuch der Österreichischen Byzantinistik*, 32/2 (1982), pp. 105–14.

Karamesine-Oikonomidou, M. 'Nomismata ek ton mouseiou ton Bolou', *Thessalika*, 5 (1966).

Karayannopulos, J. 'Ho hypsosis tes times tou sitou epi Parapinake', *Byzantina*, 5 (1973), pp. 106–9.

'Ein Problem der spätbyzantinischen Agrargeschichte', *Jahrbuch der Österreichischen Byzantinistik*, 30 (1981), pp. 207–37.

Karlin-Hayter, P. 'Notes sur les archives de Patmos comme source pour la démographie et l'économie de l'île', *Byzantinische Forschungen*, 5 (1977), pp. 189–215.

Karpozelos, A. 'Realia in Byzantine Epistolography X–XIIc', *Byzantinische Zeitschrift*, 77 (1984), pp. 20–37.

Kazhdan, A. P. 'Some Questions Addressed to Scholars Who Believe in the Authenticity of Kameniates' "Capture of Thessalonica"', *Byzantinische Zeitschrift*, 71 (1978), pp. 301–14.

'La byzantinologie soviétique en 1974–75', *Byzantion,* 49 (1979), pp. 506–53.

'Remarques sur le XIᵉ siècle byzantin à propos d'un livre récent de Paul Lemerle', *Byzantion*, 49 (1979), pp. 491–503.

'Two Notes on Byzantine Demography of the Eleventh and Twelfth Centuries', *Byzantinische Forschungen*, 8 (1982), pp. 115–22.

Kazhdan, A. P. and Constable, G. *People and Power in Byzantium. An Introduction to Modern Byzantine Studies* (Dumbarton Oaks, 1982).

Kazhdan, A. P. and Cutler, A. 'Continuity and Discontinuity in Byzantine History', *Byzantion*, 52 (1982), pp. 429–78.

Kazhdan, A. P. and Epstein, A. W. *Change in Byzantine Culture in the Eleventh and Twelfth Centuries* (Berkeley, 1985).

Kazhdan, A. P. and Franklin, S. *Studies on Byzantine Literature of the Eleventh and Twelfth Centuries* (Cambridge, 1984).

Kerblay, B. 'Chayanov and the Theory of Peasantry as a Specific Type of Economy', in T. Shanin (ed.), *Peasants and Peasant Societies* (Harmondsworth, 1971), pp. 150–60.

Bibliography

283

Koder, J. *Negroponte. Untersuchungen zur Topographie und Siedlungsgeschichte der Insel Euboia während der Zeit der Venezianerherrschaft* (Vienna, 1973).

Koder, J. and Hild, F. *Tabula Imperii Byzantini, I, Hellas und Thessalia* (Vienna, 1976).

Kolodny, E. Y. *La Population des îles de la Grèce* (2 vols., Aix-en-Provence, 1974).

Konidares, I. M.. *To dikaion tes monateriakes periousias apo tou 9ou mechri tou 12ou aiona* (Athens, 1979).

Köpstein, H. 'Zu den Agrarverhältnissen', in F. Winkelmann *et al.*, *Byzanz im 7. Jahrhundert. Untersuchungen zur Herausbildung des Feudalismus* (Berlin, 1978), pp. 1–72.

Köpstein, H. and Winkelmann F. (eds.). *Studien zum 7. Jahrhundert in Byzanz. Probleme der Herausbildung des Feudalismus* (Berlin, 1976).

Koukoules, Ph. *Byzantinon bios kai politismos* (6 vols., Athens, 1948–55).

Kraemer, C. J. *Excavations at Nessana, III, Non-Literary Papyri* (Princeton, 1958).

Krautheimer, R. *Early Christian and Byzantine Architecture* (Harmondsworth, 1965).

Krekic, B. *Dubrovnik (Raguse) et le Levant au moyen âge* (Paris, 1961).

Kula, W. *An Economic Theory of the Feudal System. Towards a Model of the Polish Economy 1500–1800* (London, 1976).

Laiou, A. E. 'A Note on the Farmer's Law, Chapter 67', *Byzantion*, 41 (1971), pp. 197–204.

Laiou-Thomadakis, A. E. *Peasant Society in the Late Byzantine Empire. A Social and Demographic Study* (Princeton, 1977).

Leake, W. M. *Journal of a Tour in Asia Minor, with Comparative Remarks on the Ancient and Modern Geography of that Country* (London, 1824).

Travels in the Morea (3 vols., London, 1830).

Travels in Northern Greece (4 vols., London, 1835).

Leclerq, J. 'Aux origines bibliques du vocabulaire de la pauvreté', in M. Mollat (ed.), *Études sur l'histoire de la pauvreté* (2 vols., Paris, 1974), I, pp. 35–43.

Lefort J. *Villages de Macédoine. Notices historiques et topographiques sur la Macédoine orientale au moyen âge, I, La Chalcidique occidentale* (Paris, 1982).

'En Macédoine orientale au Xe siècle: habitat rural, communes et domaines', in *Actes du XIe congrès de la société des historiens mediévalistes de l'enseignement supérieur public, Dijon 1978* (Paris, 1979), pp. 251–72.

'Une grande fortune foncière aux X–XIIIe siècles: les biens du monastère d'Iviron', in *Structures féodales et féodalisme dans l'Occident méditerranéen (X–XIIIe siècles). Bilan et perspectives de recherches* (Collection de l'École Française de Rome 44) (Rome, 1980), pp. 727–42.

'Le cadastre de Radolibos (1103), les géomètres et leurs mathématiques', *Travaux et Mémoires*, 8 (1981), pp. 269–313.

'Radolibos: population et paysage', *Travaux et Mémoires*, 9 (1985), pp. 195–234.

284   *Bibliography*

Lemerle, P. *Cinq études sur le XIe siècle byzantin* (Paris, 1977).

The Agrarian History of Byzantium from the Origins to the Twelfth Century. The Sources and Problems (Galway, 1979).

'Notes sur la date de trois documents athonites et sur trois fonctionnaires du XIe siècle', *Revue des Études Byzantines*, 10 (1952), pp. 109–13.

'Les archives du monastère des Amalfitains au Mont Athos', *Epeteris Hetaireias Byzantinon Spoudon*, 23 (1953), pp. 548–66.

'Notes sur l'administration byzantine à la veille de la IVe crusade d'après deux documents inédits des archives de Lavra', *Revue des Études Byzantines*, 19 (1961), pp. 258–72.

'Un aspect du rôle des monastères à Byzance: les monastères donnés à des laïcs, les charisticaires', *Comptes-rendu des séances de l'Académie des Inscriptions et Belles-Lettres* (1967), pp. 9–28.

Lilie, R.-J. *Die byzantinische Reaktion auf die Ausbreitung der Araber. Studien zur Strukturwandlung des byzantinischen Staates im 7. und 8. Jahrhundert* (Munich, 1976).

Handel und Politik zwischen dem byzantinischen Reich und den italienischen Kommunen Venedig, Pisa und Genua in der Epoche der Komnenen und der Angeloi (1081–1204) (Amsterdam, 1984).

'"Thrakien" und "Thrakesion". Zur byzantinischen Provinzorganisation am Ende des 7. Jahrhunderts', *Jahrbuch der Österreichischen Byzantinistik*, 26 (1977), pp. 7–47.

'Die zweihundertjährige Reform: Zu den Anfängen der Themenorganisation im 7. und 8. Jahrhundert. II. Die "Soldatenbauern"', *ByzantinoSlavica*, 45 (1984), pp. 190–201.

Lipchits, E. 'La fin du régime esclavagiste et le début du féodalisme à Byzance', in *Le Féodalisme à Byzance. Problèmes du mode de production de l'empire byzantin, Recherches Internationales à la Lumière du Marxisme*, 79 (1974), pp. 19–30.

'La ville et le village à Byzance: du VIe siècle jusqu'à la première moitié du IXe siècle', *Le Féodalisme à Byzance. Problèmes du mode de production de l'empire byzantin, Recherches Internationales à la Lumière du Marxisme*, 79 (1974), pp. 51–64.

Litavrin, G. G. 'Zur Lage der byzantinischen Bauernschaft im 10.–11. Jh. Strittige Fragen', in V. Vavrinek (ed.), *Beiträge zur byzantinischen Geschichte im 9.–11. Jahrhundert* (Prague, 1978), pp. 47–70.

Loos, M. 'Quelques remarques sur les communautés rurales et la grande propriété terrienne à Byzance (VIIe–XIe siècles)', *ByzantinoSlavica*, 39 (1978), pp. 3–18.

Lopez, R. S. 'The Silk Industry in the Byzantine Empire', *Speculum*, 20 (1945), pp. 1–42.

McDonald, W. A., Coulson, W. D. E. and Rosser, J. *Excavations at Nichoria in Southwest Greece, III, Dark Age and Byzantine Occupation* (Minneapolis, 1983).

Magdalino, P. 'The Byzantine Aristocratic Oikos', in M. Angold (ed.), *The Byzantine Aristocracy, IX to XIII Centuries* (Oxford, 1984), pp. 92–111.

Malamut, E. 'Les îles de la mer Égée de la fin du XIe siècle à 1204', *Byzantion*, 52 (1982), pp. 310–50.

Mango, C. *Byzantium. The Empire of New Rome* (London, 1980).

Le Développement urbain de Constantinople (IVe–VIIe siècles) (Paris, 1985).

'Les monuments de l'architecture du XIe siècle et leur signification historique et sociale', *Travaux et Mémoires*, 6 (1976), pp. 351–65.

Matschke, K.-P. 'Sozialschichten und Geisteshaltungen', *XVI Internationaler Byzantinistenkongress. Akten, Jahrbuch der Österreichischen Byzantinistik*, 31/1 (1981), pp. 189–212.

Metcalf, D. M. 'Bronze Coinage and City Life in Central Greece AD 1000', *Annual of the British School at Athens*, 60 (1965), pp. 1–40.

'Interpretation of the Byzantine "Rex Regnantium" Folles of Class "A", c. 970–1030', *Numismatic Chronicle*, 7th series, 10 (1970), pp. 199–218.

'Corinth in the Ninth Century: The Numismatic Evidence', *Hesperia*, 42 (1973), pp. 180–251.

Miller, E. and Hatcher, J. *Medieval England. Rural Society and Economic Change 1086–1348* (London, 1978).

Miller, J. I. *The Spice Trade of the Roman Empire, 29 BC to AD 641* (Oxford, 1969).

Miller, S. G. 'Excavations at Nemea, 1973–4', *Hesperia*, 44 (1975), pp. 143–72.

'Excavations at Nemea, 1975', *Hesperia*, 45 (1976), pp. 174–202.

Minchinton, W. 'Patterns and Structure of Demand 1500–1700', in C. Cipolla (ed.), *The Fontana Economic History of Europe*, II, *The Sixteenth and Seventeenth Centuries* (London, 1974), pp. 83–176.

Ministry of Agriculture, Fisheries and Food. *Manual of Nutrition*, 8th edn (London, 1976).

Morgan, C. H. *Corinth, XI, The Byzantine Pottery* (Harvard, 1942).

Morgan, G. 'The Venetian Claims Commission of 1278', *Byzantinische Zeitschrift*, 69 (1976), pp. 411–38.

Moritz, L. A. *Grain Mills and Flour in Classical Antiquity* (Oxford, 1958).

Morris, R. 'The Byzantine Church and the Land in the Tenth and Eleventh Centuries' (unpublished D. Phil. thesis, Oxford, 1978).

'The Powerful and the Poor in Tenth-Century Byzantium: Law and Reality', *Past and Present*, 73 (1976), pp. 3–27.

'The Political Saint of the Eleventh Century', in S. Hackel (ed.), *The Byzantine Saint* (Studies Supplementary to Sobornost 5) (London, 1981), pp. 43–50.

Morrisson, C. 'La dévaluation de la monnaie byzantine au XIe siècle: essai d'interprétation', *Travaux et Mémoires*, 6 (1976), pp. 3–48.

'La logarikè: réforme monétaire et réforme fiscale sous Alexis 1er Comnène', *Travaux et Mémoires*, 7 (1979), pp. 419–64.

Müller-Wiener, W. *Bildlexicon zur Topographie Istanbuls* (Tübingen, 1977).

Nasturel, P. S. and Beldiceanu, N. 'Les églises byzantines et la situation économique de Drama, Serrès et Zichna aux XIVᵉ et XVᵉ siècles', *Jahrbuch der Österreichischen Byzantinistik*, 27 (1978), pp. 269–85.

Nelson, J. L. 'Charles the Bald and the Church in Town and Countryside', in D. Baker (ed.), *The Church in Town and Countryside* (Oxford, 1979), pp. 103–18.

Nesbitt, J. W. 'Mechanisms of Agricultural Production on Estates of the Byzantine Praktika' (unpublished Ph.D. thesis, University of Wisconsin, 1972).

'The Life of St Philaretos (702–792) and its Significance for Byzantine Agriculture', *Greek Orthodox Theological Review*, 14 (1969), pp. 150–8.

Oberländer-Tarnoveanu, E. 'Quelques aspects de la circulation monétaire dans la zone de l'embouchure du Danube au XIIᵉ siècle', *Dacia*, 23 (1979), pp. 265–73.

Oikonomides, N. *Hommes d'affaires grecs et latins à Constantinople (XIIIᵉ–XVᵉ siècles)* (Paris, Montreal, 1979).

'Recherches sur l'histoire du Bas-Danube aux Xᵉ–XIᵉ siècles: la Mésopotamie de l'Occident', *Revue des Études Sud-Est Européennes*, 3 (1965), pp. 57–79.

'The Donations of Castles in the Last Quarter of the 11th Century', *Polychronion. Festschrift F. Dölger* (Heidelberg, 1966), pp. 413–17.

'He dianome ton basilikon episkepseon tes Kretes (1170–71) kai he demosionomike politike tou Manouel I Komnenou', in *Pepragmena tou III Diethnous Kretologikou Synedriou*, III (Athens, 1968), pp. 195–201.

'L'évolution de l'organisation administrative de l'empire byzantin au XIᵉ siècle (1025–1118)', *Travaux et Mémoires*, 6 (1976), pp. 125–52.

'La décomposition de l'empire byzantin à la veille de 1204 et les origines de l'empire de Nicée: à propos de la "Partitio Romaniae"', in *Actes du XVᵉ congrès international d'études byzantines. Athènes, septembre 1976*, I, *Histoire*, pp. 1–28.

'Hoi authentai ton Kretikon to 1118', in *Pepragmena tou IV Diethnous Kretologikou Synedriou*, II, *Byzantinoi kai mesoi chronoi* (Athens, 1981), pp. 308–17.

Ostrogorsky, G. *Pour l'histoire de la féodalité byzantine* (Brussels, 1954).

Quelques problèmes d'histoire de la paysannerie byzantine (Brussels, 1956).

History of the Byzantine State, 2nd English edn, trans. J. M. Hussey (Oxford, 1968).

'Die ländliche Steuergemeinde des byzantinischen Reiches im X. Jahrhundert', *Vierteljahrschrift für Sozial- und Wirtschaftsgeschichte*, 20 (1927), pp. 1–108.

'Über die vermeintliche Reformtätigkeit der Isaurer', *Byzantinische Zeitschrift*, 30 (1930), pp. 394–400.

'Löhne und Preise in Byzanz', *Byzantinische Zeitschrift*, 32 (1932), pp. 293–333.

'The Peasant's Pre-emption Right: An Abortive Reform of the Macedonian Emperors', *Journal of Roman Studies*, 37 (1947), pp. 117–26.

'Byzantine Cities in the Early Middle Ages', *Dumbarton Oaks Papers*, 13 (1959), pp. 47–66.

'La commune rurale byzantine. Loi agraire – Traité fiscal – Cadastre de Thèbes', *Byzantion*, 32 (1962), pp. 139–66.

'Die Pronoia unter den Komnenen', *Zbornik Radova Vizantološkog Instituta*, 12 (1970), pp. 41–54.

Oudaltsova, Z. 'À propos de la genèse du féodalisme à Byzance', in *Le Féodalisme à Byzance. Problèmes du mode de production de l'empire byzantin, Recherches Internationales à la Lumière du Marxisme*, 79 (1974), pp. 31–50.

Papachryssanthou, D. 'Un évêché byzantin: Hiérissos en Chalcidique', *Travaux et Mémoires*, 8 (1981), pp. 373–96.

Parsons, A. W. 'A Roman Water-Mill in the Athenian Agora', *Hesperia*, 5 (1936), pp. 70–90.

Patlagean, E. *Pauvreté économique et pauvreté sociale à Byzance, 4ᵉ–7ᵉ siècles* (Paris, 1977).

'"Économie paysanne" et "féodalité byzantine"', *Annales ESC*, 30 (1975), pp. 1371–96.

Picard, O. 'Trésors et circulation monétaire à Thasos du IVᵉ au VIIᵉ siècle après J.C.', *Thasiaca. Bulletin de Correspondance Hellénique*, supplement 5, pp. 411–54.

Pococke, R. *A Description of the East and Some Other Countries* (2 vols., London, 1743–5).

Postan, M. M. (ed.). *The Cambridge Economic History of Europe*, I, *The Agrarian Life of the Middle Ages*, 2nd edn (Cambridge, 1971).

Pounds, N. J. G. *An Economic History of Medieval Europe* (London, 1974).

Rackham, O. 'Observations on the Historical Ecology of Boeotia', *Annual of the British School at Athens*, 78 (1983), pp. 291–351.

Razi, Z. *Life, Marriage and Death in a Medieval Parish. Economy, Society and Demography in Halesowen 1270–1400* (Cambridge, 1980).

Richard, J. 'Une économie coloniale? Chypre et ses resources agricoles au moyen âge', *Byzantinische Forschungen*, 5 (1977), pp. 331–52.

Robert, L. 'Les kordakia de Nicée, le combustible de Synnada et les poissons-scies. Sur des lettres d'un métropolite de Phrygie au Xᵉ siècle. Philologie et réalités', *Journal des Savants* (1961), pp. 97–166.

Robinson, H. S. and Weinberg, S. S. 'Excavations at Corinth, 1959', *Hesperia*, 29 (1960), pp. 225–53.

Rouche, M. 'La faim à l'époque carolingienne: essai sur quelques types de rations alimentaires', *Revue Historique*, 250 (1973), pp. 295–320.

Rouillard, G. 'La dîme des bergers valaques sous Alexis Iᵉʳ Comnène', in *Mélanges offerts à M. Nicolas Iorga* (Paris, 1933), pp. 779–86.

Runciman, S. *Byzantine Civilisation* (London, 1933).

Rupp, D. W. and King, R. H., 'Canadian Palaipaphos Survey Project', in D. R. Keller and D. W. Rupp, *Archaeological Survey in the Mediterranean Area* (Oxford, 1983), pp. 323–7.

Saranti-Mendelovici, H. 'À propos de la ville de Patras aux 13ᵉ–15ᵉ siècles', *Revue des Études Byzantines*, 38 (1980), pp. 219–32.

Schilbach, E. *Byzantinische Metrologie* (Munich, 1970).

Schreiner, P. 'Untersuchungen zu den Niederlassungen westlicher Kaufleute im byzantinischen Reich des 11. und 12. Jahrhunderts', *Byzantinische Forschungen*, 7 (1979), pp. 175–91.

Scranton, R. L. *Corinth, XVI, Medieval Architecture in the Central Area of Corinth* (Princeton, 1957).

Seibt, W. *Die Skleroi. Eine prosopographisch-sigillographische Studie* (Vienna, 1976).

Semple, E. C. *The Geography of the Mediterranean Region. Its Relation to Ancient History* (London, 1932).

Setton, K. M. 'The Archaeology of Medieval Athens', in *Essays in Medieval Life and Thought Presented in Honor of Austin Patterson Evans* (New York, 1955), pp. 227–58.

Shanin, T. (ed.). *Peasants and Peasant Societies* (Harmondsworth, 1971).

Shear, T. L. 'The Athenian Agora: Excavations of 1972', *Hesperia*, 42 (1973), pp. 359–407.

Simon, D. 'Provinzialrecht und Volksrecht', in D. Simon (ed.), *Fontes Minores*, I (Frankfurt am Main, 1976), pp. 102–16.

Siouzioumov, M. I. 'Le village et la ville à Byzance aux IXᵉ–Xᵉ siècles', *Le Féodalisme à Byzance. Problèmes du mode de production de l'empire byzantin, Recherches Internationales à la Lumière du Marxisme*, 79 (1974), pp. 65–74.

Sorlin, I. 'Les recherches soviétiques sur l'histoire byzantine de 1945 à 1962', *Travaux et Mémoires*, 2 (1967), pp. 489–564.

  'Publications soviétiques sur le XIᵉ siècle', *Travaux et Mémoires*, 6 (1976), pp. 367–98.

Soulis, G. 'On the Slavonic Settlement in Hierissos in the Tenth Century', *Byzantion*, 23 (1953), pp. 67–72.

Stannard, J. 'Aspects of Byzantine Materia Medica', *Dumbarton Oaks Papers*, 38 (1984), pp. 205–11.

Starr, J. *The Jews in the Byzantine Empire 641–1204* (Athens, 1939).

Stauridou-Zaphraka, A. 'He angareia sto Byzantio', *Byzantina*, 11 (1982), pp. 23–54.

Stefan, G., Barnea, I., Comsa, M. and Comsa, E. *Dinogetia, I, Asezarea feudala timpurie de la Bisericuta–Garvan* (Bucharest, 1967).

Svoronos, N. 'Recherches sur le cadastre byzantin et la fiscalité aux XIᵉ et XIIᵉ siècles: le cadastre de Thèbes', *Bulletin de Correspondance Hellénique*, 83 (1959), pp. 1–145.

  'Les privilèges de l'Église à l'époque des Comnènes: un rescrit inédit de Manuel 1ᵉʳ Comnène', *Travaux et Mémoires*, 1 (1965), pp. 325–91.

  'Société et organisation intérieure dans l'empire byzantin au XIᵉ siècle: les principaux problèmes', *Proceedings of the XIIIth International Congress of Byzantine Studies, Oxford 1966* (London, 1967), pp. 373–89.

Bibliography

'L'épibolè à l'époque des Comnènes', *Travaux et Mémoires*, 3 (1968), pp. 375–95.

'Remarques sur les structures économiques de l'empire byzantin au XIe siècle', *Travaux et Mémoires*, 6 (1976), pp. 49–67.

'Notes sur l'origine et la date du code rural', *Travaux et Mémoires*, 8 (1981), pp. 487–500.

Tafrali, O. *Thessalonique au quatorzième siècle* (Paris, 1913).

Topographie de Thessalonique (Paris, 1913).

Tavernier, J. B. *The Six Voyages of John Baptista Tavernier, Baron of Aubonne: Through Turkey into Persia and the East Indies* (London, 1678).

Tchalenko, G. *Villages antiques de la Syrie du Nord. Le massif du Bélus à l'époque romaine* (3 vols., Paris, 1953–8).

Teall, J. L. 'The Grain Supply of the Byzantine Empire, 330–1025', *Dumbarton Oaks Papers*, 13 (1959), pp. 89–139.

'The Byzantine Agricultural Tradition', *Dumbarton Oaks Papers*, 25 (1971), pp. 35–59.

Theocharides, G. I. 'Mia exasphanistheisa megale mone tes Thessalonikes, he mone tou Prodromou', *Makedonika*, 28 (1978), pp. 1–26.

Thiriet, F. *La Romanie vénitienne au moyen âge. Le développement et l'exploitation du domaine colonial vénitien (XIIe–XVe siècles)*. (Paris, 1959).

'Agriculteurs et agriculture à Corfu au XVème siècle', *Kerkyraika Chronika*, 23 (1980), pp. 315–28.

Thompson, H. A. 'Activities in the Athenian Agora: 1956', *Hesperia*, 26 (1957), pp. 99–107.

Thompson, M. *The Athenian Agora, II, Coins from the Roman through the Venetian Period* (Princeton, 1954).

Thorner, D. 'Peasant Economy as a Category in Economic History', in T. Shanin (ed.), *Peasants and Peasant Societies* (Harmondsworth, 1971), pp. 202–18.

Titow, J. Z. *English Rural Society 1200–1350* (London 1969).

Tivchev, P. 'Sur les cités byzantines aux XIe–XIIe siècles', *ByzantinoBulgarica*, 1 (1962), pp. 145–82.

Tournefort, M. *A Voyage into the Levant* (2 vols., London, 1718).

Toynbee, A. *Constantine Porphyrogenitus and his World* (London, 1973).

Travlos, I. N. *Poleodomike exelexis ton Athenon* (Athens, 1960).

Treadgold, W. T. *The Byzantine State Finances in the Eighth and Ninth Centuries* (New York, 1982).

Trojanos, S. 'Kastroktisia. Einige Bemerkungen über die finanziellen Grundlagen des Festbaues im byzantinischen Reich', *Byzantina*, 1 (1969), pp. 41–57.

Udal'cova, Z. V. and Chvostova, K. V. 'Les structures sociales et économiques dans la Basse-Byzance', *XVI Internationaler Byzantinistenkongress. Akten, Jahrbuch der Österreichischen Byzantinistik*, 31/1 (1981), pp. 131–47.

Unger, R. W. *The Ship in the Medieval Economy* (London, 1980).

290 *Bibliography*

Van Andel, T. H., Runnels, C. N. and Pope, K. O. 'Five Thousand Years of Land Use and Abuse in Southern Argolid Greece', *Hesperia*, 55 (1986), pp. 103–28.

Van der Osten, H. H. *The Alishar Huyuk. Seasons of 1930–2*, part 3 (Chicago, 1937).

Vannier, J. F. *Familles byzantines. Les Argyroi (IXᵉ–XIIᵉ siècles)* (Paris, 1975).

Vasiliev, A. 'Harun-lbn-Yahya and his Description of Constantinople', *Seminarium Kondakovianum*, 5 (1932), pp. 149–63.

Vavrinek, V. (ed.). *Beiträge zur byzantinischen Geschichte im 9.–11. Jahrhundert* (Prague, 1978).

Vita-Finzi, C. *The Mediterranean Valleys. Geological Changes in Historical Times* (Cambridge, 1969).

Volk, R. *Gesundheitswesen und Wohltätigkeit im Spiegel der byzantinischen Klostertypika* (Munich, 1983).

Vryonis, S. *The Decline of Medieval Hellenism in Asia Minor and the Process of Islamization from the Eleventh through the Fifteenth Century* (Berkeley, Los Angeles, London, 1971).

'The Will of a Provincial Magnate, Eustathius Boilas (1059)', *Dumbarton Oaks Papers*, 11 (1957), pp. 263–77.

'An Attic Hoard of Byzantine Gold Goins (668–741) from the Thomas Whittemore Collection and the Numismatic Evidence for the Urban History of Byzantium', *Zbornik Radova Vizantološkog Instituta*, 8, part 1 (1963), pp. 291–300.

'The Peira as a Source for the History of Byzantine Aristocratic Society in the First Half of the Eleventh Century', in *Near Eastern Numismatics, Iconography, Epigraphy and History. Studies in Honor of George C. Miles* (Beirut, 1974), pp. 279–84.

'The Panegyris of the Byzantine Saint: A Study in the Nature of a Medieval Institution, its Origins and Fate', in S. Hackel (ed.), *The Byzantine Saint* (Studies Supplementary to Sobornost 5) (London, 1981), pp. 196–226.

Waage, D. B. *'Antioch on the Orantes*, IV, part 2, *Greek, Roman, Byzantine and Crusaders' Coins* (Princeton, 1952).

Waldbaum, J. C. *Metalwork from Sardis. The Finds through 1974* (Cambridge, Massachusetts, 1983).

Walpole, R. (ed.). *Memoires relating to European and Asiatic Turkey and Other Countries of the East* (London, 1812).

Weiss, G. *Oströmische Beamte im Spiegel der Schriften des Michael Psellos* (Munich, 1973).

'Vermögensbildung der Byzantiner in Privathand. Methodische Fragen einer quantitativen Analyse', *Byzantina*, 11 (1982), pp. 77–92.

White, K. D. *Agricultural Implements of the Roman World* (Cambridge, 1967).
Roman Farming (London, 1970).
Farm Equipment of the Roman World (Cambridge, 1975).

Bibliography 291

White, L. *Medieval Technology and Social Change* (Oxford, 1962).

'The Expansion of Technology 500–1500', in C. Cipolla (ed.), *The Fontana Economic History of Europe*, I, *The Middle Ages* (London, 1972), pp. 143–74.

Wickham, C. J. *Early Medieval Italy. Central Power and Local Society 400–1000* (London, 1981).

'Historical and Topographical Notes on Early Medieval South Etruria: Part II', *Papers of the British School at Rome*, 47 (1979), pp. 66–95.

'The Uniqueness of the East', *Journal of Peasant Studies*, 12, parts 2–3 (1985), pp. 166–96.

Wilson, N. G. 'Books and Readers in Byzantium', in *Byzantine Books and Bookmen* (Dumbarton Oaks, 1975), pp. 1–15.

Winkelmann, F., Köpstein, H., Ditten, H. and Rochow, I. *Byzanz im 7. Jahrhundert. Untersuchungen zur Herausbildung des Feudalismus* (Berlin, 1978).

Wolf, E. R. *Peasants* (New Jersey, 1966).

Woodward, A. M. 'Excavations at Sparta, 1924–5', *Annual of the British School at Athens*, 26 (1924–5), pp. 116–310.

Xanalatos, D. *Beiträge zur Wirtschafts- und Sozialgeschichte Makedoniens im Mittelalter, hauptsächlich auf Grund der Briefe des Erzbischofs Theophylaktos von Achrida* (Munich, 1937).

Yannopoulos, P. A. *La Société profane dans l'empire byzantin des VIIe VIIIe et IXe siècles* (Louvain, 1975).

Zakythinos, D. A. *Le Despotat grec de Morée. Vie et institutions*, 2nd edn (London, 1975).

Zivojinovic, M. 'Sur l'époque de la formation de l'évêché d'Hiérissos', *Zbornik Radova Vizantološkog Instituta*, 14–15 (1973), pp. 155–8 (French summary, p. 158).

Index

Abydos, 208, 232
Adrameri, 62, 77, 201
Adrianople, 28, 236
aerikon, 103–4, 105
agriculture: alluvial soils, 135–40;
  arable cultivation, 122–8, 137–41;
  arboriculture, 144–9; crop rotation,
  125–6; implements, 122–5; irrigation,
  134–5; legumes, 126–7; viticulture,
  142–6, 148; water-mills, 128–33
agridion, 35–6
Ainos, 233, 239
aktemon, 49, 51–2, 110, 151, 209
Alexios I, *see* Komnenos
Alexios II, *see* Komnenos
Alexios III, *see* Angelos
Alopekai (*episkepsis*), 68
Amalfitan monastery, 60, 72, 116, 239
Amorion, 25
Anatolikon, 41, 42, 78
Andronikos I, *see* Komnenos
Andronikos II, *see* Palaiologos
angareia, 108, 109, 110, 113, 249
Angelos, Alexios III, 219, 240
Angelos, Isaac II, 240
Ankara, 25, 152, 199, 211
antikaniskion, 109, 110
aplekton, 107
aporos, 37, 40, 110, 117, 209
archontes, 48, 74, 216
Argos, 214, 217, 267
Argyros, Romanos III, 45, 109, 188
aristocratic estates, 40–1, 71, 78–9, 227,
  232–3
Armeniakon, 103
Artabasdos, Nikephoros, 90, 91, 96
Artze, 212
Asmalou, 51, 52–3, 95, 100, 131,
  252
ateleis (*paroikoi*), 48, 53–4

Athanasios, St, 135, 145, 178, 190,
  235, 258
Athens: coin finds, 21, 86, 88; industry,
  28, 218, 219, 235; landowners, 228;
  taxation, 112, 166
Athos: agriculture, 132, 135, 146, 153,
  154–5; archives, 74, 247, 250; boats,
  238–9; monasteries, 65, 71, 230;
  property, 58, 76; workshops, 235
Attaleia, 27, 164, 184, 213, 267
Attaleiates, Michael: charitable
  foundations, 165, 178, 189, 206;
  history, 114, 236–7; properties, 69,
  227; *typikon*, 184
autourgion, 121, 143, 227

Bačkovo, 84, 115, 140, 185, 186, 189,
  225, 231
Baris (property of Andronikos Doukas),
  123, 126, 142, 165, 189
Baris (property of Lembiotissa), 247–8,
  249
Barzachanion, 51, 95, 131
Basil I, 32, 34, 58, 87, 154
Basil II: confiscation of lands, 67; grant
  of maritime privileges, 238; grants of
  revenues, 82, 105, 233; legislation,
  38, 41, 43–4, 45, 235; taxation, 113,
  114
bee-keeping, 157–8
Benjamin of Tudela, 219, 226
Bithynia, 23
boidatos, 52, 103, 110, 209
boidion, 60
Boilas, Eustathios: book collection, 195;
  church-building, 189; colonisation,
  64–5, 125, 159–60, 246; construction
  of water-mills, 131; freed slaves, 60,
  85; improvements to properties, 134,
  135, 146

293

294 Index

Boiotia, 18, 65, 74, 136, 219, 245
Book of Ceremonies, 183
Book of the Eparch, 170, 183, 193, 203
Botaneiates, Nikephoros III, 56, 83, 86, 93
building, 186–93
Bulgaria, 65, 66, 88, 113, 175, 245, 246, 267

Cappadocia, 41, 78
chalkeus, 125
Chalkidike, 54, 74, 118, 230, 245, 251, 253
Chalkis, 74, 219, 228
Chantax, 254, 256
charistikarios, 66, 159
Chilandar, 241
Chios, 146, 173, 175
Choirospaktes, Michael, 42
Chonai, 26
Choniates, Michael: Athenian economy, 218, 219; fiscal exactions, 107, 166; *Hypomnestikon*, 112; supply of Constantinople, 146, 222; wine, 146, 175
Choniates, Niketas, 73, 202, 215, 219
chorion, 35, 37, 44
Chostiane, 55, 69, 73, 125
Christodoulos, 64, 69, 112, 146, 155–6
Chrysoupolis, 233–4
Chrystoupolis, 232, 233
clothing, 182–6
coinage, *see* monetary circulation
coinage debasement, 89–91
colonisation, 64–6
colonus adscripticius, 15, 33
Constans II, 21
Constantine IV, 21
Constantine V, 21, 22
Constantine VII Porphyrogenitos, 33, 37, 54, 86, 87, 110, 167, 195
Constantine VIII, 114
Constantine IX, *see* Monomachos
Constantine X, *see* Doukas
Constantinople: centre of consumption, 2, 23, 169–70, 172, 174, 185; charities, 84, 206; coin production, 20, 21, 85; early medieval decline, 23–4; industries, 183, 193, 196, 204, 226–7; monasteries, 56, 72, 84, 188; rents, 226–7; social classes, 204–6; supplies, 23, 139, 146, 203–4, 237–8; tax-payments, 90, 95, 99;

trade with provinces, 27, 110, 164, 208, 212–13, 217, 222–3, 231, 236–7, 239–41
Corfu, 56, 158
Corinth: coinage, 21, 86; industry, 28, 214–15, 261; trade, 147, 216
Crete: archaeological survey, 18; fiscal revenues, 83; independent peasant community, 77; irrigation, 134; *pronoia*, 73; water-mills, 132–3; wine, 146, 175
Cyprus, 166, 223, 245, 267
Cyril Phileotes, St, 84, 173

Dalassena, Anna, 95
Danielis, 32, 81 n5, 235
dekateia, 46, 157, 238, 239, 240–1
Delphinas, Nikoulitzas, 114, 221
Demetrias, 221–2
demosiarioi, 48
demosion, 48, 68, 102
diet, 164–79; bread, 165–7; cheese, 172; fishing, 170–1; fruit, 173; meat, 167–70; spices, 174–5; vegetables, 172–3; wine, 175
dikeraton, 97–8, 99
Dinogetia: agriculture, 123, 125, 165; coinage, 87, 224; demand for industrial goods, 194, 224–5; fishing, 158; housing, 191; workshops, 225
Dobrobikeia, 61
Docheiariou, 94, 190, 191
Dorylaion, 212
Doukas, Andronikos: estates, 51, 67, 68–9, 137; house at Baris, 189; *praktikon*, 137, 151; revenues, 102, 103, 104
Doukas, Constantine X, 115
Doukas, John, 70, 90
Doukas, Michael VII, 69, 91
Doxompous, 254, 257, 260
Drama, 199
dromos, 48, 99, 111
dynatos, 37, 40–2, 44
Dyrrachion, 223

elatikon, 98–9
ennomion, 103–4, 151
epereia, 113, 239
Ephesos: coinage, 21, 88; early medieval decline, 25, 26–7; economic revival, 209–10; harbour, 27, 136–7
epibole, 64, 93–5, 100

Index

episkepsis, 68, 69, 228
Esphigmenou, 95, 98, 105, 251, 252, 253
Euboia, 146, 175
Euchaita, 211–12, 236
Euergetes, 71
exkousseia, 108

Farmer's Law, 14–19, 123
feudalism, 6–12, 33, 225–6, 264–7
fiscal privileges, 69–70
fiscal reform, 96–102
Fiscal Treatise, 35–7
fishing, 158–9, 254

Galaidai, 51, 138
genikon sekreton, 43
Genoese, 222, 223
Geoponika, 120, 127, 143, 145
georgos, 15
Gerontios, 124, 126, 151
Gomatou, 151, 253
Gregory Dekapolites, St, 27

Hagia Sophia, 55–6, 236, 238
Halmyros, 221–2, 223
Harun-Ibn-Yahya, 220
hemiseia, 16–17
Heraklios, 21, 29
hexafollon, 98–9
Hierissos: Athonite property, 229–30;
  commercial fair, 260; harbour, 230;
  pastoral farming, 154; properties of
  residents, 57–8, 76, 117, 142, 192

idiosystaton, 38
inheritance customs, 255–6
Isaac I, *see* Komnenos
Isaac II, *see* Angelos
Iviron: confiscation of property, 70, 95;
  grant of fiscal revenues, 82–3; land
  disputes, 62, 146; maritime privileges,
  238; *paroikoi*, 49–50, 253; properties,
  49–50, 61, 72, 228, 230, 231, 260

Justinian II, 30

Kalamaria, 63, 153, 251
Kamateros, Demetrios, 90
Kameniates, John, 220, 222
kaniskion, 105–6, 109, 166, 170
kanonikon, 104, 165, 170
kapnikon, 33, 103
Kareai, 83, 116

Kassandra peninsula, 54, 57, 70, 98,
  111, 117, 153, 155, 252
kastroktisia, 109
Kataphloron, John, 92, 93, 94, 98, 100,
  105
kathisma, 105, 106
Kecharitomene, 189, 195
Kekaumenos, 90, 115, 121, 221, 222
Kenchreiai, 86
Kephalas, Leo, 55, 59 n88, 69, 196
klasmatic land, 57–9, 61
klerikos, 29, 56, 96
Kolobou, 54, 58, 154, 230
kommerkion, 208, 213, 217, 226, 237,
  238, 239
Komnene, Anna, 134, 188, 200
Komnene, Irene, 189
Komnenos, Adrian, 70
Komnenos, Alexios I: chrysobull to the
  Venetians, 224 n107, 226, 238;
  coinage, 85, 87, 89, 91; concentration
  of power by family, 70, 189;
  'conservatism', 9; grants of fiscal
  privileges, 50, 53, 56, 69–70, 83,
  93–4, 99–100; grants of maritime
  privileges, 239–40, 241; restoration of
  imperial authority, 79, 265;
  restoration of orphanage, 188, 206;
  taxation reform, 96–102, 259
Komnenos, Alexios II, 55
Komnenos, Andronikos I, 88
Komnenos, Isaac I, 83, 104
Komnenos, Isaac (brother of Alexios I),
  70, 184
Komnenos, Isaac (founder of
  Kosmosotira): boats, 239; building,
  190; cash payments, 84–5; foundation
  of Kosmosotira, 225–6; improvements
  to properties, 135; properties, 71, 233;
  typikon, 115
Komnenos, Manuel I: coinage, 86, 87,
  88; grants of commercial privileges,
  223; grants of fiscal privileges, 53, 55,
  83, 102, 145; military campaigns,
  107, 264; *pronoia*, 73
Korone, 147, 217
Korykos, 202–3
Kos, 69, 112
Kosmosotira: building, 189–90; cash
  payments, 84–5; fishing, 158–9;
  foundation, 226; improvements to
  properties, 135; mills, 131, 132;
  properties, 71; treasure, 115

296 Index

Kyzikos, 20, 208

Lagoudes, Constantine, 60, 117, 142, 231
Lampsakos, 110, 198, 209
land disputes, 62, 249–50
Larissa, 139, 157, 221–2
Latros, 102, 145
Lavra: boats, 238–9, 241; building, 190; donations of land, 94, 99–100 (imperial), 142 (other); expenditure, 145, 190; fiscal privileges, 54–5, 82, 100–1, 111, 233; food allowances, 176–7; irrigation, 135; land disputes, 60, 62; mills, 131, 132; number of monks, 65; pastoral farming, 154, 156, 157; properties, 51–3, 71, 99–100, 228, 229, 233, 252–3; revenues, 162, 260; tax-payments, 92–5, 99–101
Lazaros, St, 65, 83
Leipso, 53, 69
Lembiotissa, 247–50
Lemnos, 82
Leo III, 30
Leo VI, 21, 33, 110, 154, 220
Leo of Synnada, 164, 167
Leros, 53, 69, 145, 155, 201, 247
Lesbos, 146
libellikon, 57
Limenites, Achillios, 77, 116, 134
logisimon, 69, 70, 82, 99, 111, 160
Lorotomou, 51–2, 95, 100, 251–2
Luke the Stylite, St, 39, 121

Macedonia: agricultural resources, 139; aristocratic estates, 32, 69, 74, 78, 231; tax-collection, 90, 99
Mangana, 72, 114, 188
Mankaphas, Theodore, 267
maritime privileges, 238–41
Melanoudion, 49
Meletios, St, 66, 83, 108
Melissenos, Nikephoros, 70
Mesembria, 28, 29
Methone, 214, 217
Michael II, 20, 103
Michael IV, 188
Michael VI, 82, 83
Michael VII, *see* Doukas
Michael VIII, *see* Palaiologos
Miletos, 67, 126, 137, 211; *episkepsis*, 68
misthios, 156

mitaton, 107, 109
modios: boat capacity, 238–40; surface area, 50–4, 57, 71, 93–5, 138; volume of produce, 126, 138, 176–8, 180
Moglena, 55, 69, 73, 157
Moirokouboulos, Thomas, 57–8
Monembasia, 29, 146, 217
monetary circulation, 80–5; contraction, 20–1; increase in volume, 86–9; markets, 234–6, 260; peasant producers, 115, 116–18
Monomachos, Constantine IX: agricultural improvements, 146; building, 114, 188; coinage, 89, 93; grants of revenues, 83; military expenditure, 264; *typikon* for Athos, 155, 233, 239
morte, 16–17, 46, 79, 248
Mosynoupolis, 71, 189, 232
Mylasa, 49
Mystikos, Nicolas, *see* Nicolas I, patriarch

Nauplion, 214, 217, 267
Nea Mone, 48, 71, 111, 116
Nemea, 125
Nicaea, 25, 27, 77, 148, 208
Nicolas I, patriarch, 107, 108
Nikephoritzes, 9, 72, 236
Nikephoros I, 31, 33, 103
Nikephoros II, *see* Phokas
Nikephoros III, *see* Botaneiates
Nikephoros, St, 33
Niketas, *patrikios*, 32, 128
Nikomedia, 20, 25, 158, 173, 204, 208
Nikon Metanoeite, St, 42, 116 n162, 144, 216, 217

oikomodion, 106
Opsikion, 78, 103
orphanotropheion, 33, 99, 188, 206

Pakouriane, Kale, 60, 85, 116
Pakourianos, Gregory: building, 189, 225, 232; colonisation, 64–5, 66, 160, 246; fiscal privileges, 69, 160, 196; *paroikoi*, 108; pastoral farming, 152–3; properties, 71, 131, 140, 225, 232; treasure, 193; *typikon*, 84, 115, 184, 232
Pakourianos, Symbatios, 81 n5, 116, 153, 184, 193

Index

pakton, 102
Palaiologos, Andronikos II, 217
Palaiologos, Michael VIII, 217
Panteleemon, 98, 105, 111, 123, 125
Pantokrator: charitable distributions, 84, 206; diet, 168, 172, 173; food allowances, 140, 165, 178; properties, 131, 228–9, 231–2, 233
Paphlagonia, 30, 41, 78
paroikos: belonging to pronoia holders, 7, 62, 73; belonging to the state, 67; grants to landowners, 6, 33, 56, 64; legal status, 15, 45–6, 76; obligations, 46–7, 102, 108, 248–9; see also peasantry
pastoral farming, 149–57
Patmos, monastery of St John: fiscal exactions, 109, 112; fiscal privileges, 69, 83; improvements to properties, 146; maritime privileges, 239, 240; properties, 53, 66, 125, 201
Patras, 29, 33, 214, 217
peasantry: economic stratification, 16–18, 37–8; independent peasants, 14–16, 77; monetary circulation, 115, 116–18, 260; poverty, 249–50; smallholdings, 63–4, 250–5
Peira, 42–4
Peloponnesos, 32, 110, 136, 147, 148, 153, 192, 214, 235
penes, 37, 42, 44
Pergamon, 27, 210
periorismos, 58–9, 62
Peristerai: land dispute, 62; monastery of St Andrew, 54, 57, 59, 144, 228; property conceded to the state, 99, 100, 131
Peritheorion, 232
Philaretos, 30–1, 134, 152, 158, 169
Philippikos, 21
Philippoupolis, 28, 71, 85, 175
Philokales, 38
Phokas, Nikephoros II, 39, 82, 83, 107, 111, 190
Pinsson, 74, 101, 260
Pisans, 232, 233
Pontos, 23, 30, 125, 173, 185, 212
population: early medieval decline, 22; growth, 47–67, 245–8, 250–5
praktikon, 4, 49; Andronikos Doukas, 137–9, 151; fourteenth-century, 125, 185, 234, 251, 253, 254, 260; monastery of Patmos, 53, 66

proasteion, 36, 64
pronoia, 6–7, 62, 72–3, 256
proskynetikion, 105, 107
Prousa, 208
Psellos, Michael, 135, 146, 159, 172, 188
Ptochoprodromos, 167, 169, 171–5 passim, 185
ptochos, 37, 75
Pylai, 208

Radochosta, 77, 131, 144
Radolibos, 50, 254
Raidestos, 227, 232, 236–8
Rhodes, 146, 175, 268
Romaios, Eustathios, 43–4
Romanos I, 38, 42, 110
Romanos II, 54
Romanos III, see Argyros
Rossikon, 190

salt, 158
Samos, 38, 112
Sardis: alluvial deposits, 136; coinage, 21, 88; early medieval decline, 27; economic revival, 210–11; housing, 191; water-mills, 129
Seleukia, 183, 184
self-sufficiency, 121–2
Serdika, 28
Serres, 199, 202, 255
Sgouros, Leo, 112, 267
Skaranos, Theodosios, 124, 126, 166, 259
Skleraina, Maria, 83, 116
Skleros, Basil, 42–3
Skleros, Romanos, 43
Skylitzes, John, 114, 115, 125
Smyrna, 27, 77, 209, 232
solemnion, 82–3, 162
Spanopoulos, George, 97
Sparta: coinage, 87; commerce, 223; early medieval decline, 29; economic revival, 214, 216–17; olive cultivation, 145, 147
Stagoi, 56, 131, 148
state properties, 67–8
Stenimachos, 65, 108, 140, 189, 225
strateia, 20, 38–9, 109, 110–12
stratiotes, 38–40, 42; pronoia holder, 62, 73
stratiotika ktemata, 20, 38
Strymitza, 50–1, 56, 83, 153

298 *Index*

Strymon, 48, 60, 92, 158, 185, 253–4
sympatheia, 55, 61, 63
synetheia, 98–9
Synnada, 164, 166, 167
synone, 103

taxation: basic land-tax, 90–102;
  commutation into cash payments,
  109–15; supplementary charges,
  102–9
telos, 46, 102, 103
textile production, 215, 216, 219
Thasos, 87
Thebes: coinage, 85; commerce, 223;
  early medieval decline, 29; economic
  revival, 218–19, 261; tax-register,
  58–9, 61, 63–4, 74–6, 130, 228
Theodore, St, 108, 124, 170
Theodosioupolis, 212
Theophanes, 24, 30
Theophilos, 20, 86
Theophylaktos, 61, 96, 104, 109
Thessalonike: administrative functions,
  48, 57, 62, 92, 99, 101; coin
  production, 20, 85; economic revival,
  220–1; housing, 191; monastic
  properties, 228–9; secular landowners,
  229; traders, 158, 221, 238, 239
Thessaly: grain exports, 28, 139, 222;
  peasant poverty, 250; rebellion, 114,
  115, 157; silk production, 148
Thrace: agricultural production, 30, 139,
  175, 236; commerce, 217, 236; large
  estates, 78, 231; tax-collection, 90, 99

Thrakesion, 78, 164, 195
Timarion, 168, 169
towns: centres of consumption, 202–3;
  early medieval decline, 24–30; size,
  198–9; urban revenues, 226–7
Trebizond, 174, 213
Tzechlianes, 99, 100, 131
Tzimiskes, John I, 82, 86, 224, 238

Vatopedi: estates, 72, 232, 233; grants
  of fiscal revenues, 82–3; land disputes,
  145, 231; livestock, 132, 154; tax-
  payment, 110
Venetians: commercial privileges, 217,
  218, 220, 232, 238; trade, 139,
  146–8, 175, 216, 217, 219, 222–4;
  urban property, 222, 226
Vicina, 87, 194
village communities, 18–19, 76–7; fiscal
  burdens, 34

Xenophon, 63, 72, 145, 153, 157
Xeropotamou, 57, 60, 126, 253
Xeros, Gregory, 94, 95, 100
Xiphilinos, Niketas, 93, 94, 95, 100

zeugaratos, 49, 50, 51–3, 103, 110, 209
zeugarion, 60, 61, 104
zeugologion, 104
Zichna, 199, 255
Zonaras, John, 96, 189
Zygos, 58

For EU product safety concerns, contact us at Calle de José Abascal, 56–1°, 28003 Madrid, Spain or eugpsr@cambridge.org.

www.ingramcontent.com/pod-product-compliance
Ingram Content Group UK Ltd.
Pitfield, Milton Keynes, MK11 3LW, UK
UKHW011322060825
461487UK00005B/282